# THE ULTIMATE BOOK OF
# BAKING

# THE ULTIMATE BOOK OF
# BAKING

Over 400 recipes for pies, tarts, buns, muffins, breads, cookies
and cakes, shown in 1800 color step-by-step photographs

## Martha Day

HERMES
HOUSE

This edition is published by Hermes House

Hermes House is an imprint of Anness Publishing Ltd
Hermes House, 88–89 Blackfriars Road, London SE1 8HA
tel. 020 7401 2077; fax 020 7633 9499; info@anness.com

A CIP catalogue record for this book is available from the British Library.

Publisher: Joanna Lorenz
Project Editor: Felicity Forster
Text: Carole Clements
Designer: Sheila Volpe
Photography, Styling: Amanda Heywood
Food Styling: Elizabeth Wolf-Cohen, Carla Capalbo,
steps by Cara Hobday, Teresa Goldfinch, Nicola Fowler
Additional Recipes: Carla Capalbo and Laura Washburn,
Frances Cleary, Norma MacMillan
Illustrations: Anna Koska
Index: Dawn Butcher
Editorial Reader: Marion Wilson

Main front cover image shows American-style Apple Pie, for recipe see page 24

Previously published as *Complete Baking*

1 3 5 7 9 10 8 6 4 2

NOTES

Standard spoon and cup measures are level.

Large eggs are used unless otherwise stated.

# CONTENTS

| | |
|---|---|
| Introduction | 6 |
| Ingredients, Equipment & Techniques | 8 |
| Cookies & Bars | 40 |
| Muffins & Quick Breads | 98 |
| Pies & Tarts | 154 |
| Cakes & Tortes | 236 |
| Low-Fat Desserts | 314 |
| Classic Breads | 362 |
| International Breads | 424 |
| Index | 506 |

# INTRODUCTION

Nothing equals the satisfaction of home baking. No commercial cake mix or store-bought cookie can match one that is made from the best fresh ingredients with all the added enjoyment that baking at home provides – the enticing aromas that fill the house and stimulate appetites, the delicious straight-from-the-oven flavor, as well as the pride of having created such wonderful goodies yourself.

This book is filled with familiar favorites as well as many other lesser known recipes. Explore the wealth of cookies, bars, muffins, quick breads, pies, tarts, cakes and breads within these pages. Even if you are a novice baker, the easy-to-follow and clear step-by-step photographs will help you achieve good results. For the more experienced home baker, the range of recipes will provide some new dishes to add to your repertoire.

Baking is an exact science and needs to be approached in an ordered way. First read through the recipe from beginning to end. Set out all the required ingredients before you begin. Large eggs are assumed unless specified otherwise, and they should be at room temperature for best results. Sift the flour after you have measured it, and incorporate other dry ingredients as specified in the individual recipes. If you sift the flour from a fair height, it will have more chance to aerate and lighten.

When a recipe calls for folding one ingredient into another, it should be done in a way that incorporates as much air as possible into the mixture. Use either a large metal spoon or a long rubber or plastic scraper. Gently plunge the spoon or scraper deep into the center of the batter and, scooping up a large amount of the batter, fold it over. Turn the bowl slightly so each scoop folds over another part of the batter.

No two ovens are alike. Buy a reliable oven thermometer and test the temperature of your oven. When possible bake in the center of the oven where the heat is more likely to be constant. If using a fan-assisted oven, follow the manufacturer's guidelines for baking. Good quality baking pans can improve your results, as they conduct heat more efficiently.

Practice, patience and enthusiasm are the keys to confident and successful baking. The recipes that follow will inspire you to start sifting flour, breaking eggs and stirring up all sorts of delectable homemade treats – all guaranteed to bring great satisfaction to both the baker and those lucky enough to enjoy the results.

# INGREDIENTS, EQUIPMENT & TECHNIQUES

KEEPING YOUR KITCHEN STOCKED WITH THE RIGHT INGREDIENTS AND EQUIPMENT, AS WELL AS MASTERING THESE BASIC TECHNIQUES, WILL ENSURE BAKING SUCCESS EVERY TIME.

# BAKING INGREDIENTS

This guide highlights a few of the most essential items that every baker should keep in their pantry and refrigerator.

## BUTTER AND MARGARINE

Butter gives the best flavor for baking and should be used whenever possible, especially when there is a high fat content, as in shortbread.

Sometimes butter needs to be at room temperature before being used. It is usually either melted or diced before being added to the other ingredients to make a batter. This is then beaten by hand or in an electric mixer. For some bread recipes, the butter is kneaded into the dough after the initial rising, since large quantities of butter can inhibit the action of the yeast.

For a low-fat alternative to butter, try polyunsaturated margarine instead. Low-fat spreads are ideal for spreading on breads and tea breads, but are unfortunately not suitable for baking because they have a high water content.

## EGGS

Eggs are a staple ingredient in most baking recipes. They should be stored and used at room temperature, so if you keep them in the refrigerator, take out the number you want at least 30 minutes before starting a recipe.

*Above: Properly fed hens lay the best and tastiest eggs.*

*Above: There are many different types of flour, each with different properties, so make sure you select the one that is best for your recipe.*

## FLOURS

Highly refined flours are fine for most baking purposes, but for the very best results choose organic stone-ground flours because they will add flavor as well as texture to your home baking.

### Bread flour

Made from hard wheat, which contains a high proportion of gluten, this flour is the one to use for bread-making.

### Cake flour

This flour, sometimes called sponge flour, contains less gluten than all-purpose flour and is ideal for light cakes and cookies.

### Whole-wheat flour

Because this flour contains the complete wheat kernel, it gives a coarser texture and a good wholesome flavor to bread.

### Rye flour

This dark-colored flour has a low gluten content and makes a dense loaf with a good flavor. It is best mixed with strong wheat flour to give a lighter loaf.

## SWEETENERS

### Sugars

Most baking recipes call for sugar. Granulated sugar is the best sweetener to use for the creaming method because the crystals dissolve easily and quickly when creamed with the fat. Granulated sugar can also be used for rubbed-in mixtures and when the sugar is heated with the fat or liquid until it dissolves.

Demerara sugar can be used when the sugar is dissolved over heat before being added to the dry ingredients. Light and dark brown sugars are used when a richer flavor and color are called for.

Raw sugar is unrefined sugar which is uncolored and pure—it also has more flavor than refined sugars, and contains some minerals.

### Fruit juice

Concentrated fruit juices are very useful for baking. They have no added sweeteners or preservatives and can be diluted as required. Use them in their concentrated form for baking or for sweetening fillings.

### Pear and apple spread

This is a very concentrated fruit juice spread with no added sugar. It has a

*Above: Fruits add natural sweetness to baked goods.*

sweet-and-sour taste and can be used as a spread or blended with fruit juice and added to baking recipes as a sweetener.

### Dried fruits

These are a traditional addition to cakes and tea breads, and there is a very wide range available, including more unusual varieties such as peach, pineapple, banana, mango and papaya. The natural sugars add sweetness to baked goods and keep them moist, making it possible to use less fat.

Chop and add dried fruits to breads by hand rather than putting them in an electric mixer or food processor, as the blades will chop the fruit and spoil the appearance and flavor of the loaf.

### Honey

Good honey has a strong flavor so you can use less of it than the equivalent amount of sugar. It also contains traces of minerals and vitamins.

### Malt extract

This is a sugary byproduct of barley. It has a strong flavor and is good to use in bread, cakes and tea breads, as it adds a moistness of its own.

### Molasses

This is the residue left after the first stage of refining sugar cane. It has a strong, smoky and slightly bitter taste which gives a good flavor to cakes and baked goods. Black treacle can be used as a substitute for molasses.

### MILK

Tea breads, sweet breads and cakes are often made with milk, whereas savory loaves tend to be made using water. Breads made with milk are softer both in the crumb and the crust than those using water.

There are many low-fat alternatives to whole milk: skim milk and 1 or 2 percent milk have a much lower fat content than whole milk, and they don't taste as rich.

### HERBS AND SPICES

Chopped fresh herbs add a great deal of interest to baking. They add flavor to breads, scones and soda breads. In the absence of fresh herbs, dried herbs can be used; less is needed, but the flavor is generally not as good.

Spices can add either strong or subtle flavors depending on the amount and variety used. The most commonly used sweet spices for baking are cinnamon, nutmeg, cloves and ginger, and the savory spices are cumin, fennel, caraway and anise. Mace, pepper and coriander seeds can be used for both sweet and savory dishes. Spices can be added with the flour or kneaded in with other ingredients.

### SALT

Many baking recipes add salt at the beginning, stirring or sifting it into the flour. Salt is one of the few essential ingredients in bread-making, both for flavor and for the effect it has on the yeast and dough.

*Above: Check that your pantry supplies are kept fresh and plentiful, and stock up on the ingredients you use most often.*

# BAKING EQUIPMENT

**Baking sheet**
Choose a large, heavy baking sheet that will not warp at high temperatures.

**Cake boards**
Silver cake boards are perfect for presenting finished cakes. They come in a variety of shapes and sizes, in circles, squares and rectangles.

**Cake tester**
A simple implement that, when inserted into a cooked cake, will come out clean if the cake is ready.

**Chef's knife**
This has a heavy, wide blade and is ideal for chopping.

**Deep round cake pan**
A deep pan useful for baking fruit cakes.

**Electric mixer**
Perfect for beating egg whites and incorporating air into light mixtures.

**Frosting smoother**
This will give a wonderfully uniform finish to cakes.

**Honey twirl**
For spooning honey without making a mess!

**Juicer**
Used for squeezing the juice from citrus fruits.

**Loaf pan**
Available in various sizes and used for making loaf-shaped breads and tea breads.

**Measuring pitcher**
Absolutely essential for measuring any kind of liquid accurately.

**Measuring spoons**
Standard measuring spoons are essential for measuring small quantities.

**Mixing bowls**
A set of different-sized mixing bowls is essential in any kitchen for whisking and mixing.

**Nonstick baking paper**
For lining pans and baking sheets to ensure that cakes, meringues and cookies do not stick.

**Nylon sieve**
Suitable for most baking purposes, and particularly for sieving foods that react adversely with metal.

**Pastry brush**
Useful for brushing excess flour from pastry and brushing glazes onto pastries, breads and tarts.

**Pastry (cookie) cutters**
A variety of shapes and sizes of cutter is useful when stamping out pastry, cookies and scones.

**Plastic cutting board**
Use this as a smooth, flat surface for cutting or rolling ingredients.

**Plastic scrapers**
These can be used to create all sorts of "combing" patterns in butter frosting.

**Rectangular cake pan**
For making sheet cakes and other baked goods to be served cut into slices.

**Ring mold**
Perfect for making angel food cakes and other ring-shaped cakes.

**Rolling pin**
Use a heavy rolling pin for rolling out bread dough, marzipan and fondant.

**Sable paint brushes**
These are expensive, but are well worth the extra cost when painting fine details onto cakes.

**Scale**
This is essential for accuracy when weighing all your ingredients for baking.

**Serrated knives**
Sharp knives are essential for cutting fruit and vegetables, and those with a serrated edge will let you cut cakes without having them break into pieces.

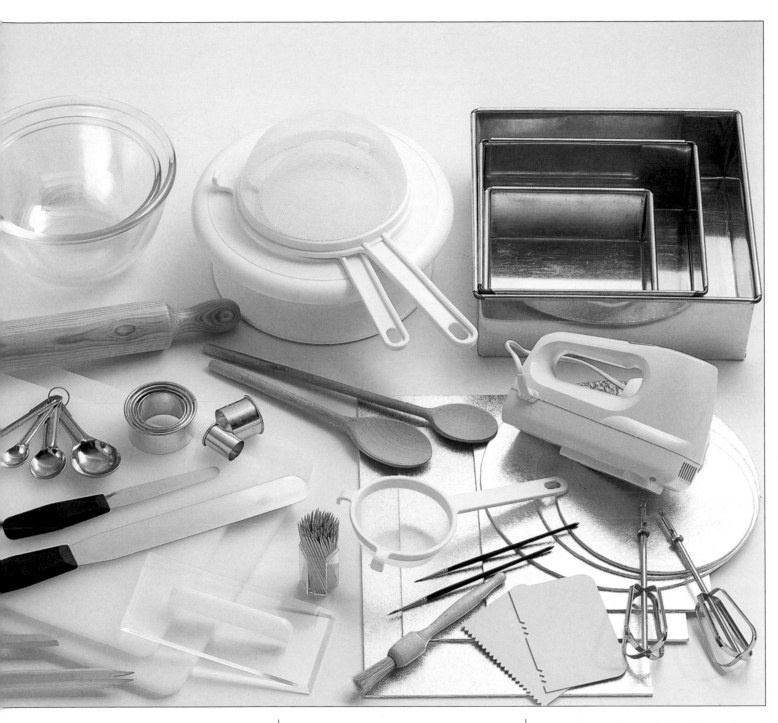

## Spatulas

These are used for loosening pies, tarts and breads from baking sheets and for smoothing frosting on cakes.

## Toothpicks

These can be used to make designs on cakes, or to support pieces of cake to make a particular shape. Always remove them before serving.

## Vegetable knife

A useful knife for preparing fruit and vegetables for your baked goods. Always keep your knives sharp, and wash and dry them immediately after use.

## Wooden spoons

Essential for mixing ingredients for baking and for creaming mixtures. These are available in a wide variety of sizes.

*Above: To be able to bake efficiently and with pleasure, you need good equipment. That is not to say that you should invest in an extensive and expensive collection of pans, tools and gadgets, but a basic range is essential. In addition, buy the best equipment you can afford, adding more as your budget allows. Well-made equipment lasts and is a sound investment; inexpensive pans are likely to dent or break.*

# BAKING TECHNIQUES

Baking your own muffins and breads is easy and satisfying, even if you're a beginner. Just follow the recipes and the tips, hints, and step-by-step techniques and you'll get perfect results every time.

**1 ▲ For liquids measured in cups:** Use a glass or clear plastic measuring cup. Put the cup on a flat surface and pour in the liquid. Bend down and check that the liquid is exactly level with the marking on the cup, as specified in the recipe.

**2 ▲ For measuring dry ingredients in a cup or spoon:** Fill the cup or spoon. Level the surface even with the rim of the cup or spoon, using the straight edge of a knife.

**3 ▲ For liquids measured in spoons:** Pour the liquid into the measuring spoon, to the brim, and then pour it into the mixing bowl.

**4 ▲ For measuring flour in a cup or spoon:** Scoop the flour from the canister in the measuring cup or spoon. Hold it over the canister and level the surface.

**5 ▲ For measuring butter:** With a sharp knife, cut off the specified amount following the markings on the wrapper.

**6 ▲ For rectangular and square cake pans:** Fold the paper and crease it with your fingernail to fit snugly into the corners of the pan. Then press the bottom paper lining into place.

**7 ▲ To line muffin cups:** Use paper cupcake liners of the required size. Or grease and flour the cups.

# MAKING SCONES

Scone dough may be rolled out and cut into shapes for baking in the oven or cooking on a griddle. To ensure light, well-risen scones, do not handle the dough too much and do not roll it out too thinly.

Drop scones are made from a batter that has the consistency of thick cream. The batter is dropped in spoonfuls onto a hot griddle or frying pan.

**1** Sift the dry ingredients into a bowl (flour, baking powder with or without baking soda, salt, sugar, ground spices, etc).

**2 ▲** Add the fat (butter, margarine, vegetable oil, etc). With a pastry blender or two knives used scissor-fashion, cut the fat into the dry ingredients until the mixture resembles fine crumbs, or rub in the fat with your fingertips.

**3 ▲** Add the liquid ingredients (milk, cream, buttermilk, eggs). Stir with a fork until the dry ingredients are thoroughly moistened and will come together in a ball of fairly soft dough in the center of the bowl.

### Date Oven Scones
Sift 2 cups self-rising flour with a pinch of salt and rub in 4 tablespoons butter. Add 2 ounces chopped dates. Mix to a soft dough with ⅔ cup milk. Roll out and cut 2-inch rounds. Glaze with egg or milk. Bake at 450°F for 8–10 minutes, or until risen and golden brown. *Makes about 12.*

**4 ▲** Turn the dough onto a lightly floured surface. Knead it very lightly, folding and pressing to mix evenly, about 30 seconds. Roll or pat out the dough to ¾-inch thickness.

**6 ▲ For griddle scones:** If using a well-seasoned cast-iron griddle, there is no need to grease it. Heat it slowly and evenly. Put scone triangles or rounds on the hot griddle and cook for 4–5 minutes on each side, or until golden brown and cooked through.

**5 ▲ For oven-baked scones:** With a floured, sharp-edged cutter, cut out rounds or other shapes. Or cut diamond shapes or triangles with a floured knife. Arrange on an ungreased baking sheet, not touching. Brush the tops with beaten egg, milk or cream if the recipe specifies. Bake until risen and golden brown.

### Cutting tips
• Be sure the cutter or knife is sharp so that the edges of the scone shapes are not compressed; this would inhibit rising.
• Cut the shapes close together so that you won't have to reroll the dough more than once.
• If necessary, a short, sturdy drinking glass can be pressed into service as a cutter. Flour the rim well and do not press too hard.

# MAKING QUICK BREADS AND MUFFINS

These sorts of bread are very quick and easy to make. The rising agent reacts quickly with moisture and heat to make the breads and muffins rise, without the need for a rising (or proving) period before baking.

The rising agent is usually baking soda or baking powder, which is a mixture of baking soda and an acid salt such as cream of tartar. Many recipes use self-rising flour, which conveniently includes a rising agent. Remember that the rising agent will start to work as soon as it comes into contact with liquid, so don't mix the dry and liquid ingredients until just before you are ready to fill the pan or pans and bake.

**1 ▲ For muffins:** Combine the dry ingredients in a bowl. It is a good idea to sift the flour with the rising agent, salt and any spices to mix them evenly. Add the liquid ingredients and stir just until the dry ingredients are moistened; the mixture will not be smooth. Do not overmix by attempting to remove all the lumps. If you do, the muffins will be tough and will have air holes in them.

**2 ▲** Divide the mixture evenly among the greased or paper-lined muffin pans, filling them about two-thirds full. Bake until golden brown and a wooden skewer inserted in the center comes out clean. To prevent soggy bottoms, remove the muffins immediately from the pans to a wire rack. Cool, and serve warm or at room temperature.

### Granola Muffins
Make the batter from 1 cup all-purpose flour, 1 tablespoon baking powder, 3 tablespoons sugar, 1 cup milk, 4 tablespoons melted butter or corn oil and 1 egg, adding 7 ounces toasted oat cereal with raisins to the dry ingredients. Pour into muffin pans. Bake in a 200°C oven for 20 minutes, or until golden brown. *Makes 10.*

**3 ▲ For fruit and/or nut breads:** Method 1: Stir together all the liquid ingredients. Add the dry ingredients and beat just until smoothly blended. Method 2: Beat the butter with the sugar until the mixture is light and fluffy. Beat in the eggs followed by the other liquid ingredients. Stir in the dry ingredients. Pour the mixture into a prepared pan (typically a loaf pan). Bake until a wooden skewer inserted in the center comes out clean. If the bread is browning too quickly, cover the top with foil.

**4 ▲** Cool in the pan for 5 minutes, then turn out onto a wire rack to cool completely. A lengthwise crack on the surface is characteristic of quick breads. For easier slicing, wrap the bread in waxed paper and then in foil, and store overnight at room temperature.

# MAKING SIMPLE MERINGUE

There are two types of this egg-white-and-sugar foam: a soft meringue used as an insulating topping for pies and baked Alaska and a firm meringue that can be shaped into containers or cake layers for luscious fillings.

Take care when separating the egg whites and yolks because even the smallest trace of yolk will prevent the whites from being beaten to their maximum volume. All equipment used must be scrupulously clean and free of grease.

**1 ▲** Put the egg whites in a large, scrupulously clean and greasefree bowl. With a whisk or electric mixer, beat the whites until they are foamy. If not using a copper bowl, add a pinch of cream of tartar.

**2 ▲** Continue beating until the whites hold soft peaks when the whisk or beaters are lifted (the tips of the peaks will flop over).

**Meringue Nests**
Make a firm meringue using 2 egg whites and ½ cup superfine sugar. Spoon large mounds of meringue onto a baking sheet lined with parchment paper. Slightly hollow out the center of each with the back of the spoon, to make a nest shape. Alternatively, put the meringue into a pastry bag fitted with a ½-inch plain tip and pipe the nest shapes. Sprinkle lightly with a little extra sugar. Dry in a preheated 200°F oven until crisp and firm to the touch but not brown, 3–4 hours. Let cool. To serve, fill with sweetened whipped cream and fresh berries or other fruit. *Makes 4–6.*

**3 ▲ For a soft meringue:** Sprinkle the sugar over the whites, beating constantly. Continue beating until the meringue is glossy and holds stiff peaks when the whisk or beaters are lifted, about 1 minute. The meringue is now ready to be spread over a pie filling or used for baked Alaska.

**Sweetened Whipped Cream**
This is used as a topping and filling for many hot and cold desserts. Whip 1 cup chilled whipping cream until it starts to thicken. Add 2 tablespoons sifted confectioners' sugar and continue whipping until the cream holds a soft peak on the beaters. If desired, the cream may be flavored with ½ teaspoon vanilla extract, ¼ teaspoon almond extract, or 2 teaspoons Cognac or liqueur, added with the sugar.

**4 ▲ For a firm meringue:** Add a little of the sugar (about ½ tablespoon for each egg white). Continue beating until the meringue is glossy and holds stiff peaks.

**5 ▲** Add the remaining sugar to the bowl, with a flavoring if the recipe directs. With a rubber spatula, fold the sugar into the meringue as lightly as possible by cutting down with the spatula to the bottom of the bowl and then turning the mixture over. The meringue is now ready to be shaped into containers or cake layers.

# MAKING BASIC PIE PASTRY

A meltingly tender, flaky pastry sets off any filling to perfection, whether sweet or savory. The pastry dough can be made with half butter or margarine and half vegetable shortening or with all one kind of fat.

### FOR A 9-INCH SINGLE-CRUST PIE

| |
| --- |
| 2 cups all-purpose flour |
| ¼ teaspoon salt |
| 4 ounces fat, chilled and diced |
| 3–4 tablespoons iced water |

**1 ▲** Sift the flour and salt into a bowl. Add the fat. Rub it into the flour with your fingertips until the mixture is crumblike.

**2 ▲** Sprinkle 3 tablespoons water over the mixture. With a fork, toss gently to mix and moisten it.

### Pastry-making tips

- It helps if the fat is cold and firm, particularly if making the dough in a food processor. Cold fat has less chance of warming and softening too much when it is being rubbed into the flour, resulting in an oily pastry. Use block margarine rather than the soft tub-type.
- When rubbing the fat into the flour, if it begins to soften and feel oily, put the bowl in the refrigerator to chill for 20–30 minutes. Then continue making the dough.
- Liquids used should be ice-cold so that they will not soften or melt the fat.
- Take care when adding the water: start with the smaller amount (added all at once, not in a dribble), and add more only if the mixture will not come together into a dough. Too much water will result in tough pastry.
- When gathering the mixture together into a ball of dough, handle it as little as possible: overworked pastry will be tough.
- To avoid shrinkage, refrigerate the pastry dough before rolling out and baking. This "resting time" will allow any elasticity developed during mixing to relax.

**3 ▲** Press the dough into a ball. If it is too dry to form a dough, add the remaining water.

**4 ▲** Wrap the ball of dough with plastic wrap or waxed paper and refrigerate it for at least 30 minutes.

**5 ▲ To make pastry in a food processor:** Combine the flour, salt and cubed fat in the work bowl. Process, turning the machine on and off, just until the mixture is crumbly. Add the ice water and process again briefly – just until the dough starts to pull away from the sides of the bowl. It should still look crumbly. Remove the dough from the processor and gather it into a ball. Wrap and refrigerate.

### Pastry variations

- For *Nut Pie Pastry*: Add 1 ounce finely chopped walnuts or pecans to the flour mixture.
- For *Rich Pie Pastry*: Use 2 cups flour and 12 tablespoons fat (preferably all butter), plus 1 tablespoon sugar if making a sweet pie. Bind with 1 egg yolk and 2–3 tablespoons water.
- For a *Double-crust Pie*, increase the proportions for these pastries by 50 percent. Thus the amounts needed for basic pie pastry are: 3 cups flour, ½ teaspoon salt, 12 tablespoons fat, 5–6 tablespoons water. For Nut Pie Pastry, as above with 2 ounces nuts. For Rich Pie Pastry, as above but using 9 ounces fat, 4–5 tablespoons water and 1 egg yolk.

# MAKING TART PASTRY

The pastry for tarts, flans and quiches is made with butter or margarine, giving a rich and crumbly result. The more fat used, the richer the pastry will be – almost like a cookie dough – and the harder to roll out. If you have difficulty rolling it, you can press it into the pan instead, or roll it out between sheets of plastic wrap. Tart pastry, like pie pastry, can be made by hand or in a food processor. Tips for making, handling and using pie pastry apply equally to tart pastry.

**FOR A 9-INCH PASTRY SHELL**

| |
|---|
| 1¾ cups all-purpose flour |
| ½ teaspoon salt |
| 1 stick (8 tablespoons) butter or margarine, chilled |
| 1 egg yolk |
| ¼ teaspoon lemon juice |
| 2–3 tablespoons iced water |

**1 ▲** Sift the flour and salt into a bowl. Add the butter or margarine. Rub into the flour until the mixture resembles fine crumbs.

**2 ▲** In a small bowl, mix the egg yolk, lemon juice and 2 tablespoons water. Add to the flour mixture. With a fork, toss gently to mix and moisten.

**3 ▲** Press the dough into a rough ball. If it is too dry to come together, add the remaining water. Turn onto the work surface or a pastry board.

**4 ▲** With the heel of your hand, push small portions of dough away from you, smearing them on the surface.

**Tart pastry variations**
● For *Sweet Tart Pastry:* Reduce the amount of salt to ¼ teaspoon; add 1 tablespoon sugar with the flour.
● For *Rich Tart Pastry:* Use 1¾ cups flour, ½ teaspoon salt, 10 tablespoons butter, 2 egg yolks, and 1–2 tablespoons water.
● For *Rich Sweet Tart Pastry:* Make rich tart pastry, adding 3 tablespoons sugar with the flour and, if desired, ½ teaspoon vanilla extract with the egg yolks.

**5 ▲** Continue mixing the dough in this way until it feels pliable and can be peeled easily off the surface.

**6 ▲** Press the dough into a smooth ball. Wrap in plastic wrap and chill for at least 30 minutes.

# ROLLING OUT AND LINING A PIE PLATE

A neat crust that doesn't distort or shrink in baking is the desired result. The key to success is handling the dough gently.

First remove the chilled dough from the refrigerator and let it soften slightly at room temperature. Unwrap and put it on a lightly floured surface. Flatten the dough into a neat, round disk. Sprinkle the top with a little flour. Lightly flour the rolling pin.

**Rolling Out and Lining Tips**

• A pastry cloth and a stockinette cover for your rolling pin will ensure that your pastry dough does not stick when rolling out.
• Reflour the surface and rolling pin if the dough starts to stick.
• Should the dough tear, patch the hole with a small piece of moistened dough.
• When rolling out and lining the pie plate, do not stretch the dough. It will only shrink back during baking, spoiling the shape of the pie shell.
• Once or twice during rolling out, gently push in the edges of the dough with your cupped palms, to keep the circular shape.
• A pastry scraper will help lift the dough from the work surface, to wrap it around the rolling pin.
• Pie plates made from heat-resistant glass or dull-finish metal such as heavyweight aluminum will give a crisp crust.
• When finishing the edge, be sure to hook the dough over the rim all the way around or to press the dough firmly to the rim. This will prevent the dough pulling away should it start to shrink slightly during baking.
• To prevent the edge of the pie-crust from overbrowning, cover it with foil. Remove the foil halfway through baking.

**1 ▲** Using even pressure, start rolling out the dough, working from the center to the edge each time and easing the pressure slightly as you reach the edge.

**2 ▲** Lift up the dough and give it a quarter turn from time to time during the rolling. This will prevent the dough sticking to the surface, and will help keep the thickness even.

**3 ▲** Continue rolling out until the dough circle is about 2 inches larger all around than the pie plate. The dough will be about ⅛-inch thick.

**4 ▲** Set the rolling pin on the dough, near one side of the circle. Fold the outside edge of dough over the pin, then roll the pin over the dough to wrap the dough around it. Do this gently and loosely.

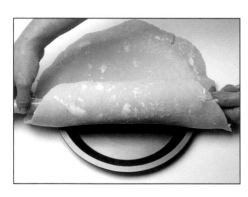

**5 ▲** Hold the pin over the pie plate and gently unroll the dough so it drapes into the plate, centering it as much as possible.

**6 ▲** With your fingertips, ease the dough into the plate, gently pressing it smoothly over the bottom and up the side. With kitchen scissors or a knife, trim the dough according to the edge to be made.

# LINING A TART PAN OR FLAN RING

A tart pan is shallow, with no rim. Its straight sides (smooth or fluted) give a tart or quiche the traditional shape. The most useful pans have removable bottoms, making it easy to unmold a tart. Flan rings, also called tart bands, are straight-sided metal rings that are set on a baking sheet. In addition to these, there are porcelain quiche dishes and small, individual tartlet tins or molds, both plain and fluted.

**Pecan Tartlets**
Line six 4-inch tartlet shells with tart pastry. Divide 1½ cups pecan halves among them. In a bowl, beat 3 eggs to mix. Add 2 tablespoons melted butter, 1 cup light corn syrup, and ½ teaspoon vanilla extract. In another bowl, sift together 1 cup sugar and 1 tablespoon flour. Add to the egg mixture and stir until evenly blended. Divide among the tartlet shells and let stand until the nuts rise to the surface. Bake in a preheated 350°F oven until a knife inserted in the filling near the center comes out clean, 35–40 minutes. Let cool on a wire rack before.serving. *Makes 6.*

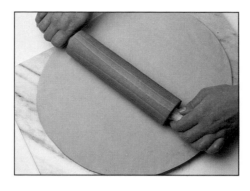

**1** ▲ Remove the chilled dough from the refrigerator and let it soften slightly at room temperature. Roll out to a circle that is about 2 inches larger all around than the tart pan. It will be about ⅛-inch thick.

**3** ▲ With your fingertips, ease the dough into the pan, gently pressing it smoothly over the bottom, without stretching it.

**5** ▲ Roll the rolling pin over the top of the pan to cut off excess pastry dough. Smooth the cut edge and press it against the side of the pan, if necessary, to keep it in place.

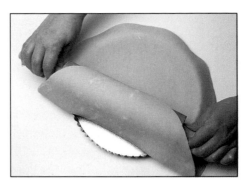

**2** ▲ Roll up the dough around the rolling pin, then unroll it over the pan, draping it gently.

**4** ▲ Fold the overhanging dough down inside the pan, to thicken the side of the pastry shell. Smooth and press the side of the shell against the side of the pan.

**6** ▲ **For tartlet molds**: Arrange them close together and unroll the dough over the molds, draping it loosely. Roll the rolling pin over the top to cut off excess pastry. Press into the bottom and sides of the molds.

# FINISHING THE EDGE OF A PIE

**1 ▲ For a fork-finished edge:** Trim the dough even with the rim and press it flat. Firmly and evenly press the tines of a fork all around the edge. If the fork sticks, dip it in flour.

**2 ▲ For a fluted or pinched edge:** Trim the dough to leave a ½-inch overhang all around. Fold the extra dough under to build up the edge. Put the knuckle or tip of the index finger of one hand inside the edge, pointing directly out. With the thumb and index finger of your other hand, pinch the dough edge around your index finger into a "V" shape. Continue all the way around the edge.

**3 ▲ For a ruffled or scalloped edge:** Trim the dough to leave a ½-inch overhang all around. Fold the extra dough under to build up the edge. Hold the thumb and index finger of one hand 1 inch apart, inside the edge, pointing directly out. With the index finger of your other hand, gently pull the dough between them, to the end of the rim. Continue all the way around the edge.

**Apple and Cherry Streusel Pie**
Mix together 3 cups peeled, cored, and sliced apples, 2 cups pitted tart red cherries, and ½ cup firmly packed light brown sugar. Put the fruit mixture into a 9-inch pie shell and spread out evenly. For the topping, combine ⅔ cup flour, ½ cup firmly packed brown sugar, and 1 teaspoon ground cinnamon. Cut in 6 tablespoons butter until the mixture resembles coarse crumbs. Sprinkle evenly over the fruit. Bake in a preheated 375°F oven until golden brown, about 45 minutes. *Serves 6.*

**4 ▲ For a cutout edge:** Trim the dough even with the rim of the pie plate and press it flat on the rim. With a small cookie cutter, cut out shapes from the dough trimmings. Moisten the edge of the pastry shell and press the cutouts in place, overlapping them slightly if desired.

**5 ▲ For a ribbon edge:** Trim the dough even with the rim of the pie plate and press it flat on the rim. Cut long strips, about ¾-inch wide, from the dough trimmings. Moisten the edge and press one end of a strip onto it. Twist the strip gently and press it onto the edge again. Continue all the way around the edge.

# BAKING A PASTRY SHELL WITHOUT A FILLING

Baked custard and cream fillings can make pastry soggy, so the shells for these pies and tarts are often prebaked before the filling is added and the final baking is done. Such prebaking is referred to as baking "blind." The technique is also used for pastry shells that are to be filled with an uncooked or precooked mixture.

The purpose of using weights is to prevent the bottom of the pastry shell from rising too much and becoming distorted, thus keeping its neat shape.

**1 ▲** Set the pie plate, tart pan, or flan ring on a sheet of parchment paper or foil. Draw or mark around its base. Cut out a circle about 3 inches larger all around than the drawn or marked one.

**2 ▲** Roll out the pastry dough and use to line the pie plate, tart pan, or flan ring set on a baking sheet. Prick the bottom of the pastry shell all over with a fork.

**Fresh Strawberry Tart**
Make the shell using sweet tart pastry or rich sweet tart pastry. Bake it "blind" and then let it cool. Combine 14 ounces cream cheese, ¼ cup sugar, 1 egg yolk, and ¼ cup whipping cream. Beat until smooth. Fold in 1 stiffly beaten egg white. Pour the mixture into the tart shell and spread it evenly. Bake at 350°F until the filling is softly set, 15–20 minutes; it will set further as it cools. Let cool. Arrange halved strawberries neatly over the surface in concentric circles. Heat ½ cup red currant jelly until it melts; brush it all over the berries to glaze them. Let cool and set before serving. *Serves 6.*

**3 ▲** Lay the circle of parchment paper or foil in the pastry shell and press it smoothly over the bottom and up the side.

**4 ▲** Put enough dried beans or pie weights in the shell to cover the bottom thickly.

**5 ▲ For partially baked pastry:** Bake the shell in a preheated 400°F oven until it is slightly dry and set, 15–20 minutes. Remove the paper or foil and beans. It is now ready to be filled and baked further.

**6 ▲ For fully baked pastry:** After baking 15 minutes, remove the paper or foil and beans. Prick the bottom again with a fork. Return to the oven and continue baking until golden brown, 5–10 minutes longer. Let cool completely before adding the filling.

# MAKING A DOUBLE-CRUST PIE

Two tender pastry layers enveloping a sweet filling – what could be nicer? It is easy to see why the double-crust pie is an American institution.

**Apple Pie**
Combine 6 cups peeled, cored, and thinly sliced apples, 1 tablespoon flour, ½ cup sugar, and ¾ teaspoon apple pie spice. Toss together until the fruit is evenly coated with the sugar and flour. Use to fill the pie (use spice pie pastry if desired). Bake in a preheated 375°F oven until the pastry is golden brown and the fruit is tender (test with a skewer through a slit in the crust), about 45 minutes. Cool on a rack.

**1 ▲** Roll out half of the pastry dough on a floured surface and line a pie plate. Trim the dough even with the rim of the pie plate.

**2 ▲** Put in the filling. Brush the edge of the pie shell evenly with water to moisten it.

**3 ▲** Roll out a second piece of dough to a circle that is about 1 inch larger all around than the pie plate. Roll it up around the rolling pin and unroll it over the pie. Press the edges together.

**4 ▲** Trim the edge of the top crust to leave a ½-inch overhang. Cut slits or a design in the center. These will act as steam vents during baking.

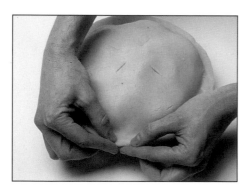

**5 ▲** Fold the overhang under the edge of the bottom crust. Press the two crusts together gently and evenly to seal. Finish the edge, as desired.

**6 ▲** Brush the top crust with milk or cream for a shiny finish. Or, brush with 1 egg yolk mixed with 1 teaspoon water for a glazed golden-brown finish. Or, brush with water and then sprinkle with sugar or cinnamon-sugar for a sugary crust.

**7 ▲** If desired, cut out decorative shapes from the dough trimmings, rolled out as thinly as possible. Moisten the cutouts with a little water and press them onto the top crust. Glaze the decorations before baking.

# MAKING A LATTICE TOP

A woven pastry lattice is a very attractive finish for a pie. Prepare pastry dough for a double-crust pie.

Roll out half of the pastry dough and line the pie plate. Trim the dough to leave a ½-inch overhang all around. Put in the filling. Roll out the second piece of dough into a circle that is about 2 inches larger all around than the pie plate.

**Apricot Lattice Pie**
Combine 6 cups peeled, pitted, thinly sliced apricots, 2 tablespoons flour, and ½ cup sugar. Toss to coat the fruit evenly. Fill the pie shell and make a lattice top. Glaze with milk and bake in a preheated 375°F oven until the pastry is golden brown and the filling is bubbling, about 45 minutes. Cool on a wire rack.

**1 ▲** With the help of a ruler, cut neat, straight strips of dough that are about ½-inch wide, using a knife or fluted pastry wheel.

**2 ▲ For a square woven lattice**: Lay half of the strips across the pie filling, keeping them neatly parallel and spacing them evenly.

**3 ▲** Fold back every other strip from the center. Lay another strip across the center, on the flat strips, at right angles to them. Lay the folded strips flat again.

**4 ▲** Now fold back those strips that were not folded the first time. Lay another strip across those that are flat now, spacing this new strip evenly from the center strip.

**5 ▲** Continue folding the strips in this way until half of the lattice is completed. Repeat on the other half of the pie.

**6 ▲** Trim the ends of the strips even with the rim of the pie plate. Moisten the edge of the bottom crust and press the strips gently to it to seal. Finish the edge.

**7 ▲ For a diamond lattice**: Weave as above, laying the intersecting strips diagonally instead of at right angles. Or, lay half the strips over the filling and the remaining strips on top.

# MAKING A CRUMB CRUST

A crumb crust is one of the simplest piecrusts to make, and the variations in flavoring are almost endless. Crumbs from any dry cookie can be used as well as cracker crumbs. You can also use bread crumbs and cake crumbs. Most crumb crusts are sweet, to hold sweet fillings, but there are also unsweetened crumb crusts for savory cheesecakes.

**MAKES AN 8- OR 9-INCH CRUST**

| 1¾ cups fine crumbs (see below) |
| ½ cup butter, melted |
| 3–4 tablespoons sugar (optional) |

**1 ▲** Combine the crumbs, melted butter, and sugar, plus other flavorings, if using. Stir well to mix.

**2 ▲** Turn the crumb mixture into a buttered 8-inch springform cake pan or 9-inch pie plate. Spread it evenly over the bottom and up the side.

### Crumb Crust Flavorings
- Use graham crackers, plain or cinnamon-flavored. Sweeten with sugar to taste. For plain crackers, add 1 teaspoon ground cinnamon or ginger or ½ teaspoon freshly grated nutmeg.
- Use plain graham crackers and sweeten with sugar to taste. Add 1 teaspoon grated lemon rind or 2 teaspoons grated orange rind.
- Use 1 cup graham cracker crumbs and ½ cup ground or very finely chopped nuts (almonds, hazelnuts, pecans, or walnuts).
- Use vanilla or chocolate wafers, gingersnaps, shortbread, amaretti cookies, or crisp macaroons. No sugar is needed.
- Use saltines or crackers for cheese, without adding sugar, for a savory filling.

**3 ▲** With the back of a large spoon or your fingers, press the crumb mixture firmly against the pie plate, to pack the crumbs into a solid crust.

**4 ▲** According to recipe directions, refrigerate the crust to set it, usually at least 1 hour. Or, bake the crust in a preheated 350°F oven 8–10 minutes; let cool before filling.

### Crushing the Crumbs
To make fine crumbs, break the cookies or crackers into small pieces. Put them, a small batch at a time, in a heavy-duty plastic bag and roll over them with a rolling pin. Or, grind finely in a blender or food processor.

**Easy Chocolate Cream Pie**
Prepare the crumb crust using chocolate wafers and pressing it into a 9-inch pie plate. Bake and let cool. Melt 6 ounces semisweet chocolate with 3 tablespoons milk; let cool. Whip 2 cups heavy whipping cream until thick. Fold the cream into the cooled chocolate. Spread evenly in the crust. Cover and refrigerate until firm. Just before serving, garnish with chocolate curls or grated chocolate. *Serves 6.*

# MAKING CREAM-PUFF PASTRY

Unlike other pastries, in which the fat is rubbed into the flour, with cream-puff pastry the butter is melted with water and then the flour is added, followed by eggs. The result is more of a paste than a pastry. It is easy to make, but care must be taken in measuring the ingredients.

**FOR 18 SMALL PUFFS OR 12 ECLAIRS**

1 stick (8 tablespoons) butter, cut into small pieces

1 cup water

2 teaspoons sugar (optional)

¼ teaspoon salt

1¼ cups all-purpose flour

4 eggs, beaten to mix

---

**Shaping cream-puff pastry**
● For *large puffs*: Use two large spoons dipped in water. Drop the paste in 2–2½-inch wide blobs on the paper-lined baking sheet, leaving 1½-inch between each. Neaten the blobs as much as possible. Alternatively, for well-shaped puffs, pipe the paste using a piping bag fitted with a ¾-inch plain nozzle.
● For *small puffs* or *profiteroles*: Use two small spoons or a piping bag fitted with a ½-inch nozzle and shape 1-inch blobs.
● For *éclairs*: Use a piping bag fitted with a ¾-inch nozzle. Pipe strips 4–5 inches long.
● For a *ring*: Draw a 12-inch circle on the paper. Spoon the paste in large blobs on the circle to make a ring. Or pipe two rings around the circle and a third on top.

---

**Baking times for cream-puff pastry**
Bake large puffs and éclairs 30–35 minutes, small puffs 20–25 minutes, rings 40–45 minutes.

**1 ▲** Combine the butter, water, sugar, if using, and salt in a large, heavy saucepan. Bring to a boil over moderately high heat, stirring occasionally.

**3 ▲** Return the pan to moderate heat and cook, stirring, until the mixture forms a ball, pulling away from the side of the pan. This will take about 1 minute. Remove from the heat again and allow to cool for 3–5 minutes.

**5 ▲** While still warm, shape large cream puffs, éclairs, small puffs or profiteroles or large rings on a baking sheet lined with baking parchment.

**2 ▲** As soon as the mixture is boiling, remove the pan from the heat. Add the flour all at once and beat vigorously with a wooden spoon to mix the flour into the liquid.

**4 ▲** Add a little of the beaten egg and beat well with the spoon or an electric mixer to incorporate. Add a little more egg and beat in well. Continue beating in the eggs until the mixture becomes a smooth, shiny paste thick enough to hold its shape.

**6 ▲** Glaze with 1 egg beaten with 1 teaspoon cold water. Put into a 425°F oven, then reduce the heat to 400°F. Bake until puffed and golden brown.

# MAKING A BUTTER CAKE

The butter cake, with its tender crumb and rich, moist flavor, is always popular. It is delicious enough to be served plain, with just a dusting of sugar, or it can be filled and iced.

To make a butter cake, the fat and sugar are "creamed" – or beaten – together before the eggs and dry ingredients are added. The fat (usually butter or margarine) should be soft enough to be beaten, so if necessary remove it from the refrigerator and leave it at room temperature for at least 30 minutes. For best results, the eggs should be at room temperature.

**Mocha Butter Cake**
Make the mixture using ¾ cup each butter or margarine, sugar and self-rising flour and 3 eggs. Divide between two bowls. To one add 1 tablespoon strong black coffee; to the other add 1 tablespoon cocoa powder mixed to a paste with 1–2 tablespoons boiling water. Place alternate spoonfuls of each flavor, side by side, in 2 greased and lined 7-inch round cake pans. Lightly smooth the tops. Bake at 350°F for 25–30 minutes. Turn out onto a wire rack and cool. Sandwich the cakes together with coffee butter frosting. Cover the top, or top and sides, with butter frosting.

1 ▲ Sift the flour with the salt, rising agent(s) and any other dry ingredients, such as spices or cocoa powder. Set aside.

3 ▲ Add the sugar to the creamed fat gradually. With the mixer at medium-high speed, beat it into the fat until the mixture is pale and very fluffy. The sugar should be completely incorporated. This will take 4–5 minutes. During this process, air will be beaten into the mixture, which will help the cake to rise.

5 ▲ Add the dry ingredients to the mixture, beating at low speed just until smoothly combined. Or fold in with a large metal spoon.

2 ▲ Put the fat in a large, deep bowl and beat with an electric mixer at medium speed or with a wooden spoon, until the texture is soft and pliable.

4 ▲ Add the eggs or egg yolks, one at a time, beating well after each addition (about 45 seconds). Scrape the bowl often so all the ingredients are evenly combined. When you add the eggs, the mixture may begin to curdle, especially if the eggs are cold. If this happens, add 1 tablespoon of the measured flour.

6 ▲ If the recipe calls for any liquid, add it in small portions alternately with portions of the dry ingredients.

**7 ▲** If the recipe directs, beat egg whites separately until frothy, add sugar, and continue beating until stiff peaks form. Fold into the batter.

**8 ▲** Pour the batter into a cake pan or pans, prepared according to recipe directions, and bake as directed.

**9 ▲** To test butter cakes for doneness, insert a cake tester, skewer, or wooden toothpick into the center; it should come out clean.

# MAKING SEVEN-MINUTE FROSTING

This fluffy white frosting has an attractive gloss and a texture like divinity candy. It is ideal for filling and frosting layer cakes.

**MAKES ENOUGH TO FROST THE TOP AND SIDES OF TWO 9-INCH CAKE LAYERS**

| |
|---|
| 1½ cups sugar |
| ¼ teaspoon cream of tartar |
| 2 egg whites |
| ¼ cup cold water |
| 1 tablespoon light corn syrup |
| 2 teaspoons vanilla extract |

**1 ▲** Combine the sugar, cream of tartar, egg whites, water, and corn syrup in a large heatproof bowl or large double boiler. Stir just to mix.

**2 ▲** Set the bowl over a saucepan of boiling water. The base of the bowl should not touch the water.

**Seven-Minute Frosting Variations**
● For *Orange Frosting*: Use orange juice instead of water and add 1 teaspoon grated orange rind. Reduce the vanilla to ½ teaspoon.
● For *Lemon Frosting*: Use 2 tablespoons each lemon juice and water and add ½ teaspoon grated lemon rind. Reduce the vanilla to ½ teaspoon.

**3 ▲** Beat with a handheld electric mixer at high speed until the frosting is thick and white, and will form stiff peaks, about 7 minutes.

**4 ▲** Remove from the heat. Add the vanilla and continue beating until the frosting has cooled slightly, about 3 minutes. Use immediately.

# MAKING A ONE-BOWL CAKE

Many cakes are made by an easy one-bowl method where all the ingredients are combined in a bowl and beaten thoroughly. The mixture can also be made in a food processor, but take care not to overprocess. A refinement on the one-bowl method is to separate the eggs and make the mixture with the yolks. The whites are beaten separately and then folded in.

**1 ▲** Sift the dry ingredients (flour, salt, rising agent, spices, etc.) into a bowl.

**2 ▲** Add the liquid ingredients (eggs, melted or soft fat, milk, fruit juices, etc.) and beat until smooth, with an electric mixer for speed. Pour into the prepared pans and bake as specified in the recipe.

# MAKING BUTTER FROSTING

Quick to make and easy to spread, butter frosting is ideal for all kinds of cakes, from simple to fancy. The basic vanilla frosting can be varied with many other flavors, and it can be tinted with food coloring, too.

**MAKES ENOUGH TO COVER THE TOP AND SIDE OF A 7–8-INCH CAKE**

| |
|---|
| 1 stick (8 tablespoons) butter, preferably unsalted, at room temperature |
| 1 cup confectioners' sugar, sifted |
| 1 teaspoon vanilla extract |
| about 2 tablespoons milk |

**1 ▲** Put the butter in a deep mixing bowl and beat it with an electric mixer at medium speed, or with a wooden spoon, until it is soft and pliable.

**2 ▲** Gradually add the sugar and beat at medium-high speed. Continue beating until the mixture is pale and fluffy.

**3 ▲** Add the vanilla extract and 1 tablespoon milk. Beat until smooth and of a spreading consistency. If it is too thick, beat in more milk. If too thin, beat in more sugar.

**Butter frosting variations**

● For *Orange or Lemon Butter Frosting*, grate the zest from 1 small orange or ½ lemon; squeeze the juice. Beat in the zest with the sugar; use the juice instead of the vanilla and milk.

● For *Chocolate Butter Frosting*, add 4 tablespoons cocoa powder, beating it in with the sugar. Increase the milk to 3–4 tablespoons.

● For *Mocha Butter Frosting*: Warm the milk and dissolve 1 teaspoon instant coffee powder in it; cool and use to make chocolate butter frosting, adding more milk if needed.

● For *Coffee Butter Frosting*, warm the milk and dissolve 1 tablespoon of instant coffee powder in it; cool before adding to the butter frosting.

# MAKING CAKES BY THE MELTING METHOD

Cakes made by the melting method are wonderfully moist and keep quite well. Ingredients such as sugar, syrup (molasses, honey, golden syrup) and fat are warmed together until melted and smoothly combined before being added to the dry ingredients.

**Fruit Cake**

Sift 1½ cups self-rising flour, a pinch of salt and 1 teaspoon apple-pie spice. Melt together 1 stick (8 tablespoons) butter or margarine, ⅔ cup light brown sugar, ⅔ cup water and the grated zest and juice of 1 orange. When smooth, add 4 ounces each golden raisins, currants and raisins and simmer gently for about 10 minutes, stirring occasionally. Cool. Add the fruit mixture to the dry ingredients. Add 2 ounces each chopped candied cherries and chopped mixed citrus peel, 1 tablespoon orange marmalade and 2 beaten eggs. Mix thoroughly. Pour into a greased and lined 8-inch round cake pan. Bake at 325°F for 1½ hours, or until firm and golden; a skewer inserted in the center should come out clean. Cool in the pan for 30 minutes before turning out onto a wire rack.

**1 ▲** Sift the dry ingredients (such as flour, rising agent, salt, ground spices) into a large bowl.

**3 ▲** If recipe instructs, warm fruit in the syrup mixture. Remove from the heat and let cool slightly (if too hot, it will not combine well with dry ingredients).

**5 ▲** If called for in the recipe, stir in fruit and/or nuts (if these have not been warmed in the syrup). Turn the cake mixture into a lined pan and bake according to the recipe.

**2 ▲** Put the sugar and/or syrup and fat in a saucepan with any other ingredients specified in the recipe. Warm over low heat, stirring occasionally, until the fat has melted and the sugar dissolved. The mixture should not boil.

**4 ▲** Make a well in the center of the dry ingredients and pour in the cooled melted mixture. Add beaten eggs and any other liquid ingredients (milk, water, etc.) and beat to a smooth, thick batter.

**Maturing for flavor**
Melting-method cakes taste best if they are allowed to "mature" before serving. After the cake has cooled completely, wrap it in waxed paper and then again in foil. Keep it in a cool place for 1–2 days before cutting into slices.

# MAKING A CLASSIC SPONGECAKE

The classic spongecake contains no fat and no leavening agents – just eggs, sugar, and flour. The light, airy texture of the finished cake depends on the air beaten into the batter.

Sometimes the eggs are separated for a spongecake and sometimes the cake is enriched with butter (called a "genoise", or butter spongecake).

Spongecake can be simply dusted with confectioners' sugar, layered with sweetened whipped cream, filled with preserves or fruit if desired, or used to make a jelly roll.

If you use a countertop electric mixer to beat the eggs and sugar, or if using separated eggs, there is no need to set the bowl over a pan of simmering water.

### Basic Spongecake
Make the cake batter using 4 whole eggs, ¾ cup sugar, and ¾ cup cake flour. Pour the batter into a greased, bottom-lined, and floured 9-inch round cake pan. Bake in a preheated 350°F oven 30–35 minutes. Let the cake cool in the pan 10 minutes, then un-mold onto a wire rack and cool completely. Before serving, peel off the lining paper. Dust lightly with confectioners' sugar.

**1 ▲**  In a bowl, combine the eggs (at room temperature) and sugar. Set the bowl over a saucepan of simmering water; the base of the bowl should not touch the water.

**3 ▲**  Lift out the beaters; the mixture on the beaters should trail back onto the surface of the remaining mixture in the bowl to make a ribbon that holds it shape.

**5 ▲**  Sift the flour and fold it into the mixture, cutting in to the bottom of the bowl with a rubber spatula or large metal spoon, and turning the batter over, working gently yet thoroughly, to retain the volume of the egg and sugar mixture.

**2 ▲**  Beat with a handheld electric mixer at medium-high speed until the mixture is very thick and pale, about 10 minutes.

**4 ▲**  Remove the bowl from over the pan of water and continue beating until the mixture is cool, 2–3 minutes.

**6 ▲**  Pour the batter into the prepared pan or pans and bake as directed. To test if a spongecake is done, press the center lightly with your fingertip: the cake should spring back.

# MAKING A JELLY ROLL

A rolled spongecake reveals an attractive spiral of filling when it is sliced. Some filling ideas are sweetened whipped cream, ice cream, fruit preserves or butter frosting.

The spongecake batter can be made using whole or separated eggs.

Line the pan with wax paper or baking parchment. Grease and dust with flour.

**Chocolate Ice Cream Roll**
Make the spongecake batter using 4 eggs, separated, ⅔ cup sugar, and ⅔ cup cake flour sifted with 3 tablespoons unsweetened cocoa powder. Pour into a prepared 15- × 10-inch jelly roll pan. Bake in a preheated 375°F oven about 15 minutes. Turn out, roll up, and let cool. When cold, unroll the cake and spread with 2½ cups softened vanilla or chocolate ice cream. Roll up the cake again, wrap in foil, and freeze until firm. About 30 minutes before serving, transfer the cake to the refrigerator. Sprinkle with granulated or confectioners' sugar before serving. If desired, serve with warm bittersweet chocolate sauce.
*Serves 6–8.*

**1 ▲** Pour the batter into the prepared pan and spread it evenly into the corners with a metal spatula. Bake as directed in the recipe.

**3 ▲** Carefully peel off the lining paper from the cake. If necessary, trim off any crisp crust from the side of the cake.

**5 ▲** Remove the towel and unroll the cake. Lift off the paper. Spread the chosen filling over the cake.

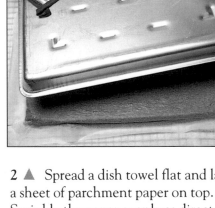

**2 ▲** Spread a dish towel flat and lay a sheet of parchment paper on top. Sprinkle the paper evenly as directed with granulated or confectioners' sugar, cocoa powder, or a spice mixture. Invert the cake onto the paper.

**4 ▲** Carefully roll up the cake, with the paper inside, starting from a short side. Wrap the towel around the cake roll and let cool on a wire rack.

**6 ▲** Roll the cake up again, using the paper to help move it forward. Sprinkle with sugar or frost, as the recipe directs.

# PREPARING CAKE PANS

Instructions vary from recipe to recipe for preparing cake pans. Some are simply greased, some are greased and floured, some are lined with paper. There are some (such as for angel food cakes) that are not greased at all. The preparation required is based on the type of cake batter and the length of the baking time.

**Flavorful Coatings**
Some cake recipes direct that the greased pan be coated with sugar, cocoa powder, or fine crumbs. Follow the method for flouring.

**1 ▲ To grease a pan**: Use butter, shortening, oil, or vegetable cooking spray. If using butter or shortening, hold a small piece in a paper towel (or use your fingers), and rub it all over the bottom and up the side of the pan to make a thin, even coating. If using oil, brush it on with a pastry brush.

**2 ▲ To flour a pan**: Put a small scoopful of flour in the center of the greased pan. Tip and rotate the pan so that the flour spreads and coats all over the bottom and up the side. Turn the pan over and shake out excess flour, tapping the base of the pan to dislodge any pockets of flour.

**3 ▲ To line the bottom of a pan**: Use wax or parchment paper. Set the pan on the paper and draw around the base. Cut out this circle, square, or rectangle, cutting just inside the drawn line. Press the paper circle smoothly onto the bottom of the pan.

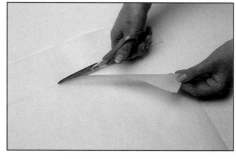

**4 ▲ To line the sides of a pan**: Cut a strip of wax or parchment paper long enough to wrap around the outside of the pan and overlap by 1½ inches. The strip should be wide enough to extend 1 inch above the rim of the cake pan.

**5 ▲** Fold the strip lengthwise at the 1-inch point and crease it firmly. With scissors, snip at regular intervals along the 1-inch fold, from the edge to the crease. Line the side of the pan, putting the snipped part of the strip on the bottom of the pan.

**6 ▲** For square and rectangular cake pans, fold the paper and crease it with your fingernail to fit snugly into the corners of the pan. Then press the bottom paper lining into place.

**7 ▲** If the recipe directs, grease the paper before you put it in the pan. If the pan is to be floured, do this after the paper is in place.

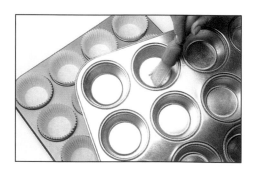

**8 ▲ To line muffin cups**: Use paper cupcake liners of the required size. Or grease and flour the cups.

**9 ▲ To line a jelly-roll pan:** Cut a rectangle of paper 2 inches larger all around than the pan. Grease the bottom of the pan lightly to prevent the paper from slipping.

**10 ▲** Lay the paper evenly in the pan. With a table knife, press the paper into the angle all around the bottom of the pan, creasing the paper firmly but not cutting it.

**11 ▲** With scissors, snip the paper in the corners from top to bottom so it will fit neatly into them. Grease the paper according to recipe instructions, unless using baking parchment.

# USING SEPARATED EGGS FOR A BEATEN SPONGE

This version of beaten sponge is easier to make than the classic one that uses whole eggs, but the results are no less light and delicious. There is no need to set the bowl over a pan of simmering water for beating, although if you are using a balloon whisk rather than an electric mixer or rotary beater, you may want to do so to speed up the thickening of the egg yolk and sugar mixture and to increase its volume. Bowls and beaters used with egg whites must be scrupulously clean.

**1 ▲** Separate the eggs, taking care that there is no trace of yolk with the whites. Put the yolks and whites in separate large bowls.

**2 ▲** Add most of the sugar to the yolks. With a handheld or tabletop electric mixer, beat at medium-high speed until the mixture is very thick and pale. Lift out the beaters: the mixture on the beaters should trail back onto the surface of the remaining mixture in the bowl to make a ribbon that holds its shape.

**3 ▲** Beat the egg whites until they form soft peaks (if not using a copper bowl, add a pinch of cream of tartar once the whites are frothy). Add the remaining sugar and continue beating until the whites will form stiff peaks.

**4 ▲** With a rubber spatula, fold the sifted flour into the egg yolk mixture, then fold in the beaten egg whites. Fold gently but thoroughly. Pour the mixture into the prepared pan and bake as instructed.

**A butter spongecake**
This sponge cake, made with whole or separated eggs, is more rich and trickier to make, as melted butter is folded in just before pouring into the pan.

# MAKING YEAST DOUGH

Making bread is a very enjoyable and satisfying culinary experience – with no other preparation do you have such "hands-on" contact. From the kneading through to the shaping of the risen dough, you are working with a living organism, yeast, not a chemical leavening agent. Yeast is available either dry or fresh. Active dry yeast keeps longer. Compressed fresh yeast should be refrigerated.

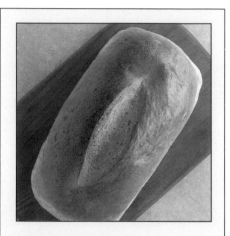

**Everyday White Bread**
Mix 2 packages active dry yeast with ⅓ cup warm water; add 1 teaspoon sugar. Sift 5½ cups flour into a large bowl with ½ table-spoon salt and 1 tablespoon sugar. Make a well in the center and add the yeast mixture, 1 cup warm milk, ¾ cup warm water, and 2 tablespoons melted and cooled butter. Mix to a soft dough, adding more flour if necessary, then knead until smooth and elastic. Let rise until doubled in bulk. Punch the dough to deflate it. Divide it in half and shape each piece into a loaf, tucking the ends under. Put in 2 greased 8½- × 4½-inch loaf pans. Leave in a warm place to rise, 30–45 minutes. If desired, lightly beat 1 egg with 1 tablespoon milk and glaze the tops of the loaves. Bake in a preheated 450°F oven 35–40 minutes. *Makes 2 loaves.*

**1 ▲** Put the yeast in a small bowl and add some of the warm liquid (105–110°F) called for in the recipe. Let dry yeast soak for 1 minute, then whisk to dissolve; mash fresh yeast to blend. Add a little sugar if the recipe directs.

**3 ▲** Using your fingers or a spoon, gradually draw the flour into the liquids. Continue until all the flour is incorporated and the dough pulls away from the sides of the bowl. If the dough feels too soft and wet, work in a little more flour. If it will not come together, add a little more liquid.

**5 ▲** Shape the dough into a ball. Put it in a lightly greased bowl and rotate the dough so that the surface is lightly greased all over. Cover the bowl with a towel or plastic wrap. Set it aside in a warm, draft-free place (about 80°F).

**2 ▲** Sift the flour into a large warm bowl (with other dry ingredients such as salt). Make a well in the center and add the yeast mixture plus any other liquid ingredients.

**4 ▲** Turn the dough onto a lightly floured surface. Fold the dough over onto itself toward you, and then press it down away from you with the heels of your hands. Rotate the dough slightly and fold and press it again. Knead until the dough looks satiny and feels elastic, about 10 minutes.

**6 ▲** Let the dough rise until it is doubled in bulk, 1–1½ hours. To test if it is sufficiently risen, press a finger about 1 inch into the dough and withdraw it quickly: the indentation should remain.

**7** ▲ Gently punch the center of the dough with your fist to deflate it and fold the edges to the center. Turn the dough onto a lightly floured surface and knead it again for 2–3 minutes. If the recipe directs, shape it into a ball again and let rise a second time.

**8** ▲ Shape the dough into loaves, rolls, or other shapes as directed. Put into prepared pans or onto baking sheets. Cover and let rise in a warm place again, ¾–1 hour. If the recipe directs, glaze the loaves or rolls before baking.

**9** ▲ Bake in the center of a preheated oven until well risen and golden brown. To test for doneness, turn out of the pan and tap the base with your knuckle. If it sounds hollow, it is fully cooked. Immediately transfer to a wire rack for cooling.

# SHAPING ROLLS

A basket of freshly baked rolls, in decorative shapes, is a delightful accompaniment for soups or salads. After shaping, arrange the rolls on a baking sheet, leaving space around each roll for spreading, and let rise for 30 minutes before baking.

### Working with Yeast

● A ¼-ounce package of active dry yeast contains 1 tablespoon. One cake of compressed fresh yeast is equivalent to a package of dry yeast. For quick-rising dry yeast, combine it with the flour and other dry ingredients, then add the liquids (which should be warmer than for ordinary active dry yeast). Or, follow recipe directions.

● If you are in any doubt about the freshness of the yeast, it is a good idea to "proof" it: set the yeast mixture in a warm place. After 5–10 minutes, the mixture should be foamy. If it isn't, discard it and start again.

**1** ▲ **For Parker House rolls:** Roll out the risen dough to ¼-inch thickness and cut out 2½- to 3-inch rounds, using a floured cutter. Brush the rounds with melted butter. Fold them in half, slightly off-center so the top overlaps the bottom. Press the folded edge firmly. Arrange on a greased baking sheet.

**2** ▲ **For butterhorn rolls:** Roll out the risen dough to a large round about ¼-inch thick. Brush with melted butter. With a sharp knife, cut into wedges that are 2½–3 inches at their wide end. Roll up each wedge, from the wide end. Set the rolls on a greased baking sheet, placing the points underneath.

**3** ◄ **For bowknot rolls:** Divide the risen dough into pieces. Roll each with your palms on a lightly floured surface to make ropes that are about ½-inch thick. Divide the ropes into 9-inch lengths. Tie each length of dough loosely into a knot, tucking the ends under. Arrange the rolls on a greased baking sheet.

# MAKING PIZZA DOUGH

The range of toppings for a pizza is virtually limitless. Although you can buy pizza bases, it's very easy to make your own at home, and takes much less time than you would expect.

**MAKES A 14-INCH PIZZA BASE**

| |
|---|
| 2 teaspoons active dry yeast |
| ¾ cup warm water (105–110°F) |
| 2¼ cups flour |
| 1 teaspoon salt |
| 1½ tablespoons olive oil |

**Tomato and Mozzarella Pizza**
Spread 1 cup tomato-garlic sauce over the pizza base, not quite to the edges. Scatter 1 cup shredded mozzarella cheese evenly over the sauce (plus thinly sliced pepperoni or salami if desired). Finish with a sprinkling of 2 tablespoons freshly grated Parmesan cheese and a drizzle of olive oil. Bake in a preheated 475°F oven for 15–20 minutes.

**Food Processor Pizza Dough**
Combine the flour, salt, yeast mixture, and olive oil in the processor container. Process briefly, then add the rest of the warm water. Work until the dough begins to form a ball. Process 3–4 minutes to knead the dough, then knead it by hand for 2–3 minutes.

**1 ▲** Put the yeast in a small bowl, add ¼ cup of the water, and let it soak 1 minute. Whisk lightly with a fork until dissolved.

**3 ▲** Using your fingers, gradually draw the flour into the liquids. Continue mixing until all the flour is incorporated and the dough will just hold together.

**5 ▲** Cover the bowl with plastic wrap. Set aside in a warm place to let the dough rise until doubled in bulk, about 1 hour. Turn the dough onto the lightly floured surface again. Gently punch down the dough to deflate it. Knead lightly until smooth.

**2 ▲** Sift the flour and salt into a large warm bowl. Make a well in the center and add the yeast mixture, olive oil, and remaining warm water.

**4 ▲** Turn the dough onto a lightly floured surface. Knead it until it is smooth and silky, about 10 minutes. Shape the dough into a ball. Put it in an oiled bowl and rotate to coat the surface with oil.

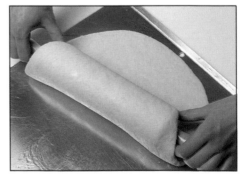

**6 ▲** Roll out the dough into a round or square about ¼-inch thick. Transfer it to a lightly oiled metal pizza tray or baking sheet. Add the topping as directed in the recipe. Bake until the pizza crust is puffy and well browned. Serve hot.

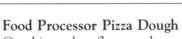

# MAKING FOCACCIA AND BREAD STICKS

Italian flatbreads, such as focaccia, and bread sticks can be topped with herbs and seeds for tasty accompaniments or starters. Personalize them with combinations of your favorite ingredients for unusual snacks or split and fill flatbreads with ham or cheese for an Italian-style sandwich.

This basic dough can be used for other recipes, such as pizza. The dough may be frozen before it is baked, and thawed before filling.

**1 ▲ For focaccia:** Warm a mixing bowl by swirling some hot water in it. Drain. Place the yeast in the bowl, and pour on the warm water. Stir in the sugar, mix with a fork, and allow to stand until the yeast has dissolved and starts to foam, 5–10 minutes.

### Working with Yeast

● A ¼-ounce package of active dry yeast contains 1 tablespoon. One cake of compressed fresh yeast is equivalent to a package of dry yeast. For quick-rising dry yeast, combine it with the flour and other dry ingredients, then add the liquids (which should be warmer than for ordinary active dry yeast). Or, follow recipe directions.

● If you are in any doubt about the freshness of the yeast, it is a good idea to "proof" it: set the yeast mixture in a warm place. After 5–10 minutes, the mixture should be foamy.

**2 ▲** Use a wooden spoon to mix in the salt and about one-third of the flour. Mix in another third of the flour, stirring with the spoon until the dough forms a mass and begins to pull away from the sides of the bowl.

**3 ▲** Sprinkle some of the remaining flour onto a smooth work surface. Remove the dough from the bowl and begin to knead it, working in the remaining flour a little at a time. Knead for 8–10 minutes. By the end the dough should be elastic and smooth. Form it into a ball.

**4** Lightly oil a mixing bowl. Place the dough in the bowl. Stretch a damp dish towel or plastic wrap across the top of the bowl, and leave it to stand in a warm place until the dough has doubled in volume, about 40–50 minutes or more, depending on the type of yeast used. To test whether the dough has risen enough, poke two fingers into the dough. If the indentations remain, the dough is ready.

**5 ▲** Punch the dough down with your fist to release the air. Knead for 1–2 minutes.

**6 ▲** Brush a pan with oil. Press the dough into the pan with your fingers to a layer 1-inch thick. Cover and leave to rise for 30 minutes. Preheat the oven. Make indentations all over the focaccia with your fingers. Brush with oil, add filling and bake until pale golden.

**7 ▲ For bread sticks:** There's no need for the first rising. Divide dough into large walnut-size pieces and roll out on a floured surface with your hands, into thin sausage shapes. Transfer to a greased cookie sheet, cover and leave in a warm place for 10–15 minutes. Bake until crisp.

# COOKIES
# & BARS

KEEP THE COOKIE JAR FILLED WITH
THIS WONDERFUL ARRAY OF
COOKIES AND BARS – SOME SOFT
AND CHEWY, SOME CRUNCHY AND
NUTTY, SOME RICH AND SINFUL,
AND SOME PLAIN AND WHOLESOME.
ALL ARE IRRESISTIBLE.

# Granola Cookies

**MAKES 18**

½ cup (1 stick) butter or margarine, at room temperature

½ cup light brown sugar, firmly packed

⅓ cup crunchy peanut butter

1 egg

½ cup flour

½ teaspoon baking powder

½ teaspoon cinnamon

⅛ teaspoon salt

2 cups granola cereal

⅓ cup raisins

½ cup walnuts, chopped

**1** Preheat oven to 350°F. Grease a cookie sheet.

**2** With an electric mixer, cream the butter or margarine and sugar until light and fluffy. Beat in the peanut butter. Beat in the egg.

**3** ▲ Sift the flour, baking powder, cinnamon, and salt over the peanut butter mixture and stir to blend. Stir in the granola, raisins, and walnuts. Taste the mixture to see if it needs more sugar, as granolas vary.

**4** ▲ Drop rounded tablespoonfuls of the batter onto the prepared cookie sheet about 1 inch apart. Press gently with the back of a spoon to spread each mound into a circle.

**5** Bake until lightly colored, about 15 minutes. With a metal spatula, transfer to a rack to cool. Store in an airtight container.

---

# Oatmeal and Cereal Cookies

**MAKES 14**

¾ cup (1½ sticks) butter or margarine, at room temperature

¾ cup sugar

1 egg yolk

1½ cups flour

1 teaspoon baking soda

½ teaspoon salt

½ cup rolled oats

½ cup small crunchy nugget cereal

~ **VARIATION** ~

For Nutty Oatmeal Cookies, substitute an equal quantity of chopped walnuts or pecans for the cereal, and prepare as described.

**1** ▲ With an electric mixer, cream the butter or margarine and sugar together until light and fluffy. Mix in the egg yolk.

**2** Sift over the flour, baking soda, and salt, then stir into the butter mixture. Add the oats and cereal and stir to blend. Refrigerate for at least 20 minutes.

**3** Preheat the oven to 375°F. Grease a cookie sheet.

**4** ▲ Roll the dough into balls. Place them on the cookie sheet and flatten with the bottom of a floured glass.

**5** Bake until golden, 10–12 minutes. With a metal spatula, transfer to a rack to cool completely. Store in an airtight container.

*Granola Cookies (top), Oatmeal and Cereal Cookies*

# Coconut Oatmeal Cookies

**MAKES 48**

2 cups quick-cooking oats

1 cup shredded coconut

1 cup (2 sticks) butter or margarine, at
  room temperature

½ cup granulated sugar

¼ cup dark brown sugar, firmly packed

2 eggs

4 tablespoons milk

1½ teaspoons vanilla extract

1 cup flour

½ teaspoon baking soda

½ teaspoon salt

1 teaspoon ground cinnamon

**1** Preheat the oven to 400°F. Lightly
grease 2 cookie sheets.

**2 ▲** Spread the oats and coconut on
an ungreased baking sheet. Bake until
golden brown, 8–10 minutes, stirring
occasionally.

**3** With an electric mixer, cream the
butter or margarine and both sugars
until light and fluffy. Beat in the eggs,
1 at a time, then the milk and vanilla.
Sift over the dry ingredients and fold
in. Stir in the oats and coconut.

**4 ▼** Drop spoonfuls of the dough 1–2
inches apart on the prepared sheets
and flatten with the bottom of a
greased glass dipped in sugar. Bake
until golden, 8–10 minutes. Transfer
to a rack to cool.

---

# Crunchy Jumbles

**MAKES 36**

½ cup (1 stick) butter or margarine, at
  room temperature

1 cup sugar

1 egg

1 teaspoon vanilla extract

1¼ cups flour

½ teaspoon baking soda

⅛ teaspooon salt

2 cups crisped rice cereal

1 cup chocolate chips

~ **VARIATION** ~

For even crunchier cookies, add
½ cup walnuts, coarsely chopped,
with the cereal and chocolate chips.

**1** Preheat the oven to 350°F. Lightly
grease 2 cookie sheets.

**2 ▲** With an electric mixer, cream
the butter or margarine and sugar until
light and fluffy. Beat in the egg and
vanilla. Sift over the flour, baking
soda, and salt and fold in.

**3 ▼** Add the cereal and chocolate
chips. Stir to mix thoroughly.

**4** Drop the dough by spoonfuls 1–2
inches apart on the sheets. Bake until
golden, 10–12 minutes. Transfer to a
rack to cool.

*Coconut Oatmeal Cookies (top), Crunchy Jumbles*

# Ginger Cookies

**MAKES 36**

1 cup granulated sugar

½ cup light brown sugar, firmly packed

½ cup (1 stick) butter, at room temperature

½ cup (1 stick) margarine, at room temperature

1 egg

⅓ cup molassses

2¼ cups flour

2 teaspoons ground ginger

½ teaspoon grated nutmeg

1 teaspoon ground cinnamon

2 teaspoons baking soda

½ teaspoon salt

**1** Preheat the oven to 325°F. Line 2–3 cookie sheets with wax paper and grease lightly.

**2 ▲** With an electric mixer, cream ½ cup of the granulated sugar, the brown sugar, butter, and margarine until light and fluffy. Add the egg and continue beating to blend well. Add the molasses.

**3 ▲** Sift the dry ingredients 3 times, then stir into the butter mixture. Refrigerate for 30 minutes.

**4 ▲** Place the remaining sugar in a shallow dish. Roll tablespoonfuls of the dough into balls, then roll the balls in the sugar to coat.

**5** Place the balls 2 inches apart on the prepared sheets and flatten slightly. Bake until golden around the edges but soft in the middle, 12–15 minutes. Let stand for 5 minutes before transferring to a rack to cool.

~ **VARIATION** ~

To make Gingerbread Men, increase the amount of flour by ¼ cup. Roll out the dough and cut out shapes with a special cutter. Decorate with icing, if wished.

# Orange Cookies

**MAKES 30**

½ cup (1 stick) butter, at room
    temperature

1 cup sugar

2 egg yolks

1 tablespoon fresh orange juice

grated rind of 1 large orange

1 cup all-purpose flour

½ cup cake flour

½ teaspoon salt

1 teaspoon baking powder

**1 ▲** With an electric mixer, cream
the butter and sugar until light and
fluffy. Add the yolks, orange juice and
rind, and continue beating to blend.
Set aside.

**2** In another bowl, sift together the
flours, salt, and baking powder. Add
to the butter mixture and stir until it
forms a dough.

**3 ▲** Wrap the dough in wax paper
and refrigerate for 2 hours.

**4** Preheat the oven to 375°F. Grease
2 cookie sheets.

**5 ▲** Roll spoonfuls of the dough into
balls and place 1–2 inches apart on
the prepared sheets.

**6 ▼** Press down with a fork to
flatten. Bake until golden brown,
8–10 minutes. With a metal spatula
transfer to a rack to cool.

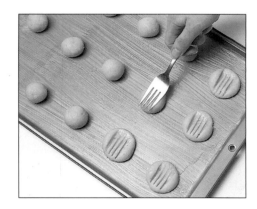

# Snickerdoodles

**MAKES 30**

½ cup (1 stick) butter, at room temperature

1½ cups sugar

1 teaspoon vanilla extract

2 eggs

¼ cup milk

3½ cups flour

1 teaspoon baking soda

½ cup walnuts or pecans, finely chopped

FOR THE COATING

5 tablespoons sugar

2 tablespoons ground cinnamon

**1**  With an electric mixer, cream the butter until light. Add the sugar and vanilla and continue until fluffy. Beat in the eggs, then the milk.

**2 ▲**  Sift the flour and baking soda over the butter mixture and stir to blend. Stir in the nuts. Refrigerate for 15 minutes. Preheat the oven to 375°F. Grease 2 cookie sheets.

**3 ▲**  For the coating, mix the sugar and cinnamon. Roll tablespoonfuls of the dough into walnut-size balls. Roll the balls in the sugar mixture. You may need to work in batches.

**4**  Place 2 inches apart on the prepared sheets and flatten slightly. Bake until golden, about 10 minutes. Transfer to a rack to cool.

---

# Chewy Chocolate Cookies

**MAKES 18**

4 egg whites

2½ cups confectioners' sugar

1 cup unsweetened cocoa powder

2 tablespoons flour

1 teaspoon instant coffee

1 tablespoon water

1 cup walnuts, finely chopped

**1**  Preheat the oven to 350°F. Line 2 cookie sheets with wax paper and grease the paper.

### ~ VARIATION ~

If wished, add ½ cup chocolate chips to the dough with the nuts.

**2**  With an electric mixer, beat the egg whites until frothy.

**3 ▼**  Sift the sugar, cocoa, flour, and coffee into the whites. Add the water and continue beating on low speed to blend, then on high for a few minutes until the mixture thickens. With a rubber spatula, fold in the walnuts.

**4 ▲**  Place generous spoonfuls of the mixture 1 inch apart on the prepared sheets. Bake until firm and cracked on top but soft on the inside, 12–15 minutes. With a metal spatula, transfer to a rack to cool.

*Snickerdoodles (top), Chewy Chocolate Cookies*

# Chocolate Pretzels

**MAKES 28**

1 cup flour

⅛ teaspoon salt

3 tablespoons unsweetened cocoa powder

½ cup (1 stick) butter, at room temperature

⅔ cup sugar

1 egg

1 egg white, lightly beaten, for glazing

sugar crystals, for sprinkling

**1** Sift together the flour, salt and cocoa powder. Set aside. Grease 2 cookie sheets.

**2 ▲** With an electric mixer, cream the butter until light. Add the sugar and continue beating until light and fluffy. Beat in the egg. Add the dry ingredients and stir to blend. Gather the dough into a ball, wrap in wax paper, and refrigerate for 1 hour or freeze for 30 minutes.

**3 ▲** Roll the dough into 28 small balls. If the dough is sticky, flour your hands. Refrigerate the balls until needed. Preheat the oven to 375°F.

**4 ▲** Roll each ball into a rope about 10 inches long. With each rope, form a loop with the two ends facing you. Twist the ends and fold back on to the circle, pressing in to make a pretzel shape. Place on the prepared sheets.

**5 ▲** Brush the pretzels with the egg white. Sprinkle sugar crystals over the tops and bake until firm, 10–12 minutes. Transfer to a rack to cool.

# Cream Cheese Spirals

**MAKES 32**

1 cup (2 sticks) butter, at room
    temperature

8 ounces cream cheese

2 teaspoons granulated sugar

2 cups flour

1 egg white beaten with 1 tablespoon
    water, for glazing

granulated sugar, for sprinkling

**FOR THE FILLING**

1 cup walnuts or pecans, finely chopped

½ cup light brown sugar, firmly packed

1 teaspoon ground cinnamon

**1** With an electric mixer, cream the
butter, cream cheese, and sugar until
soft. Sift over the flour and mix to
form a dough. Gather into a ball and
divide in half. Flatten each half, wrap
in wax paper and refrigerate for at
least 30 minutes.

**2** Meanwhile, make the filling. Mix
together the chopped walnuts or
pecans, the brown sugar, and the
cinnamon. Set aside.

**3** Preheat the oven to 375°F. Grease
2 cookie sheets.

**4 ▲** Working with one half of the
dough at a time, roll out thinly into a
circle about 11 inches in diameter.
Trim the edges with a knife, using a
dinner plate as a guide.

**5 ▼** Brush the surface with the egg
white glaze and sprinkle the dough
evenly with half the filling.

**6** Cut the dough into quarters, and
each quarter into 4 sections, to form
16 triangles.

**7 ▲** Starting from the base of the
triangles, roll up to form spirals.

**8** Place on the sheets and brush with
the remaining glaze. Sprinkle with
granulated sugar. Bake until golden,
15–20 minutes. Cool on a rack.

# Vanilla Crescents

**MAKES 36**

1¼ cups unblanched almonds

1 cup flour

½ teaspoon salt

1 cup (2 sticks) unsalted butter, at room
   temperature

½ cup granulated sugar

1 teaspoon vanilla extract

confectioners' sugar, for dusting

**1**  Grind the almonds with a few
tablespoons of the flour in a food
processor, blender, or nut grinder.

**2**  Sift the remaining flour with the
salt. Set aside.

**3**  With an electric mixer, cream the
butter and sugar together until light
and fluffy.

**4 ▼**  Add the almonds, vanilla, and
the flour mixture. Stir to mix well.
Gather the dough into a ball, wrap in
wax paper, and refrigerate for at least
30 minutes.

**5**  Preheat the oven to 325°F. Lightly
grease 2 cookie sheets.

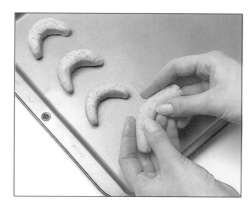

**6 ▲**  Break off walnut-size pieces of
dough and roll into small cylinders
about ½ inch in diameter. Bend into
small crescents and place on the
prepared cookie sheets.

**7**  Bake until dry but not brown,
about 20 minutes. Transfer to a rack
to cool only slightly. Set the rack over
a baking sheet and dust with an even
layer of confectioners' sugar.

# Walnut Crescents

**MAKES 72**

1 cup walnuts

1 cup (2 sticks) unsalted butter, at room
   temperature

¾ cup granulated sugar

½ teaspoon vanilla extract

2 cups flour

¼ teaspoon salt

confectioners' sugar, for dusting

**1**  Preheat the oven to 350°F.

**2**  Grind the walnuts in a food
processor, blender, or nut grinder
until they are almost a paste. Transfer
to a bowl.

**3**  Add the butter to the walnuts and
mix with a wooden spoon until
blended. Add the granulated sugar
and vanilla and stir to blend.

**4 ▼**  Sift the flour and salt into the
walnut mixture. Work into a dough
with your hands.

**5**  Shape the dough, a teaspoonful at a
time, into small cylinders about 1½
inches long. Bend into crescents and
place evenly spaced on an ungreased
cookie sheet.

**6 ▲**  Bake until lightly browned,
about 15 minutes. Transfer to a rack
to cool only slightly. Set the rack over
a baking sheet and dust lightly with
confectioners' sugar.

*Vanilla Crescents (top), Walnut Crescents*

# Pecan Puffs

**MAKES 24**

½ cup (1 stick) unsalted butter, at room
   temperature

2 tablespoons granulated sugar

⅛ teaspoon salt

1 teaspoon vanilla extract

1 cup pecans

1 cup sifted cake flour

confectioners' sugar, for dusting

**1** Preheat the oven to 300°F. Grease
2 cookie sheets.

**2 ▲** With an electric mixer, cream
the butter and sugar until light and
fluffy. Stir in the salt and vanilla.

**3** Grind the nuts in a food processor,
blender, or nut grinder. Stir several
times to prevent the nuts becoming
oily. If necessary, grind in batches.

**4 ▲** Force the ground nuts through a
strainer set over a bowl to aerate
them. Pieces too large to go through
the strainer can be ground again.

**5 ▲** Sift the cake flour before
measuring. Stir the nuts and flour into
the butter mixture.

**6** Roll the dough into marble-size
balls between the palms of your hands.
Place on the prepared sheets and bake
for 45 minutes.

**7 ▲** While the puffs are still hot,
roll in confectioners' sugar. Let cool
completely, then roll once more in
confectioners' sugar.

# Pecan Tassies

**MAKES 24**

4 ounces cream cheese

½ cup (1 stick) butter, at room temperature

1 cup flour

FOR THE FILLING

2 eggs

¾ cup dark brown sugar, firmly packed

1 teaspoon vanilla extract

⅛ teaspoon salt

2 tablespoons butter, melted

1 cup pecans

**1** Place a baking sheet in the oven and preheat to 350°F. Grease 2 12-cup mini-muffin tins.

**2** Cut the cream cheese and butter in pieces. Put in a mixing bowl. Sift over the flour and mix to form a dough.

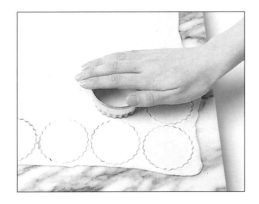

**3 ▲** Roll the dough out thinly. With a fluted pastry cutter, stamp out 24 2½-inch rounds. Line the muffin cups with the rounds and refrigerate while making the filling.

**4** For the filling, lightly whisk the eggs in a bowl. Gradually whisk in the brown sugar, a few tablespoons at a time, and add the vanilla, salt, and butter. Set aside.

**5 ▼** Reserve 24 undamaged pecan halves and chop the rest coarsely with a sharp knife.

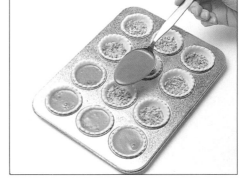

**6 ▲** Place a spoonful of chopped nuts in each muffin cup and cover with the filling. Set a pecan half on the top of each.

**7** Bake on the hot baking sheet until puffed and set, about 20 minutes. Transfer to a rack to cool. Serve at room temperature.

---

### ~ VARIATION ~

To make Jam Tassies, fill the cream cheese pastry shells with raspberry or blackberry jam, or other fruit jam. Bake as described.

# Lady Fingers

**MAKES 24**

⅔ cup flour

⅛ teaspoon salt

4 eggs, separated

½ cup granulated sugar

½ teaspoon vanilla extract

confectioners' sugar, for sprinkling

**1** Preheat the oven to 300°F. Grease 2 cookie sheets, then coat lightly with flour, and shake off the excess.

**2** Sift the flour and salt twice.

---

~ **COOK'S TIP** ~

To make the cookies all the same length, mark parallel lines 4 inches apart on the greased cookie sheet, and pipe between the lines.

---

**3** With an electric mixer, beat the egg yolks with half the sugar until thick enough to leave a ribbon trail when the beaters are lifted.

**4** ▲ In another bowl, beat the egg whites until stiff. Beat in the remaining sugar until glossy.

**5** Sift the flour over the yolks and spoon a large dollop of egg whites over the flour. Carefully fold in with a large metal spoon, adding the vanilla. Gently fold in the remaining whites.

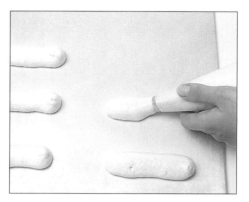

**6** ▲ Spoon the mixture into a pastry bag fitted with a large plain nozzle. Pipe out 4-inch long lines on the prepared sheets about 1 inch apart. Sift over a layer of confectioners' sugar. Quickly turn the sheet upside down to dislodge any excess sugar.

**7** Bake until crusty on the outside but soft in the center, about 20 minutes. Allow to cool slightly on the cookie sheet before transferring to a rack to cool completely.

---

# Walnut Cookies

**MAKES 60**

½ cup (1 stick) butter or margarine, at room temperature

¾ cup sugar

1 cup flour

2 teaspoons vanilla extract

1 cup walnuts, finely chopped

---

~ **VARIATION** ~

To make Almond Cookies, use an equal amount of finely chopped unblanched almonds instead of walnuts. Replace half the vanilla with ½ teaspoon almond extract.

---

**1** Preheat the oven to 300°F. Grease 2 cookie sheets.

**2** ▲ With an electric mixer, cream the butter or margarine until soft. Add ⅓ cup of the sugar and continue beating until light and fluffy. Stir in the flour, vanilla, and walnuts.

**3** Drop teaspoonfuls of the batter 1–2 inches apart on the sheets and flatten slightly with a fork. Bake until deep golden, about 25 minutes.

**4** ▼ Transfer to a rack set over a baking sheet and sprinkle with the remaining sugar.

*Lady Fingers (top), Walnut Cookies*

# Italian Almond Cookies

**MAKES 48**

1 cup unblanched almonds

1½ cups flour

½ cup sugar

⅛ teaspoon salt

⅛ teaspoon ground saffron

½ teaspoon baking soda

2 eggs

1 egg white, lightly beaten

~ COOK'S TIP ~

Serve these cookies after a meal, for dunking in glasses of sweet white wine, such as an Italian *Vin Santo* or a French *Muscat de Beaumes-de-Venise.*

**1** Preheat the oven to 375°F. Grease and flour 2 cookie sheets.

**2 ▲** Spread the almonds in a baking tray and bake until lightly browned, about 15 minutes. When cool, grind ¼ cup of the almonds in a food processor, blender, or nut grinder until pulverized. Coarsely chop the remaining almonds in 2 or 3 pieces each. Set aside.

**3 ▲** Combine the flour, sugar, salt, saffron, baking soda, and ground almonds in a bowl and mix to blend. Make a well in the center and add the 2 eggs. Stir from the center to form a rough dough. Transfer to a floured surface and knead until well blended. Knead in the chopped almonds.

**4 ▲** Divide the dough into 3 equal parts. With your hands, roll into logs about 1 inch in diameter. Place on one of the prepared sheets; leave room for spreading. Brush with the egg white. Bake for 20 minutes.

**5 ▲** Remove from the oven and lower the heat to 275°F. With a very sharp knife, cut at an angle into ½-inch slices. Return the slices to the oven and bake for 25 minutes more. Transfer to a rack to cool.

# Christmas Cookies

**MAKES 30**

¾ cup (1½ sticks) unsalted butter, at room temperature

1¼ cups sugar

1 egg

1 egg yolk

1 teaspoon vanilla extract

grated rind of 1 lemon

¼ teaspoon salt

2½ cups flour

FOR DECORATING (OPTIONAL)

colored icing and small candies such as silver balls, red hots, colored sugar sprinkles, etc.

**1 ▲** With an electric mixer, cream the butter until soft. Add the sugar gradually and continue beating until light and fluffy.

**2 ▲** Using a wooden spoon, slowly mix in the whole egg and the egg yolk. Add the vanilla, lemon rind and salt. Stir to mix well.

**3** Add the flour and stir to blend. Gather the dough into a ball, wrap, and refrigerate for 30 minutes.

**4 ▼** Preheat the oven to 375°F. On a floured surface, roll out the dough about ⅛ inch thick.

**5 ▲** Stamp out shapes or rounds with cookie cutters.

**6** Bake until lightly colored, about 8 minutes. Transfer to a rack and let cool completely before decorating, if wished, with icing and candies.

# Toasted Oat Meringues

**MAKES 12**

¾ cup old-fashioned oats

2 egg whites

⅛ teaspoon salt

1½ teaspoons cornstarch

¾ cup sugar

**1** Preheat the oven to 275°F. Spread the oats in a baking tray and toast in the the oven until golden, about 10 minutes. Lower the heat to 250°F. Grease and flour a baking sheet.

~ **VARIATION** ~

Add ½ teaspoon ground cinnamon with the oats, and fold in gently.

**2** ▼ With an electric mixer, beat the egg whites and salt until they start to form soft peaks.

**3** Sift over the cornstarch and continue beating until the whites hold stiff peaks. Add half the sugar and whisk until glossy.

**4** ▲ Add the remaining sugar and fold in, then fold in the oats.

**5** Gently spoon the mixture onto the prepared sheet and bake for 2 hours.

**6** When done, turn off the oven. Lift the meringues from the tray, turn over, and set in another place on the sheet to prevent sticking. Leave in the oven as it cools down.

# Meringues

**MAKES 24**

4 egg whites

⅛ teaspoon salt

1¼ cups sugar

½ teaspoon vanilla or almond extract (optional)

1 cup whipped cream (optional)

**1** Preheat the oven to 225°F. Grease and flour 2 large cookie sheets.

**2** With an electric mixer, beat the egg whites and salt in a very clean metal bowl on low speed. When they start to form soft peaks, add half the sugar and continue beating until the mixture holds stiff peaks.

**3** ▲ With a large metal spoon, fold in the remaining sugar and vanilla or almond extract, if using.

**4** ▼ Pipe the meringue mixture or gently spoon it on the prepared sheet.

**5** Bake for 2 hours. Turn off the oven. Loosen the meringues, invert, and set in another place on the sheets to prevent sticking. Leave in the oven as it cools. Serve sandwiched with whipped cream, if desired.

*Toasted Oat Meringues (top), Meringues*

# Old-Fashioned Sugar Cookies

**MAKES 36**

3 cups flour

1 teaspoon baking soda

2 teaspoons baking powder

¼ teaspoon grated nutmeg

½ cup (1 stick) butter or margarine, at room temperature

1 cup sugar

½ teaspoon vanilla extract

1 egg

½ cup milk

colored sugar, for sprinkling

**1** Sift the flour, baking soda, baking powder, and nutmeg into a small bowl. Set aside.

**2 ▲** With an electric mixer, cream the butter or margarine, sugar, and vanilla together until the mixture is light and fluffy. Add the egg and beat to mix well.

**3 ▲** Add the flour mixture alternately with the milk, stirring with a wooden spoon to make a soft dough. Wrap the dough in plastic wrap and refrigerate at least 30 minutes, or overnight.

**4 ▲** Preheat the oven to 350°F. Roll out the dough on a lightly floured surface to ⅛-inch thickness. Cut into rounds or other shapes with cookie cutters.

**5 ▲** Transfer the cookies to ungreased cookie sheets. Sprinkle each cookie with colored sugar.

**6** Bake until golden brown, 10–12 minutes. With a slotted spatula, transfer the cookies to a wire rack and let cool.

# Chocolate Chip and Macadamia Nut Cookies

**MAKES 36**

1 cup flour

1 teaspoon baking powder

¼ teaspoon salt

6 tablespoons butter or margarine, at room temperature

½ cup granulated sugar

¼ cup light brown sugar, firmly packed

1 egg

1 teaspoon vanilla extract

¾ cup chocolate chips

½ cup macadamia nuts, chopped

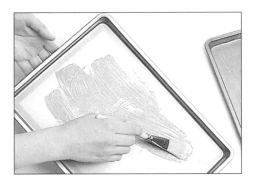

**1 ▲** Preheat the oven to 350°F. Grease 2–3 cookie sheets.

**2** Sift the flour, baking powder, and salt into a small bowl. Set aside.

**3 ▲** With an electric mixer, cream the butter or margarine and sugars together. Beat in the egg and vanilla.

**4** Add the flour mixture and beat well with the mixer on low speed.

**5 ▼** Stir in the chocolate chips and ¼ cup of the macadamia nuts using a wooden spoon.

**6** Drop the mixture by teaspoons onto the prepared cookie sheets, to form ¾-inch mounds. Space the cookies 1–2 inches apart.

**7 ▲** Flatten each cookie lightly with a wet fork. Sprinkle the remaining macadamia nuts on top of the cookies and press lightly into the surface.

**8** Bake until golden brown, about 10–12 minutes. With a slotted spatula, transfer the cookies to a wire rack and let cool.

# Chocolate Macaroons

**MAKES 24**

2 1-ounce squares unsweetened
chocolate

1 cup blanched almonds

1 cup granulated sugar

⅓ cup egg whites (about 2 eggs)

½ teaspoon vanilla extract

¼ teaspoon almond extract

confectioners' sugar, for dusting

**1** Preheat the oven to 300°F. Line 2 cookie sheets with wax paper and grease the paper.

**2 ▼** Melt the chocolate in the top of a double boiler, or in a heatproof bowl set over a pan of hot water.

**3 ▲** Grind the almonds finely in a food processor, blender, or nut grinder. Transfer to a mixing bowl.

**4 ▲** In a mixing bowl, whisk the egg whites until they form soft peaks, Fold in the sugar, vanilla and almond extract, ground almonds and cooled melted chocolate. Refrigerate for 15 minutes.

**5 ▲** Use a teaspoon and your hands to shape the dough into walnut-size balls. Place on the sheets and flatten slightly. Brush each ball with a little water and sift over a thin layer of confectioners' sugar. Bake until just firm, 20-25 minutes. With a metal spatula, transfer to a rack to cool.

~ **VARIATION** ~

For Chocolate Pine Nut Macaroons, spread ¾ cup pine nuts in a shallow dish. Press the balls of chocolate macaroon dough into the nuts to cover one side and bake as described, nut-side up.

# Coconut Macaroons

**MAKES 24**

⅓ cup flour

⅛ teaspoon salt

2½ cups shredded coconut

⅔ cup sweetened condensed milk

1 teaspoon vanilla extract

**1** Preheat the oven to 350°F. Grease 2 cookie sheets.

**2** Sift the flour and salt into a bowl. Stir in the coconut.

**3 ▲** Pour in the milk. Add the vanilla and stir from the center to make a very thick batter.

**4 ▼** Drop heaped tablespoonfuls of batter 1 inch apart on prepared sheets. Bake until golden brown, about 20 minutes. Cool on a rack.

*Chocolate Macaroons (top), Coconut Macaroons*

# Almond Tiles

**MAKES 40**

| |
|---|
| ½ cup blanched almonds |
| ½ cup sugar |
| 3½ tablespoons unsalted butter |
| 2 egg whites |
| ⅓ cup cake flour |
| ½ teaspoon vanilla extract |
| 1 cup sliced almonds |

**1** Grind the blanched almonds with 2 tablespoons of the sugar in a food processor, blender, or nut grinder.

**2** Preheat the oven to 425°F. Grease 2 cookie sheets.

**3** ▲ With an electric mixer, cream the butter and remaining sugar together until light and fluffy.

**4** Add the egg whites and stir until just blended. Sift over the flour and fold in with a metal spoon. Fold in the ground almonds and vanilla.

**5** ▲ Working in small batches, drop tablespoonfuls of the batter 3 inches apart on one of the prepared sheets. With the back of a spoon, spread out into thin, almost transparent circles about 2½ inches in diameter. Sprinkle each circle with some of the sliced almonds.

**6** Bake until the outer edges have browned slightly, about 4 minutes.

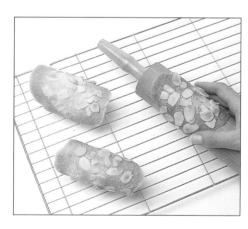

**7** ▲ Remove from the oven. With a metal spatula, quickly transfer the cookies to a rolling pin to form a curved shape. Transfer to a rack when firm. If the cookies harden too quickly to shape, reheat briefly. Repeat the baking and shaping process until the batter is used up. Store the cookies in an airtight container.

# Florentines

**MAKES 36**

3 tablespoons butter

½ cup whipping cream

⅔ cup sugar

1½ cups sliced almonds

¼ cup candied orange peel, finely chopped

2 tablespoons chopped candied cherries

½ cup flour, sifted

8 1-ounce squares semisweet chocolate

1 teaspoon vegetable oil

**1** Preheat the oven to 350°F. Grease 2 cookie sheets.

**2 ▲** Melt the butter, cream, and sugar together and slowly bring to the boil. Take off the heat and stir in the almonds, orange peel, cherries, and flour until blended.

**3** Drop teaspoonfuls of the batter 1–2 inches apart on the prepared sheets and flatten with a fork.

**4** Bake until the cookies brown at the edges, about 10 minutes. Remove from the oven and correct the shape by quickly pushing in any thin uneven edges with a knife or a round cookie cutter. Work fast or they will cool and harden while still on the sheets. If necessary, return to the oven for a few moments to soften. While still hot, use a metal spatula to transfer the cookies to a clean, flat surface.

**5** Melt the chocolate in the top of a double boiler or in a heatproof bowl set over a pan of hot water. Add the oil and stir to blend.

**6 ▲** With a metal spatula, spread the smooth underside of the cooled cookies with a thin coating of the melted chocolate.

**7 ▼** When the chocolate is about to set, draw a serrated knife across the surface with a slight sawing motion to make wavy lines. Store in an airtight container in a cool place.

# Nut Lace Cookies

**MAKES 18**

½ cup blanched almonds

4 tablespoons butter

3 tablespoons flour

½ cup sugar

2 tablespoons heavy cream

½ teaspoon vanilla extract

**1** Preheat the oven to 375°F. Grease 1–2 cookie sheets.

**2** With a sharp knife, chop the almonds as finely as possible. Alternatively, use a food processor, blender, or nut grinder to chop the nuts very finely.

**3** ▼ Melt the butter in a saucepan over low heat. Remove from the heat and stir in the remaining ingredients and the almonds.

**4** Drop teaspoonfuls 2½ inches apart on the prepared sheets. Bake until golden, about 5 minutes. Cool on the sheets briefly, just until the cookies are stiff enough to lift off.

**5** ▲ With a metal spatula, transfer to a rack to cool completely.

~ **VARIATION** ~

Add ¼ cup finely chopped candied orange peel to the batter.

---

# Oatmeal Lace Cookies

**MAKES 36**

⅔ cup (10⅔ tablespoons) butter or margarine

1½ cups rolled oats

¾ cup dark brown sugar, firmly packed

¾ cup granulated sugar

3 tablespoons flour

¼ teaspoon salt

1 egg, lightly beaten

1 teaspoon vanilla extract

½ cup pecans or walnuts, finely chopped

**1** Preheat the oven to 350°F. Grease 2 cookie sheets.

**2** Melt the butter or margarine in a saucepan over low heat. Set aside.

**3** In a mixing bowl, combine the oats, brown sugar, granulated sugar, flour, and salt.

**4** ▲ Make a well in the center and add the butter or margarine, the egg, and vanilla.

**5** ▼ Mix until blended, then stir in the chopped nuts.

**6** Drop rounded teaspoonfuls of the batter about 2 inches apart on the prepared sheets. Bake until lightly browned on the edges and bubbling, 5–8 minutes. Let cool on the sheet for 2 minutes, then transfer to a rack to cool completely.

*Nut Lace Cookies (top), Oatmeal Lace Cookies*

# Raspberry Sandwich Cookies

**MAKES 32**

1 cup blanched almonds

1½ cups flour

¾ cup (1½ sticks) butter, at room temperature

½ cup sugar

grated rind of 1 lemon

1 teaspoon vanilla extract

1 egg white

⅛ teaspoon salt

⅓ cup slivered almonds

1 cup raspberry jam

1 tablespoon fresh lemon juice

**1** Place the blanched almonds and 3 tablespoons of the flour in a food processor, blender, or nut grinder and process until finely ground. Set aside.

**2** With an electric mixer, cream the butter and sugar together until light and fluffy. Stir in the lemon rind and vanilla. Add the ground almonds and remaining flour and mix well to form a dough. Gather into a ball, wrap in wax paper, and refrigerate for at least 1 hour.

**3** Preheat oven to 325°F. Line 2 cookie sheets with wax paper.

**4** Divide the dough into 4 equal parts. Working with one section of the dough at a time, roll out to a thickness of ⅛ inch on a lightly floured surface. With a 2½-inch fluted pastry cutter, stamp out circles. Gather the dough scraps, roll out, and stamp out more circles. Repeat with the remaining dough.

**5** ▲ With the small end of a piping tip, or with a ¾-inch cutter, stamp out the centers from half the circles. Place dough rings and circles ½ inch apart on the prepared sheets.

**6** ▲ Whisk the egg white with the salt until just frothy. Chop the slivered almonds. Brush only the cookie rings with the egg white, then sprinkle over the almonds. Bake until very lightly browned, 12–15 minutes. Let cool for a few minutes on the sheets before transferring to a rack.

**7** ▲ In a saucepan, melt the jam with the lemon juice until it comes to a simmer. Brush the jam over the cookie circles and sandwich together with the rings. Store in an airtight container with sheets of wax paper between the layers.

# Brandy Snaps

**MAKES 18**

4 tablespoons butter, at room temperature

⅔ cup sugar

l rounded tablespoon corn syrup

⅓ cup flour

½ teaspoon ground ginger

FOR THE FILLING

1 cup whipping cream

2 tablespoons brandy

**1** With an electric mixer, cream together the butter and sugar until light and fluffy, then beat in the corn syrup. Sift over the flour and ginger and mix to a rough dough.

**2 ▲** Transfer the dough to a work surface and knead until smooth. Cover and refrigerate for 30 minutes.

**3** Preheat the oven to 375°F. Grease a cookie sheet.

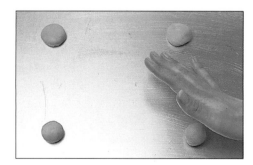

**4 ▲** Working in batches of 4, form walnut-size balls of dough. Place far apart on the prepared sheet and flatten slightly. Bake until golden and bubbling, about 10 minutes.

**5 ▼** Remove from the oven and let cool a few moments. Working quickly, slide a metal spatula under each one, turn over, and wrap around the handle of a wooden spoon (have four spoons ready). If they firm up too quickly, reheat for a few seconds to soften. When firm, slide the snaps off and place on a rack to cool.

**6 ▲** When all the brandy snaps are cool, prepare the filling. Whip the cream and brandy until soft peaks form. Fill a pastry bag with the brandy cream. Pipe into each end of the brandy snaps just before serving.

# Pepper-Spice Cookies

**MAKES 48**

1¾ cups flour

½ cup cornstarch

2 teaspoons baking powder

½ teaspoon ground cardamom

½ teaspoon ground cinnamon

½ teaspoon grated nutmeg

½ teaspoon ground ginger

½ teaspoon ground allspice

½ teaspoon salt

½ teaspoon freshly ground black pepper

1 cup (2 sticks) butter or margarine, at room temperature

½ cup light brown sugar, firmly packed

½ teaspoon vanilla extract

1 teaspoon finely grated lemon rind

¼ cup whipping cream

⅔ cup finely ground almonds

2 tablespoons confectioners' sugar

**1** Preheat the oven to 350°F.

**2** Sift the flour, cornstarch, baking powder, spices, salt, and pepper into a bowl. Set aside.

**3** With an electric mixer, cream the butter or margarine and brown sugar together until light and fluffy. Beat in the vanilla and lemon rind.

**4** ▲ With the mixer on low speed, add the flour mixture alternately with the cream, beginning and ending with flour. Stir in the ground almonds.

**5** ▲ Shape the dough into ¾-inch balls. Place them on ungreased cookie sheets about 1 inch apart. Bake until the cookies are golden brown underneath, 15–20 minutes.

**6** Let the cookies cool on the cookie sheets about 1 minute before transferring them to a wire rack to cool completely. Before serving, sprinkle them lightly with confectioners' sugar.

---

# Five-Layer Bars

**MAKES 24**

2 cups graham cracker crumbs

¼ cup sugar

⅛ teaspoon salt

½ cup (1 stick) butter or margarine, melted

1 cup shredded coconut

1½ cups semisweet chocolate chips

1 cup sweetened condensed milk

1 cup walnut pieces, chopped

**1** Preheat the oven to 350°F.

**2** ▼ In a bowl, combine the graham-cracker crumbs, sugar, salt, and butter or margarine. Press the mixture evenly over the bottom of an ungreased 13- × 9-inch baking dish.

**3** ▲ Sprinkle the coconut over the crumb crust, then scatter over the chocolate chips. Pour the condensed milk evenly over the chocolate. Sprinkle the walnuts on top.

**4** Bake 30 minutes. Unmold onto a wire rack and let cool, preferably overnight. When cooled, cut into bars.

*Pepper-Spice Cookies (top), Five-Layer Bars*

# Shortbread

**MAKES 8**

⅔ cup (10⅔ tablespoons) unsalted
    butter, at room temperature

½ cup sugar

1¼ cups all-purpose flour

½ cup rice flour

¼ teaspoon baking powder

⅛ teaspoon salt

**1** Preheat the oven to 325°F. Grease
a shallow 8-inch cake pan.

**2** With an electric mixer, cream the
butter and sugar together until light
and fluffy. Sift over the flours, baking
powder, and salt and mix well.

**3** ▲ Press the dough neatly into the
prepared pan, smoothing the surface
with the back of a spoon.

**4** Prick all over with a fork, then
score into 8 equal wedges.

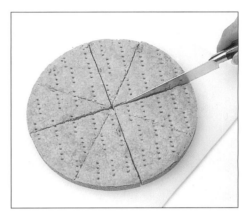

**5** ▲ Bake until golden, 40–45
minutes. Leave in the pan until cool
enough to handle, then unmold and
recut the wedges while still hot. Store
in an airtight container.

# Oatmeal Wedges

**MAKES 8**

4 tablespoons butter

1 rounded tablespoon dark corn syrup

⅓ cup dark brown sugar, firmly packed

1¼ cups quick-cooking oats

⅛ teaspoon salt

**1** ▲ Preheat the oven to 350°F. Line
an 8-inch shallow cake pan with wax
paper and grease the paper.

**2** ▼ Place the butter, corn syrup,
and sugar in a pan over low heat.
Cook, stirring, until melted and
combined.

~ **VARIATION** ~

If wished, add 1 teaspoon ground
ginger to the melted butter.

**3** ▲ Remove from the heat and add
the oats and salt. Stir to blend.

**4** Spoon into the prepared pan and
smooth the surface. Place in the
center of the oven and bake until
golden brown, 20–25 minutes. Leave
in the pan until cool enough to
handle, then unmold and cut into
wedges while still hot.

*Shortbread (top), Oatmeal Wedges*

# Chocolate-Nut Refrigerator Cookies

**MAKES 50**

| |
|---|
| 1 1-ounce square semisweet chocolate |
| 1 1-ounce square unsweetened chocolate |
| 2 cups flour |
| ½ teaspoon salt |
| 1 cup (2 sticks) unsalted butter, at room temperature |
| 1 cup sugar |
| 2 eggs |
| 1 teaspoon vanilla extract |
| 1 cup walnuts, finely chopped |

**1** Melt the chocolates in the top of a double boiler, or in a heatproof bowl set over a pan of gently simmering water. Set aside.

**2 ▼** In a small bowl, sift together the flour and salt. Set aside.

**3** With an electric mixer, cream the butter until soft. Add the sugar and continue beating until the mixture is light and fluffy.

**4** Mix the eggs and vanilla, then gradually stir into the butter mixture.

**5 ▲** Stir in the chocolate, then the flour. Stir in the nuts.

**6 ▲** Divide the dough into 4 parts, and roll each into 2-inch diameter logs. Wrap tightly in foil and refrigerate or freeze until firm.

**7** Preheat the oven to 375°F. Grease 2 cookie sheets.

**8** With a sharp knife, cut the dough into ¼-inch slices. Place the rounds on the prepared sheets and bake until lightly colored, about 10 minutes. Transfer to a rack to cool.

~ **VARIATION** ~

For two-tone cookies, melt only 1 ounce of chocolate. Combine all the ingredients, except the chocolate, as above. Divide the dough in half. Add the chocolate to one half. Roll out the plain dough to a flat sheet. Roll out the chocolate dough, place on top of the plain dough and roll up. Wrap, slice and bake as described.

# Cinnamon Refrigerator Cookies

**MAKES 50**

2⅛ cups flour

½ teaspoon salt

2 teaspoons ground cinnamon

1 cup (2 sticks) unsalted butter, at room temperature

1 cup sugar

2 eggs

1 teaspoon vanilla extract

**1** In a bowl, sift together the flour, salt, and cinnamon. Set aside.

**2 ▲** With an electric mixer, cream the butter until soft. Add the sugar and continue beating until the mixture is light and fluffy.

**3** Beat the eggs and vanilla, then gradually stir into the butter mixture.

**4 ▲** Stir in the dry ingredients.

**5 ▲** Divide the dough into 4 parts, then roll each into 2-inch diameter logs. Wrap tightly in foil and refrigerate or freeze until firm.

**6** Preheat the oven to 375°F. Grease 2 cookie sheets.

**7 ▼** With a sharp knife, cut the dough into ¼-inch slices. Place the rounds on the prepared sheets and bake until lightly colored, about 10 minutes. With a metal spatula, transfer to a rack to cool.

# Coffee Ice Cream Sandwiches

**MAKES 8**

½ cup (1 stick) butter or margarine, at room temperature

¼ cup granulated sugar

1 cup flour

2 tablespoons instant coffee

confectioners' sugar, for sprinkling

1 pint coffee ice cream

2 tablespoons unsweetened cocoa powder

**1** Lightly grease 2–3 cookie sheets.

**2** With an electric mixer or wooden spoon, beat the butter or margarine until soft. Beat in the granulated sugar.

**3 ▲** Add the flour and coffee and mix by hand to form an evenly blended dough. Wrap in a plastic bag and refrigerate at least 1 hour.

**4** Lightly sprinkle the work surface with confectioners' sugar. Knead the dough on the sugared surface for a few minutes to soften it slightly.

**5 ▼** Using a rolling pin dusted with confectioners' sugar, roll out the dough to ⅛-inch thickness. With a 2½-inch fluted cookie cutter, cut out 16 rounds. Transfer the rounds to the prepared cookie sheets. Refrigerate for at least 30 minutes.

**6** Preheat the oven to 300°F. Bake the cookies until they are lightly golden, about 30 minutes. Let the cookies cool and firm up before removing them from the sheets to a wire rack to cool completely.

**7** Remove the ice cream from the freezer and let soften 10 minutes at room temperature.

**8 ▲** With a metal spatula, spread ¼ cup of the ice cream on the flat side of half of the cookies, leaving the edges clear. Top the ice cream with the remaining cookies, flat-side down.

**9** Arrange the cookie sandwiches on a baking sheet. Cover and freeze at least 1 hour, longer if a firmer sandwich is desired. Sift the cocoa powder over the tops before serving.

# Hazelnut Brownies

**MAKES 9**

2 1-ounce squares unsweetened chocolate

5 tablespoons butter or margarine

1 cup sugar

7 tablespoons flour

½ teaspoon baking powder

2 eggs, beaten

½ teaspoon vanilla extract

1 cup skinned hazelnuts, roughly chopped

**1** Preheat the oven to 350°F. Grease an 8-inch square baking pan.

**2** ▲ In a heatproof bowl set over a pan of barely simmering water, or in a double boiler, melt the chocolate and butter or margarine. Remove the bowl from the heat.

**3** ▲ Add the sugar, flour, baking powder, eggs, vanilla, and ½ cup of the hazelnuts to the melted mixture and stir well with a wooden spoon.

**4** ▼ Pour the batter into the prepared pan. Bake 10 minutes, then sprinkle the reserved hazelnuts over the top. Return to the oven and continue baking until firm to the touch, about 25 minutes.

**5** ▲ Let cool in the pan, set on a wire rack for 10 minutes, then unmold onto the rack and let cool completely. Cut into squares for serving.

# Peanut Butter Cookies

**MAKES 24**

1 cup flour

½ teaspoon baking soda

½ teaspoon salt

½ cup (1 stick) butter, at room temperature

¾ cup light brown sugar, firmly packed

1 egg

1 teaspoon vanilla extract

1 cup crunchy peanut butter

**1** Sift together the flour, baking soda, and salt and set aside.

**2** With an electric mixer, cream the butter and sugar together until light and fluffy.

**3** In another bowl, mix the egg and vanilla, then gradually beat into the butter mixture.

**4** ▲ Stir in the peanut butter and blend thoroughly. Stir in the dry ingredients. Refrigerate for at least 30 minutes, or until firm.

**5** Preheat the oven to 350°F. Grease 2 cookie sheets.

**6** Spoon out rounded teaspoonfuls of the dough and roll into balls.

**7** ▲ Place the balls on the prepared sheets and press flat with a fork into circles about 2½ inches in diameter, making a criss-cross pattern. Bake until lightly colored, 12–15 minutes. Transfer to a rack to cool.

> **~ VARIATION ~**
>
> Add ½ cup peanuts, coarsely chopped, with the peanut butter.

# Tollhouse Cookies

**MAKES 24**

½ cup (1 stick) butter or margarine, at room temperature

¼ cup granulated sugar

½ cup dark brown sugar, firmly packed

1 egg

½ teaspoon vanilla extract

1⅛ cup flour

½ teaspoon baking soda

⅛ teaspoon salt

1 cup chocolate chips

½ cup walnuts, chopped

**1** Preheat the oven to 350°F. Grease 2 large cookie sheets.

**2** ▼ With an electric mixer, cream the butter or margarine and two sugars together until light and fluffy.

**3** In another bowl, mix the egg and vanilla, then gradually beat into the butter mixture. Sift over the flour, baking soda, and salt. Stir to blend.

**4** ▲ Add the chocolate chips and walnuts, and mix to combine well.

**5** Place heaped teaspoonfuls of the dough 2 inches apart on the prepared sheets. Bake until lightly colored, 10–15 minutes. With a metal spatula, transfer to a rack to cool.

*Peanut Butter Cookies (top), Tollhouse Cookies*

# Applesauce Cookies

**MAKES 3 DOZEN**

½ cup sugar

4 tablespoons butter or shortening, at room temperature

¾ cup thick applesauce

⅛ teaspoon grated lemon rind

1 cup flour

½ teaspoon baking powder

¼ teaspoon baking soda

¼ teaspoon salt

½ teaspoon ground cinnamon

½ cup chopped walnuts

~ **COOK'S TIP** ~

If the applesauce is runny, put it in a strainer over a bowl and let it drain for 10 minutes.

**1** Preheat the oven to 375°F.

**2** In a medium-size bowl, beat together the sugar and butter or shortening until well mixed. Beat in the applesauce and lemon rind.

**3** ▲ Sift the flour, baking powder, baking soda, salt, and cinnamon into the mixture, and stir to blend. Fold in the chopped walnuts.

**4** ▲ Drop teaspoonfuls of the dough on a lightly greased cookie sheet, spacing them about 2 inches apart.

**5** Bake the cookies in the center of the oven until they are golden brown, 8–10 minutes. Transfer the cookies to a wire rack to cool.

---

# Toffee Bars

**MAKES 32**

2 cups light brown sugar, firmly packed

2 cups (4 sticks) butter or margarine, at room temperature

2 egg yolks

1½ teaspoons vanilla extract

4 cups all-purpose or whole-wheat flour

½ teaspoon salt

2 4-ounce bars of milk chocolate, broken in pieces

1 cup chopped walnuts or pecans

**1** Preheat the oven to 350°F.

**2** Beat together the sugar and butter or margarine until light and fluffy. Beat in the egg yolks and vanilla. Stir in the flour and salt.

**3** ▼ Spread the dough in a greased 13- × 9- × 2-inch baking pan. Bake until lightly browned, 25–30 minutes. The texture will be soft.

**4** ▲ Remove from the oven and immediately place the chocolate pieces on the hot cookie base. Let stand until the chocolate softens, then spread it evenly with a spatula. Sprinkle with the nuts.

**5** While still warm, cut into bars about 2 × 1½ inches.

*Applesauce Cookies (top), Toffee Bars*

# Chocolate Chip Brownies

**MAKES 24**

4 1-ounce squares unsweetened
  chocolate

½ cup (1 stick) butter

3 eggs

1½ cups sugar

1 teaspoon vanilla extract

pinch of salt

¾ cup flour

1 cup chocolate chips

**1 ▼** Preheat the oven to 350°F. Line the bottom and sides of a 13- × 9-inch pan with wax paper and grease.

**2 ▲** Melt the chocolate and butter in the top of a double boiler, or in a heatproof bowl set over a pan of gently simmering water.

**3 ▲** Beat together the eggs, sugar, vanilla, and salt. Stir in the chocolate mixture. Sift over the flour and fold in. Add the chocolate chips.

**4 ▲** Pour the batter into the prepared pan and spread evenly. Bake until just set, about 30 minutes. Do not overbake; the brownies should be slightly moist inside. Cool in the pan.

**5** To unmold, run a knife all around the edge and invert onto a cookie sheet. Remove the paper. Place another sheet on top and invert again so the brownies are right-side up. Cut into squares for serving.

# Marbled Brownies

**MAKES 24**

| 8 1-ounce squares semisweet chocolate |
| 6 tablespoons butter |
| 4 eggs |
| 1½ cups sugar |
| 1 cup flour |
| ½ teaspoon salt |
| 1 teaspoon baking powder |
| 2 teaspoons vanilla extract |
| 1 cup walnuts, chopped |

FOR THE PLAIN BATTER

| 4 tablespoons butter, at room temperature |
| 6 ounces cream cheese |
| ½ cup sugar |
| 2 eggs |
| 2 tablespoons flour |
| 1 teaspoon vanilla extract |

**1** Preheat the oven to 350°F. Line the bottom and sides of a 13- × 9-inch pan with wax paper and grease.

**2** Melt the chocolate and butter over very low heat, stirring constantly. Set aside to cool.

**3** Meanwhile, beat the eggs until light and fluffy. Gradually add the sugar and continue beating until blended. Sift over the flour, salt, and baking powder and fold to combine.

**4 ▲** Stir in the cooled chocolate mixture. Add the vanilla and walnuts. Measure and set aside 2 cups of the chocolate batter.

**5 ▲** For the plain batter, cream the butter and cream cheese with an electric mixer.

**6** Add the sugar and continue beating until blended. Beat in the eggs, flour, and vanilla.

**7** Spread the unmeasured chocolate batter in pan. Pour over the cream cheese mixture. Drop spoonfuls of the reserved chocolate batter on top.

**8 ▲** With a metal spatula, swirl the mixtures to marble. Do not blend completely. Bake until just set, 35–40 minutes. Unmold when cool and cut into squares for serving.

# Chocolate Pecan Squares

**MAKES 16**

2 eggs

2 teaspoons vanilla extract

⅛ teaspoon salt

1½ cups pecans, coarsely chopped

½ cup flour

¼ cup sugar

½ cup dark corn syrup

3 1-ounce squares semisweet chocolate, finely chopped

3 tablespoons butter

16 pecan halves, for decorating

**1** Preheat the oven to 325°F. Line the bottom and sides of an 8-inch square baking pan with wax paper and grease lightly.

**2 ▼** Whisk together the eggs, vanilla, and salt. In another bowl, mix together the pecans and flour. Set both aside.

**3** In a saucepan, bring the sugar and corn syrup to a boil. Remove from the heat and stir in the chocolate and butter to blend thoroughly with a wooden spoon.

**4 ▲** Mix in the beaten eggs, then fold in the pecan mixture.

**5** Pour the batter into the prepared pan and bake until set, about 35 minutes. Cool in the pan for 10 minutes before unmolding. Cut into 2-inch squares and press pecan halves into the tops while warm. Cool completely on a rack.

# Raisin Brownies

**MAKES 16**

½ cup (1 stick) butter or margarine

½ cup unsweetened cocoa powder

2 eggs

1 cup sugar

1 teaspoon vanilla extract

⅓ cup flour

¾ cup walnuts, chopped

½ cup raisins

**1** Preheat the oven to 350°F. Line the bottom and sides of an 8-inch square baking pan and grease.

**2 ▼** Gently melt the butter or margarine in a small saucepan. Remove from the heat and stir in the cocoa powder.

**3** With an electric mixer, beat the eggs, sugar, and vanilla together until light. Add the cocoa mixture and stir to blend.

**4 ▲** Sift the flour over the cocoa mixture and gently fold in. Add the walnuts and raisins and scrape the batter into the prepared pan.

**5** Bake in the center of the oven for 30 minutes. Do not overbake. Leave in the pan to cool before cutting into 2-inch squares and removing. The brownies should be soft and moist.

*Chocolate Pecan Squares (top), Raisin Brownies*

# Chocolate Walnut Bars

**MAKES 24**

½ cup walnuts

⅓ cup granulated sugar

¾ cup flour, sifted

6 tablespoons cold unsalted butter, cut in pieces

FOR THE TOPPING

2 tablespoons unsalted butter

⅓ cup water

⅓ cup unsweetened cocoa powder

½ cup granulated sugar

1 teaspoon vanilla extract

⅛ teaspoon salt

2 eggs

confectioners' sugar, for dusting

**1** Preheat the oven to 350°F. Grease the sides and bottom of an 8-inch square baking pan.

**2 ▼** Grind the walnuts with a few tablespoons of the sugar in a food processor, blender, or nut grinder.

**3** In a bowl, combine the ground walnuts, remaining sugar, and flour. With a pastry blender, cut in the butter until the mixture resembles coarse crumbs. Alternatively, combine all the ingredients in a food processor and process until the mixture resembles coarse crumbs.

**4 ▲** Pat the walnut mixture into the bottom of the prepared pan in an even layer. Bake for 25 minutes.

**5 ▲** Meanwhile, for the topping, melt the butter with the water. Whisk in the cocoa and sugar. Remove the pan from the heat, stir in the vanilla and salt and let cool for 5 minutes. Whisk in the eggs until blended.

**6 ▲** Pour the topping over the crust when baked.

**7** Return to the oven and bake until set, about 20 minutes. Set the pan on a rack to cool. Cut into 2½- × 1-inch bars and dust with confectioners' sugar. Store in the refrigerator.

# Pecan Bars

**MAKES 36**

2 cups flour

pinch of salt

½ cup granulated sugar

1 cup (2 sticks) cold butter or
   margarine, cut in pieces

1 egg

finely grated rind of 1 lemon

**FOR THE TOPPING**

¾ cup (1½ sticks) butter

¼ cup honey

¼ cup granulated sugar

¾ cup dark brown sugar, firmly packed

5 tablespoons whipping cream

4 cups pecan halves

**1** Preheat the oven to 375°F. Lightly grease a 15½- × 10½- × 1-inch jelly roll pan.

**2 ▲** For the crust, sift the flour and salt into a mixing bowl. Stir in the sugar. With a pastry blender, cut in the butter or margarine until the mixture resembles coarse crumbs. Add the egg and lemon rind and blend with a fork until the mixture just holds together.

**3 ▼** Spoon the mixture into the prepared pan. With floured fingertips, press into an even layer. Prick the pastry all over with a fork and refrigerate for 10 minutes.

**4** Bake the pastry crust for 15 minutes. Remove the pan from the oven, but keep the oven on while making the topping.

**5 ▲** Melt the butter, honey, and both sugars. Bring to a boil. Boil, without stirring, for 2 minutes. Off the heat, stir in the cream and pecans. Pour over the crust, return to the oven and bake for 25 minutes.

**6** When cool, run a knife around the edge. Invert onto a baking sheet, place another sheet on top and invert again. Dip a sharp knife into very hot water and cut into squares for serving.

# Fig Bars

**MAKES 48**

2 cups dried figs

3 eggs

¾ cup granulated sugar

¾ cup flour

1 teaspoon baking powder

½ teaspoon ground cinnamon

¼ teaspoon ground cloves

¼ teaspoon grated nutmeg

¼ teaspoon salt

¾ cup walnuts, finely chopped

2 tablespoons brandy or cognac

confectioners' sugar, for dusting

**1** Preheat the oven to 325°F. Line a 12- × 8- × 1½-inch pan with wax paper and grease.

**2 ▲** With a sharp knife, chop the figs roughly. Set aside.

**3** In a bowl, whisk the eggs and sugar until well blended. In another bowl, sift together the dry ingredients, then fold into the egg mixture in several batches.

**4 ▼** Stir in the figs, walnuts, and brandy or cognac.

**5** Scrape the mixture into the prepared pan and bake until the top is firm and brown, 35–40 minutes. It should still be soft underneath.

**6** Let cool in the pan for 5 minutes, then unmold and transfer to a sheet of wax paper lightly sprinkled with confectioners' sugar. Cut into bars.

---

# Lemon Bars

**MAKES 36**

½ cup confectioners' sugar

1½ cups flour

½ teaspoon salt

¾ cup (1½ sticks) butter, cut in small
   pieces

FOR THE TOPPING

4 eggs

1½ cups granulated sugar

grated rind of 1 lemon

½ cup fresh lemon juice

¾ cup whipping cream

confectioners' sugar, for dusting

**1** Preheat the oven to 325°F. Grease a 13- × 9-inch baking pan.

**2** Sift the sugar, flour, and salt into a bowl. With a pastry blender, cut in the butter until the mixture resembles coarse crumbs.

**3 ▲** Press the mixture into the bottom of the prepared pan. Bake until golden brown, about 20 minutes.

**4** Meanwhile, for the topping, whisk the eggs and sugar together until blended. Add the lemon rind and juice and mix well.

**5 ▲** Lightly whip the cream and fold into the egg mixture. Pour over the still warm crust, return to the oven, and bake until set, about 40 minutes.

**6** Cool completely before cutting into bars. Dust with confectioners' sugar.

*Fig Bars (top), Lemon Bars*

# Apricot Bars

½ cup light brown sugar, firmly packed

¾ cup flour

6 tablespoons cold unsalted butter, cut in pieces

FOR THE TOPPING

1 cup dried apricots

1 cup water

grated rind of 1 lemon

⅓ cup granulated sugar

2 teaspoons cornstarch

½ cup walnuts, chopped

**1** Preheat the oven to 350°F.

**2** ▲ In a bowl, combine the brown sugar and flour. With a pastry blender, cut in the butter until the mixture resembles coarse crumbs.

**3** ▲ Transfer to an 8-inch square baking pan and press into an even layer. Bake for 15 minutes. Remove from the oven but leave the oven on.

**4** Meanwhile, for the topping, combine the apricots and water in a saucepan and simmer until soft, about 10 minutes. Strain the liquid and reserve. Chop the apricots.

**5** ▲ Return the apricots to the saucepan and add the lemon rind, granulated sugar, cornstarch, and 4 tablespoons of the soaking liquid. Cook for 1 minute.

**6** ▲ Cool slightly before spreading the topping over the base. Sprinkle over the walnuts and continue baking for 20 minutes more. Let cool in the pan before cutting into bars.

# Almond Bars

**MAKES 36**

| |
|---|
| 6 tablespoons butter, at room temperature |
| ¼ cup sugar |
| 1 egg yolk |
| grated rind and juice of ½ lemon |
| ½ teaspoon vanilla extract |
| 2 tablespoons whipping cream |
| 1 cup flour |
| FOR THE TOPPING |
| 1 cup sugar |
| ¾ cup sliced almonds |
| 4 egg whites |
| ½ teaspoon ground ginger |
| ½ teaspoon ground cinnamon |

**1** ▲ Preheat the oven to 375°F. Line a 13- × 9-inch jelly-roll pan with wax paper and grease.

**2** With an electric mixer, cream the butter and sugar until light and fluffy. Beat in the egg yolk, lemon rind and juice, vanilla and cream.

**3** ▲ Gradually stir in the flour until mixed. Gather into a ball of dough.

**4** With lightly floured fingers, press the dough into the pan in a thin even layer. Bake for 15 minutes. Remove from the oven but leave the oven on.

**5** ▲ For the topping, combine all the ingredients in a heavy saucepan. Cook, stirring constantly, until the mixture comes to a boil.

**6** Continue boiling until just golden, about 1 minute. Pour it over the dough, spreading it evenly.

**7** ▲ Return to the oven and bake until golden, about 45 minutes. Remove and score into bars. Cool completely before cutting and serving.

# Hermits

**MAKES 30**

¾ cup flour

1½ teaspoons baking powder

1 teaspoon ground cinnamon

½ teaspoon grated nutmeg

¼ teaspoon ground cloves

¼ teaspoon ground allspice

1½ cup raisins

½ cup (1 stick) butter or margarine, at room temperature

½ cup sugar

2 eggs

½ cup molasses

½ cup walnuts, chopped

**1** Preheat the oven to 350°F. Line the bottom and sides of a 13- × 9-inch pan with wax paper and grease.

**2** Sift together the flour, baking powder, and spices.

**3 ▲** Place the raisins in another bowl and toss with a few tablespoons of the flour mixture.

**4 ▲** With an electric mixer, cream the butter or margarine and sugar together until light and fluffy. Beat in the eggs, 1 at a time, then the molasses. Stir in the flour mixture, raisins, and walnuts.

**5** Spread evenly in the pan. Bake until just set, 15–18 minutes. Let cool in the pan before cutting into bars.

# Butterscotch Meringue Bars

**MAKES 12**

4 tablespoons butter

1 cup dark brown sugar, firmly packed

1 egg

½ teaspoon vanilla extract

½ cup flour

½ teaspoon salt

¼ teaspoon grated nutmeg

**FOR THE TOPPING**

1 egg white

⅛ teaspoon salt

l tablespoon light corn syrup

½ cup granulated sugar

½ cup walnuts, finely chopped

**1 ▲** Combine the butter and brown sugar in a pan and cook until bubbling. Set aside to cool.

**2** Preheat oven to 350°F. Line the bottom and sides of an 8-inch square cake pan with wax paper and grease.

**3** Beat the egg and vanilla into cooled sugar mixture. Sift over the flour, salt, and nutmeg and fold in. Spread in the bottom of the pan.

**4 ▲** For the topping, beat the egg white with the salt until it holds soft peaks. Beat in the corn syrup, then the sugar and continue beating until the mixture holds stiff peaks. Fold in the nuts and spread on top. Bake for 30 minutes. Cut into bars when cool.

*Hermits (top), Butterscotch Meringue Bars*

# Strawberry Shortcake

**SERVES 6**

1½ pints strawberries, hulled and halved or quartered, depending on size

3 tablespoons confectioners' sugar

1 cup whipping cream

mint leaves, for garnishing

**FOR THE BISCUITS**

2 cups flour

6 tablespoons granulated sugar

1 tablespoon baking powder

½ teaspoon salt

1 cup whipping cream

**1** Preheat the oven to 400°F. Lightly grease a baking sheet.

**2 ▲** For the biscuits, sift the flour into a mixing bowl. Add 4 tablespoons of the granulated sugar, the baking powder, and salt. Stir well.

**3 ▲** Gradually add the cream, tossing lightly with a fork until the mixture forms clumps.

**4 ▲** Gather the clumps together, but do not knead the dough. Shape the dough into a 6-inch log. Cut into 6 slices and place them on the prepared baking sheet.

**5 ▲** Sprinkle with the remaining 2 tablespoons granulated sugar. Bake until light golden brown, about 15 minutes. Let cool on a wire rack.

**6 ▲** Meanwhile, combine 1 cup of the strawberries with the confectioners' sugar. Mash with a fork. Stir in the remaining strawberries. Let stand 1 hour at room temperature.

**7 ▲** In a bowl, whip the cream until soft peaks form.

**8 ▲** To serve, slice each biscuit in half horizontally using a serrated knife. Put the bottom halves on individual dessert plates. Top each biscuit half with some of the whipped cream. Divide the berries among the 6 biscuits. Replace the biscuit tops and garnish with mint. Serve with the remaining whipped cream.

~ **COOK'S TIP** ~

For best results when whipping cream, refrigerate the bowl and beaters until thoroughly chilled. If using an electric mixer, increase speed gradually, and turn the bowl while beating to incorporate as much air as possible.

# MUFFINS & QUICK BREADS

EASY TO MAKE AND SATISFYING TO EAT, THESE MUFFINS AND QUICK BREADS WILL FILL THE HOUSE WITH HOMEY SCENTS AND LURE YOUR FAMILY AND FRIENDS TO LINGER OVER BREAKFAST, COFFEE OR TEA – AND THEY ARE GREAT FOR SNACKS OR LUNCH.

# Raisin Bran Muffins

**MAKES 15**

4 tablespoons butter or margarine

⅔ cup all-purpose flour

½ cup whole-wheat flour

1½ teaspoons baking soda

⅛ teaspoon salt

1 teaspoon ground cinnamon

½ cup bran

½ cup raisins

⅓ cup dark brown sugar, firmly packed

¼ cup granulated sugar

1 egg

1 cup buttermilk

juice of ½ lemon

**1** Preheat the oven to 400°F. Grease 15 muffin cups or use paper liners.

**2 ▲** Place the butter or margarine in a saucepan and melt over gentle heat. Set aside.

**3** In a mixing bowl, sift together the all-purpose flour, whole-wheat flour, baking soda, salt, and cinnamon.

**4 ▲** Add the bran, raisins, and sugars and stir until blended.

**5** In another bowl, mix together the egg, buttermilk, lemon juice, and melted butter.

**6 ▲** Add the buttermilk mixture to the dry ingredients and stir lightly and quickly just until moistened; do not mix until smooth.

**7 ▲** Spoon the batter into the prepared muffin cups, filling them almost to the top. Half-fill any empty cups with water.

**8** Bake until golden, 15–20 minutes. Serve warm or at room temperature.

# Raspberry Crumble Muffins

**MAKES 12**

| |
|---|
| 1½ cups flour |
| ¼ cup granulated sugar |
| ¼ cup light brown sugar, firmly packed |
| 2 teaspoons baking powder |
| ⅛ teaspoon salt |
| 1 teaspoon ground cinnamon |
| ½ cup (1 stick) butter, melted |
| 1 egg |
| ½ cup milk |
| 1¼ cups fresh raspberries |
| grated rind of 1 lemon |
| FOR THE CRUMBLE TOPPING |
| ¼ cup pecans, finely chopped |
| ¼ cup dark brown sugar, firmly packed |
| 3 tablespoons flour |
| 1 teaspoon ground cinnamon |
| 3 tablespoons butter, melted |

**1** Preheat the oven to 350°F. Grease a 12-cup muffin pan or use paper liners.

**2** Sift the flour into a bowl. Add the sugars, baking powder, salt, and cinnamon and stir to blend.

**3 ▲** Make a well in the center. Place the butter, egg, and milk in the well and mix until just combined. Stir in the raspberries and lemon rind. Spoon the batter into the prepared muffin cups, filling them almost to the top.

**4 ▼** For the crumble topping, mix the pecans, dark brown sugar, flour, and cinnamon in a bowl. Add the melted butter and stir to blend.

**5 ▲** Spoon some of the crumble over each muffin. Bake until browned, about 25 minutes. Transfer to a rack to cool slightly. Serve warm.

# Carrot Muffins

**MAKES 12**

¾ cup margarine, at room temperature

½ cup dark brown sugar, firmly packed

1 egg, at room temperature

1 tablespoon water

2 cups grated carrots

1¼ cups flour

1 teaspoon baking powder

½ teaspoon baking soda

1 teaspoon ground cinnamon

¼ teaspoon grated nutmeg

½ teaspoon salt

**1** Preheat the oven to 350°F. Grease a 12-cup muffin pan or use paper liners.

**2** With an electric mixer, cream the margarine and sugar until light and fluffy. Beat in the egg and water.

**3 ▲** Stir in the carrots.

**4** Sift over the flour, baking powder, baking soda, cinnamon, nutmeg, and salt. Stir to blend.

**5 ▼** Spoon the batter into the prepared muffin cups, filling them almost to the top. Bake until the tops spring back when touched lightly, about 35 minutes. Let stand 10 minutes before transferring to a rack.

# Dried Cherry Muffins

**MAKES 16**

1 cup plain yogurt

1 cup dried cherries

½ cup (1 stick) butter, at room temperature

¾ cup sugar

2 eggs, at room temperature

1 teaspoon vanilla extract

1¾ cups flour

2 teaspoons baking powder

1 teaspoon baking soda

⅛ teaspoon salt

**1** In a mixing bowl, combine the yogurt and cherries. Cover and let stand for 30 minutes.

**2** Preheat the oven to 350°F. Grease 16 muffin cups or use paper liners.

**3** With an electric mixer, cream the butter and sugar together until light and fluffy.

**4 ▼** Add the eggs, 1 at a time, beating well after each addition. Add the vanilla and the cherry mixture and stir to blend. Set aside.

**5 ▲** In another bowl, sift together the flour, baking powder, baking soda, and salt. Fold into the cherry mixture in 3 batches; do not overmix.

**6** Fill the prepared cups two-thirds full. For even baking, half-fill any empty cups with water. Bake until the tops spring back when touched lightly, about 20 minutes. Transfer to a rack to cool.

*Carrot Muffins (top), Dried Cherry Muffins*

# Blueberry Muffins

**MAKES 12**

1¼ cups flour

⅓ cup sugar

2 teaspoons baking powder

¼ teaspoon salt

2 eggs

4 tablespoons butter, melted

¾ cup milk

1 teaspoon vanilla extract

1 teaspoon grated lemon rind

1 cup fresh blueberries

**1** Preheat the oven to 400°F.

**2 ▼** Grease a 12-cup muffin pan or use paper liners.

**3 ▲** Sift the flour, sugar, baking powder, and salt into a bowl.

**4** In another bowl, whisk the eggs until blended. Add the melted butter, milk, vanilla, and lemon rind and stir to combine.

**5** Make a well in the dry ingredients and pour in the egg mixture. With a large metal spoon, stir just until the flour is moistened, not until smooth.

**6 ▲** Fold in the blueberries.

**7 ▲** Spoon the batter into the cups, leaving room for the muffins to rise.

**8** Bake until the tops spring back when touched lightly, 20–25 minutes. Let cool in the pan for 5 minutes before unmolding.

# Apple Cranberry Muffins

**MAKES 12**

4 tablespoons butter or margarine

1 egg

½ cup sugar

grated rind of 1 large orange

½ cup fresh orange juice

1 cup flour

1 teaspoon baking powder

½ teaspoon baking soda

1 teaspoon ground cinnamon

½ teaspoon grated nutmeg

½ teaspoon ground allspice

¼ teaspoon ground ginger

¼ teaspoon salt

1–2 apples

1 cup cranberries

½ cup walnuts, chopped

confectioners' sugar, for dusting
   (optional)

**1** Preheat the oven to 350°F.
Grease a 12-cup muffin pan or
use paper liners.

**2** Melt the butter or margarine over
gentle heat. Set aside to cool.

**3 ▲** Place the egg in a mixing bowl
and whisk lightly. Add the melted
butter or margarine and whisk
to combine.

**4** Add the sugar, orange rind, and
juice. Whisk to blend, then set aside.

**5** In a large bowl, sift together the
flour, baking powder, baking soda,
cinnamon, nutmeg, allspice, ginger,
and salt. Set aside.

**6 ▲** Quarter, core, and peel the
apples. With a sharp knife, chop in a
coarse dice to obtain 1¼ cups.

**7** Make a well in the dry ingredients
and pour in the egg mixture. With a
spoon, stir until just blended.

**8 ▲** Add the apples, cranberries, and
walnuts and stir to blend.

**9** Fill the cups three-quarters full and
bake until the tops spring back when
touched lightly, 25–30 minutes.
Transfer to a rack to cool. Dust with
confectioners' sugar, if desired.

# Chocolate Chip Muffins

**MAKES 10**

½ cup (1 stick) butter or margarine, at room temperature

⅓ cup granulated sugar

2 tablespoons dark brown sugar

2 eggs, at room temperature

1½ cups cake flour

1 teaspoon baking powder

½ cup milk

1 cup semisweet chocolate chips

1  Preheat the oven to 375°F. Grease 10 muffin cups or use paper liners.

2 ▼  With an electric mixer, cream the butter or margarine until soft. Add both sugars and beat until light and fluffy. Beat in the eggs, 1 at a time.

3  Sift together the flour and baking powder, twice. Fold into the butter mixture, alternating with the milk.

4 ▲  Divide half the mixture between the muffin cups. Sprinkle several chocolate chips on top, then cover with a spoonful of the batter. To ensure even baking, half-fill any empty cups with water.

5  Bake until lightly colored, about 25 minutes. Let stand 5 minutes before unmolding.

# Chocolate Walnut Muffins

**MAKES 12**

¾ cup (1½ sticks) unsalted butter

4 1-ounce squares semisweet chocolate

1 1-ounce square unsweetened chocolate

1 cup granulated sugar

¼ cup dark brown sugar, firmly packed

4 eggs

1 teaspoon vanilla extract

¼ teaspoon almond extract

¾ cup flour

1 cup walnuts, chopped

1  Preheat the oven to 350°F. Grease a 12-cup muffin pan or use paper liners.

2 ▼  Melt the butter with the two chocolates in the top of a double boiler or in a heatproof bowl set over a pan of hot water. Transfer to a large mixing bowl.

3  Stir both the sugars into the chocolate mixture. Mix in the eggs, 1 at a time, then add the vanilla and almond extracts.

4  Sift over the flour and fold in.

5 ▲  Stir in the walnuts.

6  Fill the prepared cups almost to the top and bake until a cake tester inserted in the center barely comes out clean, 30–35 minutes. Let stand 5 minutes before transferring to a rack to cool completely.

*Chocolate Chip Muffins (top), Chocolate Walnut Muffins*

# Oatmeal Buttermilk Muffins

**MAKES 12**

- 1 cup rolled oats
- 1 cup buttermilk
- ½ cup (1 stick) butter, at room temperature
- ½ cup dark brown sugar, firmly packed
- 1 egg, at room temperature
- 1 cup flour
- 1 teaspoon baking powder
- ½ teaspoon baking soda
- ¼ teaspooon salt
- ¼ cup raisins

~ COOK'S TIP ~

If buttermilk is not available, add 1 teaspoon lemon juice or vinegar per cup of milk. Let the mixture stand a few minutes to curdle.

1 ▲ In a bowl, combine the oats and buttermilk and let soak for 1 hour.

2 ▲ Grease a 12-cup muffin pan or use paper liners.

3 ▲ Preheat the oven to 400°F. With an electric mixer, cream the butter and sugar until light and fluffy. Beat in the egg.

4 In another bowl, sift together the flour, baking powder, baking soda, and salt. Stir into the butter mixture, alternating with the oat mixture. Fold in the raisins. Do not overmix.

5 Fill the prepared cups two-thirds full. Bake until a cake tester inserted in the center comes out clean, 20–25 minutes. Transfer to a rack to cool.

# Pumpkin Muffins

**MAKES 14**

- ½ cup (1 stick) butter or margarine, at room temperature
- ¾ cup dark brown sugar, firmly packed
- ⅓ cup molasses
- 1 egg, at room temperature, beaten
- 1 cup cooked or canned pumpkin (about 8 ounces)
- 1 ¾ cups flour
- ¼ teaspoon salt
- 1 teaspoon baking soda
- 1½ teaspoons ground cinnamon
- 1 teaspoon grated nutmeg
- ¼ cup currants or raisins

1 Preheat the oven to 400°F. Grease 14 muffin cups or use paper liners.

2 With an electric mixer, cream the butter or margarine until soft. Add the sugar and molasses and beat until light and fluffy.

3 ▲ Add the egg and pumpkin and stir until well blended.

4 Sift over the flour, salt, baking soda, cinnnamon, and nutmeg. Fold just enough to blend; do not overmix.

5 ▼ Fold in the currants or raisins.

6 Spoon the batter into the prepared muffin cups, filling them three-quarters full.

7 Bake until the tops spring back when touched lightly, 12–15 minutes. Serve warm or cold.

*Oatmeal Buttermilk Muffins (top), Pumpkin Muffins*

# Prune Muffins

MAKES 12

| |
|---|
| 1 egg |
| 1 cup milk |
| ¼ cup vegetable oil |
| ¼ cup granulated sugar |
| 2 tablespoons dark brown sugar |
| 2 cups flour |
| 2 teaspoons baking powder |
| ½ teaspoon salt |
| ¼ teaspoon grated nutmeg |
| ¾ cup cooked pitted prunes, chopped |

**1** Preheat the oven to 400°F. Grease a 12-cup muffin tin or use paper liners.

**2** Break the egg into a mixing bowl and beat with a fork. Beat in the milk and oil.

**3 ▼** Stir in the sugars. Set aside.

**4** Sift the flour, baking powder, salt, and nutmeg into a mixing bowl. Make a well in the center, pour in the egg mixture and stir until moistened. Do not overmix; the batter should be slightly lumpy.

**5 ▲** Fold in the prunes.

**6** Fill the prepared cups two-thirds full. Bake until golden brown, about 20 minutes. Let stand 10 minutes before unmolding. Serve warm or at room temperature.

---

# Yogurt Honey Muffins

MAKES 12

| |
|---|
| 4 tablespoons butter |
| 5 tablespoons thin honey |
| 1 cup plain yogurt |
| 1 large egg, at room temperature |
| grated rind of 1 lemon |
| ¼ cup fresh lemon juice |
| 1 cup all-purpose flour |
| 1 cup whole-wheat flour |
| 1½ teaspoons baking soda |
| ⅛ teaspoon grated nutmeg |

> ~ **VARIATION** ~
>
> For Walnut Yogurt Honey Muffins, add ½ cup chopped walnuts, folded in with the flour. This makes a more substantial muffin.

**1** Preheat the oven to 375°F. Grease a 12-cup muffin pan or use paper liners.

**2** In a saucepan, melt the butter and honey. Remove from the heat and set aside to cool slightly.

**3 ▲** In a bowl, whisk together the yogurt, egg, lemon rind and juice. Add the butter and honey mixture. Set aside.

**4 ▲** In another bowl, sift together the dry ingredients.

**5** Fold the dry ingredients into the yogurt mixture just to blend.

**6** Fill the prepared cups two-thirds full. Bake until the tops spring back when touched lightly, 20–25 minutes. Let cool in the pan for 5 minutes before unmolding. Serve warm or at room temperature.

*Prune Muffins (top), Yogurt Honey Muffins*

# Banana Muffins

**MAKES 10**

2 cups flour

1 teaspoon baking powder

1 teaspoon baking soda

¼ teaspoon salt

½ teaspoon ground cinnamon

¼ teaspoon grated nutmeg

3 large ripe bananas

1 egg

⅓ cup dark brown sugar, firmly packed

¼ cup vegetable oil

¼ cup raisins

**1** Preheat the oven to 375°F.

**2** ▼ Line 10 muffin cups with paper liners or grease.

**3** Sift together the flour, baking powder, baking soda, salt, nutmeg, and cinnamon. Set aside.

**4** ▲ With an electric mixer, beat the peeled bananas at moderate speed until mashed.

**5** ▲ Beat in the egg, sugar, and oil.

**6** Add the dry ingredients and beat in gradually, on low speed. Mix just until blended. With a wooden spoon, stir in the raisins.

**7** Fill the prepared cups two-thirds full. For even baking, half-fill any empty cups with water.

**8** ▲ Bake until the tops spring back when touched lightly, 20–25 minutes.

**9** Transfer to a rack to cool.

# Maple Pecan Muffins

**MAKES 20**

| |
|---|
| 1¼ cups pecans |
| 2½ cups flour |
| 1 teaspoon baking powder |
| 1 teaspoon baking soda |
| ¼ teaspoon salt |
| ¼ teaspoon ground cinnamon |
| ½ cup granulated sugar |
| ⅓ cup light brown sugar, firmly packed |
| 3 tablespoons maple syrup |
| ⅔ cup (10⅔ tablespoons) butter, at room temperature |
| 3 eggs, at room temperature |
| 1¼ cups buttermilk |
| 60 pecan halves, for decorating |

**1** Preheat the oven to 350°F. Grease 2 12-cup muffin pans or use paper liners.

**2 ▲** Spread the pecans on a baking sheet and toast in the oven for 5 minutes. When cool, chop coarsely and set aside.

~ **VARIATION** ~

For Pecan Spice Muffins, substitute an equal quantity of molasses for the maple syrup. Increase the cinnamon to ½ teaspoon, and add 1 teaspoon ground ginger and ½ teaspoon grated nutmeg, sifted with the flour and other dry ingredients.

**3** In a bowl, sift together the flour, baking powder, baking soda, salt, and cinnamon. Set aside.

**4 ▲** In a large mixing bowl, combine the granulated sugar, light brown sugar, maple syrup, and butter. Beat with an electric mixer until light and fluffy.

**5** Add the eggs, 1 at a time, beating to incorporate thoroughly after each addition.

**6 ▲** Pour half the buttermilk and half the dry ingredients into the butter mixture, then stir until blended. Repeat with the remaining buttermilk and dry ingredients.

**7** Fold in the chopped pecans.

**8** Fill the prepared cups two-thirds full. Top with the pecan halves. For even baking, half-fill any empty cup with water.

**9** Bake until puffed up and golden, 20–25 minutes. Let stand 5 minutes before unmolding.

# Banana-Pecan Muffins

**MAKES 8**

1¼ cups flour

1½ teaspoons baking powder

4 tablespoons butter or margarine, at room temperature

¾ cup sugar

1 egg

1 teaspoon vanilla extract

¾ cup mashed bananas (about 3 medium bananas)

½ cup pecans, chopped

⅓ cup milk

~ **VARIATION** ~

Use an equal quantity of walnuts instead of the pecans.

**1** Preheat the oven to 375°F. Grease a muffin pan.

**2** Sift the flour and baking powder into a small bowl. Set aside.

**3** ▲ With an electric mixer, cream the butter or margarine and sugar together. Add the egg and vanilla and beat until fluffy. Mix in the banana.

**4** ▼ Add the pecans. With the mixer on low speed, beat in the flour mixture alternately with the milk.

**5** Spoon the batter into the prepared muffin cups, filling them two-thirds full. Bake until golden brown and a cake tester inserted into the center of a muffin comes out clean, 20–25 minutes.

**6** Let cool in the pan on a wire rack for 10 minutes. To loosen, run a knife gently around each muffin and unmold onto the wire rack. Let cool 10 minutes longer before serving.

# Blueberry-Cinnamon Muffins

**MAKES 8**

1 cup flour

1 tablespoon baking powder

⅛ teaspoon salt

⅓ cup light brown sugar, firmly packed

1 egg

¾ cup milk

3 tablespoons corn oil

2 teaspoons ground cinnamon

1 cup fresh or thawed frozen blueberries

**1** Preheat the oven to 375°F. Grease a muffin pan.

**2** With an electric mixer, beat the first 8 ingredients together until smooth.

**3** ▲ Fold in the blueberries.

**4** ▲ Spoon the batter into the muffin cups, filling them two-thirds full. Bake until a cake tester inserted in the center of a muffin comes out clean, about 25 minutes.

**5** Let cool in the pan on a wire rack for 10 minutes, then unmold the muffins onto the wire rack and allow to cool completely.

# Raspberry Muffins

**MAKES 10–12**

1 cup self-rising flour

1 cup whole-wheat self-rising flour

3 tablespoons sugar

½ teaspoon salt

2 eggs, beaten

scant 1 cup milk

4 tablespoons melted butter

6 oz raspberries, fresh or frozen
(defrosted for less than 30 minutes)

**1 ▼** Preheat the oven to 375°F. Lightly grease the muffin pan, or use paper liners. Sift both the flours, sugar and the salt together, then tip back in the whole-wheat flakes from the sifter.

**2 ▲** Beat the eggs, milk and butter with the dry ingredients to give a thick batter. Add the raspberries.

**3 ▲** Stir in the raspberries gently. (If you are using frozen raspberries, work quickly as the cold berries make the mixture solidify.) If you mix too much the raspberries begin to disintegrate and color the dough. Spoon the mixture into the tins or paper cases.

**4** Bake the muffins for 30 minutes, until well risen and just firm. Serve warm or cool.

# Cherry Marmalade Muffins

**MAKES 12**

2 cups self-rising flour

1 teaspoon apple pie spice

6 tablespoons sugar

½ cup candied cherries, quartered

2 tablespoons orange marmalade

⅔ cup skim milk

4 tablespoons soft sunflower margarine

marmalade, to brush

**1** ▲ Preheat the oven to 400°F. Lightly grease a 12-cup muffin pan with oil.

**2** ▲ Sift together the flour and spice, then stir in the sugar and cherries.

**3** Mix the marmalade with the milk and beat into the dry ingredients with the margarine. Spoon into the greased cups. Bake for 20–25 minutes, until golden brown and firm.

**4** ▼ Turn out on to a wire rack and brush the tops with warmed marmalade. Serve warm or cold.

~ **VARIATION** ~

To make Honey-Nut Lemon Muffins, substitute 2 tablespoons clear honey for the orange marmalade. Add the juice and grated rind of a lemon and ¼ cup toasted, chopped hazelnuts, instead of the candied cherries.

# Blackberry and Almond Muffins

**MAKES 12**

2½ cups plain unbleached flour

generous ¼ cup light brown sugar

4 teaspoons baking powder

pinch of salt

generous ½ cup chopped blanched
    almonds

generous ½ cup fresh blackberries

2 eggs

⅞ cup milk

4 tablespoons melted butter, plus a little
    more to grease cups, if using

1 tablespoon sloe gin

1 tablespoon rosewater

**1 ▼** Mix the flour, brown sugar,
baking powder and salt in a large bowl
and stir in the almonds and
blackberries, mixing them well to coat
completely with the flour mixture.
Preheat the oven to 400°F.

**2 ▲** In another bowl, mix the eggs
with the milk, then gradually add the
butter, sloe gin and rosewater. Make a
well in the center of the bowl of dry
ingredients and add the egg and milk
mixture. Stir well.

**3** Spoon the mixture into a greased
12-cup muffin pan or cases. Bake for
20–25 minutes or until browned. Turn
out the muffins on to a wire rack to
cool. Serve with butter.

~ **COOK'S TIP** ~

Other berries can be substituted
for the blackberries, such as
raspberries or blueberries.

~ **VARIATION** ~

For Blackberry and Apple Muffins,
substitute 2 dessert apples, peeled,
cored, and diced, for the almonds.
Add 1 teaspoon ground coriander
to the flour mixture, and instead
of the sloe gin and rosewater,
substitute 2 tablespoons
Crème de Cassis.

# Bacon Cornmeal Muffins

**MAKES 14**

| |
|---|
| 8 slices bacon |
| 4 tablespoons butter |
| 4 tablespoons margarine |
| 1 cup flour |
| 1 tablespoon baking powder |
| 1 teaspoon sugar |
| ¼ teaspoon salt |
| 1½ cups cornmeal |
| 1 cup milk |
| 2 eggs |

**1** Preheat the oven to 400°F. Grease 14 muffin cups or use paper liners.

**2** ▲ Fry the bacon until crisp. Drain on paper towels, then chop into small pieces. Set aside.

**3** Gently melt the butter and margarine and set aside.

**4** ▲ Sift the flour, baking powder, sugar, and salt into a large mixing bowl. Stir in the cornmeal, then make a well in the center.

**5** In a saucepan, heat the milk to lukewarm. In a small bowl, lightly whisk the eggs, then add to the milk. Stir in the melted fats.

**6** ▼ Pour the milk mixture into the center of the well and stir until smooth and well blended.

**7** ▲ Fold in the bacon.

**8** Spoon the batter into the prepared cups, filling them halfway. Bake until risen and lightly colored, about 20 minutes. Serve hot or warm.

# Cheese Muffins

**MAKES 9**

4 tablespoons butter

1½ cups flour

2 teaspoons baking powder

2 tablespoons sugar

¼ teaspoon salt

1 teaspoon paprika

2 eggs

½ cup milk

1 teaspoon dried thyme

2 ounces sharp cheddar cheese, cut into ½-inch dice

**1** Preheat the oven to 375°F. Thickly grease 9 muffin cups or use paper liners.

**2** Melt the butter and set aside.

**3 ▼** In a mixing bowl, sift together the flour, baking powder, sugar, salt, and paprika.

**4 ▲** In another bowl, combine the eggs, milk, melted butter, and thyme, and whisk to blend.

**5** Add the milk mixture to the dry ingredients and stir just until moistened; do not mix until smooth.

**6 ▲** Place a heaped spoonful of batter into the prepared cups. Drop a few pieces of cheese over each, then top with another spoonful of batter. For even baking, half-fill any empty muffin cups with water.

**7 ▲** Bake until puffed and golden, about 25 minutes. Let stand 5 minutes before unmolding onto a rack. Serve warm or at room temperature.

# Sweet Potato Biscuits

**MAKES ABOUT 24**

1¼ cups flour

4 teaspoons baking powder

1 teaspoon salt

1 tablespoon brown sugar

¾ cup mashed cooked sweet potatoes

⅔ cup milk

4 tablespoons butter or margarine, melted

**1** Preheat the oven to 450°F.

**2 ▲** Sift the flour, baking powder, and salt into a bowl. Add the sugar and stir to mix.

**3 ▲** In a separate bowl, combine the sweet potatoes with the milk and melted butter or margarine. Mix well until evenly blended.

**4 ▼** Stir the dry ingredients into the sweet potato mixture to make a dough. Turn onto a lightly floured surface and knead lightly just to mix, 1–2 minutes.

**5 ▲** Roll or pat out the dough to ½-inch thickness. Cut out rounds with a 1½-inch cookie cutter.

**6** Arrange the rounds on a greased cookie sheet. Bake until puffed and lightly golden, about 15 minutes. Serve the biscuits warm.

# Buttermilk Biscuits

**MAKES 15**

1½ cups flour

1 teaspoon salt

1 teaspoon baking powder

½ teaspoon baking soda

4 tablespoons cold butter or margarine

¾ cup buttermilk

**1** Preheat the oven to 425°F. Grease a baking sheet.

**2** Sift the dry ingredients into a bowl. Cut in the butter or margarine with a pastry blender until the mixture resembles coarse crumbs.

**3 ▼** Gradually pour in the buttermilk, stirring with a fork to form a soft dough.

**4 ▲** Roll out about ½ inch thick.

**5** Stamp out 2-inch circles with a cookie cutter.

**6** Place on the prepared tray and bake until golden, 12–15 minutes. Serve warm or at room temperature.

# Baking Powder Biscuits

**MAKES 8**

1⅓ cups flour

2 tablespoons sugar

3 teaspoons baking powder

⅛ teaspoon salt

5 tablespoons cold butter, cut in pieces

½ cup milk

**1** Preheat the oven to 425°F. Grease a baking sheet.

**2 ▲** Sift the flour, sugar, baking powder, and salt into a bowl.

**3** Cut in the butter with a pastry blender until the mixture resembles coarse crumbs.

**4** Pour in the milk and stir with a fork to form a soft dough.

~ **VARIATION** ~

For Berry Shortcake, split the biscuits in half while still warm. Butter one half, top with lightly sugared fresh berries, such as strawberries, raspberries or blueberries, and sandwich with the other half. Serve with dollops of whipped cream.

**5 ▲** Roll out the dough about ¼ inch thick. Stamp out circles with a 2½-inch cookie cutter.

**6** Place on the prepared sheet and bake until golden, about 12 minutes. Serve hot or warm, with butter for meals; to accompany tea or coffee, serve with butter and jam.

*Buttermilk Biscuits (top), Baking Powder Biscuits*

# Whole-Wheat Scones

**MAKES 16**

¾ cup (1½ sticks) cold butter

2 cups whole-wheat flour

1 cup all-purpose flour

2 tablespoons sugar

½ teaspoon salt

2½ teaspoons baking soda

2 eggs

¾ cup buttermilk

¼ cup raisins

**1** Preheat the oven to 400°F. Grease and flour a large baking sheet.

**2 ▲** Cut the butter into small pieces.

**3** Combine the dry ingredients in a bowl. Add the butter and cut in with a pastry blender until the mixture resembles coarse crumbs. Set aside.

**4** In another bowl, whisk together the eggs and buttermilk. Set aside 2 tablespoons for glazing.

**5** Stir the remaining egg mixture into the dry ingredients until it just holds together. Stir in the raisins.

**6** Roll out the dough about ¾ inch thick. Stamp out circles with a cookie cutter. Place on the prepared sheet and brush with the glaze.

**7** Bake until golden, 12–15 minutes. Allow to cool slightly before serving. Split in two with a fork while still warm and spread with butter and jam, if wished.

# Orange Raisin Scones

**MAKES 16**

2 cups flour

1½ teaspoons baking powder

⅓ cup sugar

½ teaspoon salt

5 tablespoons butter, diced

5 tablespoons margarine, diced

grated rind of 1 large orange

⅓ cup raisins

½ cup buttermilk

milk, for glazing

**1** Preheat the oven to 425°F. Grease and flour a large baking sheet.

**2** Combine the dry ingredients in a large bowl. Add the butter and margarine and cut in with a pastry blender until the mixture resembles coarse crumbs.

**3 ▲** Add the orange rind and raisins.

**4** Gradually stir in the buttermilk to form a soft dough.

**5 ▲** Roll out the dough about ¾ inch thick. Stamp out circles with a cookie cutter.

**6 ▲** Place on the prepared sheet and brush the tops with milk.

**7** Bake until golden, 12–15 minutes. Serve hot or warm, with butter or whipped cream, and jam.

> **~ COOK'S TIP ~**
>
> For light tender scones, handle the dough as little as possible. If you wish, split the scones when cool and toast them under a preheated broiler. Butter them while still hot.

*Whole-Wheat Scones (top), Orange Raisin Scones*

# Sunflower-Raisin Biscuits

**MAKES 10–12**

2 cups self-rising flour

1 teaspoon baking powder

2 tablespoons soft sunflower margarine

2 tablespoons sugar

⅓ cup raisins

2 tablespoons sunflower seeds

⅔ cup plain yogurt

about 2–3 tablespoons skim milk

**1** Preheat the oven to 450°F. Lightly oil a cookie sheet. Sift the flour and baking powder into a bowl and rub in the margarine evenly.

**2** Stir in the sugar, raisins, and half the sunflower seeds, then mix in the yogurt, with just enough milk to make a fairly soft, but not sticky dough.

**3 ▼** Roll out on a lightly floured surface to about ¾-inch thickness. Cut into 2½-inch flower shapes or rounds with a cookie cutter and lift onto the baking sheet.

**4 ▲** Brush with milk and sprinkle with the reserved sunflower seeds, then bake for 10–12 minutes, until puffed and golden brown.

**5** Cool the biscuits on a wire rack. Serve split and spread with butter and jam.

# Prune and Candied Peel Cookies

**MAKES 12**

2 cups flour

2 teaspoons baking powder

⅔ cup raw sugar

½ cup chopped dried prunes

⅓ cup chopped candied citrus peel

finely grated rind of 1 lemon

¼ cup sunflower oil

5 tablespoons skim milk

### ~ VARIATION ~

For Spicy Fruit Cookies, substitute ½ cup dried cranberries for the prunes, ⅓ cup raisins for the candied peel, and add 1 teaspoon apple pie spice, ¼ teaspoon ground ginger, and ¼ teaspoon ground cinnamon.

**1 ▼** Preheat the oven to 400°F. Lightly oil a large baking sheet. Sift together the flour and baking powder, then stir in the sugar, prunes, peel, and lemon rind.

**2** Mix the oil and milk, then stir into the mixture, to make a dough which just binds together.

**3 ▲** Spoon rough mounds onto the baking sheet and bake for 20 minutes, until golden. Cool on a wire rack.

# Cheese and Marjoram Biscuits

**MAKES 18**

1 cup whole-wheat flour

1 cup self-rising flour

pinch of salt

scant 3 tablespoons butter

¼ teaspoon dry mustard

2 teaspoons dried marjoram

½–⅔ cup finely grated sharp Cheddar cheese

½ cup milk, or as required to make soft dough

1 teaspoon sunflower oil (optional)

⅓ cup pecans or walnuts, chopped

**1 ▼** Gently sift the two kinds of flour into a bowl and add the salt. Cut the butter into small pieces, and rub these into the flour until it resembles fine bread crumbs.

**2 ▲** Add the mustard, marjoram and grated cheese, and mix in sufficient milk to make a soft dough. Knead the dough lightly.

**3** Preheat the oven to 425°F. Roll out the dough on a floured surface to about a ¾-inch thickness and cut it out with a 2-inch square cutter. Grease some cookie sheets with the paper from the butter (or use a little sunflower oil), and place the biscuits on the sheets.

**4** Brush the biscuits with a little milk and sprinkle the chopped pecans or walnuts over the top. Bake for 12 minutes. Serve warm.

> ### ~ VARIATION ~
>
> For Mixed Herb and Mustard Biscuits, with a light, summery flavor, use 2 tablespoons chopped fresh parsley or chives in place of the dried marjoram. Use 1 teaspoon Dijon mustard and ⅓ cup chopped pistachios for the dry mustard and the pecans.

# Cheese and Chive Biscuits

**MAKES 9**

| |
|---|
| 1 cup self-rising flour |
| 1 cup self-rising whole-wheat flour |
| ½ teaspoon salt |
| 3 oz feta cheese |
| 1 tablespoon snipped fresh chives |
| ⅔ cup skim milk, plus extra for glazing |
| ¼ teaspoon cayenne pepper |

**1 ▲** Preheat the oven to 400°F. Sift the flours and salt into a mixing bowl, adding any bran left over from the flour in the sifter.

**2 ▲** Crumble the feta cheese and rub into the dry ingredients. Stir in the chives, then add the milk and mix to a soft dough.

**3 ▼** Turn out the dough onto a floured surface and lightly knead until smooth. Roll out to ¾-inch thick and stamp out nine scones with a 2½-inch cookie cutter.

**4 ▲** Transfer the biscuits to a nonstick baking sheet. Brush with skim milk, then sprinkle over the cayenne pepper. Bake in the oven for 15 minutes, or until golden brown. Serve warm or cold.

# Dill-Potato Cakes

**MAKES 10**

2 cups self-rising flour

3 tablespoons butter, softened

pinch of salt

1 tablespoon finely chopped fresh dill

scant 1 cup mashed potato, freshly made

2–3 tablespoons milk, as required

**1 ▼** Preheat the oven to 450°F. Sift the flour into a bowl, and add the butter, salt and dill. Mix in the mashed potato and enough milk to make a soft, pliable dough.

**2 ▲** Roll out the dough on a well-floured surface until it is fairly thin. Cut into several neat rounds with a 3-inch cutter.

**3 ▲** Grease a cookie sheet, place the cakes on it, and bake for 20–25 minutes until risen and golden.

~ **VARIATION** ~

For Cheese and Herb Potato Cakes, blue cheese makes a tasty addition. Stir in about ¼ cup crumbled blue cheese, and substitute 1 tablespoon snipped fresh chives for the dill. In place of the butter, use 3 tablespoons sour cream.

# Parmesan Popovers

**MAKES 6**

| |
|---|
| ½ cup freshly grated Parmesan cheese |
| 1 cup flour |
| ¼ teaspoon salt |
| 2 eggs |
| 1 cup milk |
| 1 tablespoon butter or margarine, melted |

1 ▼ Preheat the oven to 450°F. Grease six ¾-cup popover pans. Sprinkle each pan with 1 tablespoon of the grated Parmesan. Alternatively, you can use custard cups, in which case, heat them on a baking sheet in the oven, then grease and sprinkle with Parmesan just before filling.

2 Sift the flour and salt into a small bowl. Set aside.

3 ▲ In a mixing bowl, beat together the eggs, milk, and butter or margarine. Add the flour mixture and stir until smoothly blended.

4 ▼ Divide the batter evenly among the pans, filling each one about half full. Bake for 15 minutes, then sprinkle the tops of the popovers with the remaining grated Parmesan cheese. Reduce the heat to 350°F and continue baking until the popovers are firm and golden brown, 20–25 minutes.

5 ▲ Remove the popovers from the oven. To unmold, run a thin knife around the inside of each pan to loosen the popovers. Gently ease out, then transfer to a wire rack to cool.

# Herb Popovers

**MAKES 12**

3 eggs

1 cup milk

2 tablespoons butter, melted

¾ cup flour

⅛ teaspoon salt

1 small sprig each mixed fresh herbs, such as chives, tarragon, dill, and parsley

**1** Preheat the oven to 425°F. Grease 12 small ramekins or popover cups.

**2** With an electric mixer, beat the eggs until blended. Beat in the milk and melted butter.

**3** Sift together the flour and salt, then beat into the egg mixture to combine thoroughly.

**4** ▼ Strip the herb leaves from the stems and chop finely. Mix together and measure out 2 tablespoons. Stir the herbs into the batter.

**5** ▲ Fill the prepared cups half-full.

**6** Bake until golden, 25–30 minutes. Do not open the oven door during baking time or the popovers may fall. For drier popovers, pierce each one with a knife after the 30 minute baking time and bake for 5 minutes more. Serve hot.

# Cheese Popovers

**MAKES 12**

3 eggs

1 cup milk

2 tablespoons butter, melted

¾ cup flour

¼ teaspoon salt

¼ teaspoon paprika

6 tablespoons freshly grated Parmesan cheese

---

**~ VARIATION ~**

To make Yorkshire Pudding Popovers, as an accompaniment for roast beef, omit the cheese, and use 4–6 tablespoons of the pan drippings to replace the butter. Put them into the oven in time to serve warm with the beef.

---

**1** Preheat the oven to 425°F. Grease 12 small ramekins or popover cups.

**2** ▲ With an electric mixer, beat the eggs until blended. Beat in the milk and melted butter.

**3** ▲ Sift together the flour, salt, and paprika, then beat into the egg mixture. Add the cheese and stir.

**4** Fill the prepared cups half-full and bake until golden, 25–30 minutes. Do not open the oven door during baking or the popovers may fall. For drier popovers, pierce each one with a knife after the 30 minute baking time and bake for 5 minutes more. Serve hot.

*Herb Popovers (top), Cheese Popovers*

# Orange Honey Bread

**MAKES 1 LOAF**

2½ cups flour

2½ teaspoons baking powder

½ teaspoon baking soda

½ teaspoon salt

2 tablespoons margarine

1 cup thin honey

1 egg, at room temperature, lightly beaten

1½ tablespoons grated orange rind

¾ cup freshly squeezed orange juice

¾ cup walnuts, chopped

**1** Preheat the oven to 325°F.

**2** Sift together the flour, baking powder, baking soda, and salt.

**3** Line the bottom and sides of a 9- × 5-inch loaf pan with wax paper and grease.

**4 ▲** With an electric mixer, cream the margarine until soft. Stir in the honey until blended, then stir in the egg. Add the orange rind and stir to combine thoroughly.

**5 ▲** Fold the flour mixture into the honey and egg mixture in 3 batches, alternating with the orange juice. Stir in the walnuts.

**6** Pour into the pan and bake until a cake tester inserted in the center comes out clean, 60–70 minutes. Let stand 10 minutes before unmolding onto a rack to cool.

# Applesauce Bread

**MAKES 1 LOAF**

1 egg

1 cup applesauce

4 tablespoons butter or margarine, melted

½ cup dark brown sugar, firmly packed

¼ cup granulated sugar

2 cups flour

2 teaspoons baking powder

½ teaspoon baking soda

½ teaspoon salt

1 teaspoon ground cinnamon

½ teaspoon grated nutmeg

½ cup currants or raisins

½ cup pecans, chopped

**1** Preheat the oven to 350°F. Line the bottom and sides of a 9- × 5-inch loaf pan with wax paper and grease.

**2 ▲** Break the egg into a bowl and beat lightly. Stir in the applesauce, butter or margarine, and both sugars. Set aside.

**3** In another bowl, sift together the flour, baking powder, baking soda, salt, cinnamon, and nutmeg. Fold dry ingredients into the applesauce mixture in 3 batches.

**4 ▼** Stir in the currants or raisins, and pecans.

**5** Pour into the prepared pan and bake until a cake tester inserted in the center comes out clean, about 1 hour. Let stand 10 minutes before unmolding and transferring to a cooling rack.

*Orange Honey Bread (top), Applesauce Bread*

# Malt Loaf

This is a rich and sticky loaf. If it lasts long enough to go stale, try toasting it for a delicious teatime treat.

### MAKES 1 LOAF

| |
|---|
| ⅔ cup warm skim milk |
| 1 teaspoon active dry yeast |
| pinch of granulated sugar |
| 3 cups all-purpose flour |
| ½ teaspoon salt |
| 2 tablespoons light brown sugar |
| 6 ounces (generous 1 cup) golden raisins |
| 1 tablespoon sunflower oil |
| 3 tablespoons malt extract |
| FOR THE GLAZE |
| 2 tablespoons granulated sugar |
| 2 tablespoons water |

**1 ▲** Place the warm milk in a bowl. Sprinkle the yeast on top and add the sugar. Let sit for 30 minutes, until frothy. Mix the flour and salt in a mixing bowl, stir in the brown sugar and raisins and make a well.

**2 ▲** Add the yeast mixture with the oil and malt extract. Gradually incorporate the flour and mix to a soft dough, adding a little extra milk if necessary.

**3 ▲** Turn out onto a floured surface and knead for about 5 minutes, until smooth and elastic. Grease a 1-pound loaf pan.

**4 ▲** Shape the dough and place it in the prepared loaf pan. Cover with a damp dish towel and let sit in a warm place for 1–2 hours, until the dough is well risen. Preheat the oven to 375°F.

**5 ▲** Bake the loaf for 30–35 minutes, or until it sounds hollow when tapped on the bottom.

**6 ▲** Meanwhile, prepare the glaze by dissolving the sugar in the water in a small pan. Bring to the boil, stirring, then lower the heat and simmer for 1 minute. Place the loaf on a wire rack and brush with the glaze while still hot. Leave the loaf to cool before serving.

---

### ~ COOK'S TIP ~

To make buns, divide the dough into 10 pieces, shape into rounds, leave to rise, then bake for about 15–20 minutes. Brush with the glaze while still hot.

# Lemon Walnut Bread

**MAKES 1 LOAF**

½ cup (1 stick) butter or margarine, at room temperature

½ cup sugar

2 eggs, at room temperature, separated

grated rind of 2 lemons

2 tablespoons fresh lemon juice

1½ cups cake flour

2 teaspoons baking powder

½ cup milk

½ cup walnuts, chopped

⅛ teaspooon salt

**1**  Preheat the oven to 350°F. Line the bottom and sides of a 9- × 5-inch loaf pan with wax paper and grease.

**2**  With an electric mixer, cream the butter or margarine with the sugar until light and fluffy.

**3** ▲  Beat in the egg yolks.

**4**  Add the lemon rind and juice and stir until blended. Set aside.

**5** ▲  In another bowl, sift together the flour and baking powder, 3 times. Fold into the butter mixture in 3 batches, alternating with the milk. Fold in the walnuts. Set aside.

**6** ▲  Beat the egg whites and salt until stiff peaks form. Fold a large dollop of the egg whites into the walnut mixture to lighten it. Fold in the remaining egg whites carefully just until blended.

**7** ▲  Pour the batter into the prepared pan and bake until a cake tester inserted in the center of the loaf comes out clean, 45–50 minutes. Let stand 5 minutes before unmolding onto a rack to cool completely.

# Banana Bread

**MAKES 1 LOAF**

| |
|---|
| 1½ cups flour |
| 2¼ teaspoons baking powder |
| ½ teaspoon salt |
| ¾ teaspoon ground cinnamon (optional) |
| ¼ cup wheat germ |
| 5 tablespoons butter, at room temperature, or ⅓ cup shortening |
| ⅔ cup sugar |
| ¾ teaspoon grated lemon rind |
| 1¼ cups mashed ripe bananas (2–3 bananas) |
| 2 eggs, beaten to mix |

**1** Preheat the oven to 350°F. Grease and flour an 8½- × 4½-inch loaf pan.

**2** ▲ Sift the flour, baking powder, salt, and cinnamon, if using, into a bowl. Stir in the wheat germ.

**3** ▲ In another bowl, beat the butter or shortening with the sugar and lemon rind until the mixture is light and fluffy.

**4** ▲ Add the mashed bananas and eggs and mix well.

**5** Add the dry ingredients and blend quickly and evenly.

**~ VARIATION ~**

For Banana Walnut Bread, add ½–¾ cup finely chopped walnuts with the dry ingredients.

**6** ▼ Spoon into the prepared loaf pan. Bake until a wooden skewer inserted in the center comes out clean, about 1 hour.

**7** Let the bread cool in the pan about 5 minutes, then unmold onto a wire rack to cool completely.

# Pineapple and Apricot Bread

**SERVES 10–12**

¾ cup sweet butter

¾ cup sugar

3 eggs, beaten

few drops vanilla extract

2 cups cake flour, sifted

¼ teaspoon salt

1½ teaspoons baking powder

1⅓ cups ready-to-eat dried apricots, chopped

½ cup each chopped crystallized ginger and crystallized pineapple

grated rind and juice of ½ orange

grated rind and juice of ½ lemon

a little milk

**1** ▲ Preheat the oven to 350°F. Double line an 8-inch round or 7-inch square cake pan. Cream the butter and sugar together until light and fluffy.

**2** Gradually beat the eggs into the creamed mixture with the vanilla extract, beating well after each addition. Sift together the flour, salt and baking powder, and add a little with the last of the egg, then fold in the rest.

**3** ▲ Fold in the fruit, crystallized fruits and fruit rinds gently, then add sufficient fruit juice and milk to give a fairly soft dropping consistency.

**4** ▲ Spoon into the prepared pan and smooth the top with a wet spoon. Bake for 20 minutes, then reduce the heat to 325°F for a further 1½–2 hours, or until firm to the touch and a skewer comes out of the center clean. Leave the cake to cool in the pan, turn out and wrap in fresh paper before storing in an airtight tin.

~ **COOK'S TIP** ~

This is not a long-keeping cake, but it does freeze, well-wrapped in wax paper and then foil.

# Date and Nut Malt Loaf

A moist loaf—perfect for brown-bag lunches.

**1** Sift the flours and salt into a large bowl, adding any bran from the sieve. Stir in the sugar and yeast.

**2 ▲** Mix the butter or margarine with the molasses and malt extract. Stir over low heat until melted. Let cool, then combine with the milk.

**3** Stir the liquid into the dry ingredients and knead for 15 minutes, until the dough is elastic. (If you have a dough blade on your food processor, follow the manufacturer's instructions for timing.)

**4 ▲** Knead in the fruits and nuts. Transfer the dough to an oiled bowl, cover with plastic wrap, and let sit in a warm place for about 1½ hours, until the dough has doubled in size.

**5 ▲** Grease two 1-pound loaf pans. Punch down the dough and knead lightly. Divide in half, form into loaves and place in the pans. Cover and let sit in a warm place for about 30 minutes, until risen. Meanwhile, preheat the oven to 375°F.

**6** Bake for 35–40 minutes, until the loaves are well risen and sound hollow when tapped on the bottom. Cool on a wire rack. Brush with honey while warm.

**MAKES 2 LOAVES**

| |
|---|
| 2 cups bread flour |
| 2 cups whole-wheat flour |
| 1 teaspoon salt |
| 6 tablespoons brown sugar |
| 1 teaspoon rapid-rise yeast |
| 4 tablespoons (½ stick) butter or margarine |
| 1 tablespoon molasses |
| 4 tablespoons malt extract |
| 1 cup tepid milk |
| 4 ounces (½ cup) chopped dates |
| 3 ounces (½ cup) golden raisins |
| 3 ounces (½ cup) raisins |
| 2 ounces (½ cup) chopped nuts |
| 2 tablespoons clear honey, to glaze |

# Banana Orange Loaf

For the best banana flavor and a good, moist texture, make sure the bananas are very ripe for this cake.

**MAKES 1 LOAF**

¾ cup whole-wheat flour

½ cup all-purpose flour

1 teaspoon baking powder

1 teaspoon apple pie spice

3 tablespoons sliced hazelnuts, toasted

2 large ripe bananas

1 egg

2 tablespoons sunflower oil

2 tablespoons honey

finely grated rind and juice of 1 small orange

4 orange slices, halved

2 teaspoons confectioners' sugar

**1** Preheat the oven to 350°F.

**2 ▲** Brush a 4-cup loaf pan with sunflower oil and line the bottom with baking parchment.

**3 ▲** Sift the flours with the baking powder and spice into a large bowl, adding any bran that is caught in the sieve. Stir in the toasted hazelnuts.

**4 ▲** Peel and mash the bananas. Beat together with the egg, oil, honey and orange rind and juice. Stir evenly into the dry ingredients.

**5** Spoon into the prepared pan and smooth the top. Bake for 40–45 minutes, or until firm and golden brown. Turn out and cool on a wire rack. Sprinkle the orange slices with the confectioners' sugar and broil until golden. Use to decorate the cake.

~ COOK'S TIP ~

If you plan to keep the loaf for more than 2–3 days, omit the orange slices, brush with honey and sprinkle with sliced hazelnuts.

# Apple, Apricot and Walnut Loaf

Serve warm and store what is left in an airtight container.

**1** Preheat the oven to 350°F. Line and grease a 2-pound loaf pan.

**2 ▲** Sift the flour, baking powder and salt into a large mixing bowl, then pour the bran remaining in the sieve into the mixture. Add the margarine, sugar, eggs, orange rind and juice. Stir, then beat with a handheld electric mixer until smooth.

**3 ▲** Stir in the walnuts and apricots. Peel, quarter, and core the apple, chop it roughly and add it to the mixture. Stir, then spoon into the prepared pan and level the top.

**4** Bake for 1 hour, or until a cake tester inserted into the center of the loaf comes out clean. Cool in the pan for 5 minutes, then turn out onto a wire rack and peel off the lining paper.

**MAKES 1 LOAF**

| |
|---|
| 2 cups whole-wheat flour |
| 1 teaspoon baking powder |
| pinch of salt |
| 8 tablespoons (1 stick) sunflower margarine |
| 1 cup light brown sugar |
| 2 eggs, lightly beaten |
| grated rind and juice of 1 orange |
| 2 ounces (½ cup) chopped walnuts |
| 2 ounces (½ cup) dried apricots, chopped |
| 1 large cooking apple |

# Banana and Ginger Tea Bread

Serve this tea bread in slices with low-fat spread. The ginger adds an interesting flavor.

MAKES 1 LOAF

| |
| --- |
| 1½ cups self-rising flour |
| 1 teaspoon baking powder |
| 3 tablespoons soft margarine |
| ⅓ cup dark brown sugar |
| ⅓ cup drained preserved ginger, chopped |
| 4 tablespoons skim milk |
| 2 ripe bananas, mashed |

**1 ▲** Preheat the oven to 350°F. Grease and line a 1-pound loaf pan. Sift the flour and baking powder into a mixing bowl.

**2 ▲** Rub in the margarine until the mixture resembles bread crumbs.

**3 ▲** Stir in the sugar. Add the ginger, milk and bananas and mix.

**4 ▲** Spoon into the prepared pan and bake for 40–45 minutes, or until an inserted cake tester comes out clean. Run a metal spatula around the edges, then turn the tea bread out onto a wire rack and let it cool.

# Pear and Golden Raisin Tea Bread

This is an ideal tea bread to make when pears are plentiful—an excellent use for windfalls.

**1 ▲** Preheat the oven to 350°F. Grease and line a 1-pound loaf pan. Put the oats in a bowl with the sugar, pour the pear or apple juice and oil over them, mix well and let stand for 15 minutes.

**2 ▲** Quarter, core and coarsely grate the pears. Add the fruit to the oat mixture with the flour, raisins, baking powder, apple pie spice and egg, then mix thoroughly.

**3 ▲** Spoon the mixture into the prepared loaf pan and level the top. Bake for 50–60 minutes, or until a cake tester inserted into the center comes out clean.

**4 ▲** Transfer the tea bread to a wire rack and peel off the lining paper. Allow to cool completely.

### ~ COOK'S TIP ~
Health food stores sell concentrated pear and apple juice, ready for diluting as required.

**MAKES 1 LOAF**

| |
|---|
| ¼ cup rolled oats |
| ¼ cup light brown sugar |
| 2 tablespoons pear or apple juice |
| 2 tablespoons sunflower oil |
| 1 large or 2 small pears |
| 1 cup self-rising flour |
| 4 ounces (¾ cup) golden raisins |
| ½ teaspoon baking powder |
| 2 teaspoons apple pie spice |
| 1 egg |

# Cardamom and Saffron Tea Loaf

An aromatic sweet bread ideal for afternoon tea or lightly toasted for breakfast. Using rapid-rise, or easy-blend, yeast makes tea loaf-making so simple.

### MAKES 1 LOAF

| |
|---|
| generous pinch of saffron strands |
| 3 cups lukewarm milk |
| 2 tablespoons butter |
| 8 cups bread flour |
| 2 teaspoons rapid-rise yeast |
| 3 tablespoons sugar |
| 6 cardamom pods, split open and seeds extracted |
| ⅔ cup raisins |
| 2 tablespoons honey, plus extra for brushing |
| 1 egg, beaten |

**1 ▲** Crush the saffron into a cup containing a little of the warm milk and allow to infuse for 5 minutes.

**2** Rub the butter into the flour, then mix in the yeast, sugar and cardamom seeds (these may need rubbing to separate them). Stir in the raisins.

**3 ▲** Beat the remaining milk with the honey and egg, then mix this into the flour with the saffron milk and strands, stirring well until a firm dough is formed. You may not need all the milk; it depends on the flour.

**4 ▲** Turn out the dough and knead it on a lightly floured board for about 5 minutes, until smooth.

**5** Return the dough to the mixing bowl, cover with oiled plastic wrap and let sit in a warm place until doubled in size. This could take 1–3 hours. Grease a 2-pound loaf pan. Turn the dough out onto a floured board again, punch it down, knead for 3 minutes, then shape it into a fat roll and fit it into the greased loaf pan.

**6** Cover with a sheet of lightly oiled plastic wrap and let stand in a warm place until the dough begins to rise again. Preheat the oven to 400°F. Bake the loaf for 25 minutes, until golden brown and firm on top. Turn out of the pan and as it cools, brush the top with honey. Slice when cold and spread with butter. It is also good lightly toasted.

# Blueberry Streusel Bread

**MAKES 8 PIECES**

| |
|---|
| 4 tablespoons butter or margarine, at room temperature |
| ¾ cup sugar |
| 1 egg, at room temperature |
| ½ cup milk |
| 2 cups flour |
| 2 teaspoons baking powder |
| ½ teaspoon salt |
| 2 cups fresh blueberries |
| FOR THE TOPPING |
| ½ cup sugar |
| ⅓ cup flour |
| ½ teaspoon ground cinnamon |
| 4 tablespoons butter, cut in pieces |

**1** Preheat the oven to 375°F. Grease a 9-inch square baking dish.

**2** With an electric mixer, cream the butter or margarine with the sugar until light and fluffy. Add the egg, beat to combine, then mix in the milk until blended.

**3** ▼ Sift over the flour, baking powder, and salt and stir just enough to blend the ingredients.

**4** ▲ Add the blueberries and stir.

**5** Transfer to the baking dish.

**6** ▲ For the topping, place the sugar, flour, cinnamon, and butter in a mixing bowl. Cut in with a pastry blender until the mixture resembles coarse crumbs.

**7** ▲ Sprinkle the topping over the batter in the pan.

**8** Bake until a cake tester inserted in the center comes out clean, about 45 minutes. Serve warm or cold.

# Glazed Banana Spice Loaf

MAKES 1 LOAF

1 large ripe banana

½ cup (1 stick) butter, at room
   temperature

¾ cup granulated sugar

2 eggs, at room temperature

1½ cups flour

1 teaspoon salt

1 teaspoon baking soda

½ teaspoon grated nutmeg

¼ teaspoon ground allspice

¼ teaspoon ground cloves

¾ cup sour cream

1 teaspoon vanilla extract

FOR THE GLAZE

1 cup confectioners' sugar

1–2 tablespoons fresh lemon juice

**1** Preheat the oven to 350°F. Line an
8½- × 4½-inch loaf pan with wax
paper and grease.

**2** ▼ With a fork, mash the banana in
a bowl. Set aside.

**3** With an electric mixer, cream the
butter and sugar until light and fluffy.
Add the eggs, 1 at a time, beating to
blend well after each addition.

**4** Sift together the flour, salt, baking
soda, nutmeg, allspice, and cloves.
Add to the butter mixture and stir to
combine well.

**5** ▲ Add the sour cream, banana,
and vanilla and mix just enough to
blend. Pour into the prepared pan.

**6** ▲ Bake until the top springs back
when touched lightly, 45–50 minutes.
Let cool in the pan for 10 minutes
before unmolding.

**7** ▲ For the glaze, combine the
confectioners' sugar and lemon juice,
then stir until smooth.

**8** To glaze, place the cooled loaf on a
rack set over a baking sheet. Pour the
glaze over the top of the bread and
allow to set.

# Chocolate Chip Walnut Loaf

**MAKES 1 LOAF**

½ cup granulated sugar

¾ cup cake flour

1 teaspoon baking powder

4 tablespoons potato flour or cornstarch

9 tablespoons butter, at room temperature

2 eggs, at room temperature

1 teaspoon vanilla extract

2 tablespoons currants or raisins

¼ cup walnuts, finely chopped

grated rind of ½ lemon

¼ cup semisweet chocolate chips

confectioners' sugar, for dusting

**1** Preheat the oven to 350°F. Line an 8½- × 4½-inch loaf pan with wax paper and grease.

**2** ▲ Sprinkle 1½ tablespoons of the granulated sugar into the pan and tilt to distribute the sugar in an even layer over the bottom and sides. Shake out any excess.

> ~ **COOK'S TIP** ~
>
> For best results, the eggs should be at room temperature. If they are too cold when folded into the creamed butter mixture, it may separate. If this happens, add a spoonful of the flour to help stabilize the mixture.

**3** ▼ Sift together the cake flour, baking powder, and potato flour or cornstarch, 3 times. Set aside.

**4** With an electric mixer, cream the butter until soft. Add the remaining sugar and continue beating until light and fluffy. Add the eggs, 1 at a time, beating to incorporate thoroughly after each addition.

**5** Gently fold the dry ingredients into the butter mixture, in 3 batches; do not overmix.

**6** ▲ Fold in the vanilla, currants or raisins, walnuts, lemon rind, and chocolate chips until just blended.

**7** Pour the batter into the prepared pan and bake until a cake tester inserted in the center comes out clean, 45–50 minutes. Let cool in the pan for 5 minutes before transferring to a rack to cool completely. Dust over an even layer of confectioners' sugar before serving.

# Cranberry Orange Bread

**MAKES 1 LOAF**

| |
|---|
| 2 cups flour |
| ½ cup sugar |
| 1 tablespoon baking powder |
| ½ teaspoon salt |
| grated rind of 1 large orange |
| ⅔ cup fresh orange juice |
| 2 eggs, lightly beaten |
| 6 tablespoons butter or margarine, melted |
| 1¼ cups fresh cranberries |
| ½ cup walnuts, chopped |

**1** Preheat the oven to 350°F. Line the bottom and sides of a 9- × 5-inch loaf pan with wax paper and grease.

**2** Sift the flour, sugar, baking powder, and salt into a mixing bowl.

**3 ▼** Stir in the orange rind.

**4 ▲** Make a well in the center and add the orange juice, eggs, and melted butter or margarine. Stir from the center until the ingredients are blended; do not overmix.

**5 ▲** Add the cranberries and walnuts and stir until blended.

**6** Transfer the batter to the prepared pan and bake until a cake tester inserted in the center comes out clean, 45–50 minutes.

**7 ▲** Let cool in the pan for 10 minutes before transferring to a rack to cool completely. Serve thinly sliced, toasted or plain, with butter or cream cheese, and jam.

# Dried Fruit Loaf

**MAKES 1 LOAF**

2½ cups mixed dried fruit, such as currants, raisins, chopped dried apricots, and dried cherries

1¼ cups cold strong tea

1 cup dark brown sugar, firmly packed

grated rind and juice of 1 small orange

grated rind and juice of 1 lemon

1 egg, lightly beaten

1¾ cups flour

1 tablespoon baking powder

⅛ teaspoon salt

1 ▲ In a bowl, toss together all the dried fruit, pour over the tea, and leave to soak overnight.

2 Preheat the oven to 350°F. Line the bottom and sides of a 9- × 5-inch loaf pan with wax paper and grease.

3 ▲ Strain the fruit, reserving the liquid. In a bowl, combine the sugar, orange and lemon rind, and fruit.

4 ▼ Pour the orange and lemon juice into a measuring cup; if the quantity is less than 1 cup, complete with the soaking liquid.

5 Stir the citrus juices and egg into the dried fruit mixture.

6 In another bowl, sift together the flour, baking powder, and salt. Stir into the fruit mixture until blended.

7 Transfer to the prepared pan and bake until a cake tester inserted in the center comes out clean, about 1¼ hours. Let stand 10 minutes before unmolding.

# Mango Bread

**MAKES 2 LOAVES**

2 cups flour

2 teaspoons baking soda

2 teaspoons ground cinnamon

½ teaspoon salt

½ cup margarine, at room temperature

3 eggs, at room temperature

1½ cups sugar

½ cup vegetable oil

2 cups chopped ripe mangoes (about 2–3 mangoes)

¾ cup shredded coconut

½ cup raisins

**1** Preheat the oven to 350°F. Line the bottom and sides of 2 9- × 5-inch loaf pans with wax paper and grease.

**2** Sift together the flour, baking soda, cinnamon, and salt. Set aside.

**3** With an electric mixer, cream the margarine until soft.

**4 ▼** Beat in the eggs and sugar until light and fluffy. Beat in the oil.

**5** Fold the dry ingredients into the creamed ingredients in 3 batches.

**6** Fold in the mangoes, ½ cup of the coconut, and the raisins.

**7 ▲** Spoon the batter into the pans.

**8** Sprinkle over the remaining coconut. Bake until a cake tester inserted in the center comes out clean, 50–60 minutes. Let stand for 10 minutes before transferring to a rack to cool completely.

# Zucchini Bread

**MAKES 1 LOAF**

4 tablespoons butter

3 eggs

1 cup corn oil

1½ cups sugar

2 cups grated unpeeled zucchini

2 cups flour

2 teaspoons baking soda

1 teaspoon baking powder

1 teaspoon salt

1 teaspoon ground cinnamon

1 teaspoon grated nutmeg

¼ teaspoon ground cloves

1 cup walnuts, chopped

**1** Preheat the oven to 350°F. Line the bottom and sides of a 9- × 5-inch loaf pan with wax paper and grease.

**2 ▲** In a saucepan, melt the butter over low heat. Set aside.

**3** With an electric mixer, beat the eggs and oil together until thick. Beat in the sugar. Stir in the melted butter and zucchini. Set aside.

**4 ▲** In another bowl, sift all the dry ingredients together 3 times. Carefully fold into the zucchini mixture. Fold in the walnuts.

**5** Pour into the pan and bake until a cake tester inserted in the center comes out clean, 60–70 minutes. Let stand 10 minutes before unmolding.

*Mango Bread (top), Zucchini Bread*

# PIES & TARTS

HERE IS EVERY SORT OF FILLING –
FROM ORCHARD FRUITS TO AUTUMN
NUTS, TANGY CITRUS TO LUSCIOUS
CHOCOLATE – FOR THE MOST
MEMORABLE PIES AND TARTS. SOME
ARE PLAIN AND SOME ARE FANCY,
BUT ALL ARE DELICIOUS.

# Apple Pie

**SERVES 8**

6 cups peeled and sliced tart apples, such as Granny Smith (about 2 pounds)

1 tablespoon fresh lemon juice

1 teaspoon vanilla extract

½ cup sugar

½ teaspoon ground cinnamon

1½ tablespoons butter or margarine

1 egg yolk

2 teaspoons whipping cream

FOR THE CRUST

2 cups flour

1 teaspoon salt

¾ cup shortening

4–5 tablespoons ice water

1 tablespoon quick-cooking tapioca

**1** Preheat the oven to 450°F.

**2** For the crust, sift the flour and salt into a mixing bowl. Using a pastry blender, cut in the shortening until the mixture resembles coarse crumbs.

**3 ▲** Sprinkle in the water, 1 tablespoon at a time, tossing lightly with your fingertips or with a fork until the dough will form a ball.

**4 ▲** Divide the dough in half and shape each half into a ball. On a lightly floured surface, roll out one of the balls to a circle about 12 inches in diameter.

**5 ▲** Use it to line a 9-inch pie pan, easing the dough in and being careful not to stretch it. Trim off the excess dough and use the trimmings for decorating. Sprinkle the tapioca over the bottom of the pie shell.

**6 ▲** Roll out the remaining dough to ⅛-inch thickness. With a sharp knife, cut out 8 large leaf-shapes. Cut the trimmings into small leaf shapes. Score the leaves with the back of the knife to mark veins.

**7 ▲** In a bowl, toss the apples with the lemon juice, vanilla, sugar, and cinnamon. Fill the pie shell with the apple mixture and dot with the butter or margarine.

**8 ▲** Arrange the large pastry leaves in a decorative pattern on top. Decorate the edge with small leaves.

**9 ▲** Mix together the egg yolk and cream and brush over the leaves to glaze them.

**10** Bake 10 minutes, then reduce the heat to 350°F and continue baking until the pastry is golden brown, 35–45 minutes. Let the pie cool in the pan, set on a wire rack.

# Apple-Cranberry Lattice Pie

SERVES 8

grated rind of 1 orange

3 tablespoons fresh orange juice

2 large, tart cooking apples

1 cup cranberries

½ cup raisins

¼ cup walnuts, chopped

1 cup plus tablespoon granulated sugar

½ cup dark brown sugar, firmly packed

1 tablespoon quick-cooking tapioca

FOR THE CRUST

2 cups flour

½ teaspoon salt

6 tablespoons cold butter, cut in pieces

4 tablespoons cold shortening, cut in
  pieces

¼–½ cup ice water

**1 ▼** For the crust, sift the flour and salt into a bowl. Add the butter and shortening and rub with your fingertips until the mixture resembles coarse crumbs, or use a pastry blender. With a fork, stir in just enough water to bind the dough. Gather into 2 equal balls, wrap in wax paper, and refrigerate for at least 20 minutes.

**2 ▲** Put the orange rind and juice into a mixing bowl. Peel and core the apples and grate them into the bowl. Stir in the cranberries, raisins, walnuts, 1 cup of the granulated sugar, brown sugar, and tapioca.

**3** Place a baking sheet in the oven and preheat to 400°F.

**4** On a lightly floured surface, roll out 1 ball of dough about ⅛ inch thick. Transfer to a 9-inch pie pan and trim the edge. Spoon the cranberry and apple mixture into the shell.

**5 ▲** Roll out the remaining dough to a circle about 11 inches in diameter. With a serrated pastry wheel, cut the dough into 10 strips, ¾ inch wide. Place 5 strips horizontally across the top of the tart at 1-inch intervals. Weave in 5 vertical strips. Trim the edges. Sprinkle the top with the remaining 1 tablespoon sugar.

**6** Bake for 20 minutes. Reduce the heat to 350°F and bake until the crust is golden and the filling is bubbling, about 15 minutes more.

# Rhubarb Cherry Pie

**SERVES 8**

1 pound rhubarb, cut into 1-inch pieces (about 3 cups)

1 1-pound can (2 cups) pitted tart red or black cherries, drained

1¼ cups sugar

¼ cup quick-cooking tapioca

**FOR THE CRUST**

2 cups flour

1 teaspoon salt

6 tablespoons cold butter, cut in pieces

4 tablespoons cold shortening, cut in pieces

¼–½ cup ice water

milk, for glazing

**1 ▲** For the crust, sift the flour and salt into a bowl. Add the butter and shortening to the dry ingredients and cut in with a pastry blender until the mixture resembles coarse crumbs.

**2** With a fork, stir in just enough water to bind the dough. Gather the dough into 2 balls, one slightly larger than the other. Wrap the dough in wax paper and refrigerate for at least 20 minutes.

**3** Place a baking sheet in the center of the oven and preheat to 400°F.

**4** On a lightly floured surface, roll out the larger dough ball to a thickness of about ⅛ inch.

**5 ▼** Roll the dough around the rolling pin and transfer to a 9-inch pie pan. Trim the edge to leave a ½-inch overhang all around.

**6** Refrigerate the pie shell while making the filling.

**7** In a mixing bowl, combine the rhubarb, cherries, sugar, and tapioca and spoon into the pie shell.

**8 ▲** Roll out the remaining dough and cut out leaf shapes.

**9** Transfer the dough to the pie and trim to leave a ¾-inch overhang. Fold the top edge under the bottom and flute. Roll small balls from the scraps. Mark veins in the dough leaves and place on top with the dough balls.

**10** Glaze the top and bake until golden, 40–50 minutes.

# Rhubarb Pie

SERVES 6

1½ cups flour

½ teaspoon salt

2 teaspoons sugar

6 tablespoons cold butter or shortening

¼ cup or more ice water

2 tablespoons whipping cream

FOR THE FILLING

3½ cups fresh rhubarb, cut in ½- to
    1-inch slices (about 2 pounds)

2 tablespoons cornstarch

1 egg

1½ cups sugar

1 tablespoon grated orange rind

**1** ▲ For the pastry, sift the flour, salt, and sugar into a bowl. Using a pastry blender or 2 knives, cut the butter or shortening into the dry ingredients as quickly as possible until the mixture resembles coarse meal.

**2** Sprinkle with the ice water and mix until the dough holds together. If the dough is too crumbly, add a little more water, 1 tablespoon at a time.

~ COOK'S TIP ~

Be sure to cut off and discard the green rhubarb leaves from the pink stalks, as they are toxic and not edible.

**3** ▲ Gather the dough into a ball, flatten into a disk, wrap in wax paper, and refrigerate at least 20 minutes.

**4** ▲ Roll out the dough between 2 sheets of wax paper to a thickness of about ⅛ inch. Use to line a 9-inch pie pan. Trim all around, leaving a ½-inch overhang. Fold the overhang under the edge and flute. Refrigerate the pie shell and dough trimmings 30 minutes.

**5** ▲ For the filling, put the rhubarb in a bowl and sprinkle with the cornstarch. Toss to coat.

**6** Preheat the oven to 425°F.

**7** In a small bowl beat the egg with the sugar. Mix in the orange rind.

**8** ▲ Stir the sugar mixture into the rhubarb and mix well. Spoon the fruit into the pie shell.

**9** ▲ Roll out the dough trimmings. Stamp out decorative shapes with a cookie cutter or cut shapes with a small knife, using a cardboard template as a guide, if wished.

**10** Arrange the shapes on top of the pie. Brush the trimmings and the edge of the pie shell with cream.

**11** Bake 30 minutes. Reduce the heat to 325°F and continue baking until the pastry is golden brown and the rhubarb is tender, about 15–20 minutes more.

# Plum Pie

**SERVES 8**

2 pounds red or purple plums

grated rind of 1 lemon

1 tablespoon fresh lemon juice

½–¾ cup sugar

3 tablespoons quick-cooking tapioca

⅛ teaspoon salt

½ teaspoon ground cinnamon

¼ teaspoon grated nutmeg

**FOR THE CRUST**

2 cups flour

1 teaspoon salt

6 tablespoons cold butter, cut in pieces

4 tablespoons cold shortening, cut in pieces

¼–½ cup ice water

milk, for glazing

**1** ▼  For the crust, sift the flour and salt into a bowl. Add the butter and shortening and cut in with a pastry blender until the mixture resembles coarse crumbs.

**2**  Stir in just enough water to bind the dough. Gather into 2 balls, one slightly larger than the other. Wrap and refrigerate for 20 minutes.

**3**  Place a baking sheet in the center of the oven and preheat to 425°F.

**4**  On a lightly floured surface, roll out the larger dough ball about ⅛ inch thick. Transfer to a 9-inch pie pan and trim the edge.

**5** ▲  Halve the plums, discard the pits, and cut in large pieces. Mix all the filling ingredients together (if the plums are very tart, use ¾ cup sugar). Transfer to the pie shell.

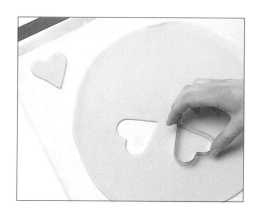

**6** ▲  Roll out the remaining dough and place on a baking tray lined with wax paper. Stamp out 4 heart shapes and reserve them. Transfer the dough to the pie using the wax paper.

**7**  Trim to leave a ¾-inch overhang. Fold the top edge under the bottom and pinch to seal. Arrange the dough hearts on top. Brush with the milk. Bake for 15 minutes. Reduce the heat to 350°F and bake 30–35 minutes more. If the crust browns too quickly, protect with a sheet of foil.

# Lattice Berry Pie

**SERVES 8**

1 pound blueberries

½ cup sugar

3 tablespoons cornstarch

2 tablespoons fresh lemon juice

2 tablespoons butter, diced

FOR THE CRUST

2 cups flour

¾ teaspoon salt

½ cup (1 stick) cold butter, cut in pieces

3 tablespoons cold shortening, cut in pieces

5–6 tablespoons ice water

1 egg beaten with 1 tablespoon water, for glazing

**1** For the crust, sift the flour and salt into a bowl. Add the butter and shortening and cut in with a pastry blender until the mixture resembles coarse crumbs. With a fork, stir in just enough water to bind the dough. Gather into 2 equal balls, wrap in wax paper, and refrigerate for 20 minutes.

**2** On a lightly floured surface, roll out one dough ball about ⅛ inch thick. Transfer to a 9-inch pie pan and trim to leave a ½-inch overhang. Brush the bottom with egg glaze.

**3** ▲ Mix all the filling ingredients together, except the butter (reserve a few blueberries for decoration). Spoon into the shell and dot with the butter. Brush the egg glaze on the edge of the lower crust.

**4** Place a baking sheet in the center of the oven and preheat to 425°F.

**5** ▼ Roll out the remaining dough on a baking tray lined with wax paper. With a serrated pastry wheel, cut out 24 thin strips of dough. Roll out the scraps and cut out leaf shapes. Mark veins in the leaves with the point of a knife.

**6** ▲ Weave the strips in a close lattice, then transfer to the pie using the wax paper. Press the edges to seal and trim. Arrange the dough leaves around the rim. Brush with egg glaze.

**7** Bake for 10 minutes. Reduce the heat to 350°F and bake until the pastry is golden, 40–45 minutes more. Decorate with reserved blueberries.

# Cherry Lattice Pie

**SERVES 8**

4 cups sour cherries, pitted (2 pounds fresh or 2 16-ounce cans, water-pack, drained)

⅓ cup sugar

¼ cup flour

1½ tablespoons fresh lemon juice

¼ teaspoon almond extract

2 tablespoons butter or margarine

**FOR THE CRUST**

2 cups flour

1 teaspoon salt

¾ cup shortening

4–5 tablespoons ice water

**1** For the crust, sift the flour and salt into a mixing bowl. Using a pastry blender, cut in the shortening until the mixture resembles coarse crumbs.

**2 ▲** Sprinkle in the water, 1 tablespoon at a time, tossing lightly with your fingertips or a fork until the dough will form a ball.

**3** Divide the dough in half and shape each half into a ball. On a lightly floured surface, roll out one of the balls to a circle about 12 inches in diameter.

**4 ▲** Use it to line a 9-inch pie pan, easing the dough in and being careful not to stretch it. With scissors, trim off excess dough, leaving a ½-inch overhang around the pie rim.

**5 ▲** Roll out the remaining dough to ⅛-inch thickness. With a sharp knife, cut out 11 strips ½ inch wide.

**6 ▲** In a mixing bowl, combine the cherries, sugar, flour, lemon juice, and almond extract. Spoon the mixture into the pie crust and dot with the butter or margarine.

**7 ▲** To make the lattice, place 5 of the pastry-dough strips evenly across the filling. Fold every other strip back. Lay the first strip across in the opposite direction. Continue in this pattern, folding back every other strip each time you add a cross strip.

**8 ▲** Trim the ends of the lattice strips even with the crust overhang. Press together so that the edge rests on the pie-pan rim. With your thumbs, flute the edge. Refrigerate 15 minutes.

**9** Preheat the oven to 425°F.

**10** Bake the pie 30 minutes, covering the edge of the crust with foil, if necessary, to prevent overbrowning. Let cool, in the pan, on a wire rack.

# Peach Leaf Pie

**SERVES 8**

2½ pounds ripe peaches

juice of 1 lemon

½ cup sugar

3 tablespoons cornstarch

¼ teaspoon grated nutmeg

½ teaspoon ground cinnamon

2 tablespoons butter, diced

**FOR THE CRUST**

2 cups flour

¾ teaspoon salt

½ cup (1 stick) cold butter, cut in
    pieces

3 tablespoons cold shortening, cut in
    pieces

5–6 tablespoons ice water

1 egg beaten with 1 tablespoon water,
    for glazing

**1** For the crust, sift the flour and salt into a bowl. Add the butter and shortening and cut in with a pastry blender until the mixture resembles coarse crumbs.

**2 ▲** With a fork, stir in just enough water to bind the dough. Gather into 2 balls, one slightly larger than the other. Wrap in wax paper and refrigerate for at least 20 minutes.

**3** Place a baking sheet in the oven and preheat to 425°F.

**4 ▲** Drop a few peaches at a time into boiling water for 20 seconds, then transfer to a bowl of cold water. When cool, peel off the skins.

**5** Slice the peaches and combine with the lemon juice, sugar, cornstarch, and spices. Set aside.

**6 ▲** On a lightly floured surface, roll out the larger dough ball about ⅛ inch thick. Transfer to a 9-inch pie pan and trim the edge. Refrigerate.

**7 ▲** Roll out the remaining dough ¼ inch thick. Cut out leaf shapes 3 inches long, using a template if needed. Mark veins with a knife. With the scraps, roll a few balls.

**8 ▲** Brush the bottom of the pie shell with egg glaze. Add the peaches, piling them higher in the center. Dot with the butter.

**9 ▲** To assemble, start from the outside edge and cover the peaches with a ring of leaves. Place a second ring of leaves above, staggering the positions. Continue with rows of leaves until covered. Place the balls in the center. Brush with glaze.

**10** Bake for 10 minutes. Lower the heat to 350°F and continue to bake for 35–40 minutes more.

### ~ COOK'S TIP ~

Baking the pie on a preheated baking sheet helps to make the bottom crust crisp. The moisture from the filling keeps the bottom crust more humid than the top, but this baking method helps to compensate for the top crust being better exposed to the heat source.

# Maryland Peach and Blueberry Pie

**SERVES 8**

2 cups flour

½ teaspoon salt

2 teaspoons sugar

10 tablespoons (1¼ sticks) cold butter or margarine

1 egg yolk

¼ cup or more ice water

2 tablespoons milk, for glazing

FOR THE FILLING

3 cups peeled, pitted, and sliced fresh peaches

2 cups fresh blueberries

¾ cup sugar

2 tablespoons fresh lemon juice

⅓ cup flour

⅛ teaspoon grated nutmeg

2 tablespoons butter or margarine, cut in pea-size pieces

**1** For the pastry, sift the flour, salt, and sugar into a bowl. Using a pastry blender or 2 knives, cut the butter or margarine into the dry ingredients as quickly as possible until the mixture resembles coarse meal.

**2** Mix the egg yolk with the ice water and sprinkle over the flour mixture. Combine with a fork until the dough holds together. If the dough is too crumbly, add a little more water, 1 tablespoon at a time. Gather the dough into a ball and flatten into a disk. Wrap in wax paper and refrigerate at least 20 minutes.

**3** Roll out two-thirds of the dough between 2 sheets of wax paper to a thickness of about ⅛ inch. Use to line a 9-inch pie pan. Trim all around, leaving a ½-inch overhang. Fold the overhang under to form the edge. Using a fork, press the edge to the rim of the pie pan.

**4 ▲** Gather the trimmings and remaining dough into a ball, and roll out to a thickness of about ¼ inch. Using a pastry wheel or sharp knife, cut strips ½ inch wide. Refrigerate both the pie shell and the strips of dough for 20 minutes.

**5** Preheat the oven to 400°F.

**6 ▲** Line the pie shell with wax paper and fill with dried beans. Bake until the pie shell is just set, 7–10 minutes. Remove from the oven and carefully lift out the paper with the beans. Prick the bottom of the pie shell all over with a fork, then return to the oven and bake 5 minutes more. Let the pie shell cool slightly before filling. Leave the oven on.

**7 ▲** In a mixing bowl, combine the peach slices with the blueberries, sugar, lemon juice, flour, and nutmeg. Spoon the fruit mixture evenly into the pie shell. Dot with the pieces of butter or margarine.

**8 ▲** Weave a lattice top with the chilled pastry strips, pressing the ends to the baked pie-shell edge. Brush the strips with the milk.

**9** Bake the pie 15 minutes. Reduce the heat to 350°F, and continue baking until the filling is tender and bubbling and the pastry lattice is golden, about 30 minutes more. If the pastry gets too brown, cover loosely with a piece of foil. Serve the pie warm or at room temperature.

# Blueberry Pie

**SERVES 6–8**

pastry for a 9-inch double-crust pie

4 cups blueberries

¾ cup plus 1 tablespoon sugar

3 tablespoons flour

1 teaspoon grated orange rind

¼ teaspoon grated nutmeg

2 tablespoons orange juice

1 teaspoon lemon juice

**1** Preheat the oven to 375°F.

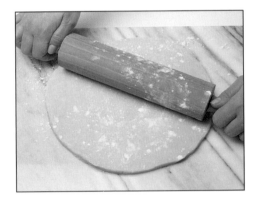

**2 ▲** On a lightly floured surface, roll out half of the pastry and use to line a 9-inch pie plate.

**3 ▲** Combine the blueberries, ¾ cup of the sugar, the flour, orange rind, and nutmeg in a bowl. Toss the mixture gently to coat the fruit evenly with the dry ingredients.

**4 ▼** Pour the blueberry mixture into the pie shell and spread it evenly. Sprinkle over the citrus juices.

**5** Roll out the remaining pastry and cover the pie. Cut out small decorative shapes or cut 2–3 slits for steam vents. Finish the edge as desired.

**6 ▲** Brush the top crust lightly with water and sprinkle evenly with the remaining sugar.

**7** Bake until the pastry is golden brown, about 45 minutes. Serve warm or at room temperature.

# Walnut and Pear Lattice Pie

**SERVES 6–8**

nut pie pastry for a 9-inch double-crust pie

6 cups peeled, cored, and thinly sliced pears

⅓ cup granulated sugar

¼ cup flour

½ teaspoon grated lemon rind

¼ cup raisins

¼ cup chopped walnuts

½ teaspoon ground cinnamon

½ cup confectioners' sugar

1 tablespoon lemon juice

about 2 teaspoons cold water

**1** Preheat the oven to 375°F.

**2** Roll out half of the pastry dough and use to line a 9-inch pie plate that is about 2 inches deep.

**3 ▲** Combine the pears, granulated sugar, flour, and lemon rind in a bowl. Toss gently to combine the fruit with the dry ingredients. Mix in the raisins, nuts, and cinnamon.

~ **COOK'S TIP** ~

For a simple cutout lattice top, roll out the dough for the top into a circle. Using a small cookie cutter, cut out shapes in a pattern, spacing them evenly and not too close together.

**4 ▲** Put the pear filling into the pie shell and spread it evenly.

**5** Roll out the remaining pastry dough and use to make a lattice top.

**6** Bake until the pastry is golden brown, about 55 minutes.

**7** Combine the confectioners' sugar, lemon juice, and water in a bowl and stir until smoothly blended.

**8 ▼** Remove the pie from the oven. With a spoon, drizzle the confectioners' sugar glaze evenly over the top of the pie, on pastry and filling. Let the pie cool on a wire rack before serving.

# Mince Pies

**MAKES 36**

1 cup blanched almonds, finely chopped

1 cup dried apricots, finely chopped

1 cup raisins

1 cup currants

1 cup candied cherries, chopped

1 cup candied citrus peel, chopped

1 cup finely chopped beef suet

grated rind and juice of 2 lemons

grated rind and juice of 1 orange

1 cup dark brown sugar, firmly packed

4 tart cooking apples, peeled, cored and chopped

2 teaspoons ground cinnamon

1 teaspoon grated nutmeg

½ teaspoon ground cloves

1 cup brandy

8 ounces cream cheese

2 tablespoons granulated sugar

confectioners' sugar, for dusting

FOR THE CRUST

3 cups flour

1¼ cups confectioners' sugar

1½ cups (3 sticks) cold butter, cut in pieces

grated rind and juice of 1 orange

milk, for glazing

**1** Mix the nuts, dried and candied fruit, suet, citrus rind and juice, brown sugar, apples, and spices in a bowl.

**2 ▲** Stir in the brandy. Cover and leave in a cool place for 2 days.

**3** For the crust, sift the flour and confectioners' sugar into a bowl. Cut in the butter until the mixture resembles coarse crumbs.

**4 ▲** Add the orange rind. Stir in just enough orange juice to bind. Gather into a ball, wrap in wax paper, and refrigerate for at least 20 minutes.

**5** Preheat the oven to 425°F. Grease 2–3 muffin pans. Beat together the cream cheese and granulated sugar.

**6 ▲** Roll out the dough ¼ inch thick. With a fluted pastry cutter, stamp out 36 3-inch rounds.

---

### ~ COOK'S TIP ~

The mincemeat mixture may be packed into sterilized jars and sealed. It will keep refrigerated for several months. Add a few tablespoonfuls to give apple pies a lift, or make small mincemeat-filled parcels using phyllo pastry.

---

**7 ▲** Transfer the rounds to the muffin pans. Fill halfway with mincemeat. Top with a teaspoonful of the cream cheese mixture.

**8 ▲** Roll out the pastry trimmings and stamp out 36 2-inch rounds with a fluted cutter. Brush the edges of the pies with milk, then set the rounds on top. Cut a small steam vent in the top of each pie.

**9 ▲** Brush lightly with milk. Bake until golden, 15–20 minutes. Let cool for 10 minutes before unmolding. Dust with confectioners' sugar.

# Pear-Apple Crumb Pie

**SERVES 8**

3 firm pears

4 tart cooking apples

¾ cup sugar

2 tablespoons cornstarch

⅛ teaspoon salt

grated rind of 1 lemon

2 tablespoons fresh lemon juice

½ cup raisins

¾ cup flour

1 teaspoon ground cinnamon

6 tablespoons cold butter, cut in pieces

**FOR THE CRUST**

1 cup flour

½ teaspoon salt

⅓ cup cold shortening, cut in pieces

2 tablespoons ice water

**1** For the crust, combine the flour and salt in a bowl. Add the shortening and cut in with a pastry blender until the mixture resembles coarse crumbs. With a fork, stir in just enough water to bind the dough. Gather into a ball and transfer to a lightly floured surface. Roll out about ⅛ inch thick.

**2 ▲** Transfer to a shallow 9-inch pie pan and trim to leave a ½-inch overhang. Fold the overhang under for a double thickness. Flute the edge with your fingers. Refrigerate.

**3** Place a baking sheet in the oven and preheat to 450°F.

**4 ▲** Peel and core the pears. Slice them into a bowl. Peel, core, and slice the apples. Add to the pears. Stir in ⅓ cup of the sugar, the cornstarch, salt, and lemon rind. Add the lemon juice and raisins and stir to blend.

**5** For the crumb topping, combine the remaining sugar, flour, cinnamon, and butter in a bowl. Blend with your fingertips until the mixture resembles coarse crumbs. Set aside.

**6 ▲** Spoon the fruit filling into the pie shell. Sprinkle the crumbs lightly and evenly over the top.

**7** Bake for 10 minutes, then reduce the heat to 350°F. Cover the top of the pie loosely with a sheet of foil and continue baking until browned, 35–40 minutes more.

# Open Apple Pie

**SERVES 8**

3 pounds sweet-tart firm eating or
   cooking apples

¼ cup sugar

2 teaspoons ground cinnamon

grated rind and juice of 1 lemon

2 tablespoons butter, diced

2–3 tablespoons honey

**FOR THE CRUST**

2 cups flour

½ teaspoon salt

½ cup (1 stick) cold butter, cut in
   pieces

3 tablespoons cold shortening, cut in
   pieces

5–6 tablespoons ice water

**1** For the crust, sift the flour and salt
into a bowl. Add the butter and
shortening and cut in with a pastry
blender until the mixture resembles
coarse crumbs.

**2 ▲** With a fork, stir in just enough
water to bind the dough. Gather into
a ball, wrap in wax paper, and
refrigerate for at least 20 minutes.

**3** Place a baking sheet in the center
of the oven and preheat to 400°F.

**4 ▼** Peel, core, and slice the apples.
Combine the sugar and cinnamon in a
bowl. Add the apples, lemon rind and
juice, and stir.

**5** On a lightly floured surface, roll out
the dough to a circle about 12 inches
in diameter. Transfer to a 9-inch
diameter deep pie dish; leave the
dough hanging over the edge. Fill
with the apple slices.

**6 ▲** Fold in the edges and crimp
loosely for a decorative border. Dot
the apples with diced butter.

**7** Bake on the hot sheet until the
pastry is golden and the apples are
tender, about 45 minutes.

**8** Melt the honey in a saucepan and
brush over the apples to glaze. Serve
warm or at room temperature.

# Brethren's Cider Pie

1½ cups flour

¼ teaspoon salt

2 teaspoons sugar

½ cup (1 stick) cold butter or
   margarine

¼ cup or more ice water

FOR THE FILLING

2½ cups apple cider

1 tablespoon butter

1 cup maple syrup

¼ cup water

¼ teaspoon salt

2 eggs, at room temperature, separated

1 teaspoon grated nutmeg

**1 ▲** For the pastry, sift the flour, salt, and sugar into a bowl. Using a pastry blender or 2 knives, cut the butter or margarine into the dry ingredients as quickly as possible until the mixture resembles coarse meal.

**2** Sprinkle the ice water over the flour mixture. Combine with a fork until the dough holds together. If the dough is too crumbly, add a little more water, 1 tablespoon at a time. Gather the dough into a ball and flatten into a disk. Wrap in wax paper and refrigerate at least 20 minutes.

**3 ▲** Meanwhile, place the cider in a medium-size heavy saucepan. Boil until only ¾ cup remains. Let cool.

**4 ▲** Roll out the dough between 2 sheets of wax paper to a thickness of about ⅛ inch. Use to line a 9-inch pie pan.

**5 ▲** Trim all around, leaving a ½-inch overhang. Fold the overhang under to form the edge. Using a fork, press the edge to the rim of the pan and press up from under with your fingers at intervals for a ruffle effect. Refrigerate 20 minutes.

**6** Preheat the oven to 350°F.

**7 ▲** For the filling, add the butter, maple syrup, water, and salt to the cider and simmer gently 5–6 minutes. Remove the pan from the heat and let the mixture cool slightly, then whisk in the beaten egg yolks.

**8 ▲** In a large bowl, beat the egg whites until they form stiff peaks. Add the cider mixture and fold gently together until evenly blended.

**9 ▲** Pour into the prepared pie shell. Dust with the grated nutmeg.

**10** Bake until the pastry is golden brown and the filling is well set, 30–35 minutes. Serve warm.

# Caramelized Upside-Down Pear Pie

**SERVES 8**

| |
| --- |
| 5–6 firm, ripe pears |
| ¾ cup sugar |
| ½ cup (1 stick) unsalted butter |
| whipped cream, for serving |
| **FOR THE CRUST** |
| ¾ cup all-purpose flour |
| ¼ cup cake flour |
| ¼ teaspoon salt |
| 9 tablespoons cold butter, cut in pieces |
| 3 tablespoons cold shortening, cut in pieces |
| ¼ cup ice water |

**1 ▲** For the crust, combine the flours and salt in a bowl. Add the butter and shortening and cut in with a pastry blender until the mixture resembles coarse crumbs. With a fork, stir in just enough water to bind the dough. Gather into a ball, wrap in wax paper, and refrigerate for at least 20 minutes.

**2** Preheat the oven to 400°F.

~ **VARIATION** ~

For Caramelized Upside-Down Apple Pie, replace the pears with 8–9 firm, tart apples. There may seem to be too many apples, but they shrink slightly as they cook.

**3 ▲** Quarter, peel and core the pears. Place in a bowl and toss with a few tablespoons of the sugar.

**4 ▲** In a 10½-inch ovenproof skillet, melt the butter over moderately high heat. Add the remaining sugar. When it starts to color, arrange the pears evenly around the edge and in the center.

**5 ▲** Continue cooking, uncovered, until caramelized, about 20 minutes.

**6 ▲** Let the fruit cool. Roll out a circle of dough slightly larger than the diameter of the skillet. Place the dough on top of the pears, tucking in around the edges.

**7** Bake for 15 minutes, then reduce the heat to 350°F. Bake until golden, about 15 minutes more.

**8 ▲** Let the pie cool in the pan for 3 minutes. To unmold, run a knife around the edge, then, using oven gloves, place a plate bottom-side up over the skillet and quickly invert the two together.

**9** If any pears stick to the skillet, remove gently with a metal spatula and replace them carefully on the pie. Serve warm, with the whipped cream passed separately.

# Lemon Meringue Pie

**SERVES 8**

| |
|---|
| grated rind and juice of 1 large lemon |
| 1 cup plus 1 tablespoon cold water |
| ½ cup plus 6 tablespoons sugar |
| 2 tablespoons butter |
| 3 tablespoons cornstarch |
| 3 eggs, separated |
| ⅛ teaspoon salt |
| ⅛ teaspoon cream of tartar |
| FOR THE CRUST |
| 1 cup flour |
| ½ teaspoon salt |
| ⅓ cup (5⅓ tablespoons) cold shortening, cut in pieces |
| 2 tablespoons ice water |

**1**  For the crust, sift the flour and salt into a bowl. Add the shortening and cut in with a pastry blender until the mixture resembles coarse crumbs. With a fork, stir in just enough water to bind the dough. Gather the dough into a ball.

**2** ▲  On a lightly floured surface, roll out the dough about ⅛ inch thick. Transfer to a 9-inch pie pan and trim the edge to leave a ½-inch overhang.

**3** ▲  Fold the overhang under and crimp the edge. Refrigerate the pie shell for at least 20 minutes.

**4**  Preheat the oven to 400°F.

**5** ▲  Prick the dough all over with a fork. Line with crumpled wax paper and fill with pie weights. Bake for 12 minutes. Remove the paper and weights and continue baking until golden, 6–8 minutes more.

**6**  In a saucepan, combine the lemon rind and juice, 1 cup of the water, ½ cup of the sugar, and butter. Bring the mixture to a boil.

**7**  Meanwhile, in a mixing bowl, dissolve the cornstarch in the remaining water. Add the egg yolks.

**8** ▲  Add the egg yolks to the lemon mixture and return to a boil, whisking continuously until the mixture thickens, about 5 minutes.

**9**  Cover the surface with wax paper to prevent a skin forming and let cool.

**10** ▲  For the meringue, using an electric mixer beat the egg whites with the salt and cream of tartar until they hold stiff peaks. Add the remaining sugar and beat until glossy.

**11** ▲  Spoon the lemon mixture into the pie shell and spread level. Spoon the meringue on top, smoothing it up to the edge of the crust to seal. Bake until golden, 12–15 minutes.

# Lime Meringue Pie

SERVES 8

| |
|---|
| 3 egg yolks |
| 1½ cups sweetened condensed milk |
| finely grated rind and juice of 4 limes |
| 7 egg whites |
| ⅛ teaspoon salt |
| squeeze of fresh lemon juice |
| ½ cup sugar |
| ½ teaspoon vanilla extract |
| FOR THE CRUST |
| 1⅓ cups flour |
| ½ teaspoon salt |
| ½ cup shortening |
| 1 egg yolk |
| 2–3 tablespoons ice water |

**1** Preheat the oven to 425°F.

**2 ▲** For the crust, sift the flour and salt into a mixing bowl. Using a pastry blender, cut in the shortening until the mixture resembles coarse crumbs. Sprinkle in the water, 1 tablespoon at a time, tossing lightly with a fork until the dough will form a ball.

---

~ **COOK'S TIP** ~

When beating egg whites with an electric mixer, start slowly, and increase speed after they become frothy. Turn the bowl constantly.

---

**3 ▲** On a lightly floured surface, roll out the dough. Use it to line a 9-inch pie pan, easing in the dough and being careful not to stretch it. With your thumbs, make a fluted edge.

**4** Using a fork, prick the bottom and sides of the pie shell all over. Bake until lightly browned, 10–15 minutes. Let cool, in the pan, on a wire rack. Reduce oven temperature to 375°F.

**5 ▲** With an electric mixer on high speed, beat the yolks and condensed milk. Stir in the lime rind and juice.

**6 ▲** In another clean bowl, beat 3 of the egg whites until stiff. Fold into lime mixture.

---

**7 ▲** Spread the lime filling in the pie crust. Bake 10 minutes.

**8 ▲** Meanwhile, beat the remaining egg whites with the salt and lemon juice until soft peaks form. Beat in the sugar, 1 tablespoon at a time, until stiff peaks form. Add the vanilla.

**9 ▲** Remove the pie from the oven. Using a metal spatula, spread the meringue over the lime filling, making a swirled design and covering the surface completely.

**10** Bake until the meringue is lightly browned and the pastry is golden brown, about 12 minutes longer. Let cool, in the pan, on a wire rack.

# Nesselrode Pie

SERVES 10

1 tablespoon rum

¼ cup candied fruit, chopped

2 cups milk

4 teaspoons unflavored gelatin

½ cup sugar

½ teaspoon salt

3 eggs, separated

1 cup whipping cream

chocolate curls, for decorating

FOR THE CRUST

1¼ cups graham cracker crumbs

5 tablespoons butter, melted

1 tablespoon sugar

**1** For the crust, mix the graham cracker crumbs, butter, and sugar. Press evenly and firmly over the bottom and sides of a 9-inch pie pan. Refrigerate until firm.

**2** ▲ In a bowl, stir together the rum and candied fruit. Set aside.

**3** Pour ½ cup of the milk into a small bowl. Sprinkle over the gelatin and let stand 5 minutes to soften.

**4** ▲ In the top of a double boiler, combine ¼ cup of the sugar, the remaining milk, and salt. Stir in the gelatin mixture. Cook over hot water, stirring, until gelatin dissolves.

**5** Whisk in the egg yolks and cook, stirring, until thick enough to coat a spoon. Do not boil. Pour the custard over the candied fruit mixture. Set in a bowl of ice water to cool.

**6** Whip the cream lightly. Set aside.

**7** With an electric mixer, beat the egg whites until they hold soft peaks. Add the remaining sugar and beat just enough to blend. Fold in a large dollop of the egg whites into the cooled gelatin mixture. Pour into the remaining egg whites and carefully fold together. Fold in the cream.

**8** ▲ Pour into the pie shell and chill until firm. Decorate the top with chocolate curls.

# Pumpkin Pie

**SERVES 8**

| |
|---|
| 2 cups cooked or canned pumpkin |
| 1 cup whipping cream |
| 2 eggs |
| ½ cup dark brown sugar, firmly packed |
| 4 tablespoons light corn syrup |
| 1½ teaspoons ground cinnamon |
| 1 teaspoon ground ginger |
| ¼ teaspoon ground cloves |
| ½ teaspoon salt |
| FOR THE CRUST |
| 1½ cup flour |
| ½ teaspoon salt |
| 6 tablespoons cold butter, cut in pieces |
| 3 tablespoons cold shortening, cut in pieces |
| 3–4 tablespoons ice water |

**1** For the crust, sift the flour and salt into a bowl. Cut in the butter and shortening with a pastry blender until the mixture resembles coarse crumbs. Stir in just enough water to bind. Gather into a ball, wrap in wax paper and refrigerate for 20 minutes.

**2** Roll out the dough ⅛ inch thick. Transfer to a 9-inch pie pan. Trim off the overhang. Roll out the trimmings and cut out leaf shapes. Moisten the edges with a brush dipped in water.

**3 ▲** Arrange the dough leaves around the edge. Refrigerate for 20 minutes. Preheat the oven to 400°F.

**4 ▲** Prick the bottom with a fork and line with crumpled wax paper. Fill with pie weights and bake for 12 minutes. Remove paper and weights and bake until golden, 6–8 minutes more. Reduce the heat to 375°F.

**5 ▼** Beat together the pumpkin, cream, eggs, sugar, corn syrup, spices, and salt. Pour into the shell and bake until set, about 40 minutes.

# Chess Pie

**SERVES 8**

2 eggs

3 tablespoons whipping cream

½ cup dark brown sugar, firmly packed

2 tablespoons granulated sugar

2 tablespoons flour

1 tablespoon bourbon or whisky

3 tablespoons butter, melted

½ cup walnuts, chopped

¾ cup pitted dates

whipped cream, for serving

FOR THE CRUST

6 tablespoons cold butter

3 tablespoons cold shortening

1½ cups flour

½ teaspoon salt

3–4 tablespoons ice water

**1 ▲** For the crust, cut the butter and shortening in small pieces.

**2** Sift the flour and salt into a bowl. With a pastry blender, cut in the butter and margarine until the mixture resembles coarse crumbs. Stir in just enough water to bind. Gather into a ball, wrap in wax paper, and refrigerate for at least 20 minutes.

**3** Place a baking sheet in the center of the oven and preheat to 375°F.

**4** Roll out the dough ⅛ inch thick. Transfer to a 9-inch pie pan and trim the edge. Roll out the trimmings, cut thin strips and braid them. Brush the edge of the pie with water and place the dough braid around the edge.

**5 ▲** In a mixing bowl, whisk together the eggs and cream.

**6** Add both sugars and beat until well combined. Sift over 1 tablespoon of the flour and stir in. Add the bourbon or whisky, the melted butter, and the walnuts. Stir to combine.

**7 ▲** Mix the dates with the remaining tablespoon of flour and stir into the walnut mixture.

**8** Pour into the pie shell and bake until the pastry is golden and the filling puffed up, about 35 minutes. Serve at room temperature, with whipped cream if desired.

# Shoofly Pie

**SERVES 8**

1 cup flour

½ cup dark brown sugar, firmly packed

¼ teaspoon each salt, ground ginger, cinnamon, mace, and grated nutmeg

6 tablespoons cold butter, cut in pieces

2 eggs

½ cup molasses

½ cup boiling water

½ teaspoon baking soda

**FOR THE CRUST**

4 ounces cream cheese, at room temperature, cut in pieces

½ cup (1 stick) cold butter, at room temperature, cut in pieces

1 cup flour

1  For the crust, put the cream cheese and butter in a mixing bowl. Sift over the flour.

2 ▲  Cut in with a pastry blender until the dough just holds together. Wrap in wax paper and refrigerate for at least 30 minutes.

3  Set a baking sheet in the center of the oven and preheat to 375°F.

4  In a bowl, mix together the flour, sugar, salt, spices, and cold butter pieces. Blend with your fingertips until the mixture resembles coarse crumbs. Set aside.

5  On a lightly floured surface, roll out the dough ⅛ inch thick and transfer to a 9-inch pie pan. Trim the overhang and flute the edges.

6 ▲  Spoon one-third of the crumbs into the pie shell.

7 ▲  To complete the filling, whisk the eggs with the molasses in a large bowl.

8  Measure the boiling water into a small bowl and stir in the soda; it will foam. Pour immediately into the egg mixture and whisk to blend. Pour carefully into the pie shell and sprinkle the remaining crumbs over the top in an even layer.

9  Bake on the hot sheet until browned, about 35 minutes. Let cool, then serve at room temperature.

# Mississippi Mud Pie

**SERVES 8**

| |
|---|
| 3 1-ounce squares semisweet chocolate |
| 4 tablespoons butter or margarine |
| 3 tablespoons corn syrup |
| 3 eggs, beaten |
| ⅔ cup sugar |
| 1 teaspoon vanilla extract |
| 4-oz chocolate bar |
| 2 cups whipping cream |
| FOR THE CRUST |
| 1⅓ cups flour |
| ½ teaspoon salt |
| ½ cup shortening |
| 2–3 tablespoons ice water |

**1** Preheat the oven to 425°F.

**2** For the crust, sift the flour and salt into a mixing bowl. Using a pastry blender, cut in the shortening until the mixture resembles coarse crumbs. Sprinkle in the water, 1 tablespoon at a time. Toss lightly with your fingers or a fork until the dough will form a ball.

**3** On a lightly floured surface, roll out the dough. Use to line an 8- or 9-inch pie pan, easing in the dough and being careful not to stretch it. With your thumbs, make a fluted edge.

**4** Using a fork, prick the bottom and sides of the pie shell all over. Bake until lightly browned, 10–15 minutes. Let cool, in the pan, on a wire rack.

**5** ▲ In a heatproof bowl set over a pan of simmering water, or in a double boiler, melt 3 squares of chocolate, the butter or margarine, and corn syrup. Remove the bowl from the heat and stir in the eggs, sugar, and vanilla.

**6** Reduce the oven temperature to 350°F. Pour the chocolate mixture into the baked crust. Bake until the filling is set, 35–40 minutes. Let cool completely in the pan, set on a rack.

**7** ▲ For the decoration, use the heat of your hands to slightly soften the chocolate bar. Draw the blade of a swivel-headed vegetable peeler along the side of the chocolate bar to shave off short, wide curls. Chill the chocolate curls until needed.

**8** Before serving, lightly whip the cream until soft peaks form. Using a rubber spatula, spread the cream over the surface of the chocolate filling. Decorate with the chocolate curls.

# Chocolate Chiffon Pie

**SERVES 8**

6 1-ounce squares semisweet chocolate

1 1-ounce square unsweetened chocolate

1 cup milk

1 tablespoon unflavored gelatin

⅔ cup sugar

2 extra-large eggs, separated

1 teaspoon vanilla extract

1½ cup whipping cream

⅛ teaspoon salt

whipped cream and chocolate curls, for decorating

FOR THE CRUST

1½ cups graham cracker crumbs

6 tablespoons butter, melted

**6 ▲** Set the top of the double boiler in a bowl of ice and stir until the mixture reaches room temperature. Remove from the ice and set aside.

**7** Whip the cream lightly. Set aside. With an electric mixer, beat the egg whites and salt until they hold soft peaks. Add the remaining sugar and beat only enough to blend.

**8** Fold a dollop of egg whites into the chocolate mixture, then pour back into the whites and fold in.

**9 ▲** Fold in the whipped cream and pour into the pastry shell. Put in the freezer until just set, about 5 minutes. If the center sinks, fill with any remaining mixture. Refrigerate for 3–4 hours. Decorate with whipped cream and chocolate curls. Serve cold.

**1** Place a baking sheet in the oven and preheat to 350°F.

**2** For the crust, mix the graham cracker crumbs and butter in a bowl. Press the crumbs evenly over the bottom and sides of a 9-inch pie pan. Bake for 8 minutes. Let cool.

**3** Chop the chocolate, then grind in a food processor or blender. Set aside.

**4** Place the milk in the top of a double boiler. Sprinkle over the gelatin. Let stand 5 minutes to soften.

**5 ▲** Set the top of the double boiler over hot water. Add ⅓ cup of the sugar, the chocolate, and egg yolks. Stir until dissolved. Add the vanilla.

# Black Bottom Pie

SERVES 8

2 teaspoons unflavored gelatin

3 tablespoons cold water

2 eggs, separated

1 cup sugar

2 tablespoons cornstarch

½ teaspoon salt

2 cups milk

2 1-ounce squares unsweetened
  chocolate, finely chopped

3 tablespoons rum

¼ teaspoon cream of tartar

chocolate curls, for decorating

FOR THE CRUST

1½ cups gingersnap cookie crumbs

⅓ cup (5⅓ tablespoons) butter, melted

**1** Preheat the oven to 350°F.

**2** For the crust, mix the cookie crumbs and melted butter.

**3** ▲ Press the mixture evenly over the bottom and sides of a 9-inch pie pan. Bake for 6 minutes. Let cool.

**4** Sprinkle the gelatin over the water and let stand to soften.

**5** Beat the egg yolks in a large mixing bowl and set aside.

**6** In a saucepan, combine half the sugar, the cornstarch, and salt. Gradually stir in the milk. Boil for 1 minute, stirring constantly.

**7** ▲ Whisk the hot milk mixture into the yolks, then pour all back into the saucepan and return to a boil, whisking. Cook for 1 minute, still whisking. Remove from the heat.

**8** ▲ Measure out 1 cup of the hot custard mixture and pour into a bowl. Add the chopped chocolate to the custard mixture, and stir until melted. Stir in half the rum and pour into the pie crust.

**9** ▲ Whisk the softened gelatin into the plain custard until it has dissolved, then stir in the remaining rum. Set the pan in cold water until it reaches room temperature.

**10** ▲ With an electric mixer, beat the egg whites and cream of tartar until they hold stiff peaks. Beat in half the remaining sugar until glossy, then fold in the rest of the sugar.

**11** ▲ Fold the custard into the egg whites, then spoon over the chocolate mixture in the pie shell. Refrigerate until set, about 2 hours.

**12** Decorate the top with chocolate curls. Keep the pie refrigerated until ready to serve.

~ COOK'S TIP ~

To make chocolate curls, melt 8 ounces semisweet chocolate over hot water, stir in 1 tablespoon of neutral vegetable oil, and mold in a small foil-lined loaf pan. For large curls, soften the bar between your hands and carve off curls from the wide side with a vegetable peeler; for small curls, grate from the narrow side using a box grater.

# Brown Sugar Pie

SERVES 8

1½ cups flour

½ teaspoon salt

2 teaspoons granulated sugar

6 tablespoons cold butter

¼ cup or more ice water

FOR THE FILLING

¼ cup flour, sifted

1 cup light brown sugar

½ teaspoon vanilla extract

1½ cups whipping cream

3 tablespoons butter, cut in tiny pieces

⅛ teaspoon grated nutmeg

**1** Sift the flour, salt, and sugar into a bowl. Using a pastry blender or 2 knives, cut in the butter until it resembles coarse meal.

**2 ▲** Sprinkle with the water and mix until the dough holds together. If it is too crumbly, add more water, 1 tablespoon at a time. Gather into a ball and flatten. Wrap in wax paper and refrigerate at least 20 minutes.

**3** Roll out the dough about ⅛ inch thick and line a 9-inch pie pan. Trim all around, leaving a ½-inch overhang. Fold it under and flute the edge. Refrigerate for 30 minutes.

**4** Preheat the oven to 425°F.

**5** Line the pie shell with a piece of wax paper that is 2 inches larger all around than the diameter of the pan. Fill the shell with dried beans. Bake until the pastry has just set, 8–10 minutes. Remove from the oven and carefully lift out the paper and beans. Prick the bottom of the pie shell all over with a fork. Return to the oven and bake 5 minutes more. Let the pie shell cool slightly before filling. Turn the oven down to 375°F.

**6 ▲** In a small bowl, mix together the flour and sugar using a fork. Spread this mixture in an even layer on the bottom of the pie shell.

**7 ▲** Stir the vanilla into the cream. Pour the flavored cream over the flour and sugar mixture and gently swirl with a fork to mix. Dot with the butter. Sprinkle the nutmeg on top.

**8** Cover the edge of the pie with foil strips to prevent overbrowning. Set on a cookie sheet and bake until the filling is golden brown and set to the touch, about 45 minutes. Serve the pie at room temperature.

# Banana Cream Pie

**SERVES 6**

| |
|---|
| 2 cups finely crushed gingersnaps |
| 5 tablespoons butter or margarine, melted |
| ½ teaspoon grated nutmeg or ground cinnamon |
| ¾ cup mashed ripe bananas |
| 1½ 8-ounce packages cream cheese, at room temperature |
| ¼ cup thick plain yogurt or sour cream |
| 3 tablespoons dark rum or 1 teaspoon vanilla extract |
| FOR THE TOPPING |
| 1 cup whipping cream |
| 3–4 bananas |

**1**  Preheat the oven to 375°F.

**2 ▲**  In a mixing bowl, combine the cookie crumbs, butter or margarine, and spice. Mix thoroughly with a wooden spoon.

**3 ▲**  Press the cookie mixture into a 9-inch pie pan, building up thick sides with a neat edge. Bake 5 minutes. Let cool, in the pan, on a wire rack.

**4 ▼**  With an electric mixer, beat the mashed bananas with the cream cheese. Fold in the yogurt or sour cream and rum or vanilla. Spread the filling in the crumb crust. Refrigerate at least 4 hours or overnight.

**5 ▲**  For the topping, whip the cream until soft peaks form. Spread on the pie filling. Slice the bananas and arrange on top in a decorative pattern.

# Georgia Peanut Butter Pie

**SERVES 8**

2 cups fine graham-cracker crumbs

¼ cup light brown sugar, firmly packed

6 tablespoons butter or margarine, melted

whipped cream or ice cream, for serving

FOR THE FILLING

3 egg yolks

½ cup granulated sugar

¼ cup light brown sugar, firmly packed

¼ cup cornstarch

⅛ teaspoon salt

2½ cups evaporated milk

2 tablespoons unsalted butter or margarine

1½ teaspoons vanilla extract

½ cup chunky peanut butter, preferably made from freshly ground peanuts

¾ cup confectioners' sugar

**1** Preheat the oven to 350°F.

**2 ▲** Combine the crumbs, sugar, and butter or margarine in a bowl and blend well. Spread the mixture in a well-greased 9-inch pie pan, pressing evenly over the bottom and sides with your fingertips.

**3** Bake the crumb crust 10 minutes. Remove from the oven and let cool. Leave the oven on.

**4 ▲** Combine the egg yolks, granulated and brown sugars, cornstarch, and salt in a heavy saucepan.

**5** Slowly whisk in the milk. Cook over medium heat, stirring constantly, until the mixture thickens, about 8–10 minutes. Reduce the heat to very low and cook until very thick, 3–4 minutes more.

**6 ▲** Beat in the butter or margarine. Stir in the vanilla. Remove from the heat. Cover the surface closely with plastic wrap and let cool.

~ **VARIATIONS** ~

If preferred, use an equal amount of finely crushed vanilla wafers or ginger snaps in place of graham crackers for the crumb crust. Or make the pie with a ready-to-use graham cracker crust.

**7 ▲** In a small bowl combine the peanut butter with the confectioners' sugar, working with your fingers to blend the ingredients to the consistency of small crumbs.

**8 ▲** Sprinkle all but 3 tablespoons of the peanut butter crumbs evenly over the bottom of the crumb crust.

**9 ▲** Pour in the filling, spreading it into an even layer. Sprinkle with the remaining crumbs. Bake 15 minutes.

**10** Let the pie cool 1 hour. Serve with whipped cream or ice cream.

# Key Lime Pie

**SERVES 8**

3 large egg yolks

1 14-ounce can sweetened condensed milk

1 tablespoon grated Key lime rind

½ cup fresh Key lime juice

green food coloring (optional)

½ cup whipping cream

**FOR THE CRUST**

1¼ cups graham cracker crumbs

5 tablespoons butter or margarine, melted

**1** Preheat the oven to 350°F.

**2 ▲** For the crust, place the graham cracker crumbs in a bowl and add the butter or margarine. Mix to combine.

~ **VARIATION** ~

If Key limes are not available, use regular limes.

**3** Press the crumbs evenly over the bottom and sides of a 9-inch pie pan. Bake for 8 minutes. Let cool.

**4 ▲** Beat the yolks until thick. Beat in the milk, lime rind and juice, and coloring, if using. Pour into the prebaked pie shell and refrigerate until set, about 4 hours. To serve, whip the cream. Pipe a lattice pattern on top, or spoon dollops around the edge.

---

# Fruit Tartlets

**MAKES 8**

¾ cup red currant or grape jelly

1 tablespoon fresh lemon juice

¾ cup whipping cream

1½ pounds fresh fruit, such as strawberries, raspberries, kiwi fruit, peaches, grapes, or blueberries, peeled and sliced as necessary

**FOR THE CRUST**

⅔ cup (10⅔ tablespoons) cold butter, cut in pieces

⅓ cup dark brown sugar, firmly packed

3 tablespoons unsweetened cocoa powder

1½ cups flour

1 egg white

**1** For the crust, combine the butter, brown sugar, and cocoa over low heat. When the butter is melted, remove from the heat and sift over the flour. Stir, then add just enough egg white to bind the mixture. Gather into a ball, wrap in wax paper, and refrigerate for at least 30 minutes.

**2 ▲** Grease 8 3-inch tartlet pans. Roll out the dough between two sheets of wax paper. Stamp out 8 4-inch rounds with a fluted cutter.

**3** Line the tartlet pans with dough. Prick the bottoms. Refrigerate for 15 minutes. Preheat the oven to 350°F.

**4** Bake until firm, 20–25 minutes. Cool, then remove from the pans.

**5 ▲** Melt the jelly with the lemon juice. Brush a thin layer in the bottom of the tartlets. Whip the cream and spread a thin layer in the tartlet shells. Arrange the fruit on top. Brush with the glaze and serve.

*Key Lime Pie (top), Fruit Tartlets*

# Chocolate Lemon Tart

SERVES 8–10

1¼ cups granulated sugar

6 eggs

grated rind of 2 lemons

⅔ cup fresh lemon juice

⅔ cup whipping cream

chocolate curls, for decorating

FOR THE CRUST

1¼ cups flour

2 tablespoons unsweetened cocoa powder

4 tablespoons confectioners' sugar

½ teaspoon salt

½ cup (1 stick) butter or margarine

1 tablespoon water

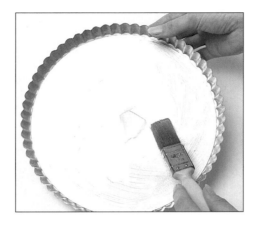

**1 ▲** Grease a 10-inch tart pan.

**2** For the crust, sift the flour, cocoa powder, confectioners' sugar, and salt into a bowl. Set aside.

**3 ▲** Melt the butter and water over low heat. Pour over the flour mixture and stir with a wooden spoon until the dough is smooth and the flour has absorbed all the liquid.

**4** Press the dough evenly over the base and sides of the prepared tart pan. Refrigerate the tart shell while preparing the filling.

**5** Place a baking sheet in the center of the oven and preheat to 375°F.

**6 ▲** Whisk the sugar and eggs until the sugar is dissolved. Add the lemon rind and juice and mix well. Add the cream. Taste the mixture and add more lemon juice or sugar if needed. It should taste tart but also sweet.

**7** Pour the filling into the tart shell and bake on the hot sheet until the filling is set, 20–25 minutes. Cool on a rack. When cool, sprinkle with the chocolate curls.

# Lemon Almond Tart

**SERVES 8**

¾ cup blanched almonds

½ cup sugar

2 eggs

grated rind and juice of 1½ lemons

½ cup (1 stick) butter, melted

strips of lemon rind, for decorating

**FOR THE CRUST**

1¼ cups flour

1 tablespoon sugar

½ teaspoon salt

½ teaspoon baking powder

6 tablespoons cold unsalted butter, cut in pieces

3–4 tablespoons whipping cream

**1** For the crust, sift the flour, sugar, salt, and baking powder into a bowl. Add the butter and cut in with a pastry blender until the mixture resembles coarse crumbs.

**2** ▲ With a fork, stir in just enough cream to bind the dough.

**3** Gather into a ball and transfer to a lightly floured surface. Roll out the dough about ⅛ inch thick and transfer to a 9-inch tart pan. Trim the edge. Prick the base all over with a fork and refrigerate for at least 20 minutes.

**4** Set a baking sheet in the center of the oven and preheat to 400°F.

**5** Line the tart shell with crumpled wax paper and fill with pie weights. Bake for 12 minutes. Remove the paper and weights and continue baking until golden, 6–8 minutes more. Reduce the oven temperature to 350°F.

**6** ▲ Grind the almonds finely with 1 tablespoon of the sugar in a food processor, blender, or nut grinder.

**7** ▲ Set a mixing bowl over a pan of hot water. Add the eggs and the remaining sugar, and beat with an electric mixer until the mixture is thick enough to leave a ribbon trail when the beaters are lifted.

**8** Stir in the lemon rind and juice, butter, and ground almonds.

**9** Pour into the prebaked shell. Bake until the filling is golden and set, about 35 minutes. Decorate with lemon rind.

# Orange Tart

**SERVES 8**

1 cup sugar

1 cup fresh orange juice, strained

2 large navel oranges

¾ cup blanched almonds

4 tablespoons butter

1 egg

1 tablespoon flour

3 tablespoons apricot jam

FOR THE CRUST

1½ cups flour

½ teaspoon salt

4 tablespoons cold butter, cut in pieces

3 tablespoons cold margarine, cut in pieces

3–4 tablespoons ice water

**1** For the crust, sift the flour and salt into a bowl. Add the butter and margarine and cut in with a pastry blender until the mixture resembles coarse crumbs. Stir in just enough water to bind the dough. Gather into a ball, wrap in wax paper, and refrigerate for at least 20 minutes.

**2** On a lightly floured surface, roll out the dough ¼ inch thick and transfer to an 8-inch tart pan. Trim off the overhang. Refrigerate until needed.

**3** In a saucepan, combine ¾ cup of the sugar and the orange juice and boil until thick and syrupy, about 10 minutes.

**4 ▲** Cut the oranges into ¼-inch slices. Do not peel. Add to the syrup. Simmer gently for 10 minutes, or until glazed. Transfer to a rack to dry. When cool, cut in half. Reserve the syrup. Place a baking sheet in the oven and heat to 400°F.

**5** Grind the almonds finely in a food processor, blender or nut grinder. With an electric mixer, cream the butter and remaining sugar until light and fluffy. Beat in the egg and 2 tablespoons of the orange syrup. Stir in the almonds and flour.

**6** Melt the jam over low heat, then brush in the tart shell. Pour in the almond mixture. Bake until set, about 20 minutes. Let cool.

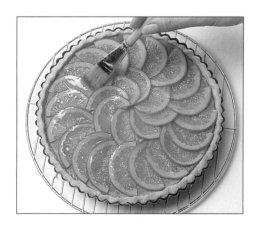

**7 ▲** Arrange overlapping orange slices on top. Boil the remaining syrup until thick. Brush on top to glaze.

# Rich Orange Cheesecake

**SERVES 8**

1½ pounds cream cheese, at room temperature

1 cup sugar

2 tablespoons flour

3 eggs

1 stick (8 tablespoons) butter, melted

1 teaspoon vanilla extract

1 tablespoon grated orange rind

8-inch crumb crust, made in a springform cake pan with graham crackers and orange rind, chilled

4 sweet oranges, peeled and sectioned

squeeze of lemon juice

1–2 tablespoons orange liqueur (optional)

**1** Preheat the oven to 300°F.

**2 ▲** Combine the cream cheese, sugar, and flour in a bowl. Beat until light and fluffy.

**3 ▲** Add the eggs, butter, vanilla, and orange rind and beat until smoothly blended.

**4 ▲** Pour the filling into the crumb crust. Set the springform pan on a baking sheet.

**5** Bake until the filling is gently set, 1–1¼ hours (it will continue to firm up as it cools). If the top browns too quickly, cover with foil. Turn off the oven and open the door.

**6** Let the cheesecake cool in the oven. When it is cold, cover and refrigerate overnight.

**7** Mix together the orange sections, lemon juice, and liqueur, if using. Serve with the cheesecake.

---

**~ VARIATIONS ~**

For Lemon Cheesecake, use 1½ teaspoons lemon rind instead of orange in the filling. For a lighter cheesecake, use a mixture of ricotta cheese and cream cheese, worked in a food processor until smooth.

---

# Blueberry-Hazelnut Cheesecake

**SERVES 6–8**

12 ounces blueberries

1 tablespoon honey

6 tablespoons granulated sugar

1 teaspoon plus 1 tablespoon fresh lemon juice

6 ounces cream cheese, at room temperature

1 egg

1 teaspoon hazelnut liqueur (optional)

½ cup whipping cream

FOR THE CRUST

1⅓ cups ground hazelnuts

⅔ cup flour

⅛ teaspoon salt

4 tablespoons butter, at room temperature

⅓ cup light brown sugar, firmly packed

1 egg yolk

**1 ▲** For the crust, put the hazelnuts in a large bowl. Sift in the flour and salt, and stir to mix. Set aside.

~ COOK'S TIP ~

The cheesecake can be prepared 1 day in advance, but add the fruit shortly before serving. Instead of covering the top completely, leave spaces to make a design, if wished.

**2** Beat the butter with the brown sugar until light and fluffy. Beat in the egg yolk. Gradually fold in the nut mixture, in 3 batches.

**3 ▲** Press the dough into a greased 9-inch pie pan, spreading it evenly against the sides. Form a rim around the top edge that is slightly thicker than the sides. Cover and refrigerate at least 30 minutes.

**4** Preheat the oven to 350°F.

**5 ▲** Meanwhile, for the topping, combine the blueberries, honey, 1 tablespoon of the granulated sugar, and 1 teaspoon lemon juice in a heavy saucepan. Cook the mixture over low heat, stirring occasionally, until the berries have given off some liquid but still retain their shape, 5–7 minutes. Remove from the heat and set aside.

**6** Place the crust in the oven and bake 15 minutes. Remove and let cool while making the filling.

**7 ▲** Beat together the cream cheese and remaining granulated sugar until light and fluffy. Add the egg, remaining lemon juice, the liqueur, if using, and the cream and beat until thoroughly incorporated.

**8 ▲** Pour the cheese mixture into the crust and spread evenly. Bake until just set, 20–25 minutes.

**9** Let the cheesecake cool completely on a wire rack, then cover and refrigerate at least 1 hour.

**10** Spread the blueberry mixture evenly over the top of the cheesecake. Serve at cool room temperature.

# Chocolate Cheesecake Pie

**SERVES 8**

12 ounces cream cheese

4 tablespoons whipping cream

1 cup sugar

½ cup unsweetened cocoa powder

½ teaspoon ground cinnamon

3 eggs

whipped cream, for decorating

chocolate curls, for decorating

FOR THE CRUST

1 cup graham cracker crumbs

½ cup crushed amaretti cookies (if unavailable, use all graham cracker crumbs for a total of 1½ cups)

6 tablespoons butter, melted

**1** Place a baking sheet in the oven and preheat to 350°F.

**2** For the crust, mix the crumbs and butter in a bowl.

**3 ▲** With a spoon, press the crumbs evenly over the bottom and sides of a 9-inch pie pan. Bake for 8 minutes. Let cool. Keep the oven on.

**4** With an electric mixer, beat the cheese and cream together until smooth. Beat in the sugar, cocoa, and cinnamon until blended.

**5 ▼** Add the eggs, 1 at a time, beating just enough to blend.

**6** Pour into the pie shell and bake on the hot sheet for 25–30 minutes. The filling will sink down as it cools. Decorate with whipped cream and chocolate curls.

# Frozen Strawberry Pie

**SERVES 8**

8 ounces cream cheese

1 cup sour cream

2 10-ounce packages frozen sliced strawberries, thawed

FOR THE CRUST

1¼ cup graham cracker crumbs

1 tablespoon sugar

5 tablespoons butter, melted

~ **VARIATION** ~

For Frozen Raspberry Pie, use raspberries in place of the strawberries and prepare the same way, or try other frozen fruit.

**1 ▲** For the crust, mix together the crumbs, sugar, and butter.

**2** Press the crumbs evenly and firmly over the bottom and sides of a 9-inch pie pan. Freeze until firm.

**3 ▼** Blend together the cream cheese and sour cream. Set aside ½ cup of the strawberries and their juice. Add the rest to the cream cheese mixture.

**4** Pour the filling into the crust and freeze 6–8 hours until firm. To serve, slice and spoon some of the reserved berries and juice on top.

*Chocolate Cheesecake Pie (top), Frozen Strawberry Pie*

# Kiwi Ricotta Cheese Tart

SERVES 8

| |
|---|
| ½ cup blanched almonds |
| ½ cup plus 1 tablespoon sugar |
| 4 cups ricotta cheese |
| 1 cup whipping cream |
| 1 egg |
| 3 egg yolks |
| 1 tablespoon flour |
| ⅛ teaspoon salt |
| 2 tablespoons rum |
| grated rind of 1 lemon |
| 2½ tablespoons lemon juice |
| ¼ cup honey |
| 5 kiwi fruit |
| FOR THE CRUST |
| 1¼ cups flour |
| 1 tablespoon sugar |
| ½ teaspoon salt |
| ½ teaspoon baking powder |
| 6 tablespoons cold butter, cut in pieces |
| 1 egg yolk |
| 3–4 tablespoons whipping cream |

**1** For the crust, sift the flour, sugar, salt, and baking powder into a bowl. Cut in the butter until the mixture resembles coarse crumbs. Mix the egg yolk and cream. Stir in just enough to bind the dough.

**2 ▲** Transfer to a lightly floured surface, flatten slightly, wrap in wax paper, and refrigerate for 30 minutes. Preheat the oven to 425°F.

**3 ▲** On a lightly floured surface, roll out the dough ⅛ inch thick and transfer to a 9-inch springform pan. Crimp the edge decoratively.

**4 ▲** Prick the bottom of the dough all over with a fork. Line with crumpled wax paper and fill with pie weights. Bake for 10 minutes. Remove the paper and weights and bake until golden, 6–8 minutes more. Let cool. Reduce the heat to 350°F.

**5 ▲** Grind the almonds finely with 1 tablespoon of the sugar in a food processor, blender, or nut grinder.

**6** With an electric mixer, beat the ricotta until creamy. Add the cream, egg, yolks, remaining sugar, flour, salt, rum, lemon rind, and 2 tablespoons of the lemon juice. Beat to combine.

**7 ▲** Stir in the ground almonds until well blended.

**8** Pour into the shell and bake until golden, about 1 hour. Let cool, then refrigerate, loosely covered, for 2–3 hours. Unmold and place on a plate.

**9** Combine the honey and remaining lemon juice for the glaze. Set aside.

**10 ▲** Peel the kiwis. Halve them lengthwise, then cut crosswise into ¼-inch slices. Arrange the slices in rows across the top of the tart. Just before serving, brush with the glaze.

# Raspberry Tart

**SERVES 8**

4 egg yolks

⅓ cup sugar

3 tablespoons flour

1¼ cups milk

⅛ teaspoon salt

½ teaspoon vanilla extract

1 pound fresh raspberries (about 1 quart)

5 tablespoons concord grape jelly

1 tablespoon fresh orange juice

FOR THE CRUST

1¼ cups flour

½ teaspoon baking powder

¼ teaspoon salt

1 tablespoon sugar

grated rind of ½ orange

6 tablespoons cold butter, cut in pieces

1 egg yolk

3–4 tablespoons whipping cream

**1** For the crust, sift the flour, baking powder, and salt into a bowl. Stir in the sugar and orange rind. Add the butter and cut in with a pastry blender until the mixture resembles coarse crumbs. With a fork, stir in the egg yolk and just enough cream to bind the dough. Gather into a ball, wrap in wax paper, and refrigerate.

**2** For the custard filling, beat the egg yolks and sugar until thick and lemon-colored. Gradually stir in the flour.

**3** In a saucepan, bring the milk and salt just to the boil, and remove from the heat. Whisk into the egg yolk mixture, return to the pan, and continue whisking over moderately high heat until just bubbling. Cook for 3 minutes to thicken. Transfer immediately to a bowl. Add the vanilla and stir to blend.

**4 ▲** Cover with wax paper to prevent a skin from forming.

**5 ▲** Preheat the oven to 400°F. On a lightly floured surface, roll out the dough about ⅛ inch thick, transfer to a 10-inch tart pan and trim the edge. Prick the bottom all over with a fork and line with crumpled wax paper. Fill with pie weights and bake for 15 minutes. Remove the paper and weights. Continue baking until golden, 6–8 minutes more. Let cool.

**6 ▲** Spread an even layer of the pastry cream filling in the tart shell and arrange the raspberries on top. Melt the jelly and orange juice in a pan and brush on top to glaze.

# Treacle Tart

**SERVES 4–6**

¾ cup dark corn syrup

1½ cups fresh white bread crumbs

grated rind of 1 lemon

2 tablespoons fresh lemon juice

**FOR THE CRUST**

1¼ cups flour

½ teaspoon salt

6 tablespoons cold butter, cut in pieces

3 tablespoons cold margarine, cut in pieces

3–4 tablespoons ice water

**1** For the crust, combine the flour and salt in a bowl. Add the butter and margarine and cut in with a pastry blender until the mixture resembles coarse crumbs.

**2 ▲** With a fork, stir in just enough water to bind the dough. Gather into a ball, wrap in wax paper, and refrigerate for at least 20 minutes.

**3** On a lightly floured surface, roll out the dough ⅛ inch thick. Transfer to an 8-inch tart pan and trim off the overhang. Refrigerate for at least 20 minutes. Reserve the trimmings for the lattice top.

**4** Place a baking sheet above the center of the oven and heat to 400°F.

**5** In a saucepan, warm the corn syrup until thin and runny.

**6 ▲** Remove from the heat and stir in the bread crumbs and lemon rind. Let sit for 10 minutes so the bread can absorb the syrup. Add more bread crumbs if the mixture is thin. Stir in the lemon juice and spread evenly in the pastry shell.

**7** Roll out the pastry trimmings and cut into 10–12 thin strips.

**8 ▼** Lay half the strips on the filling, then arrange the remaining strips to form a lattice pattern.

**9** Place on the hot sheet and bake for 10 minutes. Lower the heat to 375°F. Bake until golden, about 15 minutes more. Serve warm or cold.

# Coconut Cream Pie

**SERVES 8**

| |
|---|
| 2½ cups flaked sweetened coconut |
| ⅔ cup sugar |
| 4 tablespoons cornstarch |
| ⅛ teaspoon salt |
| 2½ cups milk |
| ¼ cup whipping cream |
| 2 egg yolks |
| 2 tablespoons unsalted butter |
| 2 teaspoons vanilla extract |
| FOR THE CRUST |
| 1 cup flour |
| ¼ teaspoon salt |
| 3 tablespoons cold butter, cut in pieces |
| 2 tablespoons cold shortening |
| 2–3 tablespoons ice water |

**1** For the crust, sift the flour and salt into a bowl. Add the butter and shortening and cut in with a pastry blender until the mixture resembles coarse crumbs.

**2 ▲** With a fork, stir in just enough water to bind the dough. Gather into a ball, wrap in wax paper, and refrigerate for at least 20 minutes.

**3** Preheat the oven to 425°F. Roll out the dough ⅛ inch thick. Transfer to a 9-inch pie pan. Trim and flute the edges. Prick the bottom. Line with crumpled wax paper and fill with pie weights. Bake for 10–12 minutes. Remove the paper and weights, reduce the heat to 350°F and bake until brown, 10–15 minutes more.

**4 ▲** Spread 1 cup of the coconut on a baking sheet and toast in the oven until golden, 6–8 minutes, stirring often. Set aside for decorating.

**5** Put the sugar, cornstarch, and salt in a saucepan. In a bowl, whisk the milk, cream, and egg yolks. Add the egg mixture to the saucepan.

**6 ▼** Cook over low heat, stirring constantly, until the mixture comes to a boil. Boil for 1 minute, then remove from the heat. Add the butter, vanilla, and remaining coconut.

**7** Pour into the prebaked pie shell. When cool, sprinkle toasted coconut in a ring in the center.

# Brandy Alexander Tart

**SERVES 8**

½ cup cold water

1 tablespoon unflavored gelatin

½ cup sugar

3 eggs, separated

4 tablespoons brandy or cognac

4 tablespoons crème de cacao

⅛ teaspoon of salt

1¼ cups whipping cream

chocolate curls, for decorating

**FOR THE CRUST**

1¼ cups graham cracker crumbs

5 tablespoons butter, melted

1 tablespoon sugar

**1** Preheat the oven to 375°F.

**2** For the crust, mix the graham cracker crumbs with the butter and sugar in a bowl.

**3** ▲ Press the crumbs evenly into the bottom and sides of a 9-inch tart pan. Bake until just brown, about 10 minutes. Cool on a rack.

**4** Place the water in the top of a double boiler set over hot water. Sprinkle over the gelatin and let stand for 5 minutes to soften. Add half the sugar and the egg yolks. Whisk continually over a very low heat until the gelatin dissolves and the mixture thickens slightly. Do not allow the mixture to boil.

**5** ▲ Remove from the heat and stir in the brandy and crème de cacao.

**6** Set the pan over ice water and stir occasionally until it cools and thickens; it should not set firmly.

**7** With an electric mixer, beat the egg whites and salt until they hold stiff peaks. Beat in the remaining sugar. Spoon a large dollop of whites into the yolk mixture and fold in to lighten.

**8** ▼ Pour the egg yolk mixture over the remaining whites and fold together gently.

**9** Whip the cream until soft peaks form, then gently fold into the filling. Spoon into the prebaked crust and chill until set, 3–4 hours. Decorate with chocolate curls before serving.

# Velvet Mocha Cream Pie

**SERVES 8**

2 teaspoons instant espresso coffee

2 tablespoons hot water

1½ cups whipping cream

6 1-ounce squares semisweet chocolate

1 1-ounce square unsweetened chocolate

½ cup whipped cream, for decorating

chocolate-covered coffee beans, for decorating

**FOR THE CRUST**

1½ cups chocolate wafer crumbs

2 tablespoons sugar

⅓ cup (5⅓ tablespoons) butter, melted

**1** ▲ For the crust, mix the chocolate wafer crumbs and sugar together, then stir in the melted butter.

**2** Press the crumbs evenly over the bottom and sides of a 9-inch pie pan. Refrigerate until firm.

**3** In a bowl, dissolve the coffee in the water and set aside.

**4** Melt both the chocolates in the top of a double boiler, or in a heatproof bowl set over a pan of hot water. Remove from the heat when nearly melted and stir to continue melting. Set the bottom of the pan in cool water to reduce the temperature. Be careful not to splash any water on the chocolate or it will become grainy.

**5** Pour the cream into a mixing bowl. Set the bowl in hot water to warm the cream, bringing it closer to the temperature of the chocolate.

**6** ▲ With an electric mixer, whip the cream until it is lightly fluffy. Add the dissolved coffee and whip until the cream just holds its shape.

**7** ▲ When the chocolate is at room temperature, fold it gently into the cream with a large metal spoon.

**8** Pour into the chilled pastry case and refrigerate until firm. To serve, pipe a ring of whipped cream rosettes around the edge, then place a chocolate-covered coffee bean in the center of each rosette.

# Chocolate Pear Tart

**SERVES 8**

4 1-ounce squares semisweet chocolate, grated

3 large firm, ripe pears

1 egg

1 egg yolk

½ cup light cream

½ teaspoon vanilla extract

3 tablespoons sugar

FOR THE CRUST

1 cup flour

⅛ teaspoon salt

2 tablespoons sugar

½ cup (1 stick) cold unsalted butter, cut into pieces

1 egg yolk

1 tablespoon fresh lemon juice

**1** For the crust, sift the flour and salt into a bowl. Add the sugar and butter. Cut in with a pastry blender until the mixture resembles coarse crumbs. With a fork, stir in the egg yolk and lemon juice until the mixture forms a dough. Gather into a ball, wrap in wax paper, and refrigerate for at least 20 minutes.

**2** Place a baking sheet in the oven and preheat to 400°F.

**3** On a lightly floured surface, roll out the dough ⅛ inch thick and trim the edge. Transfer to a 10-inch tart pan.

**4** ▲ Sprinkle the bottom of the tart shell with the grated chocolate.

**5** ▲ Peel, halve, and core the pears. Cut in thin slices crosswise, then fan them out slightly.

**6** Transfer the pear halves to the tart with the help of a metal spatula and arrange on top of the chocolate like the spokes of a wheel.

**7** ▼ Whisk together the egg and egg yolk, cream, and vanilla. Ladle over the pears, then sprinkle with sugar.

**8** Bake for 10 minutes. Reduce the heat to 350°F and cook until the custard is set and the pears begin to caramelize, about 20 minutes more. Serve at room temperature.

# Maple Walnut Pie

**SERVES 8**

3 eggs

⅛ teaspoon salt

¼ cup granulated sugar

4 tablespoons butter or margarine, melted

1 cup pure maple syrup

1 cup walnuts, chopped

whipped cream, for decorating

**FOR THE CRUST**

½ cup all-purpose flour

½ cup whole-wheat flour

⅛ teaspoon salt

4 tablespoons cold butter, cut in pieces

3 tablespoons cold shortening, cut in pieces

1 egg yolk

2–3 tablespoons ice water

**1 ▼** For the crust, mix the flours and salt in a bowl. Add the butter and shortening and cut in with a pastry blender until the mixture resembles coarse crumbs. With a fork, stir in the egg yolk and just enough water to bind the dough.

**2** Gather into a ball, wrap in wax paper, and refrigerate for 20 minutes.

**3** Preheat the oven to 425°F.

**4** On a lightly floured surface, roll out the dough about ⅛ inch thick and transfer to a 9-inch pie pan. Trim the edge. To decorate, roll out the trimmings. With a small heart-shaped cutter, stamp out enough hearts to go around the rim of the pie. Brush the edge with water, then arrange the dough hearts all around.

**5 ▲** Prick the bottom with a fork. Line with crumpled wax paper and fill with pie weights. Bake 10 minutes. Remove the paper and weights and continue baking until golden brown, 3–6 minutes more.

**6** In a bowl, whisk the eggs, salt, and sugar together. Stir in the butter or margarine and maple syrup.

**7 ▲** Set the pie shell on a baking sheet. Pour in the filling, then sprinkle the nuts over the top.

**8** Bake until just set, about 35 minutes. Cool on a rack. Decorate with whipped cream, if wished.

# Pecan Tart

**SERVES 8**

3 eggs

⅛ teaspoon of salt

1 cup dark brown sugar, firmly packed

½ cup dark corn syrup

2 tablespoons fresh lemon juice

6 tablespoons butter, melted

1½ cups pecans, chopped

½ cup pecan halves

**FOR THE CRUST**

1¼ cups flour

1 tablespoon granulated sugar

1 teaspoon baking powder

½ teaspoon salt

6 tablespoons cold unsalted butter, cut in pieces

1 egg yolk

3–4 tablespoons whipping cream

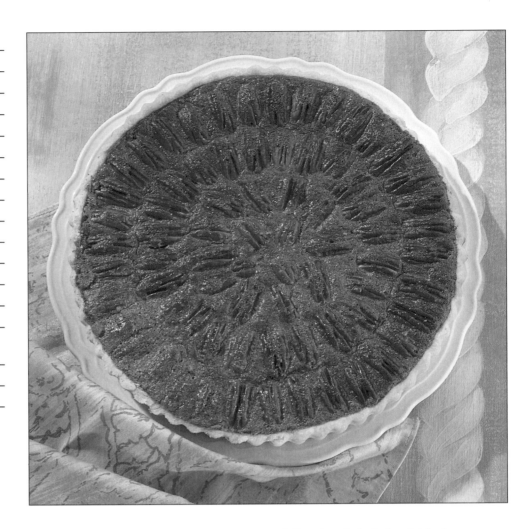

**1** For the crust, sift the flour, sugar, baking powder, and salt into a bowl. Add the butter and cut in with a pastry blender until the mixture resembles coarse crumbs.

**2** ▼ In a bowl, beat together the egg yolk and cream until blended.

**3** ▲ Pour the cream mixture into the flour mixture and stir with a fork.

**4** Gather the dough into a ball. On a lightly floured surface, roll out ⅛ inch thick and transfer to a 9-inch tart pan. Trim the overhang and flute the edge with your fingers. Refrigerate for at least 20 minutes.

**5** Set a baking sheet in the middle of the oven and preheat to 400°F.

**6** In a bowl, lightly whisk the eggs and salt. Add the sugar, corn syrup, lemon juice, and butter. Mix well and stir in the chopped nuts.

**7** ▲ Pour into the pastry shell and arrange the pecan halves in concentric circles on top.

**8** Bake for 10 minutes. Reduce the heat to 325°F; continue baking 25 minutes more.

~ COOK'S TIP ~

Serve this tart warm, accompanied by ice cream or whipped cream, if wished.

# Peach Tart with Almond Cream

**SERVES 8–10**

| |
|---|
| 4 large ripe freestone peaches |
| ⅔ cup blanched almonds |
| 2 tablespoons flour |
| 7 tablespoons unsalted butter, at room temperature |
| ½ cup plus 2 tablespoons sugar |
| 1 egg |
| 1 egg yolk |
| ½ teaspoon vanilla extract, or 2 teaspoons rum |
| FOR THE CRUST |
| 1¼ cups flour |
| ¾ teaspoon salt |
| 7 tablespoons cold unsalted butter, cut in pieces |
| 1 egg yolk |
| 2½–3 tablespoons ice water |

**4 ▲** On a lightly floured surface, roll out the dough ⅛ inch thick. Transfer to a 10-inch tart pan. Trim the edge, prick the bottom and refrigerate.

**5 ▲** Score the bottoms of the peaches. Drop the peaches, one at a time, into boiling water. Boil for 20 seconds, then dip in cold water. Peel off the skins using a sharp knife.

**7 ▲** Halve the peaches and remove the stones. Cut crosswise in thin slices and arrange on top of the almond cream like the spokes of a wheel; keep the slices of each peach half together. Fan out by pressing down gently at a slight angle.

**8 ▲** Bake until the pastry begins to brown, 10–15 minutes. Lower the heat to 350°F and continue baking until the almond cream sets, about 15 minutes more. Ten minutes before the end of the cooking time, sprinkle with the remaining 2 tablespoons of sugar.

**1 ▲** For the crust, sift the flour and salt into a bowl.

**2** Add the butter and cut in with a pastry blender until the mixture resembles coarse crumbs. With a fork, stir in the egg yolk and just enough water to bind the dough. Gather into a ball, wrap in wax paper, and refrigerate for at least 20 minutes.

**3** Place a baking sheet in the oven and preheat to 400°F.

**6 ▲** Grind the almonds finely with the flour in a food processor, blender, or nut grinder. With an electric mixer, cream the butter and ½ cup of the sugar until light and fluffy. Gradually beat in the egg and yolk. Stir in the almonds and vanilla or rum. Spread in the pastry shell.

~ **VARIATION** ~

For a Nectarine and Apricot Tart with Almond Cream, replace the peaches with nectarines, prepared and arranged the same way. Peel and chop 3 fresh apricots. Fill the spaces between the fanned-out nectarines with 1 tablespoon of chopped apricots. Bake as above.

# Almond Syrup Tart

**SERVES 6**

| |
|---|
| 1 cup fresh white bread crumbs |
| 1 cup golden or light corn syrup |
| finely grated zest of ½ lemon |
| 2 teaspoons lemon juice |
| 9-inch pastry shell, made with basic, nut or rich pie pastry |
| 1 ounce sliced almonds |

1  Preheat oven to 400°F.

2 ▲  In a mixing bowl, combine the bread crumbs with the syrup and the lemon zest and juice.

3  Spoon into the pastry shell and spread out evenly.

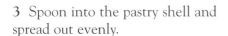

4 ▲  Sprinkle the sliced almonds evenly over the top.

5 ▼  Brush the pastry with milk to glaze, if desired. Bake for 25–30 minutes, or until the pastry and filling are golden brown.

6  Remove to a wire rack to cool. Serve warm or cold, with cream, custard or ice cream.

### ~ VARIATIONS ~

For Walnut Syrup Tart, replace the almonds with chopped walnuts. For Ginger Syrup Tart, mix 1 teaspoon ground ginger with the bread crumbs before adding the syrup and lemon zest and juice. Omit the nuts if desired. For Coconut Syrup Tart, replace ⅓ cup of the bread crumbs with ⅓ cup dried unsweetened coconut.

# Apple Maple Dumplings

**SERVES 8**

| |
|---|
| 4½ cups flour |
| 2 teaspoons salt |
| 1½ cups shortening |
| ¾–1 cup ice water |
| 8 firm, tart-sweet apples |
| 1 egg white |
| ⅔ cup sugar |
| 3 tablespoons whipping cream |
| ½ teaspoon vanilla extract |
| 1 cup maple syrup |
| whipped cream, for serving |

**1** Sift the flour and salt into a large bowl. Using a pastry blender or 2 knives, cut in the shortening until the mixture resembles coarse meal. Sprinkle with ¾ cup water and mix until the dough holds together. If it is too crumbly, add a little more water. Gather into a ball. Wrap in wax paper and refrigerate at least 20 minutes.

**2** Preheat the oven to 425°F.

**3** Peel the apples. Remove the cores, cutting from the stem end, without cutting through the base.

**4 ▲** Roll out the dough thinly. Cut squares almost large enough to enclose the apples. Brush the squares with egg white. Set an apple in the center of each square of dough.

**5** Combine the sugar, cream, and vanilla in a small bowl. Spoon some into the hollow in each apple.

**6 ▼** Pull the points of the dough squares up around the apples and moisten the edges where they overlap. Mold the dough around the apples, pleating the top. Do not cover the center hollows. Crimp the edges tightly to seal.

**7** Set the apples in a large greased baking dish, at least ¾ inch apart. Bake 30 minutes. Lower the oven temperature to 350°F and continue baking until the pastry is golden brown and the apples are tender, about 20 minutes more.

**8** Transfer the dumplings to a serving dish. Mix the maple syrup with the juices in the baking dish and drizzle over the dumplings.

**9** Serve the dumplings hot with whipped cream.

# Apple Strudel

**SERVES 10–12**

½ cup raisins

2 tablespoons brandy

5 eating apples, such as Granny Smith or Jonathan

3 large, tart cooking apples

½ cup dark brown sugar, firmly packed

1 teaspoon ground cinnamon

grated rind and juice of 1 lemon

⅓ cup dry bread crumbs

½ cup pecans, chopped

12 sheets phyllo pastry

¾ cup (1½ sticks) butter, melted

confectioners' sugar, for dusting

whipped cream, for serving

**1** Soak the raisins in the brandy for at least 15 minutes.

**2 ▼** Peel, core, and thinly slice the apples. In a bowl, combine the sugar, cinnamon, and lemon rind. Stir in the apples, and half the bread crumbs.

**3** Add the raisins, nuts and lemon juice and stir until blended.

**4** Preheat the oven to 375°F. Grease 2 baking sheets.

**5 ▲** Carefully unfold the phyllo sheets. Keep the unused sheets covered with wax paper. Lift off one sheet, place on a clean surface, and brush with melted butter. Lay a second sheet on top and brush with butter. Continue until you have a stack of 6 buttered sheets.

**6** Sprinkle a few tablespoons of bread crumbs over the last sheet and spoon half the apple mixture at the bottom edge of the strip.

**7 ▲** Starting at the apple-filled end, roll up the pastry, as for a jelly roll. Place on a baking sheet, seam-side down, and carefully fold under the ends to seal. Repeat the procedure to make a second strudel. Brush both with butter.

**8** Bake the strudels for 45 minutes. Let cool slightly. Using a small sieve, dust with a fine layer of confectioners' sugar. Serve with whipped cream.

# Cherry Strudel

**SERVES 8**

| |
|---|
| 2 cups fresh bread crumbs |
| ¾ cup (1½ sticks) butter, melted |
| 1 cup sugar |
| 1 tablespoon ground cinnamon |
| 1 teaspoon grated lemon rind |
| 4 cups sour cherries, pitted |
| 8 sheets phyllo pastry |
| confectioners' sugar, for dusting |

**1** Lightly fry the bread crumbs in 5 tablespoons of the butter until golden. Set aside to cool.

**2 ▲** In a large mixing bowl, toss together the sugar, cinnamon, and lemon rind.

**3** Stir in the cherries.

**4** Preheat the oven to 375°F. Grease a baking sheet.

**5** Carefully unfold the phyllo sheets. Keep the unused sheets covered with wax paper. Lift off one sheet, place on a flat surface lined with wax paper. Brush the pastry with melted butter. Sprinkle bread crumbs evenly over the surface, using about ¼ cup of crumbs.

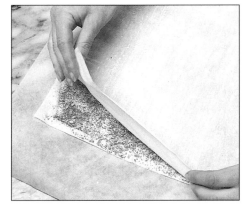

**6 ▲** Lay a second sheet of phyllo on top, brush with butter and sprinkle with crumbs. Continue until you have a stack of 8 buttered sheets.

**7** Spoon the cherry mixture at the bottom edge of the strip. Starting at the cherry-filled end, roll up the dough as for a jelly roll. Use the wax paper to help flip the strudel on to the baking sheet, seam-side down.

**8 ▼** Carefully fold under the ends to seal in the fruit. Brush the top with any remaining butter.

**9** Bake the strudel for 45 minutes. Let cool slightly. Using a small sieve, dust with a fine layer of confectioners' sugar. Serve warm.

# Chicken-Mushroom Pie

**SERVES 6**

½ ounce dried porcini mushrooms

4 tablespoons butter

2 tablespoons flour

1 cup chicken stock, warmed

¼ cup whipping cream or milk

salt and pepper

1 onion, coarsely chopped

2 carrots, sliced

2 celery stalks, coarsely chopped

2 ounces fresh mushrooms, quartered

1 pound cooked chicken meat, cubed

½ cup shelled fresh or frozen peas

beaten egg, for glazing

FOR THE CRUST

2 cups flour

¼ teaspoon salt

½ cup (1 stick) cold butter, cut
    in pieces

⅓ cup shortening

4–8 tablespoons ice water

**1 ▲** For the crust, sift the flour and salt into a bowl. With a pastry blender or 2 knives, cut in the butter and shortening until the mixture resembles coarse meal. Sprinkle with 6 tablespoons ice water and mix until the dough holds together. If the dough is too crumbly, add a little more water, 1 tablespoon at a time. Gather the dough into a ball and flatten into a disk. Wrap in wax paper and refrigerate at least 30 minutes.

**2** Place the porcini mushrooms in a small bowl. Add hot water to cover and soak until soft, about 30 minutes. Lift out of the water with a slotted spoon to leave any grit behind and drain. Discard the soaking water.

**3** Preheat the oven to 375°F.

**4 ▲** Melt 2 tablespoons of the butter in a heavy saucepan. Whisk in the flour and cook until bubbling, whisking constantly. Add the warm stock and cook over medium heat, whisking, until the mixture boils. Cook 2–3 minutes more. Whisk in the cream or milk. Season with salt and pepper. Set aside.

**5 ▲** Heat the remaining butter in a large nonstick skillet until foamy. Add the onion and carrots and cook until softened, about 5 minutes. Add the celery and fresh mushrooms and cook 5 minutes more. Stir in the chicken, peas, and drained porcini mushrooms.

**6** Add the chicken mixture to the cream sauce and stir to mix. Taste for seasoning. Transfer to a 10-cup rectangular baking dish.

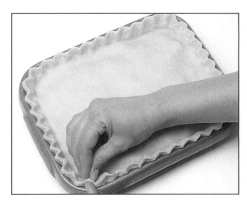

**7 ▲** Roll out the dough to about ⅛-inch thickness. Cut out a rectangle about 1 inch larger all around than the dish. Lay the rectangle of dough over the filling. Make a decorative edge, crimping the dough by pushing the index finger of one hand between the thumb and index finger of the other.

**8** Cut several vents in the top crust to allow steam to escape. Brush with the egg glaze.

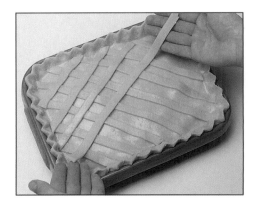

**9 ▲** Press together the dough trimmings, then roll out again. Cut into strips and lay them over the top crust. Glaze again. If desired, roll small balls of dough and set them in the "windows" in the lattice.

**10** Bake until the top crust is browned, about 30 minutes. Serve the pie hot from the dish.

# Ricotta and Basil Tart

**SERVES 8–10**

2 cups basil leaves, tightly packed

1 cup flat-leaf parsley

½ cup extra-virgin olive oil

salt and pepper

2 eggs

1 egg yolk

1¾ pounds ricotta cheese

½ cup black olives, pitted

½ cup freshly grated Parmesan cheese

**FOR THE CRUST**

1¼ cups flour

½ teaspoon salt

6 tablespoons cold butter, cut in pieces

3 tablespoons cold margarine, cut in pieces

3–4 tablespoons ice water

**1 ▲** For the crust, combine the flour and salt in a bowl. Add the butter and margarine.

**2** Cut in with a pastry blender until the mixture resembles coarse crumbs. With a fork, stir in just enough water to bind the dough. Gather into a ball, wrap in wax paper, and refrigerate for at least 20 minutes.

**3** Place a baking sheet in the center of the oven and preheat to 375°F.

**4** Roll out the dough ⅛ inch thick and transfer to a 10-inch tart pan. Prick the base with a fork and line with crumpled wax paper. Fill with pie weights and bake for 12 minutes. Remove the paper and weights and bake until golden, 3–5 minutes more. Lower the heat to 350°F.

**5 ▲** In a food processor, combine the basil, parsley, and olive oil. Season well with salt and pepper and process until finely chopped.

**6** In a bowl, whisk the eggs and yolk to blend. Gently fold in the ricotta.

**7 ▲** Fold in the basil mixture and olives until well combined. Stir in the Parmesan and adjust the seasoning.

**8** Pour into the prebaked shell and bake until set, 30–35 minutes.

# Onion and Anchovy Tart

**SERVES 8**

4 tablespoons olive oil

2 pounds onions, sliced

1 teaspoon dried thyme

salt and pepper

2–3 tomatoes, sliced

24 small black olives, pitted

1 2-ounce can anchovy fillets, drained and sliced

6 sun-dried tomatoes, cut into slivers

**FOR THE CRUST**

1¼ cups flour

½ teaspoon salt

½ cup (1 stick) cold butter, cut in pieces

1 egg yolk

2–3 tablespoons ice water

**3 ▲** Heat the oil in a frying pan. Add the onions, thyme, and seasoning. Cook over low heat, covered, for 25 minutes. Uncover and continue cooking until soft. Let cool. Preheat the oven to 400°F.

**4 ▼** Spoon the onions into the tart shell and top with the tomato slices. Arrange the olives in rows. Make a lattice pattern, alternating lines of anchovies and sun-dried tomatoes. Bake until golden, 20–25 minutes.

**1 ▲** For the crust, sift the flour and salt into a bowl. Cut in the butter with a pastry blender until the mixture resembles coarse crumbs. Stir in the yolk and just enough water to bind.

**2 ▲** Roll out the dough about ⅛ inch thick. Transfer to a 9-inch tart pan, using a rolling pin, and trim the edge. Refrigerate until needed.

# Mushroom Quiche

**SERVES 8**

1 pound fresh mushrooms

2 tablespoons olive oil

1 tablespoon butter

1 clove garlic, finely chopped

1 tablespoon fresh lemon juice

salt and pepper

2 tablespoons finely chopped parsley

3 eggs

1½ cups whipping cream

½ cup freshly grated Parmesan cheese

**FOR THE CRUST**

1¼ cups flour

½ teaspoon salt

6 tablespoons cold butter, cut in pieces

3 tablespoons cold margarine, cut in pieces

3–4 tablespoons ice water

**1** For the crust, sift the flour and salt into a bowl. Cut in the butter and margarine with a pastry blender until the mixture resembles coarse crumbs. Stir in just enough water to bind.

**2** Gather into a ball, wrap in wax paper and refrigerate for 20 minutes.

**3** Place a baking sheet in the center of the oven and preheat to 375°F.

**4** Roll out the dough ⅛ inch thick and transfer to a 9-inch tart pan. Trim the edge. Prick the base all over with a fork. Line with crumpled wax paper and fill with pie weights. Bake for 12 minutes. Remove the paper and weights and continue baking until golden, about 5 minutes more.

**5** ▲ Wipe the mushrooms with a damp paper towel to remove any dirt. Trim the ends of the stalks, place on a cutting board, and slice thinly.

**6** Heat the oil and butter in a frying pan. Stir in the mushrooms, garlic, and lemon juice. Season with salt and pepper. Cook until the mushrooms render their liquid, then raise the heat and cook until dry.

**7** ▼ Stir in the parsley and add more salt and pepper if necessary.

**8** Whisk the eggs and cream together, then stir in the mushrooms. Sprinkle the cheese in the prebaked shell and pour the mushroom filling over the top.

**9** Bake until puffed and brown, about 30 minutes. Serve the quiche warm.

# Bacon and Cheese Quiche

**SERVES 8**

4 ounces medium-thick bacon slices

3 eggs

1½ cups whipping cream

1 cup grated Swiss cheese

⅛ teaspoon grated nutmeg

salt and pepper

**FOR THE CRUST**

1¼ cups flour

½ teaspoon salt

6 tablespoons cold butter, cut in pieces

3 tablespoons cold margarine, cut in pieces

3–4 tablespoons ice water

**1** Make the crust as directed in steps 1–4 above. Maintain the oven temperature at 375°F.

**2** ▲ Fry the bacon until crisp. Drain, then crumble into small pieces. Sprinkle in the pie shell.

**3** ▲ Beat together the eggs, cream, cheese, nutmeg, salt, and pepper. Pour over the bacon and bake until puffed and brown, about 30 minutes. Serve the quiche warm.

*Mushroom Quiche (top), Bacon and Cheese Quiche*

# Asparagus, Corn, and Red Bell Pepper Quiche

**SERVES 6**

½ pound fresh asparagus, woody stalks removed

2 tablespoons butter or margarine

1 small onion, finely chopped

1 red bell pepper, seeded and finely chopped

½ cup drained canned corn or frozen corn, thawed

2 eggs

1 cup light cream

½ cup shredded cheddar cheese

salt and pepper

FOR THE CRUST

1⅔ cups flour

½ teaspoon salt

½ cup shortening

2–3 tablespoons ice water

1  Preheat the oven to 400°F.

2  For the crust, sift the flour and salt into a mixing bowl. Using a pastry blender, cut in the shortening until the mixture resembles coarse crumbs. Sprinkle in the water, 1 tablespoon at a time, tossing lightly with your fingertips or a fork until the dough will form a ball.

3 ▲ On a lightly floured surface, roll out the dough. Use it to line a 10-inch quiche dish or loose-bottomed tart pan, easing the dough in and being careful not to stretch it. Trim off excess dough.

4 ▲  Line the pie shell with wax paper and weigh it down with pie weights or dry beans. Bake 10 minutes. Remove the paper and weights or beans and bake until the pastry shell is set and beige in color, about 5 minutes longer. Let cool.

5  Trim the stem ends of 8 of the asparagus spears to make them 4 inches in length. Set aside.

6 ▲  Finely chop the asparagus trimmings and any remaining spears. Place in the bottom of the pie shell.

7 ▲  Melt the butter or margarine in a frying pan. Add the onion and red bell pepper and cook until softened, about 5 minutes. Stir in the corn and cook 2 minutes longer.

8  Spoon the corn mixture over the chopped asparagus in the pie shell.

9 ▲  In a small bowl, beat the eggs with the cream. Stir in the cheese and salt and pepper to taste. Pour into the pie shell.

10 ▲  Arrange the reserved asparagus spears like the spokes of a wheel on top of the filling.

11  Bake until the filling is set, 25–30 minutes.

~ VARIATION ~

To make individual tartlets, roll out the dough and use to line 12 3-inch tartlet molds. For the filling, cut off and reserve the asparagus tips and chop the tender part of the stalks. Mix the asparagus and the cooked vegetables into the egg mixture with the cheese. Spoon the filling into the molds and bake as directed, decreasing baking time by about 8–10 minutes.

# Cheesy Tomato Quiche

**SERVES 6–8**

10 medium-sized tomatoes

1 2-ounce can anchovy fillets, drained and finely chopped

½ cup whipping cream

2 cups grated Monterey Jack cheese

¾ cup whole-wheat bread crumbs

½ teaspoon dried thyme

salt and pepper

**FOR THE CRUST**

1½ cups flour

½ cup (1 stick) cold butter, cut in pieces

1 egg yolk

2–3 tablespoons ice water

**1** For the crust, sift the flour into a bowl. Cut in the butter with a pastry blender until the mixture resembles coarse crumbs.

**2** ▲ With a fork, stir in the egg yolk and enough water to bind the dough.

**3** Roll out the dough about ⅛ inch thick and transfer to a 9-inch tart pan. Refrigerate until needed. Preheat the oven to 400°F.

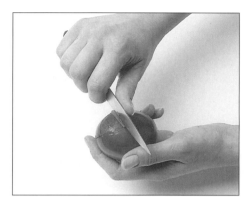

**4** ▲ Score the bottoms of the tomatoes. Plunge in boiling water for 1 minute. Remove and peel off the skin with a knife. Cut in quarters and remove the seeds with a spoon.

**5** ▲ In a bowl, mix the anchovies and cream. Stir in the cheese.

**6** Sprinkle the bread crumbs in the tart. Arrange the tomatoes on top. Season with thyme, salt, and pepper.

**7** ▲ Spoon the cheese mixture on top. Bake until golden, 25–30 minutes. Serve warm.

# Quiche Lorraine

**SERVES 6**

½ pound sliced bacon, cut across into
    ½-inch pieces

9-inch tart shell, made with tart pastry
    and partially baked "blind"

3 eggs

2 egg yolks

1½ cups whipping cream

½ cup milk

salt and pepper

1  Preheat the oven to 400°F.

2 ▲  Fry the bacon over medium heat
until it is crisp and has rendered most
of its fat. Drain on paper towels.

3 ▲  Scatter the bacon in the
partially baked tart shell.

4  Beat together the eggs, egg yolks,
cream, and milk. Season with salt
and pepper.

5 ▼  Pour the egg mixture into the
pastry shell.

6  Bake until the filling is set and
golden brown and the pastry is golden,
35–40 minutes. Serve warm or at
room temperature.

~ **VARIATIONS** ~

Add ¾ cup shredded Gruyère or
Swiss cheese with the bacon.
Replace the bacon with diced
cooked ham, if desired. For a
vegetarian quiche, omit the
bacon. Slice 1 pound zucchini and
fry in a little oil until lightly
browned on both sides. Drain on
paper towels, then arrange in the
tart shell. Scatter ½ cup shredded
cheese on top. Make the egg
mixture with 4 eggs, 1 cup cream,
¼ cup milk, ⅛ teaspoon grated
nutmeg, salt, and pepper.

# Pizza

**MAKES 2**

| |
|---|
| 3½ cups flour |
| 1 teaspoon salt |
| 2 teaspoons active dry yeast |
| 1¼ cups lukewarm water |
| ¼–½ cup extra-virgin olive oil |
| tomato sauce, grated cheese, olives, and herbs, for topping |

**1** Combine the flour and salt in a large mixing bowl. Make a well in the center and add the yeast, water, and 2 tablespoons of the olive oil. Leave for 15 minutes to dissolve the yeast.

**2** With your hands, stir until the dough just holds together. Transfer to a floured surface and knead until smooth and elastic. Avoid adding too much flour while kneading.

**3** ▲ Brush the inside of a clean bowl with 1 tablespoon of the oil. Place the dough in the bowl and roll around to coat with the oil. Cover with a plastic bag and leave to rise in a warm place until more than doubled in volume, about 45 minutes.

**4** Divide the dough into 2 balls. Preheat the oven to 400°F.

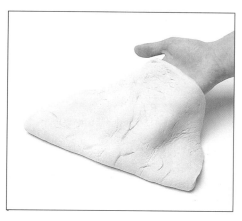

**5** ▲ Roll each ball into a 10-inch circle. Flip the circles over and onto your palm. Set each circle on the work surface and rotate, stretching the dough as you turn, until it is about 12 inches in diameter.

**6** ▲ Brush 2 pizza pans with oil. Place the dough circles in the pans and neaten the edges. Brush with oil.

**7** ▲ Cover with the toppings and bake until golden, 10–12 minutes.

# Onion, Olive, and Anchovy Pizza

**SERVES 4**

| |
|---|
| 6 tablespoons olive oil |
| 1 pound onions, thinly sliced |
| 3 garlic cloves, minced |
| 1 bay leaf |
| 2 teaspoons dried thyme |
| salt and pepper |
| 2 cans anchovy fillets, drained and blotted dry on paper towels |
| 12 olives, mixed black and green, pitted |
| FOR THE PIZZA DOUGH |
| 1 cup whole-wheat flour |
| ¾ cup all-purpose flour |
| 1¼ teaspoons active dry yeast |
| ⅛ teaspoon sugar |
| ⅔ cup tepid water |
| 2 tablespoons olive oil |
| ½ teaspoon salt |

**1** For the pizza dough, in a food processor combine the flours, yeast, and sugar. With the motor running, pour in the tepid water. Turn the motor off. Add the oil and salt. Process until a ball of dough is formed.

**2** Put the dough in an oiled bowl and turn it to coat with oil. Cover and let rise until doubled in bulk.

**3** ▲ Heat 3 tablespoons of the oil in a frying pan. Add the onions, garlic, and herbs. Cook over low heat until the onions are very soft and the moisture has evaporated, about 45 minutes. Season with salt and pepper.

**4** Preheat the oven to 500°F. Oil a 13- × 9-inch baking sheet.

**5** ▼ Transfer the risen dough onto a lightly floured surface. Punch down the dough to deflate it, and knead it briefly. Roll out the dough to a rectangle to fit the baking sheet. Lay the dough on the sheet and press it up to the edges of the pan.

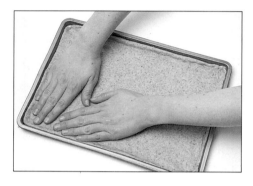

**6** Brush the dough with 1 tablespoon olive oil. Discard the bay leaf, and spoon the onion mixture onto the dough. Spread it out evenly, leaving a ½-inch border clear around the edge.

**7** ▲ Arrange the anchovies and olives on top of the onions. Drizzle the remaining 2 tablespoons olive oil over the top.

**8** Bake the pizza until the edges are puffed and browned, 15–20 minutes.

# Broccoli and Goat Cheese Pizza

**SERVES 2–3**

| |
|---|
| ½ pound broccoli florets |
| 2 tablespoons cornmeal |
| ½ cup tomato sauce |
| 6 cherry tomatoes, halved |
| 12 black olives, pitted |
| ¼ pound goat cheese, crumbled |
| ½ cup freshly grated Parmesan cheese |
| 1 tablespoon olive oil |
| FOR THE PIZZA DOUGH |
| 2–2¼ cups flour |
| 1 package active dry yeast (¼ ounce) |
| ⅛ teaspoon sugar |
| about ⅔ cup tepid water |
| 2 tablespoons olive oil |
| ½ teaspoon salt |

**1** For the pizza dough, combine ¾ cup of the flour, the yeast, and sugar in a food processor. With the motor running, pour in the tepid water. Turn the motor off. Add the olive oil, 1¼ cups of the remaining flour, and the salt.

**2 ▲** Process until a ball of dough is formed, adding more water, 1 teaspoon at a time, if the dough is too dry, or the remaining flour, 1 tablespoon at a time, if it is too wet.

**3 ▲** Put the dough in an oiled bowl and turn it so the ball of dough is oiled all over. Cover the bowl and let the dough rise in a warm place until doubled in bulk, about 1 hour.

**4 ▲** Meanwhile, cook the broccoli florets in boiling salted water or steam them until just tender, about 5 minutes. Drain well and set aside.

**5** Preheat the oven to 500°F. Oil a 12-inch round pizza pan and sprinkle with the cornmeal.

**6** When the dough has risen, turn out onto a lightly floured surface. Punch down the dough to deflate it, and knead it briefly.

> ~ **COOK'S TIP** ~
>
> If more convenient, the pizza dough can be used as soon as it is made, without any rising.

**7 ▲** Roll out the dough to a 12-inch round. Lay the dough on the pizza pan and press it down evenly.

**8 ▲** Spread the tomato sauce evenly onto the pizza base, leaving a rim of dough uncovered around the edge about ½ inch wide.

**9 ▲** Arrange the broccoli florets, tomatoes, and olives on the tomato sauce and sprinkle with the cheeses. Drizzle the olive oil over the top.

**10** Bake until the cheese melts and the edge of the pizza base is puffed and browned, 10–15 minutes.

# CAKES & TORTES

AS TASTY AS THEY ARE BEAUTIFUL, WITH HOMESPUN CHARM OR SOPHISTICATED STYLE, THESE CAKES AND TORTES MAKE ANY OCCASION MEMORABLE. THE SPECIAL SECTION ON DELIGHTFUL PARTY CAKES TAKES THE MYSTERY OUT OF CAKE DECORATION.

# Apple Ring Cake

**SERVES 12**

7 eating apples, such as Jonathan or
　Granny Smith

1½ cups vegetable oil

2 cups sugar

3 eggs

3 cups flour

1 teaspoon salt

1 teaspoon baking soda

1 teaspoon ground cinnamon

1 teaspoon vanilla extract

1 cup walnuts, chopped

1 cup raisins

confectioners' sugar, for dusting

**1** Preheat the oven to 350°F. Grease
a 9-inch tube pan.

**2 ▲** Quarter, peel, core, and slice
the apples into a bowl. Set aside.

**3** With an electric mixer, beat the oil
and sugar together until blended. Add
the eggs and continue beating until
the mixture is creamy.

**4** Sift together the flour, salt, baking
soda, and cinnamon.

**5 ▼** Fold the flour mixture into the
egg mixture with the vanilla. Stir in
the apples, walnuts, and raisins.

**6** Pour into the pan and bake until
the cake springs back when touched
lightly, about 1¼ hours. Let stand 15
minutes, then unmold and transfer to
a cooling rack. Dust with a layer of
confectioners' sugar before serving.

# Orange Cake

**SERVES 6**

1¼ cups flour

1½ teaspoons baking powder

⅛ teaspoon salt

½ cup (1 stick) butter or margarine

½ cup sugar

grated rind of 1 large orange

2 eggs, at room temperature

2 tablespoons milk

FOR THE SYRUP AND DECORATION

½ cup sugar

1 cup fresh orange juice, strained

3 orange slices, for decorating

**1** Preheat the oven to 350°F. Line an
8-inch cake pan with wax paper and
grease.

**2 ▲** Sift the flour, salt, and baking
powder onto a square of wax paper.

**3** With an electric mixer, cream the
butter or margarine until soft. Add the
sugar and orange rind and continue
beating until light and fluffy. Beat in
the eggs, 1 at a time. Fold in the flour
in 3 batches, then add the milk.

**4** Spoon into the pan and bake until
the cake pulls away from the sides,
about 30 minutes. Remove from the
oven but leave in the pan.

**5** Meanwhile, for the syrup, dissolve
the sugar in the orange juice over low
heat. Add the orange slices and
simmer for 10 minutes. Remove and
drain. Let the syrup cool.

**6 ▲** Prick the cake all over with a
fine skewer. Pour the syrup over the
hot cake. It may seem at first that
there is too much syrup for the cake to
absorb, but it will soak it all up.
Unmold when completely cooled and
decorate with small triangles of the
orange slices arranged on top.

*Apple Ring Cake (top), Orange Cake*

# Angel Food Cake

**SERVES 12–14**

| |
|---|
| 1 cup sifted cake flour |
| 1½ cups superfine sugar |
| 1¼ cups egg whites (about 10–11 eggs) |
| 1¼ teaspoons cream of tartar |
| ¼ teaspoon salt |
| 1 teaspoon vanilla extract |
| ¼ teaspoon almond extract |
| confectioners' sugar, for dusting |

**1** Preheat the oven to 325°F.

**2 ▼** Sift the flour before measuring, then sift it 4 times with ½ cup of the sugar. Transfer to a bowl.

**3** With an electric mixer, beat the egg whites until foamy. Sift over the cream of tartar and salt and continue to beat until they hold soft peaks when the beaters are lifted.

**4 ▲** Add the remaining sugar in 3 batches, beating well after each addition. Stir in the vanilla and almond extracts.

**5 ▲** Add the flour mixture, ½ cup at a time, and fold in with a large metal spoon after each addition.

**6** Transfer to an ungreased 10-inch tube pan and bake until delicately browned on top, about 1 hour.

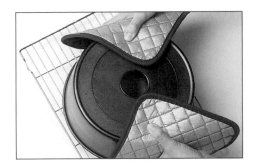

**7 ▲** Turn the pan upside down onto a cake rack and let cool for 1 hour. If the cake does not unmold, run a spatula around the edge to loosen it. Invert on a serving plate.

**8** When cool, lay a star-shaped template on top of the cake, sift over confectioners' sugar, and lift off.

# Black and White Pound Cake

**SERVES 16**

4 1-ounce squares semisweet chocolate

3 cups flour

1 teaspoon baking powder

2 cups (4 sticks) butter, at room temperature

3⅓ cups sugar

1 tablespoon vanilla extract

10 eggs, at room temperature

confectioners' sugar, for dusting

**1 ▲** Preheat the oven to 350°F. Line the bottom of a 10-inch tube pan with wax paper and grease. Dust with flour and spread evenly with a brush.

**2 ▲** Melt the chocolate in the top of a double boiler, or in a heatproof bowl set over a pan of hot water. Stir occasionally. Set aside.

**3** In a bowl, sift together the flour and baking powder. In another bowl, cream the butter, sugar, and vanilla with an electric mixer until light and fluffy. Add the eggs, 2 at a time, then gradually incorporate the flour mixture on low speed.

**4 ▲** Spoon half of the batter into the prepared pan.

**5 ▲** Stir the chocolate into the remaining batter, then spoon into the pan. With a metal spatula, swirl the two batters to create a marbled effect.

**6** Bake until a cake tester inserted in the center comes out clean, about 1 hour 45 minutes. Cover with foil halfway through baking. Let stand 15 minutes, then unmold and transfer to a cooling rack. To serve, dust with confectioners' sugar.

# Carrot Cake with Cream Cheese Frosting

**SERVES 10**

2 cups granulated sugar

1 cup vegetable oil

4 eggs

2 cups finely grated carrots
(about ½ pound)

2 cups flour

1½ teaspoons baking soda

1½ teaspoons baking powder

1 teaspoon ground allspice

1 teaspoon ground cinnamon

FOR THE FROSTING

2 cups confectioners' sugar

1 8-ounce package cream cheese, at
room temperature

4 tablespoons butter or margarine, at
room temperature

2 teaspoons vanilla extract

1½ cups walnut pieces or pecans,
chopped

**1** Preheat the oven to 375°F. Butter and flour 2 9-inch round cake pans.

**2 ▲** In a mixing bowl, combine the granulated sugar, vegetable oil, eggs, and carrots.

**3** Sift the dry ingredients into another bowl. Add by ½-cup measures to the carrot mixture, mixing well after each addition.

**4 ▲** Divide the batter evenly between the prepared cake pans. Bake until a cake tester inserted in the center comes out clean, 35–40 minutes.

**5** Let cool in the pans on wire racks for 10 minutes, then unmold the cakes from the pans onto the wire racks and let cool completely.

**6** For the frosting, combine everything but the nuts in a bowl and beat until smooth.

**7 ▲** To assemble, set 1 cake layer on a serving plate and spread with one-third of the frosting. Place the second cake layer on top. Spread the remaining frosting all over the top and sides of the cake, swirling it to make a decorative finish. Sprinkle the nuts around the top edge.

# Pound Cake

**SERVES 12**

| |
|---|
| 2 cups flour |
| 1 teaspoon baking powder |
| 1 cup (2 sticks) butter or margarine, at room temperature |
| 1 cup sugar |
| grated rind of 1 lemon |
| 1 teaspoon vanilla extract |
| 4 eggs |

**1** Preheat the oven to 325°F. Grease a 9- × 5-inch loaf pan.

**2** Sift the flour and baking powder into a small bowl. Set aside.

**3** ▲ With an electric mixer, cream the butter or margarine, adding the sugar 2 tablespoons at a time, until light and fluffy. Stir in the lemon rind and vanilla.

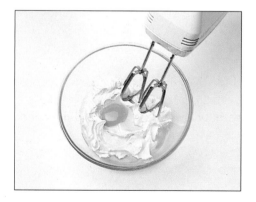

**4** ▲ Add the eggs one at a time, beating for 1 minute after each addition.

**5** ▼ Add the flour mixture and stir until just combined.

**6** ▲ Pour the batter into the pan and tap lightly. Bake until a cake tester inserted in the center comes out clean, about 1¼ hours.

**7** Let cool in the pan on a wire rack for 10 minutes, then unmold the cake from the pan onto the wire rack and let cool completely.

# Lemon Yogurt Coffee Cake

**SERVES 12**

1 cup (2 sticks) butter, at room temperature

1½ cups granulated sugar

4 eggs, at room temperature, separated

2 teaspoons grated lemon rind

⅓ cup fresh lemon juice

1 cup plain yogurt

2 cups flour

2 teaspoons baking powder

1 teaspoon baking soda

½ teaspoon salt

FOR THE GLAZE

1 cup confectioners' sugar

2 tablespoons fresh lemon juice

3–4 tablespoons plain yogurt

**1** Preheat the oven to 350°F. Grease a 12-cup bundt or tube pan and dust with flour.

**2** With an electric mixer, cream the butter and granulated sugar until light and fluffy. Add the egg yolks, 1 at a time, beating well after each addition.

**3** ▲ Add the lemon rind, juice, and yogurt and stir to blend.

**4** Sift together the flour, baking powder, and baking soda. Set aside. In another bowl, beat the egg whites and salt until they hold stiff peaks.

**5** ▲ Fold the dry ingredients into the butter mixture, then fold in a dollop of egg whites. Fold in the remaining whites until blended.

**6** Pour into the pan and bake until a cake tester inserted in the center comes out clean, about 50 minutes. Let stand 15 minutes, then unmold and transfer to a cooling rack.

**7** For the glaze, sift the confectioners' sugar into a bowl. Stir in the lemon juice and just enough yogurt to make a smooth glaze.

**8** ▲ Set the cooled cake on a rack over a sheet of wax paper or a baking sheet. Pour over the glaze and let it drip down the sides. Allow the glaze to set before serving.

# Banana Lemon Layer Cake

**SERVES 8–10**

2¼ cups cake flour

1¼ teaspoons baking powder

½ teaspoon salt

½ cup (1 stick) butter, at room temperature

1 cup granulated sugar

½ cup light brown sugar, firmly packed

2 eggs

½ teaspoon grated lemon rind

1 cup mashed very ripe bananas

1 teaspoon vanilla extract

¼ cup milk

¾ cup chopped walnuts

**FOR THE FROSTING**

½ cup (1 stick) butter, at room temperature

4½ cups confectioners' sugar

¾ teaspoon grated lemon rind

3–5 tablespoons fresh lemon juice

**1**  Preheat the oven to 350°F. Grease 2 9-inch round cake pans, and line the bottom of each with a disk of greased wax paper.

**2**  Sift the flour with the baking powder and salt.

**3** ▲  In a large mixing bowl, cream the butter with the sugars until light and fluffy. Beat in the eggs, one at a time. Stir in the lemon rind.

**4** ▲  In a small bowl mix the mashed bananas with the vanilla and milk. Add the banana mixture and the dry ingredients to the butter mixture alternately in 2 or 3 batches and stir until just blended. Fold in the nuts.

**5**  Divide the batter between the cake pans and spread it out evenly. Bake until a cake tester inserted in the center comes out clean, 30–35 minutes. Let stand 5 minutes before unmolding onto a wire rack. Peel off the wax paper.

**6**  For the frosting, cream the butter until smooth, then gradually beat in the sugar. Stir in the lemon rind and enough juice to make a spreadable consistency.

**7** ▼  Set one of the cake layers on a serving plate. Cover with about one-third of the frosting. Top with the second cake layer. Spread the remaining frosting evenly over the top and sides of the cake.

# Light Fruit Cake

**MAKES 2 LOAVES**

8 ounces ready-to-eat prunes

8 ounces dates

8 ounces currants

8 ounces golden raisins

1 cup dry white wine

1 cup rum

3 cups flour

2 teaspoons baking powder

1 teaspoon ground cinnamon

½ teaspoon grated nutmeg

1 cup (2 sticks) butter, at room temperature

1 cup sugar

4 eggs, at room temperature, lightly beaten

1 teaspoon vanilla extract

**1** Pit the prunes and dates and chop finely. Place in a bowl with the currants and raisins.

**2 ▲** Stir in the wine and rum and let stand, covered, for 48 hours. Stir occasionally.

**3** Preheat the oven to 300°F. Line 2 9- × 5- × 3-inch pans with wax paper and grease. Place a tray of hot water on the bottom of the oven.

**4** Sift together the flour, baking powder, cinnamon, and nutmeg.

**5 ▲** With an electric mixer, cream the butter and sugar together until light and fluffy.

**6** Gradually add the eggs and vanilla. Fold in the flour mixture in 3 batches. Fold in the dried fruit mixture and its macerating liquid.

**7 ▲** Divide the batter between the pans and bake until a cake tester inserted in the center comes out clean, about 1½ hours.

**8** Let stand 20 minutes, then unmold and transfer to a cooling rack. Wrap in foil or wax paper and store in an airtight container. If possible, leave for at least 1 week before serving to allow the flavors to mellow.

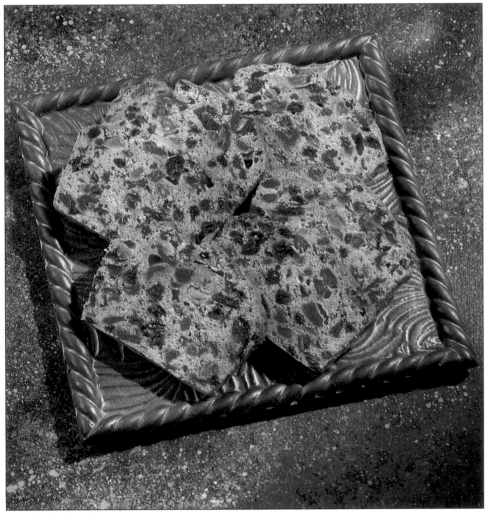

# Dark Fruit Cake

**SERVES 12**

| |
|---|
| 1 cup currants |
| 1 cup raisins |
| ⅔ cup golden raisins |
| ¼ cup candied cherries, halved |
| 3 tablespoons Madeira or sherry wine |
| ¾ cup (1½ sticks) butter |
| 1 cup dark brown sugar, firmly packed |
| 2 extra-large eggs, at room temperature |
| 1⅔ cups flour |
| 2 teaspoons baking powder |
| 2 teaspoons each ground ginger, allspice, and cinnamon |
| 1 tablespoon dark corn syrup |
| 1 tablespoon milk |
| ¼ cup mixed candied fruit, chopped |
| 1 cup walnuts or pecans, chopped |
| FOR THE DECORATION |
| 1 cup sugar |
| ½ cup water |
| 1 lemon, thinly sliced |
| ½ orange, thinly sliced |
| ½ cup orange marmalade |
| candied cherries |

**1** One day before preparing, combine the currants, both raisins, and the cherries in a bowl. Stir in the Madeira or sherry. Cover and let stand overnight to macerate.

**2** Preheat the oven to 300°F. Line a 9- × 3-inch springform pan with wax paper and grease. Place a tray of hot water on the bottom of the oven.

**3** With an electric mixer, cream the butter and sugar until light and fluffy. Beat in the eggs, 1 at a time.

**4** ▲ Sift the flour, baking powder, and spices together 3 times. Fold into the butter mixture in 3 batches. Fold in the corn syrup, milk, dried fruit and liquid, candied fruit, and nuts.

**5** ▲ Spoon into the pan, spreading out so there is a slight depression in the center of the batter.

**6** Bake until a cake tester inserted in the center comes out clean, 2½–3 hours. Cover with foil when the top is golden to prevent overbrowning. Cool in the pan on a rack.

**7** ▲ For the decoration, combine the sugar and water in a saucepan and bring to a boil. Add the lemon and orange slices and cook until candied, about 20 minutes. Work in batches, if necessary. Remove the fruit with a slotted spoon. Pour the remaining syrup over the cake and let cool. Melt the marmalade over low heat, then brush over the top of the cake. Decorate with the candied citrus slices and cherries.

# Ginger Cake with Spiced Whipped Cream

**SERVES 9**

1½ cups flour

2 teaspoons baking powder

½ teaspoon salt

2 teaspoons ground ginger

2 teaspoons ground cinnamon

1 teaspoon ground cloves

¼ teaspoon grated nutmeg

2 eggs

1 cup granulated sugar

1 cup whipping cream

1 teaspoon vanilla extract

confectioners' sugar, for sprinkling

**FOR THE SPICED WHIPPED CREAM**

¾ cup whipping cream

1 teaspoon confectioners' sugar

¼ teaspoon ground cinnamon

¼ teaspoon ground ginger

⅛ teaspoon grated nutmeg

**1** Preheat the oven to 350°F. Grease a 9-inch square baking pan.

**2** Sift the flour, baking powder, salt, ginger, cinnamon, cloves, and nutmeg into a bowl. Set aside.

**3** ▲ With an electric mixer, beat the eggs on high speed until very thick, about 5 minutes. Gradually beat in the granulated sugar.

**4** ▲ With the mixer on low speed, beat in the flour mixture alternately with the cream, beginning and ending with the flour. Stir in the vanilla.

**5** ▲ Pour the batter into the prepared pan and bake until the top springs back when touched lightly, 35–40 minutes. Let cool in the pan on a wire rack for 10 minutes.

**6** ▲ Meanwhile, to make the spiced whipped cream, combine the ingredients in a bowl and whip until the cream will hold soft peaks.

**7** Sprinkle confectioners' sugar over the hot cake, cut in 9 squares, and serve with spiced whipped cream.

# Rich, Sticky Gingerbread

**MAKES AN 8-INCH SQUARE CAKE**

| |
| --- |
| 2 cups all-purpose flour |
| pinch of salt |
| 1 teaspoon baking soda |
| 2 teaspoons ground ginger |
| 1 teaspoon apple-pie spice |
| 8 tablespoons butter or margarine |
| ½ cup golden syrup or corn syrup |
| ½ cup molasses |
| ¼ cup dark brown sugar |
| 2 eggs, beaten |
| ½ cup milk |
| 4 ounces golden raisins or chopped preserved ginger (optional) |
| FOR THE ICING (OPTIONAL) |
| ½ cup confectioners' sugar |
| about 4 teaspoons water |

**1** ▲ Preheat oven to 350°F. Grease and line an 8-inch square cake pan.

**2** ▲ Sift the flour, salt, baking soda and spices into a bowl.

**3** Put the butter or margarine, syrup, molasses and brown sugar in a saucepan and warm over gentle heat, stirring occasionally, until the fat has melted and the mixture is smooth. Remove from the heat and let cool slightly.

**4** ▼ Make a well in the center of the dry ingredients and add the melted mixture, the beaten eggs and milk. Beat with a wooden spoon until the mixture is smooth. Add the golden raisins or ginger, if using.

**5** Turn the cake mixture into the prepared pan. Bake for about 1 hour. To test if the gingerbread is done, press it lightly in the center; it should spring back. Allow to cool in the pan for 5 minutes before turning out onto a wire rack to cool completely.

**6** ▲ If icing the gingerbread, sift the confectioners' sugar into a bowl and add 3 teaspoons of the water. Stir to mix, then add more water, 1 teaspoon at a time, until the icing is smooth and a pouring consistency. Pour the icing over the gingerbread and allow to set before serving.

# Black Walnut Layer Cake

**Serves 8**

2 cups cake flour

1 tablespoon baking powder

½ teaspoon salt

½ cup (1 stick) butter or margarine,
　at room temperature

1 cup granulated sugar

2 eggs

1 teaspoon grated orange rind

1 teaspoon vanilla extract

1 cup minced black walnut pieces

¾ cup milk

black walnut halves, for decoration

**For the frosting**

½ cup (1 stick) butter

¾ cup light brown sugar, firmly packed

3 tablespoons maple syrup

¼ cup milk

1¾–2 cups confectioners' sugar, sifted

**1 ▲** Grease 2 8- × 2-inch cake pans and line the bottoms of each with a disk of greased wax paper. Preheat the oven to 375°F.

**2** Sift together the flour, baking powder, and salt.

~ **VARIATION** ~

If black walnuts are unavailable, substitute regular walnuts, or use pecans instead.

**3 ▲** Beat the butter or margarine to soften, then gradually beat in the granulated sugar until light and fluffy. Beat in the eggs, one at a time. Add the orange rind and vanilla and beat to mix well.

**4 ▲** Stir in the minced walnuts. Add the flour alternately with the milk, stirring only enough to blend after each addition.

**5 ▲** Divide the batter between the prepared cake pans. Bake until a cake tester inserted in the center comes out clean, about 25 minutes. Cool in the cake pans for 5 minutes before unmolding onto a wire rack.

**6 ▲** For the frosting, melt the butter in a medium-size saucepan. Add the brown sugar and maple syrup and boil 2 minutes, stirring constantly.

**7 ▲** Add the milk. Bring back to a boil and stir in ¼ cup of the confectioners' sugar. Remove from the heat and let cool to lukewarm. Gradually beat in the remaining confectioners' sugar. Set the pan in a bowl of ice water and stir until the frosting is thick enough to spread.

**8 ▲** Spread some of the frosting on one of the cake layers. Set the other layer on top. Spread the remaining frosting over the top and sides of the cake. Decorate with walnut halves.

# Chiffon Cake

**SERVES 16**

| |
|---|
| 2 cups flour |
| 1 tablespoon baking powder |
| 1 teaspoon salt |
| 1½ cups sugar |
| ½ cup vegetable oil |
| 7 eggs, at room temperature, separated |
| ¾ cup cold water |
| 2 teaspoons vanilla extract |
| 2 teaspoons grated lemon rind |
| ½ teaspoon cream of tartar |

FOR THE FROSTING

| |
|---|
| ⅔ cup (10⅔ tablespoons) unsalted butter, at room temperature |
| 5 cups confectioners' sugar |
| 4 teaspoons instant coffee dissolved in 4 tablespoons hot water |

**1** Preheat the oven to 325°F.

**2** ▼ Sift the flour, baking powder, and salt into a bowl. Stir in 1 cup of the sugar. Make a well in the center and add in the following order: oil, egg yolks, water, vanilla, and lemon rind. Beat with a whisk or metal spoon until the mixture is smooth.

**3** With an electric mixer, beat the egg whites with the cream of tartar until they hold soft peaks. Add the remaining ½ cup of sugar and beat until they hold stiff peaks.

**4** ▲ Pour the flour mixture over the whites in 3 batches, folding well after each addition.

**5** Transfer the batter to an ungreased 10- × 4-inch tube pan and bake until the top springs back when touched lightly, about 1 hour and 10 minutes.

**6** ▲ When baked, remove from the oven and immediately hang the cake upside-down over the neck of a funnel or a narrow bottle. Let cool. To remove the cake, run a knife around the inside to loosen, then turn the pan over and tap the sides sharply. Invert the cake onto a serving plate.

**7** For the frosting, beat together the butter and confectioners' sugar with an electric mixer until smooth. Add the coffee and beat until fluffy. With a metal spatula, spread over the sides and top of the cake.

# Forgotten Torte

**SERVES 6**

6 egg whites, at room temperature

½ teaspoon cream of tartar

⅛ teaspoon salt

1½ cups granulated sugar

1 teaspoon vanilla extract

¾ cup whipping cream

FOR THE SAUCE

12 ounces fresh or thawed frozen raspberries

2–3 tablespoons confectioners' sugar

**1** Preheat the oven to 450°F. Generously grease a 6-cup ring mold.

**2 ▲** With an electric mixer, beat the egg whites, cream of tartar, and salt until they hold soft peaks. Gradually add the sugar and beat until glossy and stiff. Fold in the vanilla.

**3 ▲** Spoon into the prepared pan and smooth the top level.

**4** Place in the oven, then turn the oven off. Leave overnight; do not open the oven door at any time.

**5 ▼** To serve, gently loosen the edge with a sharp knife and unmold onto a serving plate. Whip the cream until firm. Spread it over the top and upper sides of the meringue and decorate with any meringue crumbs.

**6 ▲** For the sauce, purée the fruit, then strain. Sweeten to taste.

~ **COOK'S TIP** ~

This recipe is not suitable for fan-assisted and solid fuel ovens.

# Pecan-Apple Torte

**SERVES 8**

1 cup pecan halves

½ cup flour

2 teaspoons baking powder

¼ teaspoon salt

2 large cooking apples

3 eggs

1 cup sugar

1 teaspoon vanilla extract

¾ cup whipping cream

**1** Preheat the oven to 325°F. Line 2 9-inch cake pans with wax paper and grease. Spread the pecans on a baking sheet and bake for 10 minutes.

**2** Finely chop the pecans. Reserve 1½ tablespoons and place the rest in a mixing bowl. Sift over the flour, baking powder, and salt and stir.

**3 ▲** Quarter, core, and peel the apples. Cut into ⅛-inch dice, then stir into the pecan-flour mixture.

**4 ▲** With an electric mixer, beat the eggs until frothy. Gradually add the sugar and vanilla and beat until a ribbon forms, about 8 minutes. Gently fold in the flour mixture.

**5** Pour into the pans and level the tops. Bake until a cake tester inserted in the center comes out clean, about 35 minutes. Let stand 10 minutes.

**6 ▲** To loosen, run a knife around the inside edge of each pan. Let cool.

**7 ▲** Whip the cream until firm. Spread half over the cake. Top with the second cake. Pipe whipped cream rosettes on top and sprinkle over the reserved pecans before serving.

# Almond Cake

**SERVES 4–6**

| |
|---|
| 1½ cups blanched whole almonds, plus more for decorating |
| 2 tablespoons butter |
| ¾ cup confectioners' sugar |
| 3 eggs |
| ½ teaspoon almond extract |
| ¼ cup flour |
| 3 egg whites |
| 1 tablespoon granulated sugar |

**1 ▲** Preheat the oven to 325°F. Line a 9-inch round cake pan with wax paper and grease.

**2 ▲** Spread the almonds in a baking tray and toast for 10 minutes. Cool, then coarsely chop 1½ cups.

**3** Melt the butter and set aside.

**4** Preheat the oven to 400°F.

**5** Grind the chopped almonds with half the confectioners' sugar in a food processor, blender, or nut grinder. Transfer to a mixing bowl.

**6 ▲** Add the whole eggs and remaining confectioners' sugar. With an electric mixer, beat until the mixture forms a ribbon when the beaters are lifted. Mix in the butter and almond extract. Sift over the flour and fold in gently.

**7** With an electric mixer, beat the egg whites until they hold soft peaks. Add the granulated sugar and beat until stiff and glossy.

**8 ▲** Fold the whites into the almond mixture in 4 batches.

**9** Spoon the batter into the prepared pan and bake in the center of the oven until golden brown, about 15–20 minutes. Decorate the top with the remaining toasted whole almonds. Serve warm.

# Walnut Coffee Torte

**SERVES 8–10**

| |
|---|
| 1¼ cups walnuts |
| ¾ cup sugar |
| 5 eggs, separated |
| ⅓ cup dry bread crumbs |
| 1 tablespoon unsweetened cocoa powder |
| 1 tablespoon instant coffee |
| 2 tablespoons rum or lemon juice |
| ⅛ teaspoon salt |
| 6 tablespoons concord grape or red currant jelly |
| chopped walnuts, for decorating |
| FOR THE FROSTING |
| 8 1-ounce squares bittersweet chocolate |
| 3 cups whipping cream |

**3 ▲** Grind the nuts with 3 tablespoons of the sugar in a food processor, blender, or nut grinder.

**4** With an electric mixer, beat the egg yolks and remaining sugar until thick and lemon-colored.

**5 ▲** Fold in the walnuts. Stir in the bread crumbs, cocoa, coffee, and rum or lemon juice.

**6 ▲** In another bowl, beat the egg whites with the salt until they hold stiff peaks. Fold carefully into the walnut mixture with a rubber spatula.

**7** Pour the meringue batter into the prepared pan and bake until the top of the cake springs back when touched lightly, about 45 minutes. Let the cake stand for 5 minutes, then unmold and transfer to a rack.

**8 ▲** When cool, slice the cake in half horizontally.

**9** With an electric mixer, beat the chocolate frosting mixture on low speed until it becomes lighter, about 30 seconds. Do not overbeat or it may become grainy.

**10 ▲** Warm the jelly in a saucepan until melted, then brush over the cut cake layer. Spread with some of the chocolate frosting, then sandwich with the remaining cake layer. Brush the top of the cake with jelly, then cover the sides and top with the remaining chocolate frosting. Make a starburst pattern by pressing gently with a table knife in lines radiating from the center. Sprinkle the chopped walnuts around the edge.

**1 ▲** For the frosting, combine the chocolate and cream in the top of a double boiler, or in a heatproof bowl set over simmering water. Stir until the chocolate dissolves. Let cool, then cover and refrigerate until the mixture is firm, or overnight.

**2** Preheat the oven to 350°F. Line a 9- × 2-inch cake pan with wax paper and grease.

# Coconut Angel Food Cake

**SERVES 10**

1½ cups confectioners' sugar

1 cup cake flour

1½ cups egg whites (about 12 egg whites)

1½ teaspoons cream of tartar

1 cup granulated sugar

¼ teaspoon salt

2 teaspoons almond extract

1 cup flaked coconut

FOR THE FROSTING

2 egg whites

½ cup granulated sugar

¼ teaspoon salt

2 tablespoons cold water

2 teaspoons almond extract

2 cups flaked coconut, toasted

**1 ▲** Preheat the oven to 350°F. Sift the confectioners' sugar and flour into a bowl. Set aside.

**2** With an electric mixer, beat the egg whites with the cream of tartar on medium speed until very thick. Turn the mixer to high speed and beat in the granulated sugar, 2 tablespoons at a time, reserving 2 tablespoons.

**3 ▲** Continue beating until stiff and glossy. Swiftly beat in the reserved 2 tablespoons of sugar, along with the salt and almond extract.

**4 ▲** Using a ¼-cup measure, sprinkle the flour mixture over the meringue, quickly folding until just combined. Fold in the flaked coconut in 2 batches.

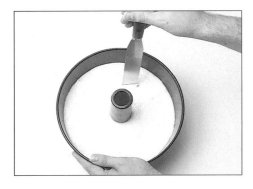

**5 ▲** Transfer the batter to an ungreased 10-inch angel cake pan, and cut gently through the batter with a metal spatula. Bake until the top of the cake springs back when touched lightly, 30–35 minutes.

**6 ▲** As soon as the cake is done, turn the pan upside down and suspend its funnel over the neck of a funnel or bottle. Let cool, about 1 hour.

**7 ▲** For the frosting, combine the egg whites, sugar, salt, and water in a heatproof bowl. Beat with an electric mixer until blended. Set the bowl over a pan of boiling water and continue beating on medium speed until the frosting is stiff, about 3 minutes. Remove the pan from the heat and stir in the almond extract.

**8 ▲** Unmold the cake onto a serving plate. Spread the frosting gently over the top and sides of the cake. Sprinkle with the toasted coconut.

# Lemon Coconut Layer Cake

**SERVES 8–10**

| |
|---|
| 1 cup flour |
| ⅛ teaspoon salt |
| 8 eggs |
| 1¾ cups granulated sugar |
| 1 tablespoon grated orange rind |
| grated rind of 2 lemons |
| juice of 1 lemon |
| ½ cup shredded coconut |
| 2 tablespoons cornstarch |
| 1 cup water |
| 6 tablespoons butter |
| FOR THE FROSTING |
| ½ cup (1 stick) unsalted butter, at room temperature |
| 1 cup confectioners' sugar |
| grated rind of 1 lemon |
| 6–8 tablespoons fresh lemon juice |
| 1 4-ounce can shredded coconut |

**1** Preheat the oven to 350°F. Line 3 8-inch cake pans with wax paper and grease. In a bowl, sift together the flour and salt and set aside.

**2** ▲ Place 6 of the eggs in a large heatproof bowl set over hot water. With an electric mixer, beat until frothy. Gradually beat in ¾ cup of the granulated sugar until the mixture doubles in volume and is thick enough to leave a ribbon trail when the beaters are lifted, about 10 minutes.

**3** ▲ Remove the bowl from the hot water. Fold in the orange rind, half the grated lemon rind, and 1 tablespoon of the lemon juice until blended. Fold in the coconut.

**4** Sift over the flour mixture in 3 batches, folding in thoroughly after each addition.

**5** ▲ Divide the mixture between the prepared pans

**6** Bake until the cakes pull away from the sides of the pan, 25–30 minutes. Let stand 3–5 minutes, then unmold and transfer to a cooling rack.

**7** In a bowl, blend the cornstarch with a little cold water to dissolve. Whisk in the remaining eggs just until blended. Set aside.

**8** ▲ In a saucepan, combine the remaining lemon rind and juice, the water, remaining sugar, and butter.

**9** Over a moderate heat, bring the mixture to a boil. Whisk in the eggs and cornstarch, and return to a boil. Whisk continuously until thick, about 5 minutes. Remove from the heat. Cover with wax paper to stop a skin forming and set aside.

**10** ▲ For the frosting, cream the butter and confectioners' sugar until smooth. Stir in the lemon rind and enough lemon juice to obtain a thick, spreadable consistency.

**11** Sandwich the 3 cake layers with the lemon custard mixture. Spread the frosting over the top and sides. Cover the cake with the coconut, pressing it in gently.

# Coconut Lime Layer Cake

**Serves 8 or more**

| |
|---|
| 2½ cups cake flour |
| 2½ teaspoons baking powder |
| ¼ teaspoon salt |
| 10 tablespoons butter, at room temperature |
| 1½ cups sugar |
| 2 teaspoons grated lime rind |
| 3 eggs |
| ½ cup fresh lime juice (from about 4–5 limes) |
| ½ cup water |
| ¾ cup sweetened flaked coconut |
| 1 recipe quantity seven-minute frosting |

1  Preheat the oven to 350°F. Grease two 9-inch layer cake pans and line the bottoms with greased wax or parchment paper.

2  Sift together the flour, baking powder, and salt.

3  In a large bowl, beat the butter until it is soft and pliable. Add the sugar and lime rind and beat until the mixture is pale and fluffy. Beat in the eggs, one at a time.

4 ▲  Beat in the sifted dry ingredients in small portions, alternating with the lime juice and water. When the mixture is smooth, gently stir in ½ cup of the coconut.

5 ▲  Divide the batter between the prepared pans and spread it evenly to the sides. Bake the cake layers until done, 30–35 minutes.

6 ▲  Remove the cake layers from the oven and set them, in their pans, on a wire rack. Let cool 10 minutes. Then unmold and peel off the lining paper. Cool completely on the rack.

7 ▲  Spread the remaining coconut in another cake pan. Bake until golden brown, stirring occasionally. Watch carefully so that the coconut does not get too dark. Let cool.

8 ▲  Put one of the cake layers, base up, on a serving plate. Spread a layer of frosting evenly over the cake.

9 ▲  Set the second layer on top, base down. Spread the remaining frosting all over the top and around sides of the cake.

10 ▲  Scatter the toasted coconut over the top of the cake and let set before serving.

# Cranberry Upside-Down Cake

**SERVES 8**

12–14 ounces fresh cranberries

4 tablespoons butter

⅔ cup sugar

FOR THE BATTER

⅔ cup flour

1 teaspoon baking powder

3 eggs

½ cup sugar

grated rind of 1 orange

3 tablespoons butter, melted

**1** Preheat the oven to 350°F. Place a baking sheet on the middle shelf of the oven.

**2** Wash the cranberries and pat dry. Thickly smear the butter on the base and sides of a 9- × 2-inch round cake pan. Add the sugar and swirl the pan to coat evenly.

**3** ▲ Add the cranberries and spread in an even layer over the bottom of the pan.

**4** For the batter, sift the flour and baking powder twice. Set aside.

**5** ▲ Combine the eggs, sugar, and orange rind in a heatproof bowl set over a pan of hot but not boiling water. With an electric mixer, beat until the eggs leave a ribbon trail when the beaters are lifted.

**6** Add the flour mixture in 3 batches, folding in well after each addition. Gently fold in the melted butter, then pour over the cranberries.

**7** Bake for 40 minutes. Let cool for 5 minutes, then run a knife around the inside edge to loosen.

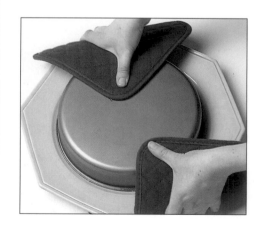

**8** ▲ To unmold, while the cake is still warm place a flat plate on top of the pan, bottom-side up. Holding the pan and plate tightly together with potholders or oven gloves, quickly flip over. Carefully lift off the pan.

# Pineapple Upside-Down Cake

**SERVES 8**

| |
|---|
| ½ cup (1 stick) butter |
| 1 cup dark brown sugar, firmly packed |
| 1 16-ounce can pineapple slices, drained |
| 4 eggs, separated |
| grated rind of 1 lemon |
| ⅛ teaspoon salt |
| ½ cup granulated sugar |
| ¾ cup flour |
| 1 teaspoon baking powder |

**1**  Preheat the oven to 350°F.

**2**  Melt the butter in an ovenproof cast-iron skillet, about 10 inches in diameter. Remove 1 tablespoon of the melted butter and set aside.

**3** ▲ Add the brown sugar to the skillet and stir until blended. Place the drained pineapple slices on top in one layer. Set aside.

~ **VARIATION** ~

For Dried Apricot Upside-Down Cake, replace the pineapple slices with 1½ cups of dried apricots. If they need softening, simmer the apricots in about ½ cup orange juice until plump and soft. Drain the apricots and discard any remaining cooking liquid.

**4**  In a bowl, whisk together the egg yolks, reserved butter, and lemon rind until well blended. Set aside.

**5** ▼  With an electric mixer, beat the egg whites with the salt until stiff. Fold in the granulated sugar, 2 tablespoons at a time. Fold in the egg yolk mixture.

**6**  Sift the flour and baking powder together. Carefully fold into the egg mixture in 3 batches.

**7** ▲  Pour the batter over the pineapple and smooth level.

**8**  Bake until a cake tester inserted in the center comes out clean, about 30 minutes.

**9**  While still hot, place a serving plate on top of the skillet, bottom-side up. Holding them tightly together with potholders or oven gloves, quickly flip over. Serve hot or cold.

# Spice Cake

**SERVES 10–12**

1¼ cups milk

2 tablespoons dark corn syrup

2 teaspoons vanilla extract

¾ cup walnuts, chopped

¾ cup (1½ sticks) butter, at room temperature

1½ cups sugar

1 egg, at room temperature

3 egg yolks, at room temperature

2 cups flour

1 tablespoon baking powder

1 teaspoon grated nutmeg

1 teaspoon ground cinnamon

½ teaspoon ground cloves

¼ teaspoon ground ginger

¼ teaspoon ground allspice

FOR THE FROSTING

6 ounces cream cheese

2 tablespoons unsalted butter, at room temperature

1¾ cups confectioners' sugar

2 tablespoons finely chopped stem ginger

2 tablespoons syrup from stem ginger

stem ginger pieces, for decorating

**1** Preheat the oven to 350°F. Line 3 8-inch cake pans with wax paper and grease. In a bowl, combine the milk, corn syrup, vanilla, and walnuts.

**2 ▼** With an electric mixer, cream the butter and sugar until light and fluffy. Beat in the egg and egg yolks. Add the milk mixture and stir well.

**3** Sift together the flour, baking powder and spices 3 times.

**4 ▲** Add the flour mixture in 4 batches, and fold in carefully after each addition.

**5** Divide the cake mixture between the pans. Bake until the cakes spring back when touched lightly, about 25 minutes. Let stand 5 minutes, then unmold and cool on a rack.

**6 ▼** For the frosting, combine all the ingredients and beat with an electric mixer. Spread the frosting between the layers and over the top. Decorate with pieces of stem ginger.

# Sour Cream Streusel Coffee Cake

**SERVES 12–14**

½ cup (1 stick) butter, at room temperature

⅔ cup granulated sugar

3 eggs, at room temperature

1½ cups flour

1 teaspoon baking soda

1 teaspoon baking powder

1 cup sour cream

**FOR THE TOPPING**

1 cup dark brown sugar, firmly packed

2 teaspoons ground cinnamon

1 cup walnuts, finely chopped

4 tablespoons cold butter, cut in pieces

**1** Preheat the oven to 350°F. Line the bottom of a 9-inch square cake pan with wax paper and grease.

**2 ▲** For the topping, place the brown sugar, cinnamon, and walnuts in a bowl. Mix with your fingertips, then add the butter and continue working with your fingertips until the mixture resembles coarse crumbs.

**3** To make the cake, cream the butter with an electric mixer until soft. Add the sugar and continue beating until the mixture is light and fluffy.

**4** Add the eggs, 1 at a time, beating well after each addition.

**5** In another bowl, sift the flour, baking soda, and baking powder together 3 times.

**6 ▲** Fold the dry ingredients into the butter mixture in 3 batches, alternating with the sour cream. Fold until blended after each addition.

**7 ▲** Pour half of the batter into the prepared pan and sprinkle over half of the walnut topping mixture.

**8** Pour the remaining batter on top and sprinkle over the remaining walnut mixture.

**9** Bake until browned, 60–70 minutes. Let stand 5 minutes, then unmold and transfer to a cooling rack.

# Carrot Cake with Maple Butter Frosting

**SERVES 12**

1 pound carrots, peeled

1½ cups flour

2 teaspoons baking powder

½ teaspoon baking soda

1 teaspoon salt

2 teaspoons ground cinnamon

4 eggs

2 teaspoons vanilla extract

1 cup dark brown sugar, firmly packed

½ cup granulated sugar

1¼ cups sunflower oil

1 cup walnuts, finely chopped

½ cup raisins

walnut halves, for decorating (optional)

FOR THE FROSTING

6 tablespoons unsalted butter, at room
    temperature

3 cups confectioners' sugar

¼ cup maple syrup

**1** Preheat the oven to 350°F. Line an
11- × 8-inch rectangular baking pan
with wax paper and grease.

**2 ▲** Grate the carrots and set aside.

**3** Sift the flour, baking powder,
baking soda, salt, and cinnamon into
a bowl. Set aside.

**4** With an electric mixer, beat the
eggs until blended. Add the vanilla,
sugars, and oil; beat to incorporate.
Add the dry ingredients, in 3 batches,
folding in well after each addition.

**5 ▲** Add the carrots, walnuts, and
raisins and fold in thoroughly.

**6** Pour the batter into the prepared
pan and bake until the cake springs
back when touched lightly, 40–45
minutes. Let stand 10 minutes, then
unmold and transfer to a rack.

**7 ▼** For the frosting, cream the
butter with half the sugar until soft.
Add the syrup, then beat in the
remaining sugar until blended.

**8** Spread the frosting over the top of
the cake. Using a metal spatula, make
decorative ridges across the top. Cut
into squares. Decorate with walnut
halves, if wished.

# Peach Torte

**SERVES 8**

| |
|---|
| 1 cup flour |
| 1 teaspoon baking powder |
| ⅛ teaspoon salt |
| ½ cup (1 stick) unsalted butter, at room temperature |
| ¾ cup sugar |
| 2 eggs, at room temperature |
| 6–7 peaches |
| sugar and lemon juice, for sprinkling |
| whipped cream, for serving (optional) |

**1** Preheat the oven to 350°F. Grease a 10-inch springform pan.

**2 ▲** Sift together the flour, baking powder, and salt. Set aside.

**3** With an electric mixer, cream the butter and sugar until light and fluffy. Add the eggs, then fold in the dry ingredients until blended.

**4 ▲** Spoon the batter into the pan and smooth it to make an even layer over the bottom.

**5 ▼** To skin the peaches, drop several at a time into a pan of gently boiling water. Boil for 10 seconds, then remove with a slotted spoon. Peel off the skin with the aid of a sharp knife. Cut the peaches in half and discard the stones.

**6 ▲** Arrange the peach halves on top of the batter. Sprinkle lightly with sugar and lemon juice.

**7** Bake until golden brown and set, 50–60 minutes. Serve warm with whipped cream, if desired.

# Plum Crumbcake

SERVES 8–10

⅔ cup (10⅔ tablespoons) butter or margarine, at room temperature

⅔ cup granulated sugar

4 eggs, at room temperature

1½ teaspoons vanilla extract

1¼ cups flour

1 teaspoon baking powder

1½ pounds purple plums, halved and pitted

FOR THE TOPPING

1 cup flour

⅔ cup light brown sugar, firmly packed

1½ teaspoons ground cinnamon

6 tablespoons butter, cut in pieces

**1** Preheat the oven to 350°F.

**2** For the topping, combine the flour, light brown sugar, and cinnamon in a bowl. Add the butter and work the mixture lightly with your fingertips until it resembles coarse crumbs. Set aside.

**3** ▲ Line a 10- × 2-inch round cake pan with wax paper and grease.

**4** Cream the butter or margarine and granulated sugar until light and fluffy.

**5** ▲ Beat in the eggs, 1 at a time. Stir in the vanilla.

**6** In a bowl, sift together the flour and baking powder, then fold into the butter mixture in 3 batches.

**7** ▲ Pour the batter into the pan. Arrange the plums on top.

**8** ▲ Sprinkle the topping over the plums in an even layer.

**9** Bake until a cake tester inserted in the center comes out clean, about 45 minutes. Let cool in the pan.

**10** To serve, run a knife around the inside edge and invert onto a plate. Invert again onto a serving plate so the topping is right-side up.

~ **VARIATION** ~

This cake can also be made with the same quantity of apricots, peeled if preferred, or pitted cherries, or use a mixture of fruit, such as red or yellow plums, greengage plums, and apricots.

# Yule Log Cake

**SERVES 8 OR MORE**

4 eggs, separated

¾ cup sugar

1 teaspoon vanilla extract

pinch of cream of tartar (if needed)

¾ cup cake flour, sifted

1 cup whipping cream

10 ounces bittersweet chocolate, chopped

2 tablespoons rum or Cognac

1 Preheat the oven to 375°F. Grease, line the bottom, and flour a 15- × 10-inch jelly roll pan.

2 Put the egg yolks in a large bowl. Reserve 2 tablespoons sugar; add the remainder to the egg yolks. Beat until pale and thick. Beat in the vanilla.

3 In another bowl, scrupulously clean and greasefree, beat the egg whites (with the cream of tartar if not using a copper bowl) until they will hold soft peaks. Add the reserved sugar and continue beating until the whites are glossy and will hold stiff peaks.

4 Add the flour to the egg yolk mixture in 2 batches and gently fold it in. Add one-quarter of the egg whites and fold in to lighten the mixture. Fold in the remaining whites.

5 ▲ Spread the batter in the prepared pan. Bake about 15 minutes.

6 Turn onto paper sprinkled with superfine sugar. Roll up and let cool.

7 Bring the cream to a boil in a small saucepan. Put the chocolate in a bowl, add the cream, and stir until the chocolate has melted.

8 ▲ Beat the chocolate mixture until it is fluffy and has thickened to a spreading consistency. Spoon one-third of the chocolate mixture into another bowl. Mix in rum or Cognac.

9 Unroll the cake. Spread the rum and chocolate mixture evenly over the surface. Roll up the cake again.

10 Cut off about one-quarter of the cake, at an angle. Place it against the side of the larger piece of cake, to resemble a branch from a tree trunk.

11 ▼ Spread the remaining chocolate mixture all over the cake. Mark with the tines of a fork to resemble bark. Before serving, add Christmas decorations, such as sprigs of holly, and dust with a little confectioners' sugar "snow", if desired.

# Orange Walnut Roll

**SERVES 8**

4 eggs, separated

½ cup sugar

1 cup walnuts, chopped very finely

⅛ teaspoon cream of tartar

⅛ teaspoon salt

confectioners' sugar, for dusting

FOR THE FILLING

1¼ cups whipping cream

1 tablespoon granulated sugar

grated rind of 1 orange

1 tablespoon orange liqueur, such as
Grand Marnier

**1** Preheat the oven to 350°F. Line a
12- × 9½-inch jelly roll pan with wax
paper and grease.

**2** With an electric mixer, beat the
egg yolks and sugar until thick.

**3** ▲ Stir in the walnuts.

**4** In another bowl, beat the egg
whites with the cream of tartar and
salt until they hold stiff peaks. Fold
gently but thoroughly into the
walnut mixture.

**5** Pour the batter into the prepared
pan and spread level with a spatula.
Bake for 15 minutes.

**6** Run a knife along the inside edge to
loosen, then invert the cake onto a
sheet of wax paper that has been
dusted with confectioners' sugar.

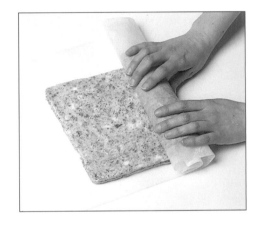

**7** ▲ Peel off the baking paper. Roll
up the cake while it is still warm with
the help of the sugared paper. Set
aside to cool.

**8** For the filling, whip the cream
until it holds soft peaks. Stir together
the granulated sugar and orange rind,
then fold into the whipped cream.
Add the liqueur.

**9** ▲ Gently unroll the cake. Spread
the inside with a layer of orange
whipped cream, then re-roll. Keep
refrigerated until ready to serve. Dust
the top with confectioners' sugar just
before serving.

# Chocolate Roll

**SERVES 10**

8 1-ounce squares semisweet chocolate

3 tablespoons water

2 tablespoons rum, brandy, or strong coffee

7 eggs, separated

¾ cup sugar

⅛ teaspoon salt

1½ cups whipping cream

confectioners' sugar, for dusting

**1** Preheat the oven to 350°F. Line a 15- × 13-inch jelly roll pan with wax paper and grease.

**2** ▲ Combine the chocolate, water, and rum or other flavoring in the top of a double boiler, or in a heatproof bowl set over hot water. Heat until melted. Set aside.

**3** With an electric mixer, beat the egg yolks and sugar until thick.

**4** ▲ Stir in the melted chocolate.

**5** In another bowl, beat the egg whites and salt until they hold stiff peaks. Fold a large dollop of egg whites into the yolk mixture to lighten it, then carefully fold in the rest of the whites.

**6** ▼ Pour the batter into the pan; spread evenly with a metal spatula.

**7** Bake for 15 minutes. Remove from the oven, cover with wax paper and a damp cloth. Let stand for 1–2 hours.

**8** With an electric mixer, whip the cream until stiff. Set aside.

**9** Run a knife along the inside edge to loosen, then invert the cake onto a sheet of wax paper that has been dusted with confectioners' sugar.

**10** Peel off the baking paper. Spread with an even layer of whipped cream, then roll up the cake with the help of the sugared paper. The cake may crack slightly.

**11** Refrigerate for several hours. Before serving, dust with an even layer of confectioners' sugar.

# Devil's Food Cake

**SERVES 10**

4 1-ounce squares semisweet chocolate

1¼ cups milk

1 cup light brown sugar, firmly packed

1 egg yolk

2¼ cups cake flour

1 teaspoon baking soda

½ teaspoon salt

⅔ cup (10⅔ tablespoons) butter or margarine, at room temperature

1⅓ cups granulated sugar

3 eggs

1 teaspoon vanilla extract

FOR THE FROSTING

8 1-ounce squares semisweet chocolate

¾ cup sour cream

¼ teaspoon salt

**1** Preheat the oven to 350°F. Line 2 8- or 9-inch round cake pans with wax paper.

**2 ▲** In a heatproof bowl set over a pan of simmering water, or in a double boiler, combine the chocolate, ½ cup of the milk, the brown sugar, and egg yolk. Cook, stirring, until smooth and thickened. Let cool.

**3 ▲** Sift the flour, baking soda, and salt into a small bowl. Set aside.

**4 ▲** With an electric mixer, cream the butter or margarine with the granulated sugar until light and fluffy. Beat in the whole eggs, one at a time. Mix in the vanilla.

**5** On low speed, beat the flour mixture into the butter mixture alternately with the remaining milk, beginning and ending with flour.

**6 ▲** Pour in the chocolate mixture and mix until just combined.

**7** Divide the batter evenly between the cake pans. Bake until a cake tester inserted in the center comes out clean, 30–40 minutes.

**8** Let cool in the pans on wire racks for 10 minutes, then unmold the cakes from the pans onto the wire racks and let cool completely.

**9 ▲** For the frosting, melt the chocolate in a heatproof bowl set over a pan of hot, not boiling, water, or in the top of a double boiler. Remove the bowl from the heat and stir in the sour cream and salt. Let cool slightly.

**10 ▲** Set 1 cake layer on a serving plate and spread with one-third of the frosting. Place the second cake layer on top. Spread the remaining frosting all over the top and sides of the cake, swirling it to make a decorative finish.

# Chocolate Frosted Layer Cake

**SERVES 8**

1 cup (2 sticks) butter or margarine, at room temperature

1½ cups sugar

4 eggs, at room temperature, separated

2 teaspoons vanilla extract

2½ cups flour

2 teaspoons baking powder

⅛ teaspoon salt

1 cup milk

FOR THE FROSTING

5 1-ounce squares semisweet chocolate

½ cup sour cream

⅛ teaspoon salt

**1** Preheat the oven to 350°F. Line 2 8-inch round cake pans with wax paper and grease. Coat the pans with flour and shake to distribute evenly. Tap to dislodge any excess flour.

**2** With an electric mixer, cream the butter or margarine until soft. Gradually add the sugar and continue beating until light and fluffy.

**3 ▲** Lightly beat the egg yolks, then mix into the creamed butter and sugar with the vanilla.

**4** Sift the flour with the baking powder 3 times. Set aside.

**5** In another bowl, beat the egg whites with the salt until they hold stiff peaks. Set aside.

**6 ▲** Gently fold the dry ingredients into the butter mixture in 3 batches, alternating with the milk.

**7** Add a large dollop of the whites and fold in to lighten the mixture. Carefully fold in the remaining whites until just blended.

**8** Divide the batter between the pans and bake until the cakes pull away from the sides of the pan, about 30 minutes. Let stand 5 minutes, then unmold and transfer to a rack.

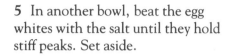

**9 ▲** For the frosting, melt the chocolate in the top of a double boiler or a bowl set over hot water. When cool, stir in the sour cream and salt.

**10** Sandwich the layers with frosting, then spread on the top and sides.

# Devil's Food Cake with Orange Frosting

**SERVES 8–10**

½ cup unsweetened cocoa powder

¾ cup boiling water

¾ cup (1½ sticks) butter, at room temperature

1½ cups dark brown sugar, firmly packed

3 eggs, at room temperature

2 cups flour

1½ teaspoons baking soda

¼ teaspoon baking powder

¾ cup sour cream

orange rind strips, for decoration

**FOR THE FROSTING**

1½ cups granulated sugar

2 egg whites

4 tablespoons frozen orange juice concentrate

1 tablespoon fresh lemon juice

grated rind of 1 orange

**4 ▼** Sift together the flour, baking soda, and baking powder twice. Fold into the cocoa mixture in 3 batches, alternating with the sour cream.

**5** Pour into the pans and bake until the cakes pull away from the sides of the pan, 30–35 minutes. Let stand 15 minutes before unmolding.

**6** Thinly slice the orange rind strips. Blanch in boiling water for 1 minute.

**7 ▲** For the frosting, place all the ingredients in the top of a double boiler or in a bowl set over hot water. With an electric mixer, beat until the mixture holds soft peaks. Continue beating off the heat until thick enough to spread.

**8** Sandwich the cake layers with frosting, then spread over the top and sides. Arrange the blanched orange rind strips on top of the cake.

**1** Preheat the oven to 350°F. Line 2 9-inch cake pans with wax paper and grease. In a bowl, mix the cocoa and water until smooth. Set aside.

**2** With an electric mixer, cream the butter and sugar until light and fluffy. Add the eggs, 1 at a time, beating well after each addition.

**3 ▲** When the cocoa mixture is lukewarm, add to the butter mixture.

# Best-Ever Chocolate Cake

**SERVES 12–14**

½ cup (1 stick) unsalted butter

1 cup cake flour

½ cup unsweetened cocoa powder

1 teaspoon baking powder

⅛ teaspoon salt

6 eggs

1 cup sugar

2 teaspoons vanilla extract

**FOR THE FROSTING**

8 1-ounce squares semisweet chocolate, chopped

6 tablespoons unsalted butter

3 eggs, separated

1 cup whipping cream

3 tablespoons sugar

**1** Preheat the oven to 350°F. Line 3 8- × 1½-inch round cake pans with wax paper and grease.

**2 ▲** Dust evenly with flour and spread with a brush. Set aside.

~ **VARIATION** ~

For a simpler frosting, combine 1 cup whipping cream with 8 ounces finely chopped semisweet chocolate in a saucepan. Stir over low heat until the chocolate has melted. Cool and whisk to spreading consistency.

**3 ▲** Melt the butter over low heat. With a spoon, skim off any foam that rises to the surface. Set aside.

**4 ▲** Sift the flour, cocoa, baking powder, and salt together 3 times and set aside.

**5** Place the eggs and sugar in a large heatproof bowl set over a pan of hot water. With an electric mixer, beat until the mixture doubles in volume and is thick enough to leave a ribbon trail when the beaters are lifted, about 10 minutes. Add the vanilla.

**6 ▲** Sift over the dry ingredients in 3 batches, folding in carefully after each addition. Fold in the butter.

**7** Divide the batter between the pans and bake until the cakes pull away from the sides of the pan, about 25 minutes. Transfer to a rack.

**8** For the frosting, melt the chopped chocolate in the top of a double boiler, or in a heatproof bowl set over hot water.

**9 ▲** Off the heat, stir in the butter and egg yolks. Return to low heat and stir until thick. Remove from the heat and set aside.

**10** Whip the cream until firm; set aside. In another bowl, beat the egg whites until stiff. Add the sugar and beat until glossy.

**11** Fold the cream into the chocolate mixture, then carefully fold in the egg whites. Refrigerate for 20 minutes to thicken the frosting.

**12 ▲** Sandwich the cake layers with frosting, stacking them carefully. Spread the remaining frosting evenly over the top and sides of the cake.

# Mississippi Mud Cake

**SERVES 8–10**

2 cups flour

⅛ teaspoon salt

1 teaspoon baking powder

1¼ cups strong brewed coffee

¼ cup bourbon or brandy

5 1-ounce squares unsweetened chocolate

1 cup (2 sticks) butter or margarine

2 cups sugar

2 eggs, at room temperature

1½ teaspoons vanilla extract

unsweetened cocoa powder

sweetened whipped cream or ice cream, for serving

**1** Preheat the oven to 275°F.

**2** Sift the flour, salt, and baking powder together.

**3** ▼ Combine the coffee, bourbon or brandy, chocolate, and butter or margarine in the top of a double boiler. Heat until the chocolate and butter have melted and the mixture is smooth, stirring occasionally.

**4** ▲ Pour the chocolate mixture into a large bowl. Using an electric mixer on low speed, gradually beat in the sugar. Continue beating until the sugar has dissolved.

**5** Raise the speed to medium and add the sifted dry ingredients. Mix well, then beat in the eggs and vanilla until thoroughly blended.

**6** Pour the batter into a well-greased 3-quart bundt pan that has been dusted lightly with cocoa powder. Bake until a cake tester inserted in the cake comes out clean, about 1 hour 20 minutes.

**7** ▲ Let cool in the pan for 15 minutes, then unmold onto a wire rack. Let cool completely.

**8** When the cake is cold, dust it lightly with cocoa powder. Serve with sweetened whipped cream or ice cream, if desired.

# Huckleberry Coffee Cake

**SERVES 10**

2 cups flour

1 tablespoon baking powder

1 teaspoon salt

⅓ cup butter or margarine, at room
temperature

¾ cup granulated sugar

1 egg

1 cup milk

½ teaspoon grated lemon rind

2 cups fresh or frozen huckleberries,
well drained

1 cup confectioners' sugar

2 tablespoons fresh lemon juice

**1**  Preheat the oven to 350°F.

**2** ▲  Sift the flour with the baking
powder and salt.

**3** ▲  In a large bowl, beat the butter
or margarine with the granulated sugar
until light and fluffy. Beat in the egg
and milk. Fold in the flour mixture,
mixing well until evenly blended to a
batter. Mix in the lemon rind.

**4** ▼  Spread half of the batter in a
greased 13- × 9- × 2-inch baking
pan. Sprinkle with 1 cup of the
berries. Top with the remaining batter
and sprinkle with the rest of the
berries. Bake until golden brown and a
cake tester inserted in the center
comes out clean, 35–45 minutes.

**5** ▲  Mix the confectioners' sugar
gradually into the lemon juice to make
a smooth glaze with a pourable
consistency. Drizzle the glaze over the
top of the warm coffee cake and allow
it to set before serving, still warm or at
room temperature.

# Chocolate Cinnamon Cake with Banana Sauce

**SERVES 6**

| |
|---|
| 4 1-ounce squares semisweet chocolate, finely chopped |
| ½ cup (1 stick) unsalted butter, at room temperature |
| 1 tablespoon instant coffee powder |
| 5 eggs, separated |
| 1 cup granulated sugar |
| 1 cup flour |
| 2 teaspoons ground cinnamon |
| FOR THE SAUCE |
| 4 ripe bananas |
| ¼ cup light brown sugar, firmly packed |
| 1 tablespoon fresh lemon juice |
| ¾ cup whipping cream |
| 1 tablespoon rum (optional) |

**1** Preheat the oven to 350°F. Grease an 8-inch round cake pan.

**2 ▲** Combine the chocolate and butter in the top of a double boiler or in a heatproof bowl set over hot water. Stir until melted. Remove from the heat and stir in the coffee. Set aside.

**3** Beat the egg yolks with the granulated sugar until thick and lemon-colored. Add the chocolate mixture and beat on low speed just to blend the mixtures evenly.

**4** Sift together the flour and cinnamon into a bowl.

**5 ▲** In another bowl, beat the egg whites until they hold stiff peaks.

**6 ▲** Fold a dollop of whites into the chocolate mixture to lighten it. Fold in the remaining whites in 3 batches, alternating with the sifted flour.

**7 ▲** Pour the batter into the prepared pan. Bake until a cake tester inserted in the center comes out clean, 40–50 minutes. Unmold the cake onto a wire rack.

**8** Preheat the broiler.

**9 ▲** For the sauce, slice the bananas into a shallow, heatproof dish. Add the brown sugar and lemon juice and stir to blend. Place under the broiler and cook, stirring occasionally, until the sugar is caramelized and bubbling, about 8 minutes.

**10 ▲** Transfer the bananas to a bowl and mash with a fork until almost smooth. Stir in the cream and rum, if using. Serve the cake and sauce warm.

> **~ VARIATION ~**
>
> For a special occasion, top the cake slices with a scoop of ice cream (rum-raisin, chocolate, or vanilla) before adding the banana sauce. With this addition, the dessert will make at least 8 portions.

# Rich Chocolate Pecan Cake

**SERVES 10**

1 cup (2 sticks) butter

8 1-ounce squares semisweet chocolate

1 cup unsweetened cocoa powder

1½ cups sugar

6 eggs

⅓ cup brandy or cognac

2 cups pecans, finely chopped

**FOR THE GLAZE**

4 tablespoons butter

5 1-ounce squares bittersweet chocolate

2 tablespoons milk

1 teaspoon vanilla extract

**1** Preheat the oven to 350°F. Line a 9- × 2-inch round cake pan with wax paper and grease.

**2** Melt the butter and chocolate together in the top of a double boiler, or in a heatproof bowl set over hot water. Set aside to cool.

**3 ▼** Sift the cocoa into a bowl. Add the sugar and eggs and stir until just combined. Pour in the melted chocolate mixture and brandy.

**4** Fold in three-quarters of the pecans, then pour the batter into the prepared pan.

**5 ▲** Set the pan inside a large pan and pour 1 inch of hot water into the outer pan. Bake until the cake is firm to the touch, about 45 minutes. Let stand 15 minutes, then unmold and transfer to a cooling rack.

**6** Wrap the cake in wax paper and refrigerate for at least 6 hours.

**7** For the glaze, combine the butter, chocolate, milk, and vanilla in the top of a double boiler or in a heatproof bowl set over hot water, until melted.

**8** Place a piece of wax paper under the cake, then drizzle spoonfuls of glaze along the edge; it should drip down and coat the sides. Pour the remaining glaze on top of the cake.

**9 ▲** Cover the sides of the cake with the remaining pecans, gently pressing them on with the palm of your hand.

# Chocolate Brownie Cake

**SERVES 8–10**

| 4 1-ounce squares unsweetened chocolate |
| --- |
| ¾ cup (1½ sticks) butter |
| 2 cups sugar |
| 3 eggs |
| 1 teaspoon vanilla extract |
| 1½ cups flour |
| 1 teaspoon baking powder |
| 1 cup walnuts, chopped |
| FOR THE TOPPING |
| 1½ cups whipping cream |
| 8 1-ounce squares semisweet chocolate |
| 1 tablespoon vegetable oil |

1 Preheat the oven to 350°F. Line two 8-inch cake pans, at least 1¾ in deep, with wax paper and grease the paper.

2 Melt the chocolate and butter together in the top of a double boiler, or in a heatproof bowl set over a saucepan of hot water.

3 ▲ Transfer to a mixing bowl and stir in the sugar. Add the eggs and vanilla and mix until well blended.

~ **VARIATION** ~

To make Chocolate Brownie Ice Cream Cake, sandwich the cake layers with softened vanilla ice cream. Freeze until serving.

4 ▲ Sift over the flour and baking powder. Stir in the walnuts.

5 Divide the batter between the prepared pans and spread level.

6 Bake until a cake tester inserted in the center comes out clean, about 30 minutes. Let stand 10 minutes, then unmold and transfer to a rack.

7 When the cakes are cool, whip the cream until firm. With a long serrated knife, carefully slice each cake in half horizontally.

8 Sandwich the layers with some of the whipped cream and spread the remainder over the top of the cake. Refrigerate until needed.

9 ▼ For the chocolate curls, melt the chocolate and oil in the top of a double boiler or a bowl set over hot water. Transfer to a non-porous surface. Spread to a ⅜-inch thick rectangle. Just before the chocolate sets, hold the blade of a straight knife at an angle to the chocolate and scrape across the surface to make curls. Place on top of the cake.

# Sachertorte

SERVES 8–10

2 1-ounce squares semisweet chocolate

2 1-ounce squares unsweetened chocolate

6 tablespoons unsalted butter, at room temperature

½ cup sugar

4 eggs, separated

1 egg white

¼ teaspoon salt

½ cup cake flour, sifted

FOR THE TOPPING

5 tablespoons apricot jam

1 cup plus 1 tablespoon water

1 tablespoon unsalted butter

6 1-ounce squares semisweet chocolate

¾ cup sugar

ready-made chocolate decorating icing (optional)

**1** Preheat the oven to 325°F. Line a 9- × 2-inch cake pan with wax paper and grease.

**2 ▲** Melt both chocolates in the top of a double boiler, or in a heatproof bowl set over hot water. Set aside.

**3** With an electric mixer, cream the butter and sugar until light and fluffy. Stir in the chocolate.

**4 ▲** Beat in the yolks, 1 at a time.

**5** In another bowl, beat the egg whites with the salt until stiff.

**6 ▲** Fold a dollop of whites into the chocolate mixture to lighten it. Fold in the remaining whites in 3 batches, alternating with the sifted flour.

**7 ▲** Pour into the pan and bake until a cake tester comes out clean, about 45 minutes. Unmold onto a rack.

**8 ▲** Meanwhile, melt the jam with 1 tablespoon of the water over low heat, then strain for a smooth consistency.

**9** For the frosting, melt the butter and chocolate in the top of a double boiler or a bowl set over hot water.

**10 ▲** In a heavy saucepan, dissolve the sugar in the remaining water over low heat. Raise the heat and boil until the mixture reaches 221°F on a sugar thermometer. Immediately plunge the bottom of the pan into cold water for 1 minute. Pour into the chocolate mixture and stir to blend. Let cool for a few minutes before using.

**11** To assemble, brush the warm jam over the cake. Starting in the center, pour over the frosting and work outward in a circular movement. Tilt the rack to spread; only use a spatula for the sides of the cake. Leave to set overnight. If wished, decorate with chocolate icing.

# Boston Cream Pie

**SERVES 8**

2 cups cake flour

1 tablespoon baking powder

½ teaspoon salt

½ cup (1 stick) butter, at room
    temperature

1 cup granulated sugar

2 eggs

1 teaspoon vanilla extract

¾ cup milk

FOR THE FILLING

1 cup milk

3 egg yolks

½ cup granulated sugar

¼ cup flour

1 tablespoon butter

1 tablespoon brandy or 1 teaspoon
    vanilla extract

FOR THE CHOCOLATE GLAZE

1-ounce square unsweetened chocolate

2 tablespoons butter or margarine

½ cup confectioners' sugar, plus extra
    for dusting

½ teaspoon vanilla extract

about 1 tablespoon hot water

**1** Preheat the oven to 375°F.

**2** Grease 2 8- × 2-inch round cake
pans, and line the bottoms with
rounds of greased wax paper.

**3** Sift the flour with the baking
powder and salt.

**4** Beat the butter and granulated
sugar together until light and fluffy.
Add the eggs one at a time, beating
well after each addition. Stir in the
vanilla. Add the milk and dry
ingredients alternately, mixing only
enough to blend thoroughly. Do not
over-beat the batter.

**5** Divide the cake batter between
the prepared pans and spread it out
evenly. Bake until a cake tester
inserted in the center comes out
clean, about 25 minutes.

**6** Meanwhile, make the filling. Heat
the milk in a small saucepan to boiling
point. Remove from the heat.

**7** ▲ In a heatproof mixing bowl,
beat the egg yolks until smooth.
Gradually add the granulated sugar
and continue beating until pale
yellow. Beat in the flour.

**8** ▲ Pour the hot milk into the egg
yolk mixture in a steady stream,
beating constantly. When all the milk
has been added, place the bowl over,
not in, a pan of boiling water, or pour
the mixture into the top of a double
boiler. Heat, stirring constantly, until
thickened. Cook 2 minutes more,
then remove from the heat. Stir in the
butter and brandy or vanilla. Let cool.

**9** ▲ When the cake layers have
cooled, use a large sharp knife to slice
off the domed top to make a flat
surface. Place one layer on a serving
plate and spread on the filling in a
thick layer. Set the other layer on top,
cut side down. Smooth the edge of the
filling layer so it is flush with the sides
of the cake layers.

**10** ▲ For the glaze, melt the
chocolate with the butter or
margarine in the top of a double
boiler. When smooth, remove from
the heat and beat in the sugar to make
a thick paste. Add the vanilla. Beat in
a little of the hot water. If the glaze
does not have a spreadable
consistency, add more water, 1
teaspoon at a time.

**11** Spread the glaze evenly over the
top of the cake, using a metal spatula.
Dust the top with confectioners' sugar.
Because of the custard filling,
refrigerate any leftover cake.

# Caramel Layer Cake

**SERVES 8–10**

| |
|---|
| 2 cups cake flour |
| 1½ teaspoons baking powder |
| ¾ cup (1½ sticks) butter, at room temperature |
| ¾ cup granulated sugar |
| 4 eggs, at room temperature, beaten |
| 1 teaspoon vanilla extract |
| 8 tablespoons milk |
| whipped cream, for decorating |
| caramel threads, for decorating (optional, see below) |

**FOR THE FROSTING**

| |
|---|
| 1⅔ cups dark brown sugar, firmly packed |
| 1 cup milk |
| 2 tablespoons unsalted butter |
| 3–5 tablespoons whipping cream |

**1** Preheat the oven to 350°F. Line 2 8-inch cake pans with wax paper and grease lightly.

**2 ▲** Sift the flour and baking powder together 3 times. Set aside.

~ COOK'S TIP ~

To make caramel threads, combine ½ cup sugar and ¼ cup water in a heavy saucepan. Boil until light brown. Dip the pan in cold water to halt cooking. Trail from a spoon on an oiled baking sheet.

**3** With an electric mixer, cream the butter and granulated sugar until light and fluffy.

**4 ▲** Slowly mix in the beaten eggs. Add the vanilla. Fold in the flour mixture, alternating with the milk.

**5 ▲** Divide the batter between the prepared pans and spread evenly, hollowing out the centers slightly.

**6** Bake until the cakes pull away from the sides of the pan, about 30 minutes. Let stand 5 minutes, then unmold and transfer to a rack.

**7 ▲** For the frosting, combine the brown sugar and milk in a saucepan.

**8** Bring to a boil, then cover and cook for 3 minutes. Remove the lid and continue to boil, without stirring, until the mixture reaches 236°F on a sugar thermometer.

**9 ▲** Immediately remove the pan from the heat and add the butter, but do not stir it in. Let cool until lukewarm, then beat until the mixture is smooth and creamy.

**10** Stir in enough cream to obtain a spreadable consistency. If necessary, refrigerate to thicken more.

**11 ▲** Spread a layer of frosting on top of one cake. Sandwich with the second cake, then spread the top and sides with the rest of the frosting and smooth the surface.

**12** To decorate, pipe whipped cream rosettes around the edge. If using, place a mound of caramel threads in the center before serving.

# Whiskey Cake

**MAKES 1 LOAF**

1½ cups walnuts, chopped

½ cup raisins, chopped

½ cup currants

1 cup flour

1 teaspoon baking powder

¼ teaspoon salt

½ cup (1 stick) butter

1 cup sugar

3 eggs, at room temperature, separated

1 teaspoon grated nutmeg

½ teaspoon ground cinnamon

⅓ cup bourbon whiskey

confectioners' sugar, for dusting

**1 ▼** Preheat the oven to 325°F. Line the bottom of a 9- × 5- × 3-inch loaf pan with wax paper and grease the paper and sides of the pan.

**2 ▲** Place the walnuts, raisins, and currants in a bowl. Sprinkle over 2 tablespoons of the flour, mix and set aside. Sift together the remaining flour, baking powder, and salt.

**3 ▲** Cream the butter and sugar until light and fluffy. Beat in the egg yolks.

**4** Mix the nutmeg, cinnamon, and whiskey. Fold into the butter mixture, alternating with the flour mixture.

**5 ▲** In another bowl, beat the egg whites until stiff. Fold into the whiskey mixture until just blended. Fold in the walnut mixture.

**6** Bake until a cake tester inserted in the center comes out clean, about 1 hour. Let cool in the pan. Dust with confectioners' sugar over a template.

# Berry Shortcake

**SERVES 8**

1¼ cups whipping cream

¼ cup confectioners' sugar

2 pints berries (strawberries or mixed
   berries), halved or sliced if large

⅓ cup granulated sugar, or to taste

FOR THE SHORTCAKE BISCUIT

2 cups flour

2 teaspoons baking powder

⅓ cup granulated sugar

1 stick (8 tablespoons) butter

⅓ cup milk

1 extra-large egg

1  Preheat the oven to 450°F. Grease
an 8-inch round cake pan.

2  For the shortcake biscuit, sift the
flour, baking powder, and sugar into a
bowl. Add the butter and cut or rub in
until the mixture resembles fine
crumbs. Combine the milk and egg.
Add to the crumb mixture and stir just
until evenly mixed to a soft dough.

3  Put the dough in the prepared pan
and pat out to an even layer. Bake
until a wooden skewer inserted in the
center comes out clean, 15–20
minutes. Let cool slightly.

4 ▲  Whip the cream until it starts to
thicken. Add the confectioners' sugar
and continue whipping until the
cream will hold soft peaks.

5  Put the berries in a bowl. Sprinkle
with the granulated sugar and toss
together lightly. Cover and set aside
for the berries to render some juice.

6 ▼  Remove the shortcake biscuit
from the pan. With a long, serrated
knife, split it horizontally into two
equal layers.

7 ▲  Put the bottom layer on a
serving plate. Top with half of the
berries and most of the cream. Set the
second layer on top and press down
gently. Spoon the remaining berries
over the top layer (or serve them
separately) and add the remaining
cream in small, decorative dollops.

# Lady Baltimore Cake

SERVES 8–10

2½ cups flour

2½ teaspoons baking powder

½ teaspoon salt

4 eggs

1½ cups sugar

grated rind of 1 large orange

1 cup freshly squeezed orange juice

1 cup vegetable oil

FOR THE FROSTING

2 egg whites

1½ cup sugar

5 tablespoons cold water

¼ teaspoon cream of tartar

1 teaspoon vanilla extract

½ cup pecans, finely chopped

½ cup raisins, chopped

3 dried figs, finely chopped

18 pecan halves, for decorating

**1** Preheat the oven to 350°F. Line 2 9-inch round cake pans with wax paper and grease.

**2** In a bowl, sift together the flour, baking powder, and salt. Set aside.

**3** ▲ With an electric mixer, beat the eggs and sugar until thick and lemon-colored. Beat in the orange rind and juice, then the oil.

**4** On low speed beat in the flour mixture in 3 batches. Divide the batter between the prepared pans.

**5** ▲ Bake until a cake tester inserted in the center comes out clean, about 30 minutes. Let stand 15 minutes. To unmold, run a knife around the inside edge, then transfer the cakes to racks to cool completely.

**6** ▲ For the frosting, combine the egg whites, sugar, water, and cream of tartar in the top of a double boiler, or in a heatproof bowl set over boiling water. With an electric mixer, beat until glossy and thick. Off the heat, add the vanilla, and continue beating until thick. Fold in the pecans, raisins, and figs.

**7** Spread a layer of frosting on top of one cake. Sandwich with the second cake, then spread the top and sides with the rest of the frosting. Arrange the pecan halves on top.

# Raspberry-Hazelnut Meringue Cake

SERVES 8

| |
|---|
| 1 cup hazelnuts |
| 4 egg whites |
| ⅛ teaspoon salt |
| 1 cup sugar |
| ½ teaspoon vanilla extract |
| FOR THE FILLING |
| 1¼ cups whipping cream |
| 1½ pounds raspberries, about 3 pints |

**1** Preheat the oven to 350°F. Line the bottom of 2 8-inch cake pans with wax paper and grease.

**2** Spread the hazelnuts on a baking sheet and bake until lightly toasted, about 8 minutes. Let cool slightly.

**3 ▲** Rub the hazelnuts vigorously in a clean dish towel to remove most of the skins.

**4** Grind the nuts in a food processor, blender, or nut grinder until they are the consistency of coarse sand.

**5** Reduce the oven heat to 300°F.

**6** With an electric mixer, beat the egg whites and salt until they hold stiff peaks. Beat in 2 tablespoons of the sugar, then fold in the remaining sugar, a few tablespoons at a time, with a rubber spatula. Fold in the vanilla and the hazelnuts.

**7 ▲** Divide the batter between the prepared pans and spread level.

**8** Bake for 1¼ hours. If the meringues brown too quickly, protect with a sheet of foil. Let stand 5 minutes, then carefully run a knife around the inside edge of the pans to loosen. Transfer to a rack to cool.

**9** For the filling, whip the cream just until firm.

**10 ▲** Spread half the cream in an even layer on one meringue round and top with half the raspberries.

**11** Top with the other meringue round. Spread the remaining cream on top and arrange the remaining raspberries over the cream. Refrigerate for 1 hour to facilitate cutting.

# Classic Cheesecake

**SERVES 8**

½ cup graham cracker crumbs

2 pounds cream cheese, at room
  temperature

1¼ cups sugar

grated rind of 1 lemon

3 tablespoons fresh lemon juice

1 teapoon vanilla extract

4 eggs, at room temperature

**1**  Preheat the oven to 325°F. Grease
an 8-inch springform pan. Place on a
round of foil 4–5 inches larger than
the diameter of the pan. Press it up
the sides to seal tightly.

**2**  Sprinkle the crumbs in the base of
the pan. Press to form an even layer.

**3**  With an electric mixer, beat the
cream cheese until smooth. Add the
sugar, lemon rind and juice, and
vanilla, and beat until blended. Beat
in the eggs, 1 at a time. Beat just
enough to blend thoroughly.

**4** ▲  Pour into the prepared pan. Set
the pan in a larger baking pan and
place in the oven. Pour enough hot
water in the outer pan to come 1 inch
up the side of the pan.

**5**  Bake until the top of the cake is
golden brown, about 1½ hours. Let
cool in the pan.

**6** ▼  Run a knife around the edge to
loosen, then remove the rim of the
pan. Refrigerate for at least 4 hours
before serving.

---

# Chocolate Cheesecake

**SERVES 10–12**

6 1-ounce squares semisweet chocolate

4 1-ounce squares unsweetened
  chocolate

2½ pounds cream cheese, at room
  temperature

1 cup sugar

2 teaspoons vanilla extract

4 eggs, at room temperature

¾ cup sour cream

FOR THE CRUST

1½ cups chocolate wafer crumbs

6 tablespoons butter, melted

½ teaspoon ground cinnamon

**1**  Preheat the oven to 350°F. Grease
the bottom and sides of a 9- × 3-inch
springform pan.

**2** ▲  For the crust, mix the chocolate
crumbs with the butter and
cinnamon. Press evenly in the bottom
of the pan.

**3**  Melt both chocolates in the top of a
double boiler, or in a heatproof bowl
set over hot water. Set aside.

**4**  With an electric mixer, beat the
cream cheese until smooth, then beat
in the sugar and vanilla. Add the eggs,
1 at a time, scraping the bowl with a
spatula when necessary.

**5**  Add the sour cream. Stir in the
melted chocolate.

**6** ▼  Pour into the crust. Bake for 1
hour. Let cool in the pan; remove rim.
Refrigerate before serving.

*Classic Cheesecake (top), Chocolate Cheesecake*

# Lemon Mousse Cheesecake

**SERVES 10–12**

2½ pounds cream cheese, at room temperature

1½ cups sugar

⅓ cup flour

4 eggs, at room temperature, separated

½ cup fresh lemon juice

grated rind of 2 lemons

1 cup graham cracker crumbs

**1** Preheat the oven to 325°F. Line a 10- × 2-inch round cake pan with wax paper and grease.

**2** With an electric mixer, beat the cream cheese until smooth. Gradually add 1¼ cups of the sugar, and beat until light. Beat in the flour.

**3 ▲** Add the egg yolks, and lemon juice and rind, and beat until smooth and well blended.

**4** In another bowl, beat the egg whites until they hold soft peaks. Add the remaining sugar and beat until stiff and glossy.

**5 ▲** Add the egg whites to the cheese mixture and gently fold in.

**6** Pour the batter into the prepared pan, then place the pan in a larger baking pan. Place in the oven and pour hot water in the outer pan to come 1 inch up the side.

**7** Bake until golden, 60–65 minutes. Let cool in the pan on a rack. Cover and refrigerate for at least 4 hours.

**8** To unmold, run a knife around the inside edge. Place a flat plate, bottom-side up, over the pan and invert onto the plate. Smooth the top with a metal spatula.

**9 ▲** Sprinkle the crumbs over the top in an even layer, pressing down slightly to make a top crust.

**10** To serve, cut slices with a sharp knife dipped in hot water.

# Marbled Cheesecake

**SERVES 10**

½ cup unsweetened cocoa powder

5 tablespoons hot water

2 pounds cream cheese, at room temperature

1 cup sugar

4 eggs

1 teaspoon vanilla extract

½ cup graham cracker crumbs

**1** Preheat the oven to 350°F. Line an 8- × 3-inch cake pan with wax paper and grease.

**2** Sift the cocoa powder into a bowl. Pour over the hot water and stir to dissolve. Set aside.

**3** With an electric mixer, beat the cheese until smooth and creamy. Add the sugar and beat to incorporate. Beat in the eggs, one at a time. Do not overmix.

**4** Divide the mixture evenly between 2 bowls. Stir the chocolate mixture into one, then add the vanilla to the remaining mixture.

**5** ▲ Pour a cupful of the plain mixture into the center of the pan; it will spread out into an even layer. Slowly pour over a cupful of chocolate mixture in the center.

**6** ▲ Repeat alternating cupfuls of the batters in a circular pattern until both are used up.

**7** Set the cake pan in a larger baking pan and pour in hot water to come 1½ inches up the sides of the cake pan.

**8** Bake until the top of the cake is golden, about 1½ hours. It will rise during baking but will sink later. Let cool in the pan on a rack.

**9** To unmold, run a knife around the inside edge. Place a flat plate, bottom-side up, over the pan and invert onto the plate.

**10** ▼ Sprinkle the crumbs evenly over the base, gently place another plate over the crumbs, and invert again. Cover and refrigerate for at least 3 hours, or overnight. To serve, cut slices with a sharp knife dipped in hot water.

# German Chocolate Cupcakes

**MAKES 24**

4 ounces sweet cooking chocolate, cut
  into small pieces

¼ cup water

2 cups cake flour

1 teaspoon baking powder

½ teaspoon baking soda

pinch of salt

1½ cups sugar

¾ cup butter or shortening, at room
  temperature

⅔ cup buttermilk or milk

1 teaspoon vanilla extract

3 eggs

1 recipe quantity butter frosting,
  flavored to taste

**1** Preheat the oven to 350°F. Grease
and flour 24 muffin pans, 2½ to 2¾
inches in diameter, or line them with
paper cupcake liners.

**2 ▲** Put the chocolate and water in a
bowl set over a pan of almost
simmering water. Heat until melted
and smooth, stirring. Remove from
the heat and let cool.

**3** Sift the flour, baking powder, soda,
salt, and sugar into a large bowl. Add
the chocolate mixture, butter,
buttermilk, and vanilla.

**4 ▲** With an electric mixer on
medium-low speed, beat until
smoothly blended. Increase the speed
to high and beat 2 minutes. Add the
eggs and beat 2 minutes.

**5** Divide the batter evenly among the
muffin pans.

**6** Bake until a toothpick inserted into
the center of a cupcake comes out
clean, 20–25 minutes. Cool in the
pans 10 minutes, then unmold and let
cool completely on a wire rack.

**7 ▼** Frost the top of each cupcake
with butter frosting, swirling it into a
peak in the center.

# Chocolate Orange Sponge Cookies

**MAKES ABOUT 14**

2 eggs

¼ cup sugar

½ teaspoon grated orange zest

⅓ cup all-purpose flour

4 tablespoons orange marmalade

1½ ounces semisweet chocolate, cut
into small pieces

1  Preheat oven to 400°F. Line 3
baking sheets with baking parchment.

2 ▲ Put the eggs and sugar in a large
bowl and set over a pan of just
simmering water. Beat until the
mixture is thick and pale.

3 ▲ Remove the bowl from the pan
of water and continue beating until
the mixture is cool. Beat in the
grated orange zest.

4  Sift the flour over the beaten
mixture and fold it in gently with a
rubber spatula.

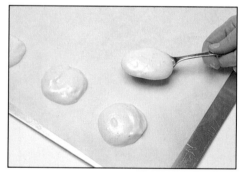

5 ▲ Using a dessert spoon, put
spoonfuls of the mixture on the
prepared baking sheets, leaving space
around each spoonful to allow for
spreading. The mixture will make
28–30 cookies.

6  Bake for about 8 minutes, or until
golden. Cool for a few minutes on the
baking sheets, then transfer to a wire
rack to cool completely.

7  Sandwich pairs of cookies together
with the orange marmalade.

8 ▼ Melt the chocolate in a double
boiler over simmering water until
smooth. Using a small spoon, drizzle
chocolate over the tops of the
cookies, or pipe it in fine lines using a
small waxed paper piping bag. Allow
to set before serving.

# Cup Cakes

## MAKES 16

½ cup (1 stick) butter, at room temperature

1 cup granulated sugar

2 eggs, at room temperature

1½ cups cake flour

¼ teaspoon salt

1½ teaspoons baking powder

½ cup plus 1 tablespoon milk

1 teaspoon vanilla extract

FOR FROSTING AND DECORATING

2 large egg whites

3½ cups sifted confectioners' sugar

1–2 drops glycerin

juice of 1 lemon

food colorings

colored sprinkles, for decorating

candied lemon and orange slices, for decorating

**1** Preheat the oven to 375°F.

**2 ▲** Fill 16 muffin cups with fluted paper baking liners, or grease.

> ~ COOK'S TIP ~
>
> Ready-made cake decorating products are widely available, and may be used, if preferred, instead of the recipes given for frosting and decorating. Colored gel in tubes with piping tips is useful.

**3** With an electric mixer, cream the butter and sugar until light and fluffy. Add the eggs, 1 at a time, beating well after each addition.

**4** Sift together the flour, salt, and baking powder. Stir into the butter mixture, alternating with the milk. Stir in the vanilla.

**5 ▲** Fill the cups half-full and bake until the tops spring back when touched lightly, about 20 minutes. Let the cup cakes stand in the pan for 5 minutes, then unmold and transfer to a rack to cool completely.

**6** For the meringue frosting, beat the egg whites until stiff but not dry. Gradually add the sugar, glycerin, and lemon juice, and continue beating for 1 minute. The consistency should be spreadable. If necessary, thin with a little water or add more sifted confectioners' sugar.

**7 ▲** Divide the frosting between several bowls and tint with food colorings. Spread different colored frostings over the cooled cup cakes.

**8 ▲** Decorate the cup cakes as wished, such as with different colored sprinkles.

**9 ▲** Other decorations include candied orange and lemon slices. Cut into small pieces and arrange on top of the cup cakes. Alternatively, use other suitable candies.

**10 ▲** To decorate with colored frostings, fill paper piping bags with different colored frostings. Pipe on faces, or make other designs.

# Heart Cake

**MAKES 1 CAKE**

1 cup (2 sticks) butter or margarine, at room temperature

1 cup sugar

4 eggs, at room temperature

1½ cups flour

1 teaspoon baking powder

½ teaspoon baking soda

2 tablespoons milk

1 teaspoon vanilla extract

FOR FROSTING AND DECORATING

3 egg whites

1½ cups granulated sugar

2 tablespoons cold water

2 tablespoons fresh lemon juice

¼ teaspoon cream of tartar

pink food coloring

¾–1 cup confectioners' sugar

**1** Preheat the oven to 350°F. Line an 8-inch heart-shaped cake pan with wax paper and grease.

**2 ▲** With an electric mixer, cream the butter or margarine and sugar until light and fluffy. Add the eggs, 1 at a time, beating thoroughly after each addition.

**3** Sift the flour, baking powder, and baking soda together. Fold the dry ingredients into the butter mixture in 3 batches, alternating with the milk. Stir in the vanilla.

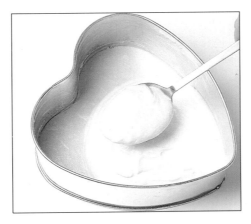

**4 ▲** Spoon the batter into the prepared pan and bake until a cake tester inserted in the center comes out clean, 35–40 minutes. Let the cake stand in the pan for 5 minutes, then unmold and transfer to a rack to cool completely.

**5** For the frosting, combine 2 of the egg whites, the granulated sugar, water, lemon juice, and cream of tartar in the top of a double boiler or in a bowl set over simmering water. With an electric mixer, beat until thick and holds soft peaks, about 7 minutes. Remove from the heat and continue beating until the mixture is thick enough to spread. Tint the frosting with the pink food coloring.

**6 ▲** Put the cake on a board, about 12 inches square, covered in foil or in paper suitable for contact with food. Spread the frosting evenly on the cake. Smooth the top and sides. Leave to set 3–4 hours, or overnight.

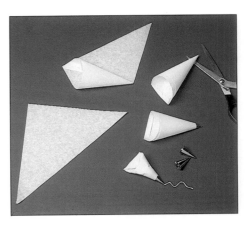

**7 ▲** For the paper piping bags, fold an 11- × 8-inch sheet of parchment or wax paper in half diagonally, then cut into 2 pieces along the fold mark. Roll over the short side, so that it meets the right-angled corner and forms a cone. To form the piping bag, hold the cone in place with one hand, wrap the point of the long side of the triangle around the cone, and tuck inside, folding over twice to secure. Snip a hole in the pointed end and slip in a small metal piping tip to extend about ¼ inch.

**8** For the piped decorations, place 1 tablespoon of the remaining egg white in a bowl and whisk until frothy. Gradually beat in enough confectioners' sugar to make a stiff mixture suitable for piping.

**9 ▲** Spoon into a paper piping bag to half-fill. Fold over the top and squeeze to pipe decorations on the top and sides of the cake.

# Snake Cake

**SERVES 10–12**

1 cup (2 sticks) butter or margarine, at room temperature

grated rind and juice of 1 small orange

1 cup granulated sugar

4 eggs, at room temperature, separated

1½ cups flour

1 teaspoon baking powder

⅛ teaspoon salt

FOR FROSTING AND DECORATING

2 tablespoons unsalted butter, at room temperature

3 cups confectioners' sugar

5 1-ounce squares semisweet chocolate

⅛ teaspoon salt

½ cup sour cream

1 egg white

green and blue food colorings

**1** Preheat the oven to 375°F. Grease 2 8½-inch ring molds and dust them with flour.

**2** With an electric mixer, cream the butter or margarine, orange rind, and sugar until light and fluffy. Beat in the egg yolks, 1 at a time.

**3** Sift the flour and baking powder. Fold the flour into the butter mixture, alternating with the orange juice.

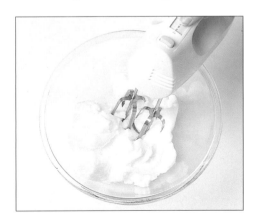

**4** ▲ In another bowl, beat the egg whites and salt until stiff.

**5** Fold a large dollop of the egg whites into the creamed butter mixture to lighten it, then gently fold in the remaining whites.

**6** Divide the batter between the prepared pans and bake until a cake tester inserted in the center comes out clean, about 25 minutes. Let stand 5 minutes, then unmold and transfer to a rack to cool.

**7** Prepare a board, about 24 × 8 inches, covered in paper suitable for contact with food, or in foil.

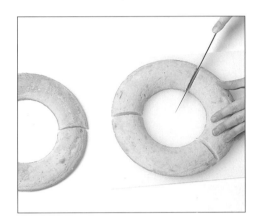

**8** ▲ Cut the cakes in 3 even pieces. Trim to level the flat side, if necessary, and shape the head by cutting off wedges from the front. Shape the tail in the same way.

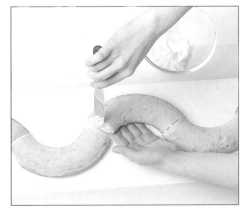

**9** ▲ For the butter frosting, mix the butter and ⅓ cup of the confectioners' sugar. Use to join the cake segments and arrange on the board.

**10** ▲ For the chocolate frosting, melt the chocolate. Stir in the salt and sour cream. When cool, spread over the cake and smooth the surface.

**11** ▲ For decorating, beat the egg white until frothy. Add enough of the remaining confectioners' sugar to obtain a thick mixture. Divide among several bowls and add food colorings.

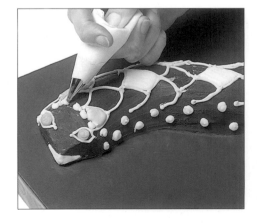

**12** ▲ Fill paper piping bags with frosting and pipe decorations.

# Sun Cake

**SERVES 10–12**

½ cup (1 stick) unsalted butter

6 eggs

1 cup sugar

1 cup cake flour

½ teaspoon salt

1 teaspoon vanilla extract

FOR FROSTING AND DECORATING

2 tablespoons unsalted butter, at room temperature

4 cups sifted confectioners' sugar

½ cup apricot jam

2 tablespoons water

2 large egg whites

1–2 drops glycerin

juice of 1 lemon

yellow and orange food colorings

**1** Preheat the oven to 350°F. Line 2 8- × 2-inch round cake pans, then grease and flour.

**2** In a saucepan, melt the butter over very low heat. Skim off any foam that rises to the surface, then set aside.

**3 ▲** Place a heatproof bowl over a saucepan of hot water. Add the eggs and sugar. Beat with an electric mixer until the mixture doubles in volume and is thick enough to leave a ribbon trail when the beaters are lifted, 8–10 minutes.

**4** Sift the flour and salt together 3 times. Sift over the egg mixture in 3 batches, folding in well after each addition. Fold in the melted butter and vanilla.

**5** Divide the batter between the pans. Level the surfaces and bake until the cakes shrink slightly from the sides of the pans, 25–30 minutes. Let stand 5 minutes, then unmold and transfer to a cooling rack.

**6** Prepare a board, about 16 inches square, covered in paper suitable for contact with food, or in foil.

**7 ▲** For the sunbeams, cut one of the cakes into 8 equal wedges. Cut away a rounded piece from the base of each so that they fit neatly up against the sides of the whole cake.

**8 ▲** For the butter frosting, mix the butter and ⅓ cup of the confectioners' sugar. Use to attach the sunbeams.

**9 ▲** Melt the jam with the water and brush over the cake. Place on the board and straighten, if necessary.

**10 ▲** For the frosting, beat the egg whites until stiff but not dry. Gradually add 3½ cups of the sugar, the glycerin, and lemon juice, and continue beating for 1 minute. The consistency should be spreadable. If necessary, thin with water or add more sugar. Tint with yellow food coloring and spread over the cake.

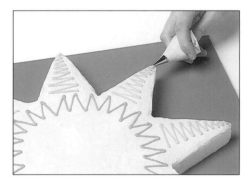

**11 ▲** Divide the remaining frosting in half and tint with more food coloring to obtain bright yellow and orange. Pipe decorative zig-zags on the sunbeams and a face in the middle.

# Jack-O'-Lantern Cake

**SERVES 8–10**

| |
|---|
| 1½ cups cake flour |
| 2½ teaspoons baking powder |
| ⅛ teaspoon salt |
| ½ cup (1 stick) butter, at room temperature |
| 1 cup granulated sugar |
| 3 egg yolks, at room temperature, well beaten |
| 1 teaspoon grated lemon rind |
| ¾ cup milk |
| FOR THE CAKE COVERING |
| 5–6 cups confectioners' sugar |
| 2 egg whites |
| 2 tablespoons liquid glucose |
| orange and black food colorings |

**1** Preheat the oven to 375°F. Line an 8-inch round cake pan with wax paper and grease.

**2** Sift together the flour, baking powder, and salt. Set aside.

**3** With an electric mixer, cream the butter and sugar until light and fluffy. Gradually beat in the egg yolks, then add the lemon rind. Fold in the flour mixture in 3 batches, alternating with the milk.

**4** Spoon the batter into the prepared pan. Bake until a cake tester inserted in the center comes out clean, about 35 minutes. Let stand 5 minutes, then unmold and transfer to a rack.

~ **COOK'S TIP** ~

If preferred, use ready-made roll-out cake covering or rolled fondant, available at specialist cake decorating supply shops and some supermarkets. Knead in food coloring, if required.

**5** For the covering, sift 4½ cups of the confectioners' sugar into a bowl. Make a well in the center, add 1 egg white, the glucose, and orange food coloring. Stir until a dough forms.

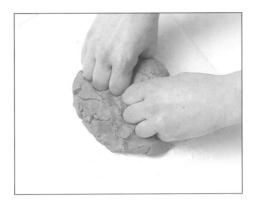

**6** ▲ Transfer to a work surface dusted with confectioners' sugar and knead briefly.

**7** ▲ Roll out the cake covering to a sheet about ⅛ inch thick.

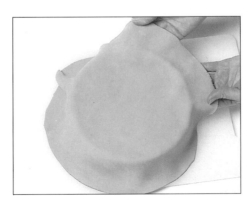

**8** ▲ Gently place the sheet on top of the cooled cake and smooth the sides. Trim the excess and reserve.

**9** ▲ From the trimmings, cut shapes for the lid. Tint the remaining cake covering trimmings with black food coloring. Roll out thinly and cut shapes for the face.

**10** ▲ Brush the undersides with water and arrange the face and lid on the cake.

**11** ▲ Place 1 tablespoon of the remaining egg white in a bowl and stir in enough confectioners' sugar to make a thick frosting. Tint with black food coloring, fill a paper piping bag, and pipe the outline of the lid.

# Stars and Stripes Cake

**SERVES 20**

1 cup (2 sticks) butter or margarine, at room temperature

1 cup dark brown sugar, firmly packed

1 cup granulated sugar

5 eggs, at room temperature

2½ cups flour

2 teaspoons baking powder

1 teaspoon baking soda

1 teaspoon ground cinnamon

1 teaspoon ground ginger

½ teaspoon ground allspice

¼ teaspoon ground cloves

¼ teaspoon salt

1½ cups buttermilk

½ cup raisins

FOR THE CAKE COVERING

2 tablespoons butter

9-10½ cups confectioners' sugar

3 egg whites

4 tablespoons liquid glucose

red and blue food colorings

**1** Preheat the oven to 350°F. Line a 9- × 12-inch baking pan with wax paper and grease.

**2** With an electric mixer, cream the butter or margarine and sugars until light and fluffy. Gradually beat in the eggs, one at a time, beating well after each addition.

**3** Sift together the flour, baking powder, baking soda, spices, and salt. Fold into the butter mixture in 3 batches, alternating with the buttermilk. Stir in the raisins.

**4** Pour the batter into the prepared pan and bake until the cake springs back when touched lightly, about 35 minutes. Let stand 10 minutes, then unmold and transfer to a rack.

**5** For assembly, make the butter frosting. Mix the butter with ⅓ cup of the confectioners' sugar.

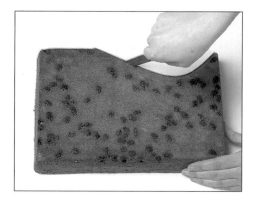

**6 ▲** When the cake is cool, cut a curved shape from the top.

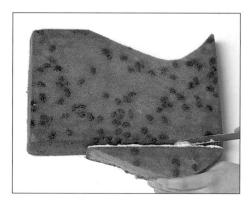

**7 ▲** Attach it to the bottom of the cake with the butter frosting.

**8** Prepare a board, about 16 × 12 inches, covered in paper suitable for contact with food, or in foil. Transfer the cake to the board.

**9** For the cake covering, sift 9 cups of the confectioners' sugar into a bowl. Add 2 of the egg whites and the liquid glucose. Stir until the mixture forms a dough.

**10** Cover and set aside half of the covering. On a work surface dusted with confectioners' sugar, roll out the remaining covering to a sheet. Transfer to the cake. Smooth the sides and trim any excess.

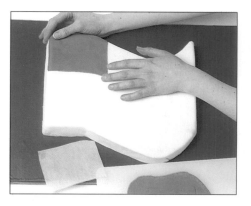

**11 ▲** Tint one-quarter of the remaining covering blue and tint the rest red. Roll out the blue to a thin sheet and cut out the background for the stars. Place on the cake.

**12 ▲** Roll out the red covering, cut out stripes, and place on the cake.

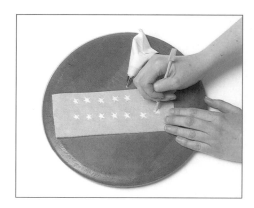

**13 ▲** For the stars, mix 1 tablespoon of the egg white with just enough confectioners' sugar to thicken. Pipe small stars on to a sheet of wax paper and leave to set. When dry, peel them off and place on the blue background.

# LOW-FAT DESSERTS

ALL THE DESSERTS IN THIS
CHAPTER ARE LOW IN FAT, IN MANY
CASES CONTAIN LITTLE OR NO
EGGS, AND OFTEN SUGAR IS
REDUCED BY USING FRUITS TO
SWEETEN THE MIXTURE.
EVERYONE WILL LOVE THESE
BAKED GOODS – THEY'RE BURSTING
WITH FLAVOR AND SUITED TO
ALL OCCASIONS.

# Spiced Apple Cake

Grated apple and chopped dates give this cake a natural sweetness.

### SERVES 8

2 cups whole-wheat flour

4 teaspoons baking powder

¼ teaspoon salt

2 teaspoons ground cinnamon

6 ounces (1 cup) chopped dates

½ cup light brown sugar

1 tablespoon pear and apple spread

½ cup apple juice

2 eggs

6 tablespoons sunflower oil

2 eating apples, cored and grated

1 tablespoon chopped walnuts

**1 ▲** Preheat the oven to 350°F. Grease and line a deep round 8-inch cake pan. Sift the flour, baking powder, salt and cinnamon into a mixing bowl, then mix in the dates and make a well in the center.

**2 ▲** Mix the sugar with the pear and apple spread in a small bowl. Gradually stir in the apple juice. Add to the dry ingredients with the eggs, oil and grated apples. Mix thoroughly.

**3 ▲** Spoon the mixture into the prepared cake pan, sprinkle with the walnuts and bake for 60–65 minutes, or until a cake tester inserted into the center of the cake comes out clean. Transfer to a wire rack, remove the lining paper and allow to cool.

NUTRITION NOTES

Per portion

| | |
|---|---|
| Calories | 331 |
| Fat | 11.41g |
| Saturated Fat | 1.68g |
| Cholesterol | 48.13mg |
| Fiber | 2.5g |

# Spiced Date and Walnut Cake

A classic flavor combination that makes a very easy low-fat, high-fiber cake.

**1** Preheat the oven to 350°F. Grease and line a 2-pound loaf pan with waxed paper.

**SERVES 10**

| |
| --- |
| 2½ cups whole-wheat flour |
| 4 teaspoons baking powder |
| ½ teaspoon salt |
| 2 teaspoons apple pie spice |
| 5 ounces (¾ cup) chopped dates |
| 2 ounces (½ cup) chopped walnuts |
| 4 tablespoons sunflower oil |
| ½ cup dark brown sugar |
| 1¼ cups skim milk |
| walnut halves, to decorate |

**2 ▲** Sift together the flour, baking powder, salt and spice. Stir in the dates and walnuts.

**4 ▲** Spoon into the prepared pan and arrange the walnut halves on top. Bake the cake for 45–50 minutes, or until golden brown and firm. Turn out the cake, remove the lining paper and let cool.

**3 ▲** Mix the oil, sugar and milk in a measuring jug, then stir evenly into the dry ingredients.

NUTRITION NOTES

Per portion

| | |
| --- | --- |
| Calories | 265 |
| Fat | 9.27g |
| Saturated Fat | 1.14g |
| Cholesterol | 0.6mg |
| Fiber | 3.51g |

# Greek Honey and Lemon Cake

Moist and tangy, a delicious afternoon snack.

**MAKES 16 SLICES**

3 tablespoons sunflower margarine

4 tablespoons honey

finely grated rind and juice of
    1 lemon

⅔ cup skim milk

1¼ cups all-purpose flour

1½ teaspoons baking powder

½ teaspoon grated nutmeg

⅓ cup semolina

2 egg whites

2 teaspoons sesame seeds

**1** Preheat the oven to 400°F. Lightly oil a 7½-inch square deep cake pan and line the bottom with baking parchment.

**2 ▲** Gently melt the margarine and 3 tablespoons of the honey. Reserve 1 tablespoon lemon juice, then stir in the rest with the lemon rind and milk. Transfer to a mixing bowl.

**3 ▲** Add the flour, baking powder and nutmeg, and stir through. Gradually beat the semolina into the mixture. Beat the egg whites until soft peaks form, then fold in evenly.

**4 ▲** Spoon into the pan and sprinkle with sesame seeds. Bake the cake for 25–30 minutes, until golden brown. Mix together the reserved honey and lemon juice and drizzle over the cake while warm. Cool in the pan, then cut into fingers to serve.

NUTRITION NOTES

Per portion

| | |
|---|---:|
| Calories | 82 |
| Fat | 2.62g |
| Saturated Fat | 0.46g |
| Cholesterol | 0.36mg |
| Fiber | 0.41g |

# Cranberry and Apple Ring

Tangy cranberries add an unusual flavor to this low-fat cake. It is best eaten very fresh.

**1 ▲** Preheat the oven to 350°F. Lightly grease a 4-cup ring mold with oil.

**2** Sift together the flour and ground cinnamon, then stir in the sugar.

**3 ▲** Toss together the diced apple and cranberries. Stir into the dry ingredients, then add the oil and apple juice and beat well.

**4 ▲** Spoon the mixture into the prepared ring mold and bake for 35–40 minutes, or until the cake is firm to the touch. Turn out and let cool completely on a wire rack.

**5** To serve, drizzle warmed cranberry jelly over the top and decorate with apple slices.

### SERVES 8

| |
|---|
| 2 cups self-rising flour |
| 1 teaspoon ground cinnamon |
| ½ cup light brown sugar |
| 1 crisp eating apple, cored and diced |
| 3 ounces (½ cup) fresh or frozen cranberries |
| 4 tablespoons sunflower oil |
| ⅔ cup apple juice |
| cranberry jelly and apple slices, to decorate |

NUTRITION NOTES
Per portion

| | |
|---|---|
| Calories | 202 |
| Fat | 5.91g |
| Saturated Fat | 0.76g |
| Cholesterol | 0 |
| Fiber | 1.55g |

### ~ COOK'S TIP ~
Fresh cranberries are available throughout the winter months and if you don't use them all at once, they can be frozen for up to a year.

# Lemon Chiffon Cake

Lemon mousse provides a tangy filling for this light lemon sponge.

**SERVES 8**

2 eggs

6 tablespoons sugar

grated rind of 1 lemon

½ cup sifted all-purpose flour

shredded lemon rind, to decorate

FOR THE FILLING

2 eggs, separated

6 tablespoons sugar

grated rind and juice of 1 lemon

½ cup water

1 tablespoon gelatin

½ cup low-fat fromage frais

FOR THE ICING

1 tablespoon lemon juice

scant 1 cup confectioners' sugar, sifted

~ COOK'S TIP ~

The mousse should be just setting when the egg whites are added. Speed up this process by placing the bowl of mousse in iced water.

NUTRITION NOTES

Per portion

| | |
|---|---|
| Calories | 202 |
| Fat | 2.81g |
| Saturated Fat | 0.79g |
| Cholesterol | 96.4mg |
| Fiber | 0.2g |

**1 ▲** Preheat the oven to 350°F. Grease and line an 8-inch loose-bottomed cake pan. Beat the eggs, sugar and lemon rind together until mousselike. Gently fold in the flour, then scrape the mixture into the prepared pan.

**2 ▲** Bake for 20–25 minutes, until the cake springs back when lightly pressed in the center. Turn onto a wire rack. Once cool, split the cake in half horizontally and return the lower half to the clean cake pan.

**3 ▲** Make the filling. Put the egg yolks, sugar, lemon rind and juice in a bowl. Beat with a handheld electric mixer until thick, pale and creamy.

**4 ▲** Pour the water into a heatproof bowl and sprinkle the gelatin on top. Let sit until spongy, then stir over simmering water until dissolved. Cool, then whisk into the yolk mixture. Fold in the fromage frais. When the mixture begins to set, beat the egg whites to soft peaks. Fold the egg whites into the mousse mixture.

**5 ▲** Pour the lemon mousse over the sponge in the cake pan, spreading it to the edges. Set the second layer of sponge on top and chill until set.

**6 ▲** Slide an icing spatula dipped in hot water between the pan and the cake to loosen it. Transfer to a plate. To make icing, add enough lemon juice to the confectioners' sugar to make a thick mixture. Pour over the cake and spread evenly to the edges. Decorate with shredded lemon rind.

# Strawberry Torte

It's hard to believe that this delicious dessert is low in fat, but it's true, so enjoy!

SERVES 6

2 eggs

⅓ cup granulated sugar

grated rind of ½ orange

½ cup all-purpose flour

strawberry leaves, to decorate (optional)

confectioners' sugar, for dusting

FOR THE FILLING

10 ounces (1¼ cups) low-fat soft cheese

grated rind of ½ orange

2 tablespoons granulated sugar

4 tablespoons low-fat fromage frais

8 ounces strawberries, halved

¼ cup chopped almonds, toasted

**1 ▲** Preheat the oven to 375°F. Grease a 12 × 8-in jelly roll pan and line with baking parchment.

**2 ▲** In a bowl, beat the eggs, sugar and orange rind together with a handheld electric mixer until thick and mousselike (when the beaters are lifted, a trail should remain on the surface of the mixture for 15 seconds).

**3 ▲** Fold in the flour with a metal spoon, being careful not to deflate. Turn into the prepared pan. Bake for 15–20 minutes, or until the cake springs back when lightly pressed. Turn the cake out onto a wire rack, remove the lining paper and let cool.

**4 ▲** Meanwhile make the filling. In a bowl, mix the cheese with the orange rind, sugar and fromage frais until smooth. Divide between two bowls. Chop half the strawberry halves and add to one bowl of filling.

**5 ▲** Cut the sponge widthwise into three equal pieces and sandwich them together with the strawberry filling. Spread two-thirds of the plain filling over the sides of the cake and press on the toasted almonds.

**6 ▲** Spread the rest of the filling over the top of the cake and decorate with strawberry halves, and strawberry leaves if desired. Dust with confectioners' sugar and transfer to a serving plate.

~ COOK'S TIP ~

Use other soft fruits in season, such as currants, raspberries, blackberries or blueberries, or try a mixture of different berries.

NUTRITION NOTES

| Per portion | |
| --- | --- |
| Calories | 213 |
| Fat | 6.08g |
| Saturated Fat | 1.84g |
| Cholesterol | 70.22g |
| Fiber | 1.02g |

# Tia Maria Cake

A featherlight coffee sponge with a creamy liqueur-flavored filling.

**SERVES 8**

¾ cup all-purpose flour

2 tablespoons instant coffee granules

3 eggs

½ cup granulated sugar

coffee beans, to decorate (optional)

FOR THE FILLING

6 ounces (¾ cup) low-fat soft cheese

1 tablespoon honey

1 tablespoon Tia Maria liqueur

2 ounces (¼ cup) preserved ginger, roughly chopped

FOR THE ICING

1¼ cups confectioners' sugar, sifted

2 teaspoons coffee extract

1 tablespoon water

1 teaspoon low-fat cocoa powder

**1 ▲** Preheat the oven to 375°F. Grease and line an 8-inch deep round cake pan. Sift the flour and coffee granules together onto a sheet of waxed paper.

**2 ▲** Beat the eggs and sugar in a bowl with a handheld electric mixer until thick and mousselike (when the beaters are lifted, a trail should remain on the surface of the mixture for at least 15 seconds).

> ~ COOK'S TIP ~
> When folding in the flour mixture in step 3, be careful not to remove the air, as it helps the cake to rise.

NUTRITION NOTES
Per portion
| | |
|---|---|
| Calories | 226 |
| Fat | 3.14g |
| Saturated Fat | 1.17g |
| Cholesterol | 75.03mg |
| Fiber | 0.64g |

**3 ▲** Gently fold in the flour mixture with a metal spoon. Pour the mixture into the prepared pan. Bake the sponge for 30–35 minutes, or until it springs back when lightly pressed. Turn out onto a wire rack to cool completely.

**4 ▲** To make the filling, mix the soft cheese with the honey in a bowl. Beat until smooth, then stir in the Tia Maria and chopped preserved ginger.

**5 ▲** Split the cake in half horizontally and sandwich the two halves together with the Tia Maria filling.

**6** Make the icing. In a bowl, mix the confectioners' sugar and coffee extract with enough of the water to create a consistency that will coat the back of a wooden spoon. Pour three-quarters of the icing over the cake, spreading it evenly to the edges. Stir the cocoa into the remaining icing until smooth. Spoon into a pastry bag fitted with a writing nozzle and pipe the mocha icing over the coffee icing. Decorate with coffee beans, if desired.

# Chocolate Banana Cake

A chocolate cake that's deliciously low in fat—it is moist enough to eat without the icing.

**SERVES 8**

| |
| --- |
| 2 cups self-rising flour |
| 3 tablespoons low-fat cocoa powder |
| ⅔ cup light brown sugar |
| 2 tablespoons malt extract |
| 2 tablespoons golden syrup or light corn syrup |
| 2 eggs |
| 4 tablespoons skim milk |
| 4 tablespoons sunflower oil |
| 2 large ripe bananas |
| FOR THE ICING |
| 2 cups confectioners' sugar, sifted |
| 7 teaspoons low-fat cocoa powder, sifted |
| 1–2 tablespoons warm water |

NUTRITION NOTES

Per portion

| | |
| --- | --- |
| Calories | 411 |
| Fat | 8.791g |
| Saturated Fat | 2.06g |
| Cholesterol | 48.27mg |
| Fiber | 2.06g |

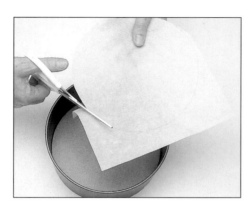

**1 ▲** Preheat the oven to 325°F. Grease and line a deep round 8-inch cake pan.

**2 ▲** Sift the flour into a mixing bowl with the cocoa. Stir in the sugar.

**3 ▲** Make a well in the center and add the malt extract, syrup, eggs, milk and oil. Mash the bananas thoroughly and stir them into the mixture until thoroughly combined.

**4 ▲** Pour the cake mixture into the prepared pan and bake for 1–1¼ hours, or until the center of the cake springs back when lightly pressed.

**5 ▲** Remove the cake from the pan and leave on a wire rack to cool.

**6 ▲** Reserve ⅓ cup confectioners' sugar and 1 teaspoon cocoa powder. Make a dark icing by beating the remaining sugar and cocoa powder with enough of the warm water to make a thick icing. Pour it over the top of the cake and spread evenly. Make a light icing by mixing the reserved sugar and cocoa powder with a few drops of water. Drizzle this icing across the top of the cake.

# Chocolate-Orange Angel Food Cake

This light-as-air sponge with its fluffy icing is virtually fat free, yet tastes heavenly.

## SERVES 10

¼ cup all-purpose flour

2 tablespoons low-fat cocoa powder

2 tablespoons cornstarch

pinch of salt

5 egg whites

½ teaspoon cream of tartar

scant ½ cup sugar

blanched and shredded rind of 1
   orange, to decorate

FOR THE ICING

1 cup sugar

1 egg white

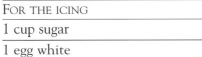

**1 ▲** Preheat the oven to 350°F. Sift the flour, cocoa powder, cornstarch and salt together three times. Beat the egg whites in a large clean, dry bowl until foamy. Add the cream of tartar, then beat until soft peaks form.

**2 ▲** Add the sugar to the egg whites a spoonful at a time, beating after each addition. Sift a third of the flour and cocoa mixture over the meringue and gently fold in. Repeat, sifting and folding in the flour and cocoa mixture two more times.

**3 ▲** Spoon the mixture into a nonstick 8-inch ring mold and level the top. Bake for 35 minutes, or until springy to the touch. Turn upside down onto a wire rack and let cool in the pan. Carefully ease out of the pan.

**4 ▲** For the icing, mix the sugar with 5 tablespoons cold water. Stir over low heat until dissolved. Boil until the syrup reaches 240°F on a candy thermometer or when a drop of the syrup makes a soft ball when dripped into a cup of cold water. Remove from the heat.

**5 ▲** Beat the egg white until stiff. Add the syrup in a thin stream, beating constantly. Continue to beat until the mixture is very thick.

**6 ▲** Spread the icing over the top and sides of the cooled cake. Sprinkle the orange rind over the top of the cake and serve.

## NUTRITION NOTES

Per portion

| | |
|---|---|
| Calories | 53 |
| Fat | 0.27g |
| Saturated Fat | 0.13g |
| Cholesterol | 0 |
| Fiber | 0.25g |

# Eggless Christmas Cake

A deliciously clever way to create a low-calorie Christmas treat!

**SERVES 12**

½ cup golden raisins

½ cup raisins

⅔ cup currants

½ cup candied cherries, halved

⅓ cup cut mixed peel

1 cup apple juice

¼ cup toasted hazelnuts

2 tablespoons pumpkin seeds

2 pieces preserved ginger in syrup

finely grated rind of 1 lemon

½ cup skim milk

½ cup sunflower oil

2 cups whole-wheat flour

4 teaspoons baking powder

2 teaspoons apple pie spice

3 tablespoons brandy or dark rum

**1 ▲** Place the golden raisins, raisins, currants, cherries and mixed peel in a bowl and stir in the apple juice. Cover and allow to soak overnight.

**2** Preheat the oven to 300°F.

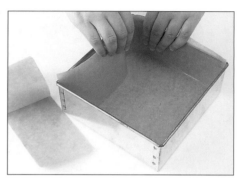

**3 ▲** Lightly grease and line a 7-inch square cake pan.

**4 ▲** Add the nuts, seeds, chopped ginger and rind to the fruit. Stir in the milk, oil, sifted flour, baking powder, and spice, and the brandy or rum.

**5 ▲** Spoon into the prepared pan and bake for 1½ hours, or until golden brown and firm to the touch. Turn out and cool on a wire rack. Brush with sieved apricot jam and decorate with candied fruits, if desired.

NUTRITION NOTES

Per portion

| | |
|---|---|
| Calories | 225 |
| Fat | 6.13g |
| Saturated Fat | 0.89g |
| Cholesterol | 0.2mg |
| Fiber | 2.45g |

# Fruit and Nut Cake

A rich fruit cake that improves with keeping.

**1 ▲** Preheat the oven to 325°F. Grease and line a deep round 8-inch cake pan. Secure a band of brown paper around the outside.

**2 ▲** Sift the flours, baking powder, salt and spice into a mixing bowl and make a well in the center.

**3 ▲** Put the apple and apricot spread in a small bowl. Gradually stir in the honey and molasses. Add to the dry ingredients with the oil, orange juice, eggs and mixed fruit. Mix thoroughly.

**4 ▲** Turn the mixture into the prepared pan and smooth the surface. Arrange the almonds and cherries in a pattern over the top. Bake for 2 hours, or until a cake tester inserted into the center comes out clean. Transfer to a wire rack and let cool, then lift out of the pan and remove the paper.

**SERVES 12–14**

| | |
|---|---|
| 1½ cups whole-wheat flour | |
| 1½ cups self-rising white flour | |
| 2¼ teaspoons baking powder | |
| 2 teaspoons apple pie spice | |
| 1 tablespoon apple and apricot spread | |
| 3 tablespoons honey | |
| 1 tablespoon molasses | |
| 6 tablespoons sunflower oil | |
| ¾ cup orange juice | |
| 2 eggs, beaten | |
| 1½ pounds (4 cups) mixed dried fruit | |
| 3 tablespoons blanched almonds | |
| 2 ounces (½ cup) candied cherries | |

NUTRITION NOTES
Per portion

| | |
|---|---|
| Calories | 333 |
| Fat | 8.54g |
| Saturated Fat | 1.12g |
| Cholesterol | 29.62mg |
| Fiber | 3.08g |

# Banana-Oatmeal Gingerbread

This gingerbread keeps well and really improves over time; it can be stored for up to two months.

## SERVES 12

1¾ cups all-purpose flour

2 teaspoons baking soda

2 teaspoons ground ginger

1¾ cups rolled oats

4 tablespoons dark brown sugar

6 tablespoons sunflower margarine

⅔ cup golden syrup or light corn syrup

1 egg, beaten

3 ripe bananas, mashed

¾ cup confectioners' sugar

## NUTRITION NOTES

Per portion

| | |
|---|---|
| Calories | 277 |
| Fat | 6.9g |
| Saturated Fat | 6.9g |
| Cholesterol | 16.4mg |
| Fiber | 1.72g |

**1** Preheat the oven to 325°F. Grease and line a 7 x 11-inch cake pan.

**2 ▲** Sift together the flour, baking soda and ginger, then stir in the oats. Melt the sugar, margarine and syrup in a saucepan, then stir into the flour mixture. Beat in the egg and mashed bananas.

**3 ▲** Spoon into the pan and bake for about 1 hour, or until firm to the touch. Allow to cool in the pan, then turn out and cut into squares.

**4 ▲** Sift the confectioners' sugar into a bowl and stir in just enough water to make a smooth, runny icing. Drizzle the icing over each square and top with a piece of preserved ginger, if desired.

~ COOK'S TIP ~

This is a nutritious, energy-giving cake that is a good choice for brown-bag lunches because it doesn't break up easily.

# Nectarine Amaretto Cake

Amaretto liqueur adds a hint of luxury to this fruity cake.

**1 ▲** Preheat the oven to 350°F. Grease an 8-inch round loose-bottomed cake pan. Beat together the egg yolks, sugar, lemon rind and juice in a bowl until the mixture is thick, pale and creamy.

**2** Fold in the semolina, almonds and flour until smooth.

**3 ▲** Beat the egg whites in a bowl until fairly stiff. Use a metal spoon to stir a generous spoonful of the whites into the semolina mixture, then fold in the remaining egg whites. Spoon the mixture into the cake pan.

**4** Bake for 30–35 minutes, until the center of the cake springs back when pressed lightly. Remove from the oven and loosen around the edge with a metal spatula. Prick the top all over with a skewer. Allow to cool in the pan.

**5** To make the syrup, heat the sugar and water in a small pan, stirring until the sugar is dissolved. Boil without stirring for 2 minutes. Add the Amaretto liqueur and drizzle the liqueur syrup over the cake in the pan.

**6 ▲** Remove the cake from the pan and transfer to a serving plate. Decorate with sliced nectarines. Brush with warm apricot glaze.

**SERVES 8**

| |
|---|
| 3 eggs, separated |
| ¾ cup sugar |
| grated rind and juice of 1 lemon |
| ⅓ cup semolina |
| ¼ cup ground almonds |
| ¼ cup all-purpose flour |
| 2 nectarines, pitted and sliced |
| 4 tablespoons apricot glaze |
| **FOR THE SYRUP** |
| ⅓ cup sugar |
| 6 tablespoons water |
| 2 tablespoons Amaretto liqueur |

NUTRITION NOTES
Per portion
| | |
|---|---|
| Calories | 264 |
| Fat | 5.7g |
| Saturated Fat | 0.85g |
| Cholesterol | 72.19mg |
| Fiber | 1.08g |

# Banana and Gingerbread Slices

Very quick to make and deliciously moist due to the addition of bananas.

**SERVES 20**

| | |
|---|---|
| ½ cup light brown sugar | |
| 2 cups all-purpose flour | |
| 4 teaspoons ground ginger | |
| 2 teaspoons apple pie spice | |
| 1 teaspoon baking soda | |
| 4 tablespoons sunflower oil | |
| 2 tablespoons molasses | |
| 2 tablespoons malt extract | |
| 2 eggs | |
| 4 tablespoons orange juice | |
| 3 bananas | |
| 4 ounces (⅔ cup) raisins | |

~ VARIATION ~

To make Spiced Honey and Banana Cake; omit the ground ginger and add another 1 teaspoon apple pie spice; omit the malt extract and the molasses and add 4 tablespoons strong-flavored honey instead; and replace the raisins with either golden raisins, coarsely chopped dried apricots, or semi-dried pineapple. If you choose to use the pineapple, then you could also replace the orange juice with fresh pineapple juice.

~ COOK'S TIP ~

The flavor of this cake develops as it keeps, so if you can, store it for a few days before eating.

NUTRITION NOTES

| Per portion | |
|---|---|
| Calories | 148 |
| Fat | 3.07g |
| Saturated Fat | 0.53g |
| Cholesterol | 19.3mg |
| Fiber | 0.79g |

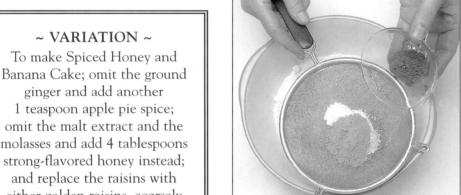

**1** ▲ Preheat the oven to 350°F. Lightly grease and line a 7 × 11-inch baking pan.

**4** ▲ Mash the bananas, then add them to the bowl with the raisins and mix together well.

**2** ▲ Mix in the sugar with some of the flour and sift it into the bowl. Sift the remaining flour into the bowl with the spices and baking soda.

**5** ▲ Pour the mixture into the prepared baking pan and bake for 35–40 minutes, or until the center springs back when lightly pressed.

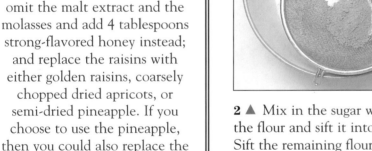

**3** ▲ Make a well in the center, add the oil, molasses, malt extract, eggs and orange juice and mix together thoroughly.

**6** ▲ Leave the cake in the pan to cool for 5 minutes, then turn out onto a wire rack and allow to cool completely. Cut into 20 slices.

# Apricot and Orange Roulade

This elegant dessert is very good served with a spoonful of plain yogurt.

SERVES 6

4 egg whites

½ cup raw sugar

½ cup all-purpose flour

finely grated rind of 1 small orange

3 tablespoons orange juice

2 teaspoons confectioners' sugar and orange zest, to decorate

FOR THE FILLING

4 ounces (⅔ cup) dried apricots

⅔ cup orange juice

NUTRITION NOTES

Per portion

| | |
|---|---|
| Calories | 203 |
| Fat | 10.52g |
| Saturated Fat | 2.05g |
| Cholesterol | 0 |
| Fiber | 2.53g |

**1** Preheat the oven to 400°F. Grease a 9 × 13-inch jelly roll pan and line it with baking parchment. Grease the paper.

**2 ▲** For the roulade, place the egg whites in a large bowl and beat them until they hold peaks. Gradually add the sugar, beating hard between each addition.

**3** Fold in the flour, orange rind and juice. Spoon the mixture into the prepared pan and spread it evenly.

**4** Bake for about 15–18 minutes, or until the sponge is firm and light golden in color. Turn out onto a sheet of baking parchment and loosely roll it up jelly-roll-style from one short side. Allow to cool.

**5 ▲** For the filling, roughly chop the apricots and place them in a saucepan with the orange juice. Cover the pan and let simmer until most of the liquid has been absorbed. Purée the apricots in a food processor.

**6 ▲** Unroll the roulade and spread with the apricot mixture. Roll up, arrange strips of paper diagonally across the roll, sprinkle lightly with lines of confectioners' sugar, remove the paper and sprinkle with orange zest to serve.

~ COOK'S TIP ~

Make and bake the sponge mixture a day in advance and keep it, rolled with the paper, in a cool place. Fill it with the fruit purée 2–3 hours before serving.

# Strawberry Roulade

A creamy fruit filling is delicious in a light roulade.

**1** Preheat the oven to 400°F. Oil a 9 × 13-inch jelly roll pan and line with baking parchment.

**2** ▲ Place the egg whites in a large bowl and beat until they form soft peaks. Gradually beat in the sugar. Fold in half of the sifted flour, then fold in the rest with the orange juice.

**3** Spoon the mixture into the prepared pan, spreading evenly. Bake for 15–18 minutes, or until golden brown and firm to the touch.

**4** ▲ Meanwhile, spread out a sheet of baking parchment and sprinkle with granulated sugar. Turn out the cake onto this and remove the lining paper. Roll up the sponge loosely from one short side, with the paper inside. Cool.

**5** Unroll and remove the paper. Stir the strawberries into the fromage frais and spread over the sponge. Re-roll and serve decorated with strawberries.

**SERVES 6**

| |
|---|
| 4 egg whites |
| ⅔ cup raw sugar |
| ⅔ cup all-purpose flour, sifted |
| 2 tablespoons orange juice |
| granulated sugar, for sprinkling |
| 4 ounces (1 cup) strawberries, chopped |
| 5 ounces (¾ cup) low-fat fromage frais |
| strawberries, to decorate |

NUTRITION NOTES
Per portion
| | |
|---|---|
| Calories | 154 |
| Fat | 0.24g |
| Saturated Fat | 0.01g |
| Cholesterol | 0.25mg |
| Fiber | 0.61g |

# Peach Jelly Roll

A featherlight sponge enclosing peach jam—delicious with tea.

**SERVES 6–8**

| |
|---|
| 3 eggs |
| ½ cup granulated sugar, plus extra for sprinkling |
| ¾ cup all-purpose flour, sifted |
| 1 tablespoon boiling water |
| 6 tablespoons peach jam |
| confectioners' sugar, for dusting (optional) |

---

~ **COOK'S TIP** ~

To decorate the jelly roll with glacé icing, make the icing with 1¾ cups confectioners' sugar and enough warm water to make a thin glacé icing. Put in a pastry bag fitted with a small writing nozzle and pipe lines over the top.

---

NUTRITION NOTES

Per portion

| | |
|---|---|
| Calories | 178 |
| Fat | 2.54g |
| Saturated Fat | 0.67g |
| Cholesterol | 82.5mg |
| Fiber | 0.33g |

**1 ▲** Preheat the oven to 400°F. Grease a 12 × 8-inch jelly roll pan and line with baking parchment. Combine the eggs and sugar in a bowl. Beat with a handheld electric mixer until thick and mousselike. (When the beaters are lifted, a trail should remain on the surface of the mixture for at least 15 seconds.)

**2 ▲** Carefully fold in the flour with a large metal spoon, then add the boiling water in the same way.

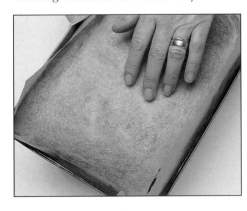

**3 ▲** Spoon into the prepared pan, spread evenly to the edges and bake for 10–12 minutes, until the cake springs back when lightly pressed.

**4 ▲** Spread a sheet of waxed paper on a flat surface, sprinkle it with granulated sugar, then invert the cake on top. Peel off the paper.

**5 ▲** Neatly trim the edges of the cake. Make a neat cut two-thirds of the way through the cake, about ½ inch from the short edge nearest you.

**6 ▲** Spread the cake with the peach jam and roll up quickly from the partially cut end. Hold in position for a minute, making sure the seam is underneath. Cool on a wire rack. Decorate with glacé icing (see Cook's Tip) or dust with confectioners' sugar before serving.

# Chestnut and Orange Roulade

This moist cake is ideal to serve as a dessert.

## SERVES 8

3 eggs, separated

½ cup granulated sugar

8 ounces (1 cup) canned unsweetened chestnut purée

grated rind and juice of 1 orange

confectioners' sugar, for dusting

### FOR THE FILLING

1 cup low-fat soft cheese

1 tablespoon honey

1 orange

**1** ▲ Preheat the oven to 350°F. Grease a 12 × 8-inch jelly roll pan and line it with baking parchment. Beat the egg yolks and sugar in a bowl until thick and creamy.

**2** ▲ Put the chestnut purée in a separate bowl. Beat in the orange rind and juice, then beat the flavored chestnut purée into the egg mixture.

**3** ▲ Beat the egg whites in a grease-free bowl until fairly stiff. Using a metal spoon, stir a generous spoonful of the whites into the chestnut mixture to lighten it, then fold in the rest. Spoon into the prepared pan and bake for 30 minutes, until firm. Cool for 5 minutes, then cover with a clean damp dish towel until completely cool.

**4** ▲ Meanwhile, make the filling. Mix the soft cheese with the honey. Finely grate the orange rind and add. Peel away all the pith from the orange, cut the fruit into segments, chop roughly and set aside. Add any juice to the cheese mixture, then beat until smooth. Mix in the orange.

**5** ▲ Dust a sheet of waxed paper thickly with confectioners' sugar. Carefully turn the roulade out onto the paper, then peel off the lining paper. Spread the filling over the roulade and roll up like a jelly roll. Transfer to a plate and dust with some more confectioners' sugar.

---

## ~ COOK'S TIP ~

Do not whisk the egg whites too stiffly or it will be difficult to fold them into the mixture and they will form lumps in the roulade.

---

## NUTRITION NOTES

Per portion

| | |
|---|---|
| Calories | 185 |
| Fat | 4.01g |
| Saturated Fat | 1.47g |
| Cholesterol | 76.25mg |
| Fiber | 1.4g |

# Chocolate, Date and Walnut Pudding

Puddings are not totally taboo when you're cutting calories or fat—this one stays within the rules! Serve hot, with yogurt or skim-milk custard.

**SERVES 4**

| |
|---|
| 1 ounce (4 tablespoons) walnuts |
| 1 ounce (2 tablespoons) dates |
| 2 eggs |
| 1 teaspoon vanilla extract |
| 2 tablespoons raw sugar |
| 3 tablespoons whole-wheat flour |
| 1 tablespoon cocoa powder |
| 2 tablespoons skim milk |

NUTRITION NOTES

| Per portion | |
|---|---|
| Calories | 169 |
| Fat | 8.1g |
| Saturated Fat | 1.7g |
| Cholesterol | 96mg |
| Fiber | 1.8g |

**1 ▲** Preheat the oven to 350°F. Grease a 5-cup pudding bowl and place a small circle of waxed paper or baking parchment in the bottom. Chop the walnuts and the dates and spoon into the bowl.

**2 ▲** Separate the eggs and place the yolks in a bowl with the vanilla and sugar. Place the bowl over a pan of hot water and beat until the mixture is thick and pale.

**3 ▲** Sift the flour and cocoa into the mixture and fold them in with a metal spoon. Stir in the milk to soften the mixture slightly. Beat the egg whites until they hold soft peaks and fold them in.

**4 ▲** Spoon the batter into the bowl and bake for 40–45 minutes, or until the pudding is well risen and firm to the touch. Run a knife around the pudding, then turn it out and serve.

# Featherlight Peach Pudding

On chilly days, try this hot fruit pudding with its tantalizing sponge topping.

**1 ▲** Preheat the oven to 350°F. Drain the peaches and place in a 4-cup pie dish with 2 tablespoons of the juice.

**2 ▲** Put all the remaining ingredients, except the confectioners' sugar, into a mixing bowl. Beat for 3–4 minutes, until well combined.

**3 ▲** Spoon the sponge mixture over the peaches and level the top evenly. Bake for 35–40 minutes, or until springy to the touch.

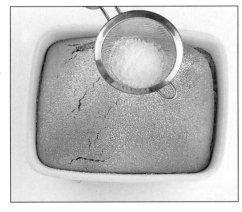

**4 ▲** Lightly dust the top with confectioners' sugar before serving hot with the custard.

~ COOK'S TIP ~

For a simple sauce, blend 1 teaspoon arrowroot with 1 tablespoon peach juice in a small saucepan. Stir in the remaining peach juice from the can and simmer for 1 minute.

## SERVES 4

| 14 ounces (3 cups) canned peach slices in natural juice |
| 4 tablespoons low-fat spread |
| ¼ cup light brown sugar |
| 1 egg, beaten |
| ¼ cup whole-wheat flour |
| ¼ cup all-purpose flour |
| 1 teaspoon baking powder |
| ½ teaspoon ground cinnamon |
| ¼ cup skim milk |
| ½ teaspoon vanilla extract |
| 2 teaspoons confectioners' sugar |
| low-fat ready-to-serve custard |

## NUTRITION NOTES
Per portion

| | |
|---|---|
| Calories | 255 |
| Fat | 6.78g |
| Saturated Fat | 1.57g |
| Cholesterol | 35mg |
| Fiber | 2.65g |

# Snowballs

A variation on the basic meringue recipe, these snowballs are made with cornstarch. They make an excellent accompaniment to ice cream.

**MAKES ABOUT 20**

| |
|---|
| 2 egg whites |
| ½ cup sugar |
| 1 tablespoon cornstarch, sifted |
| 1 teaspoon white wine vinegar |
| ¼ teaspoon vanilla extract |

NUTRITION NOTES

Per portion

| | |
|---|---|
| Calories | 29 |
| Fat | 0.01g |
| Saturated Fat | 0 |
| Cholesterol | 0 |
| Fiber | 0 |

**1 ▲** Preheat the oven to 300°F. Line two baking sheets with baking parchment. Beat the egg whites in a large grease-free bowl until very stiff.

**2 ▲** Add the sugar, beating until the meringue is very stiff. Beat in the cornstarch, vinegar and vanilla.

**3 ▲** Drop teaspoonfuls of the mixture onto the baking sheets, shaping them into mounds, and bake for 30 minutes, until crisp.

**4 ▲** Remove from the oven and allow to cool on the baking sheets. When the snowballs are cold, remove them from the baking paper with a spatula.

# Brown Sugar Meringues

These light brown meringues are extremely low in fat and are delicious served on their own or sandwiched together with a fresh-fruit soft-cheese filling.

**1 ▲** Preheat the oven to 325°F. Line two baking sheets with baking parchment. Press the sugar through a metal sieve into a bowl.

**2 ▲** Beat the egg whites in a clean, dry bowl, until very stiff and dry, then beat in the sugar, about 1 tablespoon at a time until the meringue is very thick and glossy.

**3 ▲** Spoon small mounds of the meringue mixture onto the prepared baking sheets.

**4 ▲** Sprinkle the meringues with the chopped walnuts. Bake for 30 minutes. Cool for 5 minutes on the baking sheets, then cool on a wire rack.

**MAKES ABOUT 20**

¾ cup light brown sugar

2 egg whites

1 teaspoon finely chopped walnuts

NUTRITION NOTES
Per portion

| | |
|---|---|
| Calories | 197 |
| Fat | 6.8g |
| Saturated Fat | 1.4g |
| Cholesterol | 25mg |
| Fiber | 0.7g |

# Coffee Sponge Drops

These are delicious on their own, but taste even better with a filling made by mixing low-fat soft cheese with drained and chopped preserved ginger.

### MAKES 12

| |
|---|
| ½ cup all-purpose flour |
| 1 tablespoon instant coffee granules |
| 2 eggs |
| 6 tablespoons sugar |
| FOR THE FILLING |
| 4 ounces (½ cup) low-fat soft cheese |
| 1½ ounces (¼ cup) chopped preserved ginger |

**1 ▲** Preheat the oven to 375°F. Line two baking sheets with baking parchment. Make the filling by beating together the soft cheese and ginger. Chill until required. Sift the flour and coffee granules together.

**2 ▲** Combine the eggs and sugar in a bowl. Beat with a handheld electric mixer until thick and mousselike. (When the beaters are lifted, a trail should remain on the surface of the mixture for at least 15 seconds.)

**3 ▲** Carefully add the sifted flour and coffee mixture and gently fold in with a metal spoon, being careful not to knock out any air.

**4 ▲** Spoon the mixture into a pastry bag fitted with a ½-inch plain nozzle. Pipe 1½-inch rounds on the baking sheets. Bake for 12 minutes. Cool on a wire rack, then sandwich together with the filling.

~ COOK'S TIP ~
As an alternative to preserved ginger in the filling, try walnuts.

NUTRITION NOTES
Per portion
| | |
|---|---|
| Calories | 69 |
| Fat | 1.36g |
| Saturated Fat | 0.5g |
| Cholesterol | 33.33mg |
| Fiber | 0.29g |

# Raspberry Vacherin

Meringue rounds filled with orange-flavored fromage frais and fresh raspberries make a perfect dinner-party dessert.

## SERVES 6

3 egg whites

¾ cup granulated sugar

1 teaspoon chopped almonds

confectioners' sugar, for dusting

raspberry leaves, to
   decorate (optional)

### FOR THE FILLING

6 ounces (¾ cup) low-fat soft cheese

1–2 tablespoons honey

1 tablespoon Cointreau

½ cup low-fat fromage frais

8 ounces (1¼ cups) raspberries

~ COOK'S TIP ~

When making the meringue, beat the egg whites until they are so stiff that you can turn the bowl upside down without them falling out.

NUTRITION NOTES
Per portion
Calories                   248
Fat                        2.22g
Saturated Fat              0.82g
Cholesterol                4mg
Fiber                      1.06g

**1 ▲** Preheat the oven to 275°F. Draw an 8-inch circle on two pieces of baking parchment. Turn the paper over so the marking is on the underside and use it to line two heavy baking sheets.

**2 ▲** Beat the egg whites in a grease-free bowl until very stiff, then gradually beat in the granulated sugar to make a stiff meringue mixture.

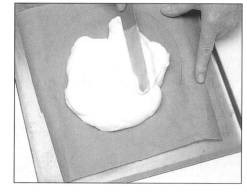

**3 ▲** Spoon the mixture onto the circles on the prepared baking sheets, spreading the meringue evenly to the edges. Sprinkle one meringue round with the chopped almonds.

**4 ▲** Bake for 1½–2 hours, then carefully lift the meringue rounds off the baking sheets, peel away the paper and cool on a wire rack.

**5 ▲** To make the filling, cream the soft cheese with the honey and liqueur in a bowl. Fold in the fromage frais and raspberries, reserving three for decoration.

**6 ▲** Place the plain meringue round on a board, spread with the filling and top with the nut-covered round. Dust with confectioners' sugar, transfer to a serving plate and decorate with the reserved raspberries and a sprig of raspberry leaves, if desired.

# Baked Blackberry Cheesecake

This light, low-fat cheesecake is best made with wild blackberries, if they're available, but cultivated ones will do; or substitute other soft fruit, such as loganberries or raspberries.

**SERVES 5**

6 ounces (¾ cup) low-fat
    cottage cheese

⅔ cup low-fat plain yogurt

1 tablespoon whole-wheat flour

2 tablespoons raw sugar

1 egg

1 egg white

finely grated rind and juice of
    ½ lemon

7 ounces (2 cups) fresh or frozen and
    thawed blackberries

### ~ COOK'S TIP ~

If you prefer to use canned blackberries, choose those in natural juice and drain the fruit well before adding it to the cheesecake mixture. The juice can be served with the cheesecake, but this will increase the total calories.

NUTRITION NOTES
Per portion
| | |
|---|---|
| Calories | 103 |
| Fat | 2g |
| Saturated Fat | 0.8g |
| Cholesterol | 41mg |
| Fiber | 1.6g |

**1 ▲** Preheat the oven to 350°F. Lightly grease and line a 7-inch layer-cake pan.

**2 ▲** Place the cottage cheese in a food processor and process until smooth. Alternatively, rub it through a sieve to obtain a smooth mixture.

**3 ▲** Add the yogurt, flour, sugar, egg and egg white, and mix. Add the lemon rind, juice and blackberries, reserving a few for decoration.

**4 ▲** Pour the mixture into the pan and bake for 30–35 minutes, or until it is just set. Turn off the oven and leave for another 30 minutes.

**5 ▲** Run a knife around the edge of the cheesecake and then turn it out. Remove the lining paper and place the cheesecake on a warm serving plate.

**6** Decorate the cheesecake with the reserved blackberries and serve it warm.

# Mango and Amaretti Strudel

Fresh mango and crushed amaretti cookies wrapped in wafer-thin filo pastry make a special treat that is equally delicious made with apricots or plums.

### SERVES 4

| |
| --- |
| 1 large mango |
| grated rind of 1 lemon |
| 2 amaretti cookies |
| 3 tablespoons raw sugar |
| 4 tablespoons whole-wheat bread crumbs |
| 2 sheets filo pastry, each 18 x 11 inches |
| 4 teaspoons soft margarine, melted |
| 1 tablespoon chopped almonds |
| confectioners' sugar, for dusting |

**1 ▲** Preheat the oven to 375°F. Lightly grease a large baking sheet. Halve, pit and peel the mango. Cut the flesh into cubes, then place them in a bowl and sprinkle with grated lemon rind.

**2 ▲** Crush the amaretti cookies and mix them with the raw sugar and the whole-wheat bread crumbs.

---

~ COOK'S TIP ~

The easiest way to prepare a mango is to cut horizontally through the fruit, keeping the knife blade close to the pit. Repeat on the other side of the pit and peel off the skin. Remove the remaining skin and flesh from around the pit.

---

NUTRITION NOTES
Per portion
| | |
| --- | --- |
| Calories | 239 |
| Fat | 8.45g |
| Saturated Fat | 4.43g |
| Cholesterol | 17.25mg |
| Fiber | 3.3g |

**3 ▲** Lay one sheet of filo on a flat surface and brush with a quarter of the margarine. Top with the second sheet, brush with one-third of the remaining margarine, then fold both sheets over to make a rectangle measuring 11 x 9 inches. Brush with half the remaining margarine.

**4 ▲** Sprinkle the filo with the amaretti mixture, leaving a 2-inch border on each long side. Arrange the mango cubes over the top.

**5 ▲** Roll up the filo from one of the long sides, jelly roll-style. Lift the strudel onto the baking sheet with the seam underneath. Brush with the remaining melted margarine and sprinkle with the chopped almonds.

**6 ▲** Bake for 20–25 minutes, until golden brown, then transfer to a board. Dust with the confectioners' sugar, slice diagonally and serve warm.

# Blueberry and Orange Crêpe Baskets

Impress your guests with these pretty, fruit-filled crêpes. When blueberries are not in season, replace them with other soft fruit, such as raspberries.

**SERVES 6**

FOR THE CRÊPES

1¼ cups all-purpose flour

pinch of salt

2 egg whites

1 cup skim milk

⅔ cup orange juice

FOR THE FILLING

4 medium-size oranges

2 cups blueberries

~ COOK'S TIP ~

Don't fill the pancake baskets until you're ready to serve them, because they will absorb the fruit juice and begin to soften. leave to rise, then bake for about 15–20 minutes. Brush with the glaze while still hot.

NUTRITION NOTES

| Per portion | |
|---|---|
| Calories | 159 |
| Fat | 0.5g |
| Saturated Fat | 0.1g |
| Cholesterol | 1mg |
| Fiber | 3.3g |

**1 ▲** Preheat the oven to 400°F. To make the crêpes, sift the flour and salt into a bowl. Make a well in the center of the flour and add the egg whites, milk and orange juice. Beat hard, until all the liquid has been incorporated and the batter is smooth and bubbly.

**2 ▲** Lightly grease a heavy or nonstick crêpe pan and heat until it is very hot. Pour in just enough batter to cover the base of the pan, swirling it to cover the pan evenly.

**3 ▲** Cook until the crêpe has set and is golden, then turn it to cook the other side. Remove the crêpe to a sheet of absorbent paper towel, and then cook the remaining batter, to make 6–8 crêpes.

**4 ▲** Place six small ovenproof bowls or molds on a baking sheet and arrange the crêpes over these. Bake the crêpes in the oven for about 10 minutes, until they are crisp and set into the shape of the molds. Lift the "baskets" off the molds.

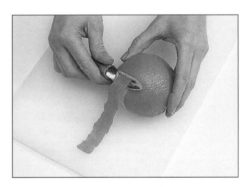

**5 ▲** For the filling, pare a thin piece of orange rind from one orange and cut it in fine strips. Blanch the strips in boiling water for 30 seconds, rinse in cold water and set aside. Cut the peel and white pith from the oranges.

**6 ▲** Divide the oranges into segments, catching the juice, combine with the blueberries and warm them gently. Spoon the fruit into the baskets and scatter the shreds of rind over the top. Serve with yogurt or light crème fraîche.

# Filo and Apricot Purses

Filo pastry is very easy to use and is low in fat. Keep a box in the freezer ready for rustling up a speedy treat.

**MAKES 12**

¾ cup dried apricots

3 tablespoons apricot compote or conserve

3 amaretti cookies, crushed

3 sheets filo pastry

4 teaspoons soft margarine, melted

confectioners' sugar, for dusting

NUTRITION NOTES

Per portion

| | |
|---|---|
| Calories | 58 |
| Fat | 1.85g |
| Saturated Fat | 0.4g |
| Cholesterol | 0.12mg |
| Fiber | 0.74g |

**1 ▲** Preheat the oven to 350°F. Grease two baking sheets. Chop the apricots, put them in a bowl and stir in the apricot compote. Add the crushed amaretti cookies and mix well.

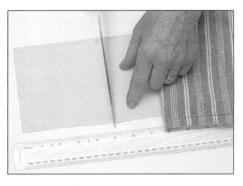

**2 ▲** Cut the pastry into twenty-four 5-inch squares, pile the squares on top of each other and cover with a clean dish towel to prevent the pastry from drying and becoming brittle.

**3 ▲** Lay one pastry square on a flat surface, brush lightly with melted margarine, and lay another square diagonally on top. Brush the top square with melted margarine. Spoon a small mound of apricot mixture in the center of the pastry, bring up the edges and pinch together in a money-bag shape. Repeat with the remaining squares to make 12 purses.

**4 ▲** Arrange the purses on the baking sheets and bake for 5–8 minutes, until golden. Transfer to a wire rack and dust with confectioners' sugar.

# Filo Scrunchies

Quick and easy to make, these pastries are ideal to serve as an afternoon snack. Eat them warm or they will lose their crispness.

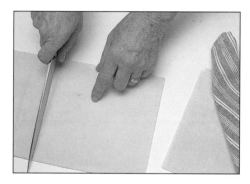

**MAKES 6**

5 apricots or plums

4 sheets filo pastry

4 teaspoons soft margarine, melted

⅓ cup raw sugar

2 tablespoons sliced almonds

confectioners' sugar, for dusting

**1 ▲** Preheat the oven to 375°F. Halve the apricots or plums, remove the pits and slice the fruit. Cut the filo pastry into twelve 7-inch squares. Pile the squares on top of each other and cover with a clean dish towel to prevent the pastry from drying out.

**4 ▲** Place the scrunchies on a baking sheet. Bake for 8–10 minutes, until golden brown, then loosen the scrunchies from the baking sheet with a metal spatula and transfer to a wire rack. Dust with confectioners' sugar and serve at once.

NUTRITION NOTES
Per portion
| | |
|---|---|
| Calories | 132 |
| Fat | 4.19g |
| Saturated Fat | 0.63g |
| Cholesterol | 0 |
| Fiber | 0.67g |

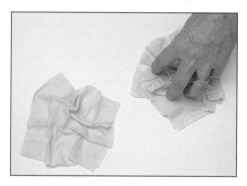

**2 ▲** Remove one square of filo and brush it with melted margarine. Lay a second filo square on top, then, using your fingers, mold the pastry into folds. Make five more scrunchies in the same way, working quickly so that the pastry does not dry out.

**3 ▲** Arrange a few slices of fruit in the folds of each scrunchie, then sprinkle generously with the raw sugar and the almonds.

# Plum Phyllo Pockets

These attractive party parcels are high in fiber as well as being a tasty treat.

**SERVES 4**

4 ounces (½ cup) non-fat milk
   soft cheese

1 tablespoon light brown sugar

½ teaspoon ground cloves

8 large, firm plums, halved and pitted

8 sheets phyllo pastry

sunflower oil, for brushing

confectioners' sugar, for sprinkling

NUTRITION NOTES

| Per portion | |
| --- | --- |
| Calories | 188 |
| Fat | 1.87g |
| Saturated Fat | 0.27g |
| Cholesterol | 0.29mg |
| Fiber | 2.55g |

**1** ▲ Preheat the oven to 425°F.
Mix together the cheese, sugar and
ground cloves.

**2** ▲ Sandwich the plum halves back
together with a spoonful of the
cheese mixture in each plum.

**3** Spread out the pastry and cut into
16 pieces, about 9 inches square.
Brush one lightly with oil and place
a second at a diagonal on top. Repeat
with the remaining squares.

**4** ▲ Place a plum on each pastry
square and gather the corners
together. Place on a baking sheet.
Bake for 15–18 minutes, until
golden, then dust lightly with
confectioners' sugar.

# Glazed Apricot Sponge

Puddings can be very high in saturated fat, but this one uses the minimum of oil and no eggs.

**1 ▲** Preheat the oven to 350°F. Lightly oil a 3¾-cup pudding bowl. Spoon in the syrup.

**2 ▲** Drain the apricots and reserve the juice. Arrange about eight halves in the bowl. Purée the rest of the apricots with the juice and set aside.

**3 ▲** Mix the flour, bread crumbs, sugar and cinnamon, then beat in the oil and milk. Spoon into the pudding bowl and bake for 50–55 minutes, or until firm and golden. Turn out and serve with the puréed fruit as a sauce.

## SERVES 4

2 teaspoons golden syrup or light corn syrup

14½-ounce can apricot halves

1¼ cups self-rising flour

1½ cups fresh bread crumbs

⅔ cup light brown sugar

1 teaspoon ground cinnamon

2 tablespoons sunflower oil

¾ cup skim milk

NUTRITION NOTES
Per portion
| | |
|---|---|
| Calories | 364 |
| Fat | 6.47g |
| Saturated Fat | 0.89g |
| Cholesterol | 0.88mg |
| Fiber | 2.37g |

# Latticed Peaches

An elegant dessert; it certainly doesn't look low in fat, but it really is. Use canned peach halves when fresh peaches are out of season, or if you're short of time.

## SERVES 6

### FOR THE PASTRY

1 cup all-purpose flour

3 tablespoons butter or
　sunflower margarine

3 tablespoons low-fat plain yogurt

2 tablespoons orange juice

skim milk, for glaze

### FOR THE FILLING

3 ripe peaches or nectarines

3 tablespoons ground almonds

2 tablespoons low-fat plain yogurt

finely grated rind of 1 small orange

¼ teaspoon almond extract

### FOR THE SAUCE

1 ripe peach or nectarine

3 tablespoons orange juice

~ COOK'S TIP ~

This dessert is best eaten fairly fresh from the oven as the pastry can toughen slightly if left to stand. Assemble the peaches in their pastry on a baking sheet, chill in the refrigerator, and bake just before serving.

NUTRITION NOTES

| | |
|---|---|
| Per portion | |
| Calories | 219 |
| Fat | 10.8g |
| Saturated Fat | 1.6g |
| Cholesterol | 1mg |
| Fiber | 2.4g |

**1 ▲** For the pastry, sift the flour into a bowl and, using your fingertips, rub in the butter or margarine evenly. Stir in the yogurt and orange juice to bind the mixture into a firm dough.

**2 ▲** Roll out about half the pastry thinly and use a pastry cutter to stamp out rounds about 3 inches in diameter, slightly larger than the circumference of the peaches. Place on a lightly greased baking sheet.

**3 ▲** Peel the peaches or nectarines, halve and remove the pits. Mix together the almonds, yogurt, orange rind and almond extract. Spoon into each peach half and place, cut side down, on the pastry rounds.

**4 ▲** Roll out the remaining pastry thinly and cut into thin strips. Arrange the strips over the peaches to form a lattice, brushing with milk to secure firmly. Trim off the ends.

**5 ▲** Chill in the refrigerator for 30 minutes. Preheat the oven to 400°F. Brush with milk and bake for 15–18 minutes, until golden brown.

**6 ▲** For the sauce, peel the peach or nectarine and halve it to remove the pit. Place the flesh in a food processor with the orange juice, and purée it until smooth. Serve the peaches hot, with the peach sauce spooned around.

# CLASSIC BREADS

THOUGH THE PACE OF TODAY'S LIFE MAY LEAVE LESS TIME FOR BAKING, BREADMAKING CAN BE THE BEST ANTIDOTE. THE PROCESS IS SIMPLE YET INFINITELY VARIABLE, AS THE LOAVES THAT FOLLOW PROVE. ROLL UP YOUR SLEEVES AND CREATE A TRADITION.

# White Bread

¼ cup lukewarm water

1 package active dry yeast

2 tablespoons sugar

2 cups lukewarm milk

2 tablespoons butter or margarine, at room temperature

2 teaspoons salt

6–6½ cups flour

**1** Combine the water, yeast, and 1 tablespoon of sugar in a measuring cup and let stand 15 minutes until the mixture is frothy.

**2 ▼** Pour the milk into a large bowl. Add the remaining sugar, the butter or margarine, and salt. Stir in the yeast mixture.

**3** Stir in the flour, 1 cup at a time, until a stiff dough is obtained. Alternatively, use a food processor.

**4 ▲** Transfer the dough to a floured surface. To knead, push the dough away from you with the palm of your hand, then fold it toward you, and push it away again. Repeat until the dough is smooth and elastic.

**5** Place the dough in a large greased bowl, cover with a plastic bag, and leave to rise in a warm place until doubled in volume, 2–3 hours.

**6** Grease 2 9- × 5-inch loaf pans.

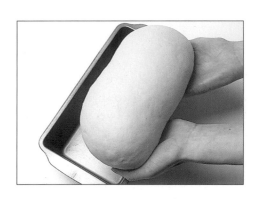

**7 ▲** Punch down the risen dough with your fist and divide in half. Form into loaf shapes and place in the pans, seam-side down. Cover and let rise in a warm place until almost doubled in volume, about 45 minutes.

**8** Preheat the oven to 375°F.

**9** Bake until firm and brown, 45–50 minutes. Unmold and tap the bottom of a loaf: if it sounds hollow the loaf is done. If necessary, return to the oven and bake a few minutes more.

**10** Let cool on a rack.

# Country Bread

**MAKES 2 LOAVES**

2½ cups whole-wheat flour

2½ cups all-purpose flour

1 cup strong flour

4 teaspoons salt

4 tablespoons butter, at room
   temperature

2 cups lukewarm milk

**FOR THE STARTER**

1 package active dry yeast

1 cup lukewarm water

1 cup all-purpose flour

¼ teaspoon sugar

**1 ▲** For the starter, combine the yeast, water, flour, and sugar in a bowl and stir with a fork. Cover and leave in a warm place for 2–3 hours, or leave overnight in a cool place.

**2** Place the flours, salt, and butter in a food processor and process just until blended, 1–2 minutes.

**3** Stir together the milk and starter, then slowly pour into the processor, with the motor running, until the mixture forms a dough. If necessary, add more water. Alternatively, the dough can be mixed by hand. Transfer to a floured surface and knead until smooth and elastic.

**4** Place in an ungreased bowl, cover with a plastic bag, and leave to rise in a warm place until doubled in volume, about 1½ hours.

**5** Transfer to a floured surface and knead briefly. Return to the bowl and leave to rise until tripled in volume, about 1½ hours.

**6 ▲** Divide the dough in half. Cut off one-third of the dough from each half and shape into balls. Shape the larger remaining portion of each half into balls. Grease a baking sheet.

**7 ▲** For each loaf, top the large ball with the small ball and press the center with the handle of a wooden spoon to secure. Cover with a plastic bag, slash the top, and leave to rise.

**8** Preheat the oven to 400°F. Dust the dough with whole-wheat flour and bake until the top is browned and the bottom sounds hollow when tapped, 45–50 minutes. Cool on a rack.

# Split Pan

**MAKES 1 LOAF**

| |
| --- |
| 5 cups unbleached white bread flour, plus extra for dusting |
| 2 teaspoons salt |
| ½ ounce fresh yeast |
| 1¼ cups lukewarm water |
| 4 tablespoons lukewarm milk |

**1** Lightly grease a 2-pound loaf pan (7¼ × 4½ inches). Sift the flour and salt together into a large bowl and make a well in the center. Mix the yeast with half the lukewarm water in a bowl, then stir in the remaining water.

As its name suggests, this homey loaf is so called because of the center split. Some bakers mold the dough in two loaves—they join together while proving but retain the characteristic crack after baking.

**2** Pour the yeast mixture into the center of the flour and, using your fingers, mix in a little flour. Gradually mix in more of the flour from around the edge of the bowl to form a batter.

**3** Sprinkle a little more flour from around the edge over the batter and leave in a warm place to "sponge." Bubbles will appear in the batter after about 20 minutes. Add the milk and remaining flour; mix to a firm dough.

**4** ▲ Place on a lightly floured surface and knead for about 10 minutes, until smooth and elastic. Place in a lightly oiled bowl, cover with lightly oiled plastic wrap and let rise, in a warm place, for 1–1¼ hours or until nearly doubled in bulk.

**5** Punch down the dough and turn out onto a lightly floured surface. Shape it into a rectangle. Roll up lengthwise, tuck the ends under and place seam side down in the pan. Cover and let rise for about 20–30 minutes, or until nearly doubled.

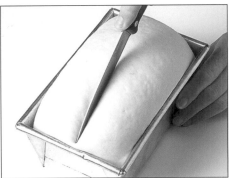

**6** ▲ Using a sharp knife, make one deep central slash the length of the bread; dust with flour. Let sit for 10–15 minutes.

**7** Meanwhile, preheat the oven to 450°F. Bake for 15 minutes, then reduce the temperature to 400°F. Bake for 20–25 minutes more or until the bread is golden and sounds hollow when tapped on the bottom.

# Braided Loaf

**MAKES 1 LOAF**

| |
|---|
| 1 package active dry yeast |
| 1 teaspoon honey |
| 1 cup lukewarm milk |
| 4 tablespoons butter, melted |
| 3 cups flour |
| 1 teaspoon salt |
| 1 egg, lightly beaten |
| 1 egg yolk beaten with 1 teaspoon milk, for glazing |

**1 ▼** Combine the yeast, honey, milk, and butter, stir, and leave for 15 minutes to dissolve.

**2** In a large bowl, mix together the flour and salt. Make a well in the center and add the yeast mixture and egg. With a wooden spoon, stir from the center, incorporating flour with each turn, to obtain a rough dough.

**3** Transfer to a floured surface and knead until smooth and elastic. Place in a clean bowl, cover, and leave to rise in a warm place until doubled in volume, about 1½ hours.

**4** Grease a baking sheet. Punch down the dough and divide into three equal pieces. Roll to shape each piece into a long thin strip.

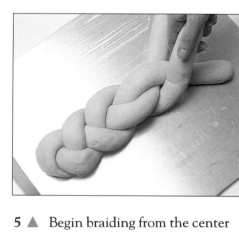

**5 ▲** Begin braiding from the center strip, tucking in the ends. Cover loosely and leave to rise in a warm place for 30 minutes.

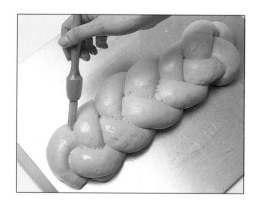

**6 ▲** Preheat the oven to 375°F. Place the bread in a cool place while oven heats. Brush with the glaze and bake until golden, 40–45 minutes. Set on a rack to cool completely.

# Sourdough Bread

**MAKES 1 LOAF**

3 cups flour

1 tablespoon salt

½ cup lukewarm water

1 cup Sourdough Starter (see below)

**1 ▲** Combine the flour and salt in a large bowl. Make a well in the center and add the starter and water. With a wooden spoon, stir from the center, incorporating more flour with each turn, to obtain a rough dough.

**2 ▲** Transfer the dough to a floured surface. To knead, push the dough away from you with the palm of your hand, then fold it towards you, and push it away again. Repeat the process until the dough has become smooth and elastic.

**3** Place in a clean bowl, cover, and leave to rise in a warm place until doubled in volume, about 2 hours.

**4** Lightly grease an 8½- × 4½-inch bread pan.

**5 ▼** Punch down the dough with your fist. Knead briefly, then form into a loaf shape and place in the pan, seam-side down. Cover with a plastic bag, and leave to rise in a warm place until the dough rises above the rim of the pan, about 1½ hours.

**6** Preheat the oven to 425°F. Dust the top of the loaf with flour, then score lengthwise. Bake for 15 minutes. Lower the heat to 375°F and bake until the bottom sounds hollow when tapped, about 30 minutes more.

# Sourdough Starter

**MAKES 3 CUPS**

1 package active dry yeast

2½ cups lukewarm water

1½ cups flour

~ **COOK'S TIP** ~

After using, or after 3 days at room temperature, feed the starter with a handful of flour and enough water to restore it to a thick batter. The starter can be refrigerated for up to 1 week, but must be brought back to room temperature before using.

**1 ▲** For the starter, combine the yeast and water, stir, and leave for 15 minutes to dissolve.

**2 ▼** Sprinkle over the flour and whisk until it forms a batter; it does not have to be smooth. Cover and leave to rise in a warm place for at least 24 hours, or preferably 2–4 days, before using.

# Rye Bread

Rye bread is popular in northern Europe and makes excellent open-faced sandwiches.

## MAKES 2 LOAVES

| |
|---|
| 3 cups whole-wheat flour |
| 2 cups rye flour |
| 1 cup bread flour |
| 1½ teaspoons salt |
| 2 tablespoons caraway seeds |
| 2 cups warm water |
| 2 teaspoons active dry yeast |
| pinch of sugar |
| 2 tablespoons molasses |

**1 ▲** Put the flours and salt in a bowl. Set aside 1 teaspoon of the caraway seeds and add the rest to the bowl.

**2 ▲** Put half the water in a jug. Sprinkle the yeast on top. Add the sugar, mix and let sit for 10 minutes.

**3 ▲** Make a well in the flour mixture, then add the yeast mixture with the molasses and the remaining water. Gradually incorporate the flour and mix to a soft dough, adding a little extra water if necessary.

**4 ▲** Transfer to a floured surface and knead for 5 minutes, until smooth and elastic. Return to the clean bowl, cover and set aside in a warm place for about 2 hours, until doubled in bulk. Grease a baking sheet.

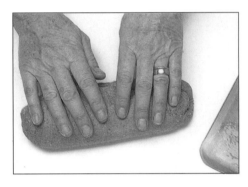

**5 ▲** Turn out the dough onto a floured surface and knead for 2 minutes. Divide the dough in half, then shape into two 9-inch-long oval loaves. Flatten the loaves slightly and place them on the baking sheet.

**6 ▲** Brush the loaves with water and sprinkle with the remaining caraway seeds. Cover and set in a warm place for about 40 minutes, until well risen. Preheat the oven to 400°F. Bake the loaves for 30 minutes, or until they sound hollow when tapped on the bottom. Cool on a wire rack.

## ~ COOK'S TIP ~

To make caraway-seed bread rolls, divide each of the two flattened loaves into eight equal portions. Place them on the baking sheet, brush with water and sprinkle with caraway seeds. Vary the topping by using poppy seeds, if you like.

# Pecan Rye Bread

MAKES 2 LOAVES

1½ packages active dry yeast

3 cups lukewarm water

5 cups all-purpose flour

3 cups rye flour

2 tablespoons salt

1 tablespoon honey

2 teaspoons caraway seeds, (optional)

½ cup (1 stick) butter, at room
   temperature

2 cups pecans, chopped

**1** Combine the yeast and ½ cup of the water. Stir and leave for 15 minutes to dissolve.

**2** In the bowl of an electric mixer, combine the flours, salt, honey, caraway seeds, and butter. With the dough hook, mix on low speed until well blended.

**3** Add the yeast mixture and the remaining water and mix on medium speed until the dough forms a ball.

**4 ▲** Transfer to a floured surface and knead in the pecans.

**5** Return the dough to a clean bowl, cover with a plastic bag, and leave in a warm place until doubled in volume, about 2 hours.

**6** Grease 2 8½- × 4½-inch bread pans.

**7 ▲** Punch down the risen dough.

**8** Divide the dough in half and form into loaves. Place in the pans, seam-side down. Dust the tops with flour.

**9** Cover with plastic bags and leave to rise in a warm place until doubled in volume, about 1 hour.

**10** Preheat the oven to 375°F.

**11 ▼** Bake until the bottoms sound hollow when tapped, 45–50 minutes. Cool on racks.

# Sourdough Rye Bread

**MAKES 2 LOAVES**

| |
|---|
| 2 teaspoons active dry yeast |
| ½ cup lukewarm water |
| 2 tablespoons butter, melted |
| 1 tablespoon salt |
| 1 cup whole-wheat flour |
| 3½–4 cups all-purpose flour |
| 1 egg mixed with 1 tablespoon of water, for glazing |

**FOR THE STARTER**

| |
|---|
| 1 package active dry yeast |
| 1½ cups lukewarm water |
| 3 tablespoons molasses |
| 2 tablespoons caraway seeds |
| 2½ cups rye flour |

**1** For the starter, combine the yeast and water, stir, and leave for 15 minutes to dissolve.

**2** ▲ Stir in the molasses, caraway seeds, and rye flour. Cover and leave in a warm place for 2–3 days.

**3** In a large bowl, combine the yeast and water, stir, and leave for 10 minutes. Stir in the melted butter, salt, whole-wheat flour, and 3½ cups of the all-purpose flour.

**4** ▲ Make a well in the center and pour in the starter.

**5** Stir to obtain a rough dough, then transfer to a floured surface and knead until smooth and elastic. Return to the bowl, cover, and leave to rise in a warm place until doubled in volume, about 2 hours.

**6** Grease a large baking sheet. Punch down the dough and knead briefly. Cut the dough in half and form each half into log-shaped loaves.

**7** ▼ Place the loaves on the baking sheet and score the tops with a sharp knife. Cover with a clean dish towel, and leave to rise in a warm place until almost doubled, about 50 minutes.

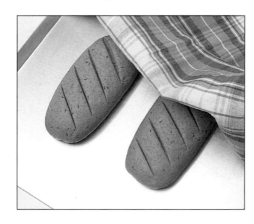

**8** Preheat the oven to 375°F.

**9** Brush the loaves with the glaze. Bake until the bottoms sound hollow when tapped, 50–55 minutes. If the tops brown too quickly, protect with a sheet of foil. Cool on a rack.

# Buttermilk Graham Bread

**MAKES 2 LOAVES**

1 package active dry yeast

½ cup lukewarm water

2 cups graham flour

3 cups all-purpose flour

1 cup cornmeal

2 teaspoons salt

2 tablespoons sugar

4 tablespoons butter, at room temperature

2 cups lukewarm buttermilk

1 beaten egg, for glazing

sesame seeds, for sprinkling

**1** Combine the yeast and water, stir, and leave for 15 minutes to dissolve.

**2** ▲ Mix the graham flour, all-purpose flour, cornmeal, salt, and sugar in a large bowl. Make a well in the center and pour in the yeast mixture, the butter and buttermilk.

**3** ▲ Stir from the center, mixing in the flour until a rough dough is formed. If too stiff, use your hands.

**4** ▲ Transfer to a floured surface and knead until smooth. Place in a clean bowl, cover, and leave in a warm place until doubled, 2–3 hours.

**5** ▲ Grease 2 8-inch square baking pans. Punch down the dough. Divide into 8 equal pieces and roll the pieces into balls. Place 4 balls in each pan. Cover and leave in a warm place until the dough rises above the rim of the pans, about 1 hour.

**6** Preheat the oven to 375°F. Brush with the glaze, then sprinkle over the sesame seeds. Bake until the bottoms sound hollow when tapped, about 50 minutes. Cool on a rack.

# Bread Stick

A bread stick, or baguette, is perfect for garlic bread or sandwiches.

**1** Combine the yeast and water, stir, and let sit for 15 minutes to dissolve. Stir in the salt.

**2** Add the flour, 1 cup at a time. Beat in with a wooden spoon, adding just enough flour to obtain a smooth dough. Alternatively, use an electric mixer with a dough hook attachment.

**3** Transfer to a floured surface and knead until smooth and elastic.

**4** Shape into a ball, place in a greased bowl, and cover with a plastic bag. Set aside to rise in a warm place until doubled in volume, 2–4 hours.

**6 ▲** Score the tops with a knife. Brush with water and place in a cold oven. Set a pan of boiling water on the bottom of the oven and set the oven to 400°F. Bake until crusty and golden, about 40 minutes. Cool on a rack.

### MAKES 2 LOAVES

| |
|---|
| 2 teaspoons active dry yeast |
| 2 cups lukewarm water |
| 1 teaspoon salt |
| 6–8 cups all-purpose flour |
| cornmeal, for sprinkling |

**5 ▲** Transfer to a lightly floured board, halve the dough and shape into two long loaves. Place on a baking sheet sprinkled with cornmeal, and let rise for 5 minutes.

# Three-Grain Bread

A mixture of grains gives this dense-textured bread a delightful nutty flavor. Make two smaller twists, if preferred.

**MAKES 1 LOAF**

| |
| --- |
| 2 cups warm water |
| 2 teaspoons active dry yeast |
| pinch of sugar |
| 2 cups bread flour |
| 1½ teaspoons salt |
| 2 cups wholemeal bread flour |
| 2 cups rye flour |
| 2 tablespoons flax seed |
| ½ cup rolled oats |
| 3 tablespoons sunflower seeds |
| 2 tablespoons malt extract |

**1 ▲** Put half the water in a jug. Sprinkle the yeast on top. Add the sugar, mix and let sit for 10 minutes.

**2 ▲** Sift the white flour and salt into a bowl and add the other flours. Set aside 1 teaspoon of the flax seed and add the rest to the flour mixture with the rolled oats and sunflower seeds. Make a well in the center. Add the yeast mixture to the bowl with the malt extract and the remaining water.

**3** Gradually incorporate the flour.

**4 ▲** Mix to a soft dough, adding extra water if necessary. Turn out onto a floured surface and knead for 5 minutes, until smooth and elastic. Return to the clean bowl, cover with a damp dish towel and let rise for 2 hours, until doubled in bulk.

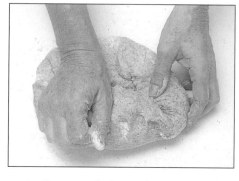

**5 ▲** Grease a baking sheet. Turn the dough onto a floured surface, knead for 2 minutes, then divide in half. Roll each half into a 12-inch sausage.

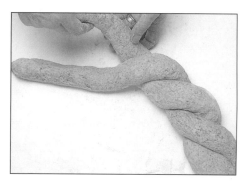

**6 ▲** Twist the two sausages together, dampen the ends and press to seal. Lift the twist onto the prepared baking sheet. Brush the braid with water, sprinkle with the remaining flax seed and cover loosely with a large plastic bag. Let sit in a warm place until well risen. Preheat the oven to 425°F.

**7 ▲** Bake the loaf for 10 minutes, then lower the oven temperature to 400°F and bake for 20 minutes more, or until the loaf sounds hollow when it is tapped on the bottom. Transfer to a wire rack to cool.

# Multi-Grain Bread

**MAKES 2 LOAVES**

| |
|---|
| 1 package active dry yeast |
| ¼ cup lukewarm water |
| 1 cup rolled oats |
| 2 cups milk |
| 2 teaspoons salt |
| ¼ cup oil |
| ¼ cup brown sugar, firmly packed |
| 2 tablespoons honey |
| 2 eggs, lightly beaten |
| ½ cup wheat germ |
| 1 cup soy flour |
| 2 cups whole-wheat flour |
| 3–3½ cups all-purpose flour |

**1** Combine the yeast and water, stir, and leave for 15 minutes to dissolve.

**2** ▲ Place the oats in a large bowl. Heat the milk until scalded, then pour over the oats.

**3** Stir in the salt, oil, sugar, and honey. Cool the mixture to 85°F.

### ~ VARIATION ~

Different flours may be used in this recipe, such as rye, barley, buckwheat or cornmeal. Try replacing the wheat germ and the soy flour with one or two of these, using the same total amount.

**4** ▲ Stir in the yeast mixture, eggs, wheat germ, soy, and whole-wheat flours. Gradually stir in enough all-purpose flour to obtain a rough dough.

**5** Transfer the dough to a floured surface and knead, adding flour if necessary, until smooth and elastic. Return to a clean bowl, cover, and leave to rise in a warm place until doubled in volume, about 2½ hours.

**6** Grease 2 8½- × 4½-inch bread pans. Punch down the risen dough with your fist and knead briefly.

**7** Divide the dough into quarters. Roll each quarter into a cylinder 1½-inch thick. Twist together 2 cylinders and place in a pan; repeat for remaining cylinders.

**8** Cover and leave to rise until doubled in size, about 1 hour.

**9** Preheat the oven to 375°F.

**10** ▲ Bake until the bottoms sound hollow when tapped lightly, 45–50 minutes. Cool on a rack.

# Sesame Seed Bread

**MAKES 1 LOAF**

| |
|---|
| 2 teaspoons active dry yeast |
| 1¼ cups lukewarm water |
| 1½ cups all-purpose flour |
| 1½ cups whole-wheat flour |
| 2 teaspoons salt |
| ½ cup toasted sesame seeds |
| milk, for glazing |
| 2 tablespoons sesame seeds, for sprinkling |

**1** Combine the the yeast and ¼ cup of the water and leave to dissolve. Mix the flours and salt in a large bowl. Make a well in the center and pour in the yeast and the remaining water.

**2 ▲** With a wooden spoon, stir from the center, incorporating flour with each turn, to obtain a rough dough.

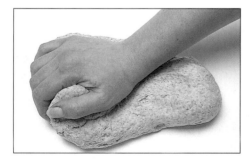

**3 ▲** Transfer to a floured surface. To knead, push the dough away from you with the palm of your hand, then fold it towards you, and push away again. Repeat until smooth and elastic, then return to the bowl and cover with a plastic bag. Leave in a warm place until doubled in volume, 1½–2 hours.

**4 ▲** Grease a 9-inch cake pan. Punch down the dough and knead in the sesame seeds. Divide the dough into 16 balls and place in the pan. Cover with a plastic bag and leave in a warm place until risen above the rim of the pan.

**5 ▼** Preheat the oven to 425°F. Brush the top of the loaf with milk and sprinkle with the sesame seeds. Bake for 15 minutes. Lower the heat to 375°F and bake until the bottom sounds hollow when tapped, about 30 minutes more. Cool on a rack.

# Granary Cob

**MAKES 1 LOAF**

4 cups Granary or malthouse flour

2 teaspoons salt

½ ounce fresh yeast

1¼ cups lukewarm water or milk and
   water mixed

FOR THE TOPPING

2 tablespoons water

½ teaspoon salt

wheat germ or cracked wheat,
   to sprinkle

**1** Lightly flour a baking sheet. Sift
the flour and salt together in a large
bowl and make a well in the center.
Place in a very low oven for 5 minutes
to warm.

Cob is an old word meaning "head." If you make a slash across the top of the
dough, the finished loaf, known as a Danish cob, will look like a large roll.
A Coburg cob has a cross cut in the top before baking.

**2 ▲** Mix the yeast with a little of the
water or milk mixture, then add the
rest. Add the yeast mixture to the
center of the flour and mix to a dough.

**3** Turn out onto a lightly floured
surface and knead for about
10 minutes. Place in a lightly oiled
bowl, cover with lightly oiled plastic
wrap and let rise, in a warm place, for
1¼ hours or until doubled in bulk.

**4 ▲** Turn the dough out onto a
lightly floured surface and punch
down. Knead for 2–3 minutes, then
roll into a ball, making sure it looks
like a plump cushion, otherwise it
will become too flat. Place in the
center of the baking sheet. Cover
with an inverted bowl and let rise, in
a warm place, for 30–45 minutes.

**5** Mix the water and salt and brush
over the bread. Sprinkle with wheat
germ or cracked wheat.

**6** Meanwhile, preheat the oven to
450°F. Bake for 15 minutes, then
reduce the oven temperature to 400°F
and bake for another 20 minutes or
until the loaf is firm to the touch and
sounds hollow when tapped on the
bottom. Cool on a wire rack.

# Oatmeal Bread

MAKES 2 LOAVES

| |
| --- |
| 2 cups milk |
| 2 tablespoons butter |
| ¼ cup dark brown sugar, firmly packed |
| 2 teaspoons salt |
| 1 package active dry yeast |
| ¼ cup lukewarm water |
| 2½ cups rolled oats (not quick-cooking) |
| 5–6 cups flour |

1 ▲   Scald the milk. Remove from the heat and stir in the butter, brown sugar and salt. Leave until lukewarm.

2   Combine the yeast and warm water in a large bowl and leave until the yeast is dissolved and the mixture is frothy. Stir in the milk mixture.

3 ▲   Add 2 cups of the oats and enough flour to obtain a soft dough.

4   Transfer to a floured surface and knead until smooth and elastic.

5 ▲   Place in a greased bowl, cover with a plastic bag, and leave until doubled in volume, 2–3 hours.

6   Grease a large baking sheet. Transfer the dough to a lightly floured surface and divide in half.

7 ▼   Shape into rounds. Place on the baking sheet, cover with a dish towel, and leave to rise until doubled in volume, about 1 hour.

8   Preheat the oven to 400°F. Score the tops and sprinkle with the remaining oats. Bake until the bottoms sound hollow when tapped, 45–50 minutes. Cool on racks.

# Granary Rolls

These make excellent picnic fare, filled with cottage cheese, tuna, salad and mayonnaise. They are also very good served warm with soup.

**MAKES 8**

| |
|---|
| 1¼ cups warm water |
| 1 teaspoon active dry yeast |
| pinch of sugar |
| 4 cups malted brown flour |
| 1 teaspoon salt |
| 1 tablespoon malt extract |
| 1 tablespoon rolled oats |

~ COOK'S TIP ~

To make a large loaf, shape the dough into a round, flatten it slightly and bake for 30–40 minutes. Test by tapping the bottom of the loaf—if it sounds hollow, it is done.

**1 ▲** Put half the warm water in a jug. Sprinkle in the yeast. Add the sugar, mix and let sit for 10 minutes.

**2 ▲** Put the malted brown flour and salt in a mixing bowl and make a well in the center. Add the yeast mixture with the malt extract and the remaining water. Gradually add in the flour and mix to a soft dough.

**3 ▲** Turn the dough onto a floured surface and knead for 5 minutes, until smooth and elastic. Return to the clean bowl, cover with a damp dish towel and set aside in a warm place to rise for about 2 hours, until doubled in bulk.

**4 ▲** Lightly grease two baking sheets. Turn out the dough onto a floured surface, knead for 2 minutes, then divide into eight pieces. Shape the pieces into balls and flatten them to make 4-inch rounds.

**5 ▲** Place the rounds on the prepared baking sheets, cover loosely with a large plastic bag (ballooning it to trap the air inside), and let stand in a warm place until the rolls are well risen. Preheat the oven to 425°F.

**6 ▲** Brush the rolls with water, sprinkle with the oats and bake for 20–25 minutes, or until they sound hollow when tapped on the bottom. Cool on a wire rack, then serve with the filling of your choice.

# Brown Soda Bread

This is very easy to make—simply mix and bake. Instead of yeast, baking soda and cream of tartar are the rising agents. This is an excellent recipe for those new to bread making.

### MAKES 1 LOAF

| |
|---|
| 4 cups all-purpose flour |
| 4 cups whole-wheat flour |
| 2 teaspoons salt |
| 1 tablespoon baking soda |
| 4 teaspoons cream of tartar |
| 2 teaspoons sugar |
| 4 tablespoons butter |
| up to 3¾ cups buttermilk or skim milk |
| extra whole-wheat flour, to sprinkle |

**1** Lightly grease a baking sheet. Preheat the oven to 375°F.

**2 ▲** Sift all the dry ingredients into a large bowl, pouring any bran from the flour back into the bowl.

**3 ▲** Rub the butter into the flour mixture, then add enough buttermilk or milk to make a soft dough. You may not need it all, so add cautiously.

**4 ▲** Knead the dough lightly until smooth, then transfer to the baking sheet and shape into a large round about 2 inches thick.

**5 ▲** Using the floured handle of a wooden spoon, make a large cross on top of the dough. Sprinkle with a little extra whole-wheat flour.

**6 ▲** Bake for 40–50 minutes, until risen and firm. Cool for 5 minutes before transferring to a wire rack.

# Sage Soda Bread

This wonderful loaf is not like bread made with yeast. It has a velvety texture and a powerful sage aroma.

**1 ▲** Preheat the oven to 425°F. Sift the dry ingredients into a mixing bowl.

**2 ▲** Stir in the sage and add enough buttermilk to make a soft dough.

**3 ▲** Shape the dough into a round loaf with your hands and place on a lightly oiled baking sheet.

**4 ▲** Cut a deep cross in the top. Bake for about 40 minutes, until the loaf is well risen and sounds hollow when tapped on the bottom. Allow to cool on a wire rack.

### MAKES 1 LOAF

| |
|---|
| 1½ cups whole-wheat flour |
| 1 cup bread flour |
| ½ teaspoon salt |
| 1 teaspoon baking soda |
| 2 tablespoons shredded fresh sage or 2 teaspoons dried sage |
| scant 1¼ cups buttermilk |

~ COOK'S TIP ~

As an alternative to the sage, try using either finely chopped rosemary or thyme.

# Rosemary Bread

Sliced thinly, this herb bread is delicious with soup for a light meal.

MAKES 1 LOAF

| |
|---|
| ¼ ounce rapid-rise yeast |
| 1½ cups whole-wheat flour |
| 1½ cups self-rising flour |
| 2 teaspoons butter, melted, plus extra to grease bowl and pan |
| ¼ cup warm water |
| 1 cup skim milk, at room temperature |
| 1 tablespoon sugar |
| 1 teaspoon salt |
| 1 tablespoon sesame seeds |
| 1 tablespoon dried chopped onion |
| 1 tablespoon fresh rosemary leaves, plus extra to decorate |
| 4 ounces (1 cup) cubed Cheddar cheese |
| coarse salt, to decorate |

**1 ▲** Mix the yeast with the flours in a large mixing bowl. Add the melted butter. Stir in the warm water, milk, sugar, salt, sesame seeds, onion and rosemary. Knead thoroughly until quite smooth.

**2 ▲** Flatten the dough, then add the cheese cubes. Quickly knead them in until they are well combined.

**3** Place the dough in a large clean bowl greased with a little butter, turning it so that it becomes lightly greased on all sides. Cover with a clean, dry cloth. Put the greased bowl and dough in a warm place for about 1½ hours, or until the dough has risen and doubled in size.

**4** Grease a 9 × 5-inch loaf pan with the remaining butter. Punch down the dough to remove some of the air, and shape it into a loaf. Put the loaf into the pan, cover with the clean cloth used earlier and set aside for about 1 hour, until it has doubled in size once again. Preheat the oven to 375°F.

**5** Bake for 30 minutes. During the last 5–10 minutes of baking, cover the loaf with aluminum foil to prevent it becoming too dark in color. Remove from the loaf pan and let cool on a wire rack. Decorate with rosemary leaves and coarse salt sprinkled on top.

# Spiral Herb Bread

**MAKES 2 LOAVES**

| |
|---|
| 2 packages active dry yeast |
| 2½ cups lukewarm water |
| 3 cups all-purpose flour |
| 3 cups whole-wheat flour |
| 3 teaspoons salt |
| 2 tablespoons butter |
| 1 large bunch of parsley, finely chopped |
| 1 bunch of scallions, finely chopped |
| 1 garlic clove, finely chopped |
| salt and freshly ground black pepper |
| 1 egg, lightly beaten |
| milk, for glazing |

**1** Combine the yeast and ¼ cup of the water, stir, and leave for 15 minutes to dissolve.

**2** Combine the flours and salt in a large bowl. Make a well in the center and pour in the yeast mixture and the remaining water. With a wooden spoon, stir from the center, working outwards to obtain a rough dough.

**3** Transfer the dough to a floured surface and knead until smooth and elastic. Return to the bowl, cover with a plastic bag, and leave until doubled in volume, about 2 hours.

**4 ▲** Meanwhile, combine the butter, parsley, scallions, and garlic in a large skillet. Cook over low heat, stirring, until softened. Season with salt and pepper and set aside.

**5** Grease 2 9- × 5-inch bread pans. When the dough has risen, cut it in half, then roll each half into a rectangle about 14 × 9 inches.

**6 ▼** Brush both with the beaten egg. Divide the herb mixture between the two, spreading just up to the edges.

**7 ▲** Roll up to enclose the filling and pinch the short ends to seal. Place in the pans, seam-side down. Cover, and leave in a warm place until the dough rises above the rim of the pans.

**8** Preheat the oven to 375°F. Brush with milk and bake until the bottoms sound hollow when tapped, about 55 minutes. Cool on a rack.

# Dill Bread

**MAKES 2 LOAVES**

| |
|---|
| 4 teaspoons active dry yeast |
| 2 cups lukewarm water |
| 2 tablespoons sugar |
| 7½ cups flour |
| ½ onion, chopped |
| 4 tablespoons oil |
| l large bunch of dill, finely chopped |
| 2 eggs, lightly beaten |
| ½ cup cottage cheese |
| 4 teaspoons salt |
| milk, for glazing |

**1** Mix together the yeast, water, and sugar in a large bowl and leave for 15 minutes to dissolve.

**2 ▼** Stir in 3 cups of the flour. Cover and leave to rise in a warm place for 45 minutes.

**3 ▲** In a skillet, cook the onion in 1 tablespoon of the oil until soft. Set aside to cool, then stir into the yeast mixture. Stir the dill, eggs, cottage cheese, salt, and remaining oil into the yeast mixture. Gradually add the remaining flour until too stiff to stir.

**4 ▲** Transfer to a floured surface and knead until smooth and elastic. Place in a bowl, cover, and leave to rise until doubled in volume, 1–1½ hours.

**5 ▲** Grease a large baking sheet. Cut the dough in half and shape into 2 rounds. Leave to rise in a warm place for 30 minutes.

**6** Preheat the oven to 375°F. Score the tops, brush with the milk, and bake until browned, about 50 minutes. Cool on a rack.

# Cheese Bread

**MAKES 1 LOAF**

| |
|---|
| 1 package active dry yeast |
| 1 cup lukewarm milk |
| 2 tablespoons butter |
| 3 cups flour |
| 2 teaspoon salt |
| 1 cup grated sharp cheddar cheese |

**1** Combine the yeast and milk, stir, and leave for 15 minutes to dissolve.

**2** Melt the butter, let cool, and add to the yeast mixture.

**3** Mix the flour and salt together in a large bowl. Make a well in the center and pour in the yeast mixture.

**4** With a wooden spoon, stir from the center, incorporating flour with each turn, to obtain a rough dough.
If the dough seems too dry, add 2–3 tablespoons water.

**5** Transfer to a floured surface and knead until smooth and elastic.
Return to the bowl, cover, and leave to rise in a warm place until doubled in volume, 2–3 hours.

**6** ▲ Grease a 9- × 5-inch bread pan. Punch down the dough with your fist. Knead in the cheese, distributing it as evenly as possible.

**7** ▼ Twist the dough, form into a loaf shape and place in the pan, tucking the ends under. Leave in a warm place until the dough rises above the rim of the pan.

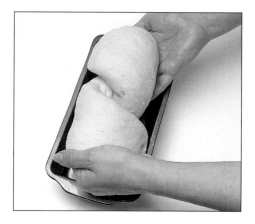

**8** ▲ Preheat the oven to 400°F. Bake for 15 minutes, then lower the heat to 375°F and bake until the bottom sounds hollow when tapped, about 30 minutes more. Cool on a rack.

# Sun-Dried Tomato Braid

This is a marvelous Mediterranean-flavored bread to serve at a summer buffet or barbecue.

MAKES 1 LOAF

1¼ cups warm water

1 teaspoon active dry yeast

pinch of sugar

2 cups whole-wheat flour

2 cups bread flour

1 teaspoon salt

¼ teaspoon freshly ground
    black pepper

⅔ cup drained sun-dried tomatoes in
    oil, chopped, plus 1 tablespoon oil
    from the jar

¼ cup freshly grated Parmesan cheese

2 tablespoons sun-dried tomato pesto

1 teaspoon coarse sea salt

**1 ▲** Put half the warm water in a jug. Sprinkle the yeast on top. Add the sugar, mix and let sit for 10 minutes.

**2 ▲** Put the whole-wheat flour in a mixing bowl. Sift in the white flour, salt and pepper. Add the yeast mixture, sun-dried tomatoes, oil, Parmesan, pesto and the remaining water. Gradually incorporate the flour and mix to a soft dough, adding a little extra water if necessary.

**3 ▲** Transfer the dough to a floured surface and knead for 5 minutes, until smooth and elastic. Return to the clean bowl, cover with a damp dish towel and set aside in a warm place to rise for about 2 hours, until doubled in bulk. Lightly grease a baking sheet.

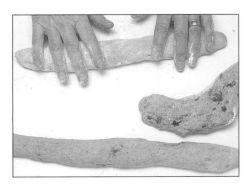

**4 ▲** Transfer the dough to a lightly floured surface and knead for a few minutes. Divide the dough into three equal pieces and shape each piece into a 12-inch-long sausage.

**5 ▲** Dampen the ends of the three sausages. Press them together at one end, braid them loosely, then press them together at the other end. Place on the baking sheet, cover and let sit in a warm place for 30 minutes, until well risen. Preheat the oven to 425°F.

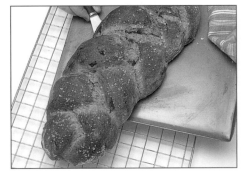

**6 ▲** Sprinkle the braid with the coarse sea salt. Bake for 10 minutes, then lower the temperature to 400°F and bake for another 15–20 minutes, or until the loaf sounds hollow when tapped on the bottom. Cool on a wire rack.

~ COOK'S TIP ~
If you can't find sun-dried tomato pesto, use 2 tablespoons chopped fresh basil mixed with 1 tablespoon sun-dried tomato paste.

# Prosciutto and Parmesan Bread

This nourishing bread is almost a meal in itself.

MAKES 1 LOAF

| |
| --- |
| 2 cups whole-wheat flour |
| 2 cups self-rising white flour |
| 3 teaspoons baking powder |
| 1¼ teaspoons salt |
| 1 teaspoon black pepper |
| 3 ounces prosciutto, chopped |
| 2 tablespoons freshly grated Parmesan cheese |
| 2 tablespoons chopped fresh parsley |
| 3 tablespoons Dijon mustard |
| 1½ cups buttermilk |
| skim milk, to glaze |

**1 ▲** Preheat the oven to 400°F. Flour a baking sheet. Place the whole-wheat flour in a bowl and sift in the white flour, baking powder and salt. Add the pepper and the prosciutto. Set aside about 1 tablespoon of the grated Parmesan and stir the rest into the flour mixture with the parsley. Make a well in the center.

**2 ▲** Mix the mustard and buttermilk, pour into the flour and quickly mix to a soft dough.

**3 ▲** Transfer the dough to a floured surface and knead briefly. Shape into an oval loaf, brush with milk and sprinkle with the reserved Parmesan. Place on the prepared baking sheet.

**4 ▲** Bake the loaf for 25–30 minutes, or until it sounds hollow when tapped on the bottom. Let cool before serving.

# Zucchini Yeast Bread

The grated zucchini gives extra moisture to this tasty loaf.

**MAKES 1 LOAF**

| |
|---|
| 1 pound (3½ cups) grated zucchini |
| 2 tablespoons salt |
| 2 teaspoons active dry yeast |
| 1¼ cups lukewarm water |
| 3½ cups all-purpose flour |
| olive oil, for brushing |

**1 ▲** In a colander, alternate layers of grated zucchini and salt. Let sit for 30 minutes, then squeeze out the moisture with your hands.

**2** Combine the yeast with ¼ cup of the lukewarm water, stir and let sit for 15 minutes to dissolve the yeast.

**6 ▲** Preheat the oven to 425°F. Brush the bread with olive oil and bake for 40–45 minutes, or until the loaf is a golden color. Cool on a rack before serving.

**3 ▲** Place the zucchini, yeast and flour in a bowl. Stir together and add just enough of the remaining water to obtain a rough dough.

**4** Transfer to a floured surface and knead until smooth and elastic. Return the dough to the bowl, cover with a plastic bag, and set aside to rise in a warm place until doubled in volume, about 1½ hours.

**5** Grease a baking sheet. Punch down the risen dough with your fist and knead into a tapered cylinder. Place on the baking sheet, cover and let rise in a warm place until doubled in volume, about 45 minutes.

# Spinach and Bacon Bread

This bread is so tasty that it is a good idea to make double the quantity and freeze some of the loaves. Use lean Canadian bacon for the best possible flavor with the minimum amount of fat.

## MAKES 2 LOAVES

| |
|---|
| scant 2 cups warm water |
| 2 teaspoons active dry yeast |
| pinch of sugar |
| 1 tablespoon olive oil |
| 1 onion, chopped |
| 4 ounces Canadian bacon slices, chopped |
| 8 ounces chopped spinach, thawed if frozen |
| 6 cups bread flour |
| 1½ teaspoons salt |
| 1½ teaspoons grated nutmeg |
| ¼ cup grated reduced-fat Cheddar cheese |

**1 ▲** Put the water in a bowl. Sprinkle the yeast on top and add the sugar. Mix well and let sit for 10 minutes. Lightly grease two 9-inch cake pans.

**2 ▲** Heat the oil in a frying pan and fry the onion and bacon for 10 minutes, until golden brown. If using frozen spinach, drain it thoroughly.

**3 ▲** Sift the flour, salt and nutmeg into a mixing bowl and make a well in the center. Add the yeast mixture. Tip in the fried bacon and onion (with the oil), then add the spinach. Gradually incorporate the flour mixture and mix to a soft dough.

**4 ▲** Transfer the dough to a floured surface and knead for 5 minutes. Return to the clean bowl, cover with a damp dish towel and set aside in a warm place to rise for about 2 hours, until doubled in bulk.

**5 ▲** Transfer the dough to a floured surface, knead briefly, then divide it in half. Shape each half into a ball, flatten slightly and place in a pan, pressing the dough to the edges. Mark each loaf into eight wedges and sprinkle with the cheese. Cover loosely with a plastic bag and set aside in a warm place until well risen. Preheat the oven to 400°F.

**6 ▲** Bake the loaves for 25–30 minutes, or until they sound hollow when they are tapped underneath. Transfer to a wire rack to cool.

~ COOK'S TIP ~

If using frozen spinach, be sure to squeeze out any excess liquid or the resulting dough will be too sticky.

# Walnut Bread

**MAKES 1 LOAF**

2½ cups whole-wheat flour

1 cup all-purpose flour

2½ teaspoons salt

2¼ cups lukewarm water

1 tablespoon honey

1 package active dry yeast

1¼ cup walnut pieces, plus more for decorating

1 beaten egg, for glazing

**1** Combine the flours and salt in a large bowl. Make a well in the center and add 1 cup of the water, the honey and the yeast.

**2** Set aside until the yeast dissolves and the mixture is frothy.

**3** Add the remaining water. With a wooden spoon, stir from the center, incorporating flour with each turn, to obtain a smooth dough. Add more flour if the dough is too sticky and use your hands if the dough becomes too stiff to stir.

**4** Transfer to a floured board and knead, adding flour if necessary, until the dough is smooth and elastic. Place in a greased bowl and roll the dough around in the bowl to coat thoroughly on all sides.

**5** ▲ Cover with a plastic bag and leave in a warm place until doubled in volume, about 1½ hours.

**6** ▲ Punch down the dough and knead in the walnuts evenly.

**7** Grease a baking sheet. Shape into a round loaf and place on the baking sheet. Press in walnut pieces to decorate the top. Cover loosely with a damp cloth and leave to rise in a warm place until doubled, 25–30 minutes.

**8** Preheat the oven to 425°F.

**9** ▲ With a sharp knife, score the top. Brush with the glaze. Bake for 15 minutes. Lower the heat to 375°F and bake until the bottom sounds hollow when tapped, about 40 minutes. Cool on a rack.

# Zucchini and Walnut Loaf

A moist and crunchy loaf—a real treat.

**1 ▲** Preheat the oven to 350°F. Grease the bottom and sides of a 2-pound loaf pan and line with waxed paper.

**2** Beat the eggs and sugar together and gradually add the oil.

**3 ▲** Sift the flour into a bowl together with the baking powder, baking soda, cinnamon and allspice.

**4 ▲** Mix into the egg mixture with the rest of the ingredients, reserving 1 tablespoon of the sunflower seeds for the top.

**5** Spoon into the prepared pan, level off the top, and sprinkle with the reserved sunflower seeds.

**6 ▲** Bake for about 1 hour, or until a skewer inserted into the center of the loaf comes out clean. Let cool slightly, then turn out onto a wire cooling rack.

**MAKES 1 LOAF**

3 eggs

½ cup light brown sugar

¼ cup sunflower oil

1½ cups whole-wheat flour

1 teaspoon baking powder

1 teaspoon baking soda

1 teaspoon ground cinnamon

½ teaspoon ground allspice

½ tablespoon green cardamom pods, seeds removed and crushed

5 ounces (1 cup) coarsely grated zucchini

2 ounces (¼ cup) walnuts, chopped

2 ounces (¼ cup) sunflower seeds

# Prune Bread

**MAKES 1 LOAF**

| |
|---|
| 1 cup dried prunes |
| 1 package active dry yeast |
| ½ cup whole-wheat flour |
| 2½–3 cups all-purpose flour |
| ½ teaspoon baking soda |
| 1 teaspoon salt |
| 1 teaspoon pepper |
| 2 tablespoons butter, at room temperature |
| ¾ cup buttermilk |
| ½ cup walnuts, chopped |
| milk, for glazing |

**1** Simmer the prunes in water to cover until soft, or soak overnight. Drain, reserving ¼ cup of the soaking liquid. Pit and chop the prunes.

**2** Combine the yeast and the reserved prune liquid, stir, and leave for 15 minutes to dissolve.

**3** In a large bowl, stir together the flours, baking soda, salt, and pepper. Make a well in the center.

**4 ▲** Add the chopped prunes, butter, and buttermilk. Pour in the yeast mixture. With a wooden spoon, stir from the center, incorporating more flour with each turn, to obtain a rough dough.

**5** Transfer to a floured surface and knead until smooth and elastic. Return to the bowl, cover with a plastic bag, and leave to rise in a warm place until doubled in volume, about 1½ hours.

**6** Grease a baking sheet.

**7 ▲** Punch down the dough with your fist, then knead in the walnuts.

**8** Shape the dough into a long, cylindrical loaf. Place on the baking sheet, cover loosely, and leave to rise in a warm place for 45 minutes.

**9** Preheat the oven to 425°F.

**10 ▼** With a sharp knife, score the top deeply. Brush with milk and bake for 15 minutes. Lower the heat to 375°F and bake until the bottom sounds hollow when tapped, about 35 minutes more. Cool on a rack.

# Orange Wheat Loaf

Perfect just with butter as a breakfast bread or tea bread and great for banana sandwiches.

**MAKES 1 LOAF**

2¼ cups whole-wheat flour

½ teaspoon salt

4 tablespoons butter

2 tablespoons light brown sugar

½ envelope rapid-rise yeast

grated rind and juice of ½ orange

**1 ▲** Sift the flour into a large bowl and return any bran caught in the sieve. Add the salt and rub in the butter lightly with your fingertips.

**5 ▲** Bake the bread for 30–35 minutes, or until it sounds hollow when tapped on the bottom. Turn out of the pan and let cool on a wire rack.

**2 ▲** Stir in the sugar, yeast and orange rind. Pour the orange juice into a measuring cup and make up to ⅞ cup with hot water (the liquid should not be more than lukewarm).

**3 ▲** Stir the liquid into the flour and mix to a ball of dough. Knead the dough on a floured surface until smooth.

**4** Place the dough in a greased 1-pound loaf pan and set aside in a warm place until nearly doubled in size. Preheat the oven to 425°F.

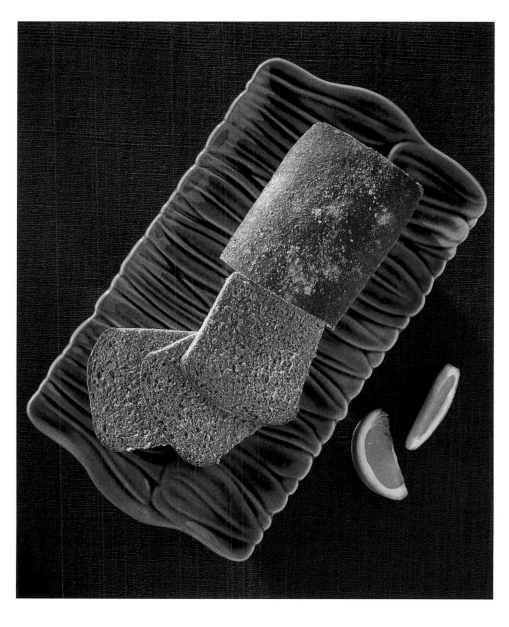

# Corn Bread

**MAKES 1 LOAF**

| |
|---|
| 1 cup flour |
| 1/3 cup sugar |
| 1 teaspoon salt |
| 1 tablespoon baking powder |
| 1½ cups cornmeal |
| 1½ cups milk |
| 2 eggs |
| 6 tablespoons butter, melted |
| 8 tablespoons margarine, melted |

**1** Preheat the oven to 400°F. Line the bottom and sides of a 9- × 5-inch loaf pan with wax paper and grease.

**2** Sift the flour, sugar, salt, and baking powder into a mixing bowl.

**3 ▼** Add the cornmeal and stir to blend. Make a well in the center.

**4 ▲** Whisk together the milk, eggs, butter, and margarine. Pour the mixture into the well. Stir until just blended; do not overmix.

**5** Pour into the pan and bake until a cake tester inserted in the center comes out clean, about 45 minutes. Serve hot or at room temperature.

---

# Tex-Mex Corn Bread

**MAKES 9 SQUARES**

| |
|---|
| 3–4 whole canned chile peppers, drained |
| 2 eggs |
| 2 cups buttermilk |
| 4 tablespoons butter, melted |
| ½ cup flour |
| 1 teaspoon baking soda |
| 2 teaspoons salt |
| 1½ cups cornmeal |
| 2 cups corn kernels |

**1** Preheat the oven to 400°F. Line the bottom and sides of a 9-inch square cake pan with wax paper and grease lightly.

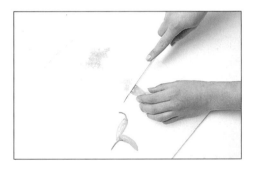

**2 ▲** With a sharp knife, chop the chiles in a fine dice and set aside.

**3 ▲** In a large bowl, whisk the eggs until frothy, then whisk in the buttermilk. Add the melted butter.

**4** In another large bowl, sift together the flour, baking soda, and salt. Fold into the buttermilk mixture in 3 batches, then fold in the cornmeal in 3 batches.

**5 ▲** Fold in the chiles and corn.

**6** Pour the batter into the prepared pan and bake until a cake tester inserted in the middle comes out clean, 25–30 minutes. Let stand for 2–3 minutes before unmolding. Cut into squares and serve warm.

*Corn Bread (top), Tex-Mex Corn Bread*

# Onion Focaccia

This pizza-like flatbread is characterized by its soft, dimpled surface.

**MAKES 2 ROUND LOAF**

| |
| --- |
| 6 cups bread flour |
| ½ teaspoon salt |
| ½ teaspoon sugar |
| 1 tablespoon rapid-rise yeast |
| 4 tablespoons extra virgin olive oil |
| 2 cups lukewarm water |
| TO FINISH |
| 2 red onions, thinly sliced |
| 3 tablespoons extra virgin olive oil |
| 1 tablespoon coarse salt |

**1** Sift the flour, salt and sugar into a large bowl. Stir in the yeast, oil and water and mix to a dough using a blunt knife. (Add a little extra water if the dough is dry.)

**2 ▲** Turn out onto a lightly floured surface and knead for 10 minutes, until smooth and elastic. Put the dough in a clean, lightly oiled bowl and cover with plastic wrap. Leave to rise in a warm place until doubled in bulk.

**3 ▲** Place two 10-inch metal flan rings on baking sheets. Oil the sides of the rings and the baking sheets.

**4 ▲** Preheat the oven to 400°F. Halve the dough and roll each piece to a 10-inch round. Press into the rings, cover with a dampened dish towel and let rise for 30 minutes.

**5 ▲** Make deep holes, about 1 inch apart, in the dough. Cover and let sit for another 20 minutes.

**6 ▲** Sprinkle the onions on top and drizzle with the oil. Sprinkle with the salt, then a little cold water, to prevent a crust from forming.

**7** Bake for about 25 minutes, sprinkling with water again during cooking. Cool on a wire rack.

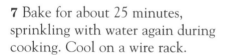

# Saffron Focaccia

A dazzling yellow bread with a distinctive flavor.

MAKES 1 ROUND LOAF

pinch of saffron threads

⅔ cup boiling water

2 cups all-purpose flour

½ teaspoon salt

1 teaspoon rapid-rise yeast

1 tablespoon olive oil

FOR THE TOPPING

2 garlic cloves, sliced

1 red onion, cut into thin wedges

rosemary sprigs

12 black olives, pitted and
   coarsely chopped

1 tablespoon olive oil

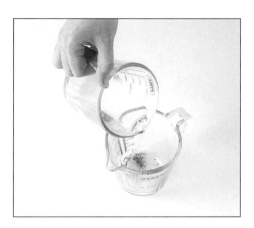

**1 ▲** Infuse the saffron in the boiling water. Let sit until cooled to lukewarm.

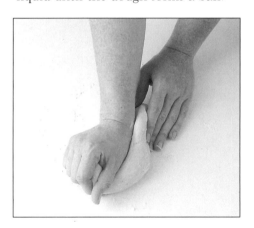

**2 ▲** Place the flour, salt, yeast and olive oil in a food processor. Turn on and gradually add the saffron and its liquid until the dough forms a ball.

**3 ▲** Transfer to a floured board and knead for 10–15 minutes. Place in a bowl, cover and let rise for 30–40 minutes, until doubled in size.

**4 ▲** Punch down the risen dough on a lightly floured surface and roll out into an oval shape ½ inch thick. Place on a lightly greased baking sheet and let rise for 20–30 minutes.

**5** Preheat the oven to 400°F. Use your fingers to press small indentations in the dough.

**6 ▲** Cover with the topping ingredients, brush lightly with olive oil, and bake for about 25 minutes, or until the loaf sounds hollow when tapped on the bottom. Allow to cool.

# Cheese and Onion Sticks

An extremely tasty bread that is very good with soups or salads. Use an extra-sharp cheese to give plenty of flavor without piling on the fat.

### MAKES 2 STICKS

| |
|---|
| 1¼ cups warm water |
| 1 teaspoon active dry yeast |
| pinch of sugar |
| 1 tablespoon sunflower oil |
| 1 red onion, finely chopped |
| 4 cups bread flour |
| 1 teaspoon salt |
| 1 teaspoon dry mustard |
| 3 tablespoons chopped fresh herbs, such as thyme, parsley, marjoram or sage |
| ¾ cup grated reduced-fat Cheddar cheese |

**1 ▲** Put the water in a jug. Sprinkle the yeast on top. Add the sugar, mix well and let sit for 10 minutes.

**2 ▲** Heat the oil in a frying pan and fry the onion until it is well colored.

**3 ▲** Stir together the flour, salt and mustard in a mixing bowl, then add the chopped herbs. Set aside 2 tablespoons of the cheese. Stir the rest into the flour mixture and make a well in the center. Add the yeast mixture with the fried onions and oil, then gradually incorporate the flour and mix to a soft dough, adding extra water if necessary.

**4 ▲** Transfer the dough to a floured surface and knead for 5 minutes, until smooth and elastic. Return to the clean bowl, cover with a damp dish towel and set aside in a warm place to rise for 2 hours, until doubled in bulk. Grease a baking sheet.

**5 ▲** Transfer the dough to a floured surface, knead briefly, then divide the mixture in half and roll each piece into a 12-inch-long stick. Place each stick on the baking sheet and make diagonal cuts along the top.

**6 ▲** Sprinkle the sticks with the reserved cheese. Cover and let sit for 30 minutes, until well risen. Preheat the oven to 425°F. Bake the sticks for 25 minutes, or until they sound hollow when tapped on the bottom.

~ COOK'S TIP ~

To make Onion and Coriander Sticks, omit the cheese, herbs and mustard. Add 1 tablespoon ground coriander and 3 tablespoons chopped fresh cilantro instead.

# Saffron and Basil Breadsticks

Saffron lends its delicate flavor, as well as rich yellow color, to these tasty breadsticks.

**MAKES 32 STICKS**

generous pinch of saffron strands

2 tablespoons hot water

4 cups bread flour

1 teaspoon salt

2 teaspoons rapid-rise yeast

1¼ cups lukewarm water

3 tablespoons olive oil

3 tablespoons chopped fresh basil

**1 ▲** Infuse the saffron strands in the hot water for 10 minutes.

**2 ▲** Sift the flour and salt into a large mixing bowl. Stir in the yeast, then make a well in the center of the dry ingredients. Pour in the lukewarm water and saffron liquid.

**3 ▲** Add the oil and basil and continue to mix to a soft dough.

**4 ▲** Turn out and knead the dough on a lightly floured surface for about 10 minutes, until smooth and elastic. Place in a greased bowl, cover with plastic wrap and let sit for about 1 hour, until it has doubled in size.

**5 ▲** Punch down and knead the dough on a lightly floured surface for 2–3 minutes.

**6 ▲** Preheat the oven to 425°F. Divide the dough into 32 pieces and shape into long sticks. Place well apart on greased baking sheets, then leave for another 15–20 minutes, until they become puffy. Bake for about 15 minutes, until crisp and golden. Serve warm.

# Flatbread with Sage

This bread is perfect served hot to accompany a pasta supper.

### MAKES 1 ROUND LOAF

| |
|---|
| 2 teaspoons active dry yeast |
| 1 cup lukewarm water |
| 3 cups all-purpose flour |
| 2 teaspoons salt |
| 5 tablespoons extra virgin olive oil |
| 12 fresh sage leaves, chopped |

**1** Combine the yeast and water, stir and let sit for 15 minutes to dissolve.

**2** Mix the flour and salt in a large bowl, and make a well in the center.

**3** Stir in the yeast mixture and 4 tablespoons of the oil. Stir from the center, incorporating flour with each turn, to obtain a rough dough.

**4 ▲** Transfer to a floured surface and knead until smooth and elastic. Place in a lightly oiled bowl. Cover and let rise in a warm place until doubled in volume, about 2 hours.

**5** Preheat the oven to 400°F and place a baking sheet in the center of the oven.

**6** Punch down the dough. Knead in the sage leaves, then roll into a 12-inch round. Let rise slightly.

**7 ▲** Dimple the surface all over with your finger. Drizzle the remaining oil on top. Slide a floured board under the bread, carry to the oven, and slide off onto the hot baking sheet. Bake for about 35 minutes, or until golden brown. Allow to cool on a wire rack.

# Sweet Sesame Loaf

**MAKES 1 OR 2 LOAVES**

| |
|---|
| ⅔ cup sesame seeds |
| 2 cups flour |
| 2½ teaspoons baking powder |
| 1 teaspoon salt |
| 4 tablespoons butter or margarine, at room temperature |
| ⅔ cup sugar |
| 2 eggs, at room temperature |
| grated rind of 1 lemon |
| 1½ cups milk |

**1** Preheat the oven to 350°F. Line a 10- × 6-inch baking pan, or 2 small loaf pans, with wax paper and grease.

**2 ▲** Reserve 2 tablespoons of the sesame seeds. Spread the rest on a baking sheet and bake until lightly toasted, about 10 minutes.

**3** Sift the flour, salt, and baking powder into a bowl.

**4 ▲** Stir in the toasted sesame seeds and set aside.

**5** With an electric mixer, cream the butter or margarine and sugar together until light and fluffy. Beat in the eggs, then stir in the lemon rind and milk.

**6 ▼** Pour the milk mixture over the dry ingredients and fold in with a large metal spoon until just blended.

**7 ▲** Pour into the pan and sprinkle over the reserved sesame seeds.

**8** Bake until a cake tester inserted in the center comes out clean, about 1 hour. Let cool in the pan for 10 minutes before unmolding.

# Apricot Nut Loaf

**MAKES 1 LOAF**

¾ cup dried apricots

1 large orange

½ cup raisins

⅔ cup sugar

⅓ cup oil

2 eggs, lightly beaten

2¼ cups flour

2 teaspoons baking powder

½ teaspoon salt

1 teaspoon baking soda

½ cup walnuts, chopped

**1** Preheat the oven to 350°F. Line the bottom and sides of a 9- × 5-inch loaf pan with wax paper and grease.

**2** Place the apricots in a bowl and add lukewarm water to cover. Let stand for 30 minutes.

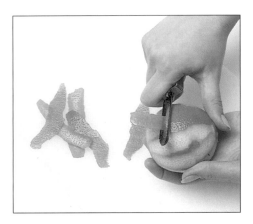

**3 ▲** With a vegetable peeler, remove the orange rind, leaving the pith.

**4** With a sharp knife, finely chop the orange rind strips.

**5** Drain the apricots and chop coarsely. Place in a bowl with the orange rind and raisins. Set aside.

**6** Squeeze the peeled orange. Measure the juice and add enough hot water to obtain ¾ cup liquid.

**7 ▼** Pour the orange juice mixture over the apricot mixture. Stir in the sugar, oil, and eggs. Set aside.

**8** In another bowl, sift together the flour, baking powder, salt, and baking soda. Fold the flour mixture into the apricot mixture in 3 batches.

**9 ▲** Stir in the walnuts.

**10** Spoon the batter into the prepared pan and bake until a cake tester inserted in the center comes out clean, 55–60 minutes. If the loaf browns too quickly, protect the top with a sheet of foil. Let cool in the pan for 10 minutes before transferring to a rack to cool completely.

# Applesauce Bread

Apples and spices such as cinnamon and nutmeg are a match made in heaven.

**1** Preheat the oven to 350°F. Line the bottom and sides of a 9 × 5-inch loaf pan with waxed paper and grease.

**2 ▲** Break the egg into a bowl and beat lightly. Stir in the apple sauce, butter or margarine and both sugars.

**3** In another bowl, sift together the flour, baking powder, baking soda, salt, cinnamon and nutmeg. Fold the dry ingredients into the applesauce mixture in three batches.

**4 ▲** Stir in the currants or raisins and chopped pecans.

**5** Pour into the prepared pan and bake for about 1 hour, or until a skewer inserted into the center comes out clean. Let stand for 10 minutes before transferring to a wire rack to cool.

**MAKES 1 LOAF**

|  |
| --- |
| 1 egg |
| 1 cup apple sauce |
| 4 tablespoons butter or margarine, melted |
| ½ cup dark brown sugar, firmly packed |
| ½ cup granulated sugar |
| 2 cups all-purpose flour |
| 2 teaspoons baking powder |
| ½ teaspoon baking soda |
| ½ teaspoon salt |
| 1 teaspoon ground cinnamon |
| ½ teaspoon grated nutmeg |
| 3 ounces (½ cup) currants or raisins |
| 6 ounces (½ cup) pecans, chopped |

# Banana and Cardamom Bread

The combination of banana and cardamom is delicious in this soft-textured moist loaf. It is perfect for teatime, served with butter and jam.

## MAKES 1 LOAF

⅔ cup warm water

1 teaspoon active dry yeast

pinch of sugar

10 cardamom pods

3½ cups bread flour

1 teaspoon salt

2 tablespoons malt extract

2 ripe bananas, mashed

1 teaspoon sesame seeds

**1 ▲** Put the warm water in a bowl. Sprinkle the yeast on top. Add the sugar, mix and let sit for 10 minutes.

**2 ▲** Split the cardamom pods. Remove the seeds and chop finely.

**3 ▲** Sift the flour and salt into a mixing bowl and make a well in the center. Add the yeast mixture with the malt extract, chopped cardamom seeds and bananas.

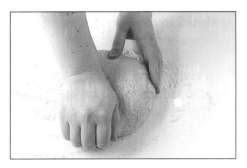

**4 ▲** Gradually incorporate the flour and mix to a soft dough, adding extra water if necessary. Turn the dough out onto a floured surface and knead for about 5 minutes. Return to the clean bowl, cover with a damp dish towel and allow to rise for 2 hours, until doubled in bulk.

**5 ▲** Grease a baking sheet. Turn the dough out onto a floured surface, knead briefly, then divide into three pieces and shape into a braid. Place the braid on the baking sheet and cover loosely with a plastic bag. Let sit until well risen. Preheat the oven to 425°F.

**6 ▲** Brush the braid lightly with water and sprinkle with the sesame seeds. Bake for 10 minutes, then lower the oven temperature to 400°F. Cook for 15 minutes more, or until the loaf sounds hollow when it is tapped on the bottom. Let cool.

## ~ COOK'S TIP ~

Make sure the bananas are really ripe so that they impart maximum flavor to the bread. If you prefer, place the dough in one piece in a 1-pound loaf pan and bake for an extra 5 minutes. In addition to being low in fat, bananas are a good source of potassium; they therefore make an ideal nutritious, low-fat snack.

# Whole-Wheat Banana Nut Bread

**MAKES 1 LOAF**

½ cup (1 stick) butter, at room
temperature

½ cup granulated sugar

2 eggs, at room temperature

1 cup all-purpose flour

1 teaspoon baking soda

¼ teaspoon salt

1 teaspoon ground cinnamon

½ cup whole-wheat flour

3 large ripe bananas

1 teaspoon vanilla extract

½ cup pecans, chopped

**1** Preheat the oven to 350°F. Line
the bottom and sides of a 9- × 5-inch
loaf pan with wax paper and grease.

**2** With an electric mixer, cream the
butter and sugar together until light
and fluffy.

**3** ▲ Add the eggs, 1 at a time,
beating well after each addition.

**4** Sift the all-purpose flour, baking
soda, salt, and cinnamon over the
butter mixture and stir to blend.

**5** ▲ Stir in the whole-wheat flour.

**6** ▲ With a fork, mash the bananas
to a purée, then stir into the batter.
Stir in the vanilla and pecans.

**7** ▲ Pour the batter into the
prepared pan and spread level.

**8** Bake until a cake tester inserted in
the center comes out clean, 50–60
minutes. Let stand 10 minutes before
transferring to a rack.

# Date-Nut Bread

MAKES 1 LOAF

| |
|---|
| 1 cup pitted dates, chopped |
| ¾ cup boiling water |
| 4 tablespoons unsalted butter, at room temperature |
| ¼ cup dark brown sugar, firmly packed |
| ¼ cup granulated sugar |
| 1 egg, at room temperature |
| 2 tablespoons brandy |
| 1⅓ cups flour |
| 2 teaspoons baking powder |
| ½ teaspoon salt |
| ¾ teaspoon freshly grated nutmeg |
| ¾ cup pecans, coarsely chopped |

**1 ▲** Place the dates in a bowl and pour over the boiling water. Set aside to cool.

**2** Preheat the oven to 350°F. Line the bottom and sides of a 9- × 5-inch loaf pan with wax paper and grease.

**3 ▲** With an electric mixer, cream the butter and sugars until light and fluffy. Beat in the egg and brandy, then set aside.

**4** Sift the flour, baking powder, salt, and nutmeg together, 3 times.

**5 ▼** Fold the dry ingredients into the sugar mixture in 3 batches, alternating with the dates and water.

**6 ▲** Fold in the pecans.

**7** Pour the batter into the prepared pan and bake until a cake tester inserted in the center comes out clean, 45–50 minutes. Let cool in the pan for 10 minutes before transferring to a rack to cool completely.

# Raisin Bread

**MAKES 2 LOAVES**

| |
|---|
| 1 package active dry yeast |
| 2 cups lukewarm milk |
| 1 cup raisins |
| ½ cup currants |
| 1 tablespoon sherry or brandy |
| ½ teaspoon grated nutmeg |
| grated rind of 1 large orange |
| ⅓ cup sugar |
| 1 tablespoon salt |
| 8 tablespoons butter, melted |
| 5–6 cups flour |
| 1 egg beaten with 1 tablespoon cream, for glazing |

**1** Stir together the yeast and ½ cup of the milk and let stand for 15 minutes to dissolve.

**2** ▲ Mix the raisins, currants, sherry or brandy, nutmeg and orange rind together and set aside.

**3** In another bowl, mix the remaining milk, sugar, salt and 4 tablespoons of the butter. Add the yeast mixture. With a wooden spoon, stir in 2–3 cups flour, 1 cup at a time, until blended. Add the remaining flour as needed for a stiff dough.

**4** Transfer to a floured surface and knead until smooth and elastic. Place in a greased bowl, cover, and leave to rise in a warm place until doubled in volume, about 2½ hours.

**5** Punch down the dough, return to the bowl, cover, and leave to rise in a warm place for 30 minutes.

**6** Grease 2 8½- × 4½- inch bread pans. Divide the dough in half and roll each half into a rectangle about 20 × 7 inches.

**7** ▲ Brush the rectangles with the remaining melted butter. Sprinkle over the raisin mixture, then roll up tightly, tucking in the ends slightly as you roll. Place in the prepared pans, cover, and leave to rise until almost doubled in volume.

**8** ▲ Preheat the oven to 400°F. Brush the top of the loaves with the glaze. Bake for 20 minutes. Lower the heat to 350°F and bake until golden, 25–30 minutes more. Cool on racks.

# Sweet Potato and Raisin Bread

The natural sweetness of sweet potato is used in this healthy loaf.

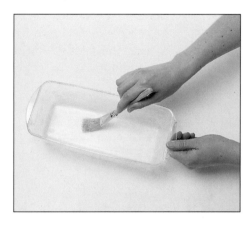

**1 ▲** Preheat the oven to 350°F. Grease a 9 × 5-inch loaf pan.

**2** Sift the flour, baking powder, salt, cinnamon and nutmeg into a small bowl. Set aside.

**3 ▲** With an electric mixer, beat the mashed sweet potatoes with the brown sugar, butter or margarine and eggs until well mixed.

**4 ▲** Add the flour mixture and the raisins. Stir with a wooden spoon until the flour is just mixed in.

**5 ▲** Transfer the batter to the prepared pan. Bake for 1–1¼ hours, or until a cake tester inserted into the center comes out clean.

**6** Cool in the pan on a wire rack for 15 minutes, then turn the bread out onto the wire rack and cool completely.

## MAKES 1 LOAF

| |
|---|
| 2½ cups all-purpose flour |
| 2 teaspoons baking powder |
| ½ teaspoon salt |
| 1 teaspoon ground cinnamon |
| ½ teaspoon grated nutmeg |
| 1 pound (2 cups) mashed cooked sweet potatoes |
| ½ cup light brown sugar, firmly packed |
| 8 tablespoons (1 stick) butter or margarine, melted and cooled |
| 3 eggs, beaten |
| 3 ounces (½ cup) raisins |

# Golden Raisin Bread

A lightly sweetened fruit bread that is delicious served warm. It is also excellent toasted and topped with butter.

MAKES 1 LOAF

⅔ cup warm water

1 teaspoon active dry yeast

1 tablespoon honey

2 cups whole-wheat flour

2 cups bread flour

1 teaspoon salt

4 ounces (⅔ cup) golden raisins

2 ounces (½ cup) walnuts, finely chopped

¾ cup warm skim milk, plus extra for glazing

~ COOK'S TIP ~

To make Apple and Hazelnut Bread, replace the golden raisins with two chopped eating apples and use chopped toasted hazelnuts instead of the walnuts. Add 1 teaspoon ground cinnamon with the flour.

**1 ▲** Put the water in a jug. Sprinkle the yeast on top. Add a few drops of the honey to activate the yeast, mix well and let stand for 10 minutes.

**2 ▲** Put the flours in a mixing bowl, with the salt and golden raisins. Set aside 1 tablespoon of the walnuts and add the rest to the bowl. Mix lightly and make a well in the center.

**3 ▲** Add the yeast and honey mixture to the flour mixture with the milk and remaining honey. Gradually incorporate the flour, mixing to a soft dough; add a little extra water if the dough feels too dry to work with.

**4 ▲** Turn the dough out onto a floured surface and knead for 5 minutes. Return to the clean bowl, cover with a damp dish towel and set aside in a warm place to rise for about 2 hours, until doubled in bulk. Grease a baking sheet.

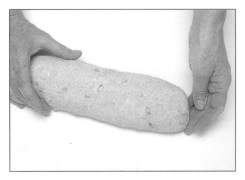

**5 ▲** Turn the dough out onto a floured surface and make an 11-inch-long sausage shape. Place on the baking sheet. Make some diagonal cuts down the length of the loaf.

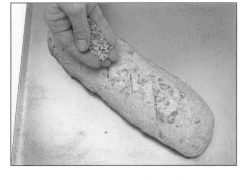

**6 ▲** Brush the loaf with milk, sprinkle with the reserved walnuts and let rise for about 40 minutes. Preheat the oven to 425°F. Bake for 10 minutes. Lower the temperature to 400°F and bake for about 20 minutes more, or until the loaf sounds hollow when tapped.

# Prune-Filled Coffee Cake

**MAKES 1 LOAF**

| |
|---|
| 1 package active dry yeast |
| ¼ cup lukewarm water |
| ¼ cup lukewarm milk |
| ¼ cup sugar |
| ½ teaspoon salt |
| 1 egg |
| 4 tablespoons butter, at room temperature |
| 3–3½ cups flour |
| 1 egg beaten with 2 teaspoons water, for glazing |

**FOR THE FILLING**

| |
|---|
| 1 cup cooked prunes |
| 2 teaspoons grated lemon rind |
| 1 teaspoon grated orange rind |
| ¼ teaspoon freshly grated nutmeg |
| 3 tablespoons butter, melted |
| ½ cup walnuts, very finely chopped |
| 2 tablespoons sugar |

**1**  In a large bowl, combine the yeast and water, stir, and leave for 15 minutes to dissolve.

**2**  Stir in the milk, sugar, salt, egg, and butter. Gradually stir in 2½ cups of the flour to obtain a soft dough.

**3**  Transfer to a floured surface and knead in just enough flour to obtain a dough that is smooth and elastic. Put into a clean bowl, cover, and leave to rise in a warm place until doubled in volume, about 1½ hours.

~ **VARIATION** ~

For Apricot-Filled Coffee Cake, replace the prunes with the same amount of dried apricots. It is not necessary to cook them, but to soften, soak them in hot tea and discard the liquid before using.

**4** ▲  Meanwhile, for the filling, combine the prunes, lemon and orange rinds, nutmeg, butter, walnuts, and sugar and stir to blend. Set aside.

**5**  Grease a large baking sheet. Punch down the dough and transfer to a lightly floured surface. Knead briefly, then roll out into a 15- × 10-inch rectangle. Carefully transfer to the baking sheet.

**6** ▲  Spread the filling in the center.

**7** ▲  With a sharp knife, cut 10 strips at an angle on either side of the filling, cutting just to the filling.

**8** ▲  For a braided pattern, fold up one end neatly, then fold over the strips from alternating sides until all the strips are folded over. Tuck excess dough at ends underneath.

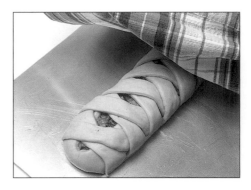

**9** ▲  Cover loosely with a dish towel and leave to rise in a warm place until almost doubled in volume.

**10** ▲  Preheat the oven to 375°F. Brush with the glaze. Bake until browned, about 30 minutes. Transfer to a rack to cool.

# INTER-NATIONAL BREADS

THIS COLLECTION INCLUDES SAVORY AND SWEET CLASSICS FROM AROUND THE WORLD, INCLUDING A GOOD SELECTION OF LESSER-KNOWN SPECIALTIES. THESE RECIPES AIM TO TAKE THE MYSTERY OUT OF BREADMAKING AND INSPIRE YOU TO TRY BAKING MANY DIFFERENT AND DELICIOUS BREADS.

# British Cottage Loaf

**MAKES 1 LOAF**

| |
|---|
| 6 cups unbleached white bread flour |
| 2 teaspoons salt |
| ¾ ounce fresh yeast |
| 1⅔ cups lukewarm water |

---

~ COOK'S TIPS ~

• To ensure a good-shaped cottage loaf the dough needs to be firm enough to support the weight of the top ball.

• Do not over-proof the dough on the second rising or the loaf may topple over—but even if it does it will still taste good.

---

Snipping the top and bottom sections of the dough at 2-inch intervals not only looks good but also helps the loaf to expand in the oven.

**1** Lightly grease 2 baking sheets. Sift the flour and salt together into a large bowl and make a well in the center.

**2** Mix the yeast in ⅔ cup of the water until dissolved. Pour into the center of the flour with the remaining water and mix to a firm dough.

**3** Knead on a lightly floured surface for 10 minutes until smooth and elastic. Place in a lightly oiled bowl, cover with lightly oiled plastic wrap and let rise, in a warm place, for about 1 hour or until doubled in bulk.

**4 ▲** Turn out onto a lightly floured surface and punch down. Knead for 2–3 minutes, then divide the dough into two-thirds and one-third; shape each to a ball. Transfer to the prepared baking sheets. Cover with inverted bowls and let rise, in a warm place, for about 30 minutes (see Cook's Tips).

**5** Gently flatten the top of the larger round of dough and cut a cross in the center, 1½ inches across. Brush with a little water and place the smaller round on top.

**6 ▲** Press a hole through the middle of the top ball, down into the lower part, using your thumb and first two fingers of one hand. Cover with oiled plastic wrap and let rest in a warm place for about 10 minutes. Preheat the oven to 425°F, and place the bread on the lower shelf. It will finish expanding as the oven heats up. Bake for 35–40 minutes or until golden brown and sounding hollow when tapped. Cool on a wire rack.

# British Grant Loaves

This quick and easy recipe was created by Doris Grant and was included in her cookbook, published in the 1940s—the dough requires no kneading and takes only a minute to mix. The loaves should keep moist for several days.

**MAKES 3 LOAVES**

| |
|---|
| 12 cups whole-wheat flour |
| 1 tablespoon salt |
| 1 tablespoon active dry yeast |
| 5 cups warm water (95–100°F) |
| 1 tablespoon brown sugar |

**1** Thoroughly grease 3 loaf pans, each about 8½ × 4½ × 2½ inches, and set aside in a warm place. Sift the flour and salt together in a large bowl and warm slightly.

**2** Sprinkle the active dry yeast over ⅔ cup of the water. After a couple of minutes stir in the sugar. Let sit for 10 minutes.

~ COOK'S TIP ~

Muscovado sugar gives this bread a rich flavor. It is a moist, unrefined cane sugar.

**3** Make a well in the center of the flour and stir in the yeast mixture and remaining water. The dough should be slippery. Mix for about 1 minute, working the sides into the middle.

**4** ▲ Divide among the prepared pans, cover with oiled plastic wrap and let rise, in a warm place, for 30 minutes or until the dough has risen to within ½ inch of the top of the pans.

**5** Meanwhile, preheat the oven to 400°F. Bake for 40 minutes or until the loaves are crisp and sound hollow when tapped on the bottom. Turn out onto a wire rack to cool.

# British Poppy-Seeded Bloomer

**MAKES 1 LOAF**

| |
|---|
| 6 cups unbleached white bread flour |
| 2 teaspoons salt |
| ½ ounce fresh yeast |
| 1⅞ cups water |
| FOR THE TOPPING |
| ½ teaspoon salt |
| 2 tablespoons water |
| poppy seeds, for sprinkling |

This satisfying white bread, which is the British version of the chunky baton loaf found throughout Europe, is made by a slower rising method and with less yeast than usual. It produces a longer-keeping loaf with a fuller flavor. The dough takes about 8 hours to rise, so you'll need to start this bread early in the morning.

**1** Lightly grease a baking sheet. Sift the flour and salt together into a large bowl and make a well in the center.

**2 ▲** Mix the yeast and ⅔ cup of the water in a cup or bowl. Mix in the remaining water. Add to the center of the flour. Mix, gradually incorporating the surrounding flour, until the mixture forms a firm dough.

**3 ▲** Turn out onto a lightly floured surface and knead the dough very well, for at least 10 minutes, until smooth and elastic. Place the dough in a lightly oiled bowl, cover with lightly oiled plastic wrap and let rise, at cool room temperature, about 60–65°F, for 5–6 hours or until doubled in bulk.

**4** Punch down the dough, turn out onto a lightly floured surface and knead it thoroughly for about 5 minutes. Return the dough to the bowl, and re-cover. Let rise, at room temperature, for another 2 hours.

**5 ▲** Punch down again and repeat the thorough kneading. Let the dough rest for 5 minutes, then roll out on a lightly floured surface into a rectangle 1-inch thick. Roll the dough up from one long side and shape it into a square-ended thick baton shape about 13 × 5 inches.

**6 ▲** Place it seam side up on a lightly floured baking sheet, cover and let rest for 15 minutes. Turn the loaf over and place on the greased baking sheet. Plump up by tucking the dough under the sides and ends then cut 6 diagonal slashes on the top. Let rest, covered, in a warm place, for 10 minutes. Meanwhile, preheat the oven to 450°F.

**7 ▲** Combine the salt and water and brush this glaze over the bread. Sprinkle with poppy seeds.

**8** Spray the oven with water, bake the bread for 20 minutes, then reduce the oven temperature to 400°F; bake for 25 more minutes, or until golden. Transfer to a wire rack to cool.

### ~ COOK'S TIP ~

The traditional cracked, crusty appearance of this loaf is difficult to achieve in a domestic oven. However, you can get a similar result by spraying the oven with water before baking. If the underneath of the loaf is not very crusty at the end of baking, turn the loaf over on the baking sheet, switch off the heat and leave in the oven for another 5–10 minutes.

# British Harvest Festival Sheaf

**MAKES 1 LOAF**

| |
| --- |
| 8 cups unbleached white bread flour |
| 1 tablespoon salt |
| ½ ounce fresh yeast |
| 5 tablespoons lukewarm milk |
| 1⅔ cups cold water |
| FOR THE TOPPING |
| 1 egg |
| 1 tablespoon milk |

This is one of the most visually stunning breads. Celebratory loaves can be seen in various forms in churches and at some bakers throughout Britain around the September harvest.

**1** Lightly grease a large baking sheet, at least 15 × 13 inches. Sift the flour and salt together into a large bowl and make a well in the center.

**2** Mix the yeast with the milk in a bowl. Add to the center of the flour with the water and mix to a stiff dough. Turn out onto a lightly floured surface and knead for 10–15 minutes, until smooth and elastic.

**3** Place in a lightly oiled bowl, cover with lightly oiled plastic wrap and let rise, at room temperature, for about 2 hours or until doubled in bulk.

**4** Turn the dough out onto a lightly floured surface, punch down and knead for about 1 minute. Cover and let rest for 10 minutes.

**5** ▲ Divide the dough in half. Roll out one piece to a 14 × 10-inch oblong. Fold loosely in half lengthwise. Using a sharp knife, cut out a half mushroom shape for the sheaf (leave the folded edge uncut). Make the stalk "base" about 7 inches long.

**6** Place the dough on the prepared baking sheet and open out. Prick all over with a fork and brush with water to prevent a skin forming. Reserve 3 ounces of the trimmings for the tie. Cover and set aside. Divide the remaining dough in two and mix the rest of the trimmings with one half. Cover and set aside. Beat together the egg and milk for the glaze.

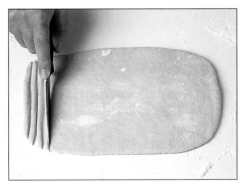

**7** ▲ Roll out the remaining dough on a lightly floured surface to a rectangle, 11 × 7 inches, and cut into 30–35 thin strips 7 inches long. Place side by side lengthwise on the base, as close as possible, to represent wheat stalks. Brush with some glaze.

**8** Take the larger piece of reserved dough and divide into four. Divide each piece into 25 and shape into oblong rolls to make 100 wheat ears. Make each roll pointed at one end.

**9** ▲ Holding one roll at a time, snip along each side toward the center, using scissors, to make wheat shapes.

**10** Preheat the oven to 425°F. Arrange the ears around the outer edge of the top of the mushroom shape, overlapping them on the baking sheet. Make a second row lower down, placing it between the first ears. Repeat until they are all used. Brush with some glaze as you work to stop the dough from drying out.

**11** ▲ Divide the smaller piece of reserved dough into 6 pieces and roll each out to a 17-inch strip. Make 2 braids, each with 3 strips. Place across the wheat stalks to make a tied bow. Brush with some glaze. Prick between the wheat ears and stalks using a sharp knife, and bake the sheaf for 15 minutes.

**12** Reduce the oven temperature to 350°F. Brush the bread with the remaining glaze and bake for another 30–35 minutes or until golden and firm. Let cool on the baking sheet.

> **~ COOK'S TIP ~**
> Harvest loaves are often baked for display, rather than for eating. If you'd like to do this, leave the baked loaf in the oven and reduce the temperature to very low (250°F) for several hours until the dough dries out.

# British Lardy Cake

## MAKES 1 LOAF

| |
|---|
| 4 cups white bread flour |
| 1 teaspoon salt |
| 1 tablespoon shortening |
| 2 tablespoons sugar |
| ¾ ounce fresh yeast |
| 1¼ cups lukewarm water |

### FOR THE FILLING

| |
|---|
| 6 tablespoons shortening |
| 6 tablespoons light brown sugar |
| ½ cup currants, slightly warmed |
| ½ cup golden raisins, slightly warmed |
| 3 tablespoons chopped candied peel |
| 1 teaspoon allspice |

### FOR THE GLAZE

| |
|---|
| 2 teaspoons sunflower oil |
| 1–2 tablespoons sugar |

This special rich fruit bread was originally made throughout many counties of England for celebrating the harvest. Using shortening (lard) rather than butter or margarine makes an authentic lardy cake.

**1** Grease a 10 × 8-inch shallow roasting pan. Sift the flour and salt into a bowl and rub in the shortening. Add the sugar. Make a well in the center.

**2** In a bowl, cream the yeast with half the water, then blend in the rest. Add to the flour and mix to a smooth dough.

**3** Turn out onto a lightly floured surface and knead for about 10 minutes until smooth and elastic. Place in a lightly oiled bowl, cover with lightly oiled plastic wrap and let rise, in a warm place, for 1 hour, or until doubled in bulk.

**4** Turn the dough out onto a lightly floured surface and punch down. Knead for 2–3 minutes. Roll into a rectangle about ¼-inch thick.

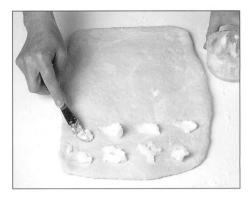

**5** ▲ Using half the shortening for the filling, cover the top two-thirds of the dough with flakes of shortening. Sprinkle on half the sugar, half the dried fruits and peel and half the allspice. Fold the bottom third up and the top third down, sealing the edges with the rolling pin.

**6** Turn the dough by 90 degrees. Roll again and cover with the remaining shortening, fruit, peel and allspice. Fold, seal and turn as before. Roll out the dough to fit the prepared pan. Cover with lightly oiled plastic wrap and let rise, in a warm place, for 30–45 minutes or until doubled in size.

**7** Meanwhile, preheat the oven to 400°F. Brush the cake with sunflower oil and sprinkle with sugar.

**8** ▲ Score a criss-cross pattern on top using a sharp knife, then bake for 30–40 minutes, until golden. Turn out onto a wire rack to cool slightly. Serve warm, cut into slices or squares.

# British Malted Currant Bread

This spiced currant bread makes a good tea or breakfast bread, sliced and spread with a generous amount of butter. It also makes superb toast.

**MAKES 2 LOAVES**

| |
|---|
| 3 tablespoons malt extract |
| 2 tablespoons corn syrup |
| ¼ cup butter |
| 4 cups white bread flour |
| 1 teaspoon allspice |
| ¾ ounce fresh yeast |
| ¾ cup lukewarm milk |
| ¾ cup currants, slightly warmed |
| FOR THE GLAZE |
| 2 tablespoons milk |
| 2 tablespoons sugar |

> ## ~ COOK'S TIP ~
> When you are making more than one loaf, the easiest way to prove them is to place the pans in a lightly oiled large plastic bag.

**4** Turn the dough out onto a floured surface, punch down, then knead in the currants. Divide the dough in half and shape into two loaves. Place in the prepared pans. Cover with oiled plastic wrap and let rise, in a warm place, for 2–3 hours or until the dough reaches the top of the pans.

**1** ▲ Lightly grease two 1-pound loaf pans. Place the malt extract, corn syrup and butter in a saucepan and heat gently until the butter has melted. Set aside to cool completely.

**2** Sift the flour and allspice together into a large bowl and make a well in the center. Mix the yeast with a little of the milk, then blend in the remaining milk. Add the yeast mixture and cooled malt mixture to the center of the flour and blend together to form a dough.

**3** Turn out the dough onto a lightly floured surface and knead for about 10 minutes until smooth and elastic. Place in a lightly oiled bowl, cover with lightly oiled plastic wrap and let rise, in a warm place, for 1½–2 hours or until doubled in bulk.

**5** ▲ Meanwhile, preheat the oven to 400°F. Bake for 35–40 minutes or until golden. While the loaves are baking, heat the milk and sugar for the glaze in a small saucepan. Turn out the loaves onto a wire rack, then invert them, so that they are the right way up. Immediately brush the glaze evenly over the loaves and let cool.

# Welsh Bara Brith

**MAKES 1 LOAF**

| |
|---|
| ¾ ounce fresh yeast |
| scant 1 cup lukewarm milk |
| 4 cups white bread flour |
| 6 tablespoons butter or shortening |
| 1 teaspoon allspice |
| ½ teaspoon salt |
| ⅓ cup light brown sugar |
| 1 egg, lightly beaten |
| ⅔ cup raisins, slightly warmed |
| scant ½ cup currants, slightly warmed |
| ¼ cup chopped candied peel |
| 1–2 tablespoons honey, for glazing |

This rich, fruity bread—the name literally means "speckled bread"—is a specialty from North Wales. The honey glaze makes a delicious topping.

**1** Grease a baking sheet. In a bowl, blend the yeast with a little of the milk, then stir in the remainder. Set aside for 10 minutes.

**2 ▲** Sift the flour into a large bowl and rub in the butter or shortening until the mixture resembles bread crumbs. Stir in the allspice, salt and sugar and make a well in the center.

**3** Add the yeast mixture and beaten egg to the center of the flour and mix into a rough dough.

**4** Turn out the dough onto a lightly floured surface and knead for about 10 minutes until smooth and elastic. Place in a lightly oiled bowl, cover with lightly oiled plastic wrap and let rise, in a warm place, for 1½ hours or until doubled in bulk.

**5 ▲** Turn out the dough onto a floured surface, punch down, and knead in the dried fruits and peel. Shape into a round and place on the baking sheet. Cover with oiled plastic wrap and let rise, in a warm place, for 1 hour or until the dough doubles in size.

**6** Meanwhile, preheat the oven to 400°F. Bake for 30 minutes or until the bread sounds hollow when tapped on the bottom. If the bread starts to over-brown, cover it loosely with foil for the last 10 minutes. Transfer the bread to a wire rack, brush with honey and let cool.

<table>
<tr><td>

### ~ VARIATION ~
The bara brith can be baked in a 6¼–7½-cup loaf pan or deep round or square cake pan, if you prefer.

</td></tr>
</table>

# Welsh Clay Pot Loaves

These breads are flavored with chives, sage, parsley and garlic. You can use any selection of your favorite herbs. For even more flavor, try adding a little grated raw onion and grated cheese to the dough.

**MAKES 2 LOAVES**

| |
| --- |
| 1 cup whole-wheat bread flour |
| 3 cups unbleached white bread flour |
| 1½ teaspoons salt |
| ½ ounce fresh yeast |
| ⅔ cup lukewarm milk |
| 1½ cups lukewarm water |
| 4 tablespoons butter, melted |
| 1 tablespoon chopped fresh chives |
| 1 tablespoon chopped fresh parsley |
| 1 teaspoon chopped fresh sage |
| 1 garlic clove, crushed |
| beaten egg, for glazing |
| fennel seeds, for sprinkling (optional) |

**4** Turn the dough out onto a lightly floured surface and punch down. Divide in half. Shape and fit into the prepared flower pots. The dough should about half fill the pots. Cover with oiled plastic wrap and let rise for 30–45 minutes, in a warm place, or until the dough is 1 inch from the tops of the pots.

**1 ▲** Lightly grease 2 clean 5½-inch diameter, 4½-inch high clay flowerpots. Sift the flours and salt together into a large bowl and make a well in the center. Blend the yeast with a little of the milk until smooth, then stir in the remaining milk. Pour into the center of the flour and sprinkle over a little of the flour from around the edge. Cover the bowl and let sit in a warm place for 15 minutes.

**2 ▲** Add the water, melted butter, herbs and garlic to the flour mixture and blend to form a dough. Turn out onto a lightly floured surface and knead for about 10 minutes, until the dough is smooth and elastic.

**3** Place in a lightly oiled bowl, cover with lightly oiled plastic wrap and let rise, in a warm place, for 1¼–1½ hours or until doubled in bulk.

**5 ▲** Meanwhile, preheat the oven to 400°F. Brush the tops with beaten egg and sprinkle with fennel seeds, if using. Bake for 35–40 minutes or until golden. Turn out onto a wire rack to cool.

# Scottish Morning Rolls

**MAKES 10 ROLLS**

4 cups unbleached plain white flour,
plus extra for dusting

2 teaspoons salt

¾ ounce fresh yeast

⅔ cup lukewarm milk

⅔ cup lukewarm water

2 tablespoons milk, for glazing

**1** Grease 2 baking sheets. Sift the flour and salt into a bowl and make a well in the center. Mix the yeast with the milk, then mix in the water. Add to the center of the flour and mix together to form a soft dough.

**2** Knead the dough lightly in the bowl, then cover with lightly oiled plastic wrap and let rise, in a warm place, for 1 hour, or until doubled in bulk. Turn the dough out onto a floured surface and punch down.

These rolls are best served warm, as soon as they are baked. In Scotland they are a popular favorite for breakfast with a fried egg and bacon.

**3** ▲ Divide the dough into 10 equal pieces. Knead lightly and, using a rolling pin, shape each piece to a flat oval 4 × 3 inches or a flat 3½-inch round .

**4** Place on the baking sheets and cover with oiled plastic wrap. Let rise, in a warm place, for about 30 minutes.

**5** ▲ Meanwhile, preheat the oven to 400°F. Press each roll in the center with the three middle fingers to equalize the air bubbles and to help prevent blistering. Brush with milk and dust with flour. Bake for 15–20 minutes or until lightly browned. Dust with more flour and cool briefly on a wire rack. Serve warm.

# Cornish Saffron Breads

Often called saffron cake, this light, delicately spiced bread contains strands of saffron and is made in a loaf pan. The flavor and texture is superb.

### MAKES 2 LOAVES

| | |
|---|---|
| 1¼ cups milk | |
| ½ teaspoon saffron strands | |
| 3½ cups all-purpose flour | |
| 1 ounce fresh yeast | |
| ½ cup ground almonds | |
| ½ teaspoon grated nutmeg | |
| ½ teaspoon ground cinnamon | |
| ¼ cup sugar | |
| ½ teaspoon salt | |
| 6 tablespoons butter, softened | |
| ⅓ cup golden raisins | |
| ¼ cup currants | |
| FOR THE GLAZE | |
| 2 tablespoons milk | |
| 1 tablespoon sugar | |

**7 ▲** Turn the dough out onto a lightly floured surface, punch down, and knead in the golden raisins and currants. Divide in half and shape into two loaves. Place in the prepared pans. Cover with oiled plastic wrap and let rise, in a warm place, for 1½ hours, or until the dough reaches the top of the pans.

**1** Grease 2 2-pound loaf pans. Heat half the milk until almost boiling.

**2 ▲** Place the saffron strands in a small heatproof bowl and pour in the milk. Stir gently, then set aside to infuse for 30 minutes.

**3** Heat the remaining milk in the same pan until it is just lukewarm.

**4** Place ½ cup flour in a small bowl, crumble in the yeast and stir in the lukewarm milk. Mix well, then let sit for about 15 minutes until the yeast starts to ferment.

**5** Combine the remaining flour, ground almonds, spices, sugar and salt in a large bowl and make a well in the center. Add the saffron infusion, yeast mixture and softened butter to the center of the flour and mix to a very soft dough.

**6** Turn out onto a floured surface and knead for 5 minutes until smooth and elastic. Place in a lightly oiled bowl, cover with lightly oiled plastic wrap and let rise, in a warm place, for 1½–2 hours, or until doubled in bulk.

**8** Meanwhile, preheat the oven to 425°F. Bake the loaves for 10 minutes, then reduce the oven temperature to 375°F and bake for 15–20 minutes or until golden.

**9** To make the glaze, heat milk and sugar together. When the loaves are cooked, brush them with the glaze, leave in the pans for 5 minutes, then turn out onto a wire rack to cool.

# French Kugelhopf

**MAKES 1 LOAF**

⅔ cup unsalted butter, softened

12 walnut halves

6 cups white bread flour

1½ teaspoons salt

¾ ounce fresh yeast

1¼ cups milk

4 ounces bacon, diced

1 onion, finely chopped

1 tablespoon vegetable oil

5 eggs, beaten

freshly ground black pepper

~ VARIATION ~

If you wish to make a sweet kugelhopf, replace the walnuts with whole almonds and the bacon and onion with 1 cup raisins and ⅓ cup candied fruits. Add ¼ cup sugar in step 2, and omit the pepper.

This inviting, fluted ring-shaped bread originates from Alsace, although Germany, Hungary and Austria all have their own variations of this popular recipe. Kugelhopf can be sweet or savory; this version is richly flavored with nuts, onion and bacon.

**1 ▲** Use 2 tablespoons of the butter to grease a 9-inch kugelhopf mold. Place 8 walnut halves around the base and chop the remainder.

**2** Sift the flour and salt into a bowl and season with pepper. Make a well in the center. In a bowl, cream the yeast with 3 tablespoons of the milk. Pour into the center of the flour with the remaining milk. Mix in a little flour to make a thick batter. Sprinkle a little of the remaining flour on top of the batter, cover with plastic wrap and let sit in a warm place for 20–30 minutes, until the yeast mixture bubbles.

**3 ▲** Fry the bacon and onion in the oil until the onion is golden.

**4** Add the eggs to the flour mixture and gradually beat in the flour, using your hand. Beat in the remaining butter to form a soft dough. Cover with oiled plastic wrap and let rise, in a warm place, for 45–60 minutes or until almost doubled in bulk. Preheat the oven to 400°F.

**5 ▲** Punch down the dough and gently knead in the bacon, onion and nuts. Place in the mold, cover with lightly oiled plastic wrap and let rise, in a warm place, for about 1 hour or until it has risen to the top of the mold.

**6** Bake for 40–45 minutes or until the loaf has browned and sounds hollow when tapped on the bottom. Cool in the mold for 5 minutes, then remove.

# French Pain Polka

This attractive, deeply cut, crusty bread is made by using a little of the previous day's dough as a starter. However, if you do not have any you can make a starter dough, the details for which are given.

**MAKES 1 LOAF**

| |
|---|
| 1 cup 6–15-hours-old French baguette dough |
| OR FOR THE STARTER |
| ¼ ounce fresh yeast |
| ½ cup lukewarm water |
| 1 cup unbleached all-purpose flour |
| FOR THE DOUGH |
| ¼ ounce fresh yeast |
| scant 1¼ cups lukewarm water |
| 4 cups unbleached white bread flour, plus extra for dusting |
| 1 tablespoon salt |

> ### ~ COOK'S TIP ~
> The piece of previously made dough can be kept covered in the fridge for up to 2 days, or frozen for up to a month. Just let it come back to room temperature and allow it to rise for an hour before using.

**2** In a bowl, mix the yeast for the dough with half of the water, then stir in the remainder. Add the previously made dough or starter (step 1) and knead to dissolve the dough. Gradually add the flour and salt and mix to a dough. Turn out onto a lightly floured surface and knead for 8–10 minutes, until the dough is smooth and elastic.

**1 ▲** Lightly flour a baking sheet. If you have French baguette dough, proceed to step 2. Make the starter. Mix the yeast with the water, then gradually stir in sufficient flour to form a batter. Beat vigorously, then gradually add the remaining flour and mix to a soft dough. Knead for 5 minutes. Place in a bowl, cover with oiled plastic wrap, and let sit at room temperature for 4–5 hours or until well risen and starting to collapse.

**3** Place the dough in an oiled bowl, cover with lightly oiled plastic wrap and let rise, in a warm place, for about 1½ hours or until doubled in bulk.

**4** Turn out the dough onto a lightly floured surface, punch down and shape into a round ball. Flatten slightly and place on the prepared baking sheet. Cover with oiled plastic wrap and let rise for 1 hour or until almost doubled in size.

**5 ▲** Dust the top of the loaf with flour and, using a sharp knife, cut the top fairly deeply in a criss-cross pattern. Let rest for 10 minutes. Meanwhile, preheat the oven to 450°F.

**6** Bake for 25–30 minutes or until browned. Spray the inside of the oven with water as soon as the bread goes into the oven, and 3 times during the first 10 minutes of baking. Transfer to a wire rack to cool.

# French Pain Bouillie

**MAKES 2 LOAVES**

**FOR THE PORRIDGE**

2 cups rye flour

1¾ cups boiling water

1 teaspoon honey

**FOR THE DOUGH**

¼ ounce fresh yeast

2 tablespoons lukewarm water

1 teaspoon caraway seeds, crushed

2 teaspoons salt

3 cups white bread flour

olive oil, for brushing

**1 ▲** Lightly grease a 9¼ × 5-inch loaf pan. Place the rye flour for the porridge in a large bowl. Pour in the boiling water and let stand for 5 minutes. Stir in the honey. Cover with plastic wrap and let sit in a warm place for about 12 hours.

**2 ▲** Make the dough. Put the yeast in a measuring cup and blend in the water. Stir the mixture into the porridge with the caraway seeds and salt. Add the white flour a little at a time. Mix first with a wooden spoon and then with your hands, until the mixture forms a firm dough.

This is an old-fashioned style of rye bread, made before sourdough starters were used. Rye flour is mixed with boiling water like a porridge and left overnight to ferment. The finished bread has a rich, earthy flavor, with just a hint of caraway.

**3** Turn out onto a lightly floured surface and knead for 6–8 minutes, until smooth and elastic. Return to the bowl, cover with lightly oiled plastic wrap and let rise, in a warm place, for 1½ hours or until doubled in bulk.

**4 ▲** Turn out the dough onto a lightly floured surface and punch down. Cut into 2 equal pieces and roll each piece into a rectangle 15 × 4½ inches. Fold the bottom third up and the top third down and seal the edges. Turn over.

**5** Brush one side of each piece of folded dough with olive oil and place side by side in the prepared pan, oiled edges next to each other. Cover with lightly oiled plastic wrap and let rise, in a warm place, for 1 hour or until the dough reaches the top of the pan.

**6** Meanwhile, preheat the oven to 425°F. Brush the tops of the loaves with olive oil and, using a sharp knife, slash with one or two cuts. Bake for 30 minutes, then reduce the oven temperature to 375°F and bake for another 25–30 minutes. Turn out onto a wire rack to cool.

~ COOK'S TIP ~

Serve very thinly sliced, with a little butter, or as an accompaniment to cold meats and cheeses.

# French Epi

This pretty, wheat shaped crusty loaf makes a good presentation bread. The recipe uses a piece of fermented French baguette dough as a starter, which improves the flavor and texture of the finished bread.

**MAKES 2 LOAVES**

| |
|---|
| ¼ ounce fresh yeast |
| generous 1 cup lukewarm water |
| ½ cup 6–10-hours-old French baguette dough |
| 2 cups white bread flour |
| ¾ cup all-purpose flour |
| 1 teaspoon salt |

> ~ COOK'S TIP ~
>
> You can use any amount up to 10 percent of previously made French baguette dough for this recipe. The épi can also be shaped into a circle to make an attractive crown.

**5** Let the dough rest between rolling for a few minutes, if necessary, to avoid tearing. Pleat a floured dish towel on a baking sheet to make 2 molds for the loaves. Place them between the pleats of the towel, cover with lightly oiled plastic wrap and let rise, in a warm place, for 30 minutes.

**1 ▲** Sprinkle a baking sheet with flour. Mix the yeast with the water in a bowl. Place the French baguette dough in a large bowl and break up. Add a little of the yeast water to soften the dough. Mix in a little of the bread flour, then alternate the additions of yeast water and both flours until incorporated. Sprinkle the salt over the dough and knead in. Turn out onto a floured surface and knead for 5 minutes, until smooth and elastic.

**2** Place in a lightly oiled bowl, cover with lightly oiled plastic wrap and let rise, in a warm place, for about 1 hour or until the dough has doubled in bulk.

**3 ▲** Punch down the dough with your fist, then cover the bowl again with the oiled plastic wrap and let rise, in a warm place, for about 1 hour.

**4** Divide the dough in half, place on a lightly floured surface and stretch each piece into a baguette.

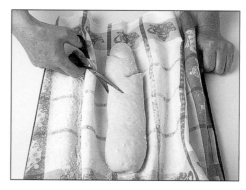

**6 ▲** Meanwhile, preheat the oven to 450°F. Using scissors, make diagonal cuts halfway through the dough about 2 inches apart, alternating the cuts along the loaf. Gently pull the dough in the opposite direction.

**7** Place on the baking sheet and bake for 20 minutes or until golden. Spray inside the oven with water 2–3 times during the first 5 minutes of baking. Transfer to a wire rack to cool.

# French Pain de Campagne Rustique

**MAKES 1 LOAF**

**FOR THE CHEF**

½ cup whole-wheat bread flour

3 tablespoons warm water

**FOR THE 1ST REFRESHMENT**

4 tablespoons warm water

¾ cup whole-wheat bread flour

**FOR THE 2ND REFRESHMENT**

½ cup lukewarm water

1 cup white bread flour

¼ cup whole-wheat bread flour

**FOR THE DOUGH**

⅔–¾ cup lukewarm water

3 cups white bread flour

2 teaspoons salt

~ COOK'S TIPS ~

• You will need to start making this bread about four days before you'd like to eat it.
• To make another loaf, keep the piece of starter dough (see step 6) in the refrigerator for up to three days. Use the reserved piece of starter dough for the 2nd refreshment in place of the *levain* in step 3, gradually mix in the water, then the flours and let rise as described.

**1 ▲** To make the *chef*, place the flour in a small bowl, add the water and knead for 3–4 minutes to form a dough. Cover with plastic wrap and let sit in a warm place for 2 days.

This superb country bread is made using a natural French *chef* starter to produce a rustic flavor and texture. In France, breads like this are often made three or four times the size of this loaf.

**2** Pull off the crust and discard, then remove 2 tablespoons of the moist center. Place in a bowl and gradually mix in the water for the 1st refreshment. Mix in the flour and knead for 3–4 minutes to form a dough or *levain*, then cover with plastic wrap and let sit in a warm place for 1 day.

**3 ▲** Discard the crust from the *levain* and gradually mix in the water for the 2nd refreshment. Mix in the flours a little at a time, mixing well after each addition to form a firm dough. Cover with lightly oiled plastic wrap and let rise, in a warm place, for about 10 hours or until doubled in bulk.

**4** Lightly flour a baking sheet. For the final stage in the preparation of the dough, gradually mix the water into the *levain* in the bowl, then gradually mix in the flour, then the salt. Turn out the dough onto a lightly floured surface and knead for about 5 minutes, until smooth and elastic.

**5** Place the dough in a large lightly oiled bowl, cover with lightly oiled plastic wrap and let rise, in a warm place, for 1½–2 hours or until the dough has almost doubled in bulk.

**6** Punch down the dough and cut off ½ cup. Set aside for making the next loaf. Shape the remaining dough into a ball—you should have about 1½ cups.

**7** Line a 4-inch high, 9-inch round basket or large bowl with a dish towel and dust with flour.

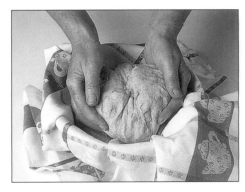

**8 ▲** Place the dough ball seam side up in the prepared basket or bowl. Cover with lightly oiled plastic wrap and let rise, in a warm place, for 2–3 hours or until almost doubled in bulk.

**9** Preheat the oven to 450°F. Invert the loaf onto the prepared baking sheet and sprinkle with flour.

**10 ▲** Using a sharp knife, slash the top of the loaf four times at right angles to each other to form a square pattern.

**11** Sprinkle with a little more flour, if desired, then bake for 30–35 minutes or until the loaf has browned and sounds hollow when tapped on the bottom. Transfer to a wire rack to cool.

# French Fougasse

**MAKES 2 LOAVES**

| |
|---|
| 4 cups white bread flour |
| 1 teaspoon salt |
| ¾ ounce fresh yeast |
| generous 1 cup lukewarm water |
| 1 tablespoon extra-virgin olive oil |
| FOR THE FILLING |
| ⅓ cup Roquefort cheese, crumbled |
| ⅓ cup walnuts, chopped |
| 2 tablespoons drained, canned anchovy fillets, soaked in milk, drained again, and chopped |
| olive oil, for brushing |

---

~ VARIATIONS ~

• Replace the cheese with
1 tablespoon chopped fresh
sage or thyme or ⅓ cup
chopped pitted olives.
• To make a sweet fougasse,
replace 1 tablespoon of the
water with orange flower water.
Include ⅓ cup chopped
candied orange peel and
2 tablespoons sugar.

---

**1 ▲** Lightly grease 2 baking sheets. Sift the flour and salt together into a large bowl and make a well in the center. In a measuring cup, cream the yeast with 4 tablespoons of the water. Pour the yeast mixture into the center of the flour with the remaining water and the olive oil and mix to a soft dough. Turn out onto a lightly floured surface and knead the dough for 8–10 minutes, until smooth and elastic.

A fougasse is a lattice-shaped, flattish loaf from the south of France. It can be cooked as a plain bread or flavored with cheese, anchovies, herbs, nuts or olives. On Christmas Eve in Provence a fougasse flavored with orange flower water is part of a table centerpiece of thirteen desserts, used to symbolize Christ and the Twelve Apostles.

**2** Place the dough in a lightly oiled bowl, cover with lightly oiled plastic wrap and let rise, in a warm place, for about 1 hour or until doubled in bulk.

**3 ▲** Turn out onto a floured surface and punch down. Divide in half and flatten one piece. Sprinkle on the cheese and walnuts and fold the dough over on itself 2–3 times to incorporate. Repeat with the other piece of dough, this time incorporating the anchovies. Shape each piece of flavored dough into a ball.

**4** Flatten each ball of dough and fold the bottom third up and the top third down, to make an oblong. Roll the cheese dough into a rectangle measuring about 11 × 6 inches. Make 4 diagonal cuts almost to the edge. Stretch the dough evenly, so that it resembles a ladder.

**5** Shape the anchovy dough into an oval with a flat base, about 10 inches long. Make 3 diagonal slits on each side toward the flat base, and pull to open the cuts. Transfer to the baking sheets, cover with oiled plastic wrap and let rise, in a warm place, for about 30–45 minutes or until nearly doubled in bulk.

**6** Meanwhile, preheat the oven to 425°F. Brush both loaves with a little olive oil and bake for 25 minutes or until golden. Transfer to a wire rack to cool.

# French Pain aux Noix

This delicious butter- and milk-enriched whole-wheat bread is filled with walnuts. It is the perfect companion for cheese.

**MAKES 2 LOAVES**

¼ cup butter

3 cups whole-wheat bread flour

1 cup white bread flour

1 tablespoon light brown sugar

1½ teaspoons salt

¾ ounce fresh yeast

generous 1 cup lukewarm milk

1½ cups chopped walnuts

**3** Knead on a lightly floured surface for 6–8 minutes. Place in a lightly oiled bowl, cover with oiled plastic wrap and let rise, in a warm place, for 1 hour or until the dough is doubled in bulk.

**4 ▲** Turn out the dough onto a lightly floured surface and gently punch down. Press or roll out to flatten and then sprinkle on the nuts. Gently press the nuts into the dough, then roll it up. Return to the oiled bowl, re-cover and let sit, in a warm place, for 30 minutes.

**5** Turn out onto a lightly floured surface, divide in half and shape each piece into a ball. Place on the baking sheets, cover with lightly oiled plastic wrap and let rise, in a warm place, for 45 minutes or until doubled in bulk.

**6** Preheat the oven to 425°F. Slash the top of each loaf 3 times. Bake for 35 minutes or until the loaves sound hollow when tapped. Transfer to a wire rack to cool.

**1 ▲** Grease 2 baking sheets. Place the butter in a small pan and heat until melted and starting to brown, then set aside to cool. Mix the flours, sugar and salt in a bowl and make a well in the center. Mix the yeast with half the milk. Add to the center of the flour with the remaining milk.

**2 ▲** Pour the cooled melted butter through a fine strainer into the center of the flour so that it joins the liquids already there. Using your hand, combine the liquids in the bowl and gradually mix in small quantities of the flour to make a batter. Continue until the mixture forms a moist dough.

# French Baguettes

**MAKES 3 LOAVES**

| |
|---|
| 5 cups white bread flour |
| 1 cup all-purpose flour |
| 2 teaspoons salt |
| ½ ounce fresh yeast |
| 2¼ cups lukewarm water |

Baguettes are difficult to reproduce at home as they require a very hot oven and steam. However, by using less yeast and a triple fermentation you can produce a bread with a superior taste and far better texture than mass-produced baguettes. These are best eaten on the day of baking.

**1** Sift the flours and salt into a bowl. Add the yeast to the water in another bowl and stir to dissolve. Gradually beat in half the flour mixture to form a batter. Cover with plastic wrap and let sit at room temperature for about 3 hours or until nearly tripled in size and starting to collapse.

**2** Add the remaining flour a little at a time, beating with your hand. Turn out onto a lightly floured surface and knead for 8–10 minutes to form a moist dough. Place in an oiled bowl, cover with oiled plastic wrap and let rise, in a warm place, for 1 hour.

**3** When the dough has almost doubled in bulk, punch it down, turn out onto a floured surface and divide into 3. Shape each into a rectangle measuring about 6 × 3 inches.

**4** Fold the bottom third up lengthwise and the top third down, and press down to make sure the pieces of dough are in contact. Seal the edges. Repeat two or three more times until each loaf is an oblong. Let rest in between folding for a few minutes, if necessary, to avoid tearing the dough.

**5 ▲** Gently stretch each piece of dough lengthwise into a 13–14-inch long loaf. Pleat a floured dish towel on a baking sheet to make 3 molds for the loaves. Place the breads between the pleats of the towel to help hold their shape while they are rising. Cover with lightly oiled plastic wrap and let rise, in a warm place, for about 45–60 minutes.

**6** Preheat the oven to maximum, at least 450°F. Roll the loaves onto a baking sheet, spaced well apart. Using a sharp knife, slash the top of each loaf several times with long diagonal slits. Bake at the top of the oven for 20–25 minutes, or until golden. Spray inside the oven with water 2–3 times during the first 5 minutes of baking. Transfer to a wire rack to cool.

# French Brioche

Rich and buttery yet light and airy, this wonderful loaf captures the essence of the classic French bread.

**MAKES 1 LOAF**

| |
|---|
| 3 cups white bread flour |
| ½ teaspoon salt |
| ½ ounce fresh yeast |
| 4 tablespoons lukewarm milk |
| 3 eggs |
| ¾ cup butter, softened |
| 2 tablespoons sugar |
| FOR THE GLAZE |
| 1 egg yolk |
| 1 tablespoon milk |

**1** Sift the flour and salt together into a large bowl and make a well in the center. Put the yeast in a measuring cup and stir in the milk.

**2** ▲ Add the yeast mixture to the center of the flour with the eggs and combine to form a soft dough.

**3** ▲ Using your hand, beat the dough for 4–5 minutes, until smooth and elastic. Cream the butter and sugar together. Gradually add the butter mixture to the dough, making sure it is incorporated before adding more. Beat until smooth, shiny and elastic.

**4** Cover the bowl with lightly oiled plastic wrap and let the dough rise, in a warm place, for 1–2 hours or until doubled in bulk.

**5** Lightly punch down the dough, then re-cover and place in the refrigerator for 8–10 hours or overnight.

**6** Lightly grease a scant 7-cup brioche mold. Turn the dough out onto a lightly floured surface. Cut off almost a quarter and set aside. Shape the rest into a ball and place in the prepared mold. Shape the reserved dough into an elongated egg shape. Using two or three fingers, make a hole in the center of the large ball of dough. Gently press the narrow end of the egg-shaped dough into the hole.

**7** Combine the egg yolk and milk for the glaze, and brush a little on the brioche. Cover with oiled plastic wrap and let rise, in a warm place, for 1½–2 hours or until the dough nearly reaches the top of the mold.

**8** Meanwhile, preheat the oven to 450°F. Brush the brioche with the remaining glaze and bake for 10 minutes. Reduce the oven temperature to 375°F and bake for another 20–25 minutes or until golden. Turn out onto a wire rack to cool.

# French Croissants

**MAKES 14 CROISSANTS**

| |
| --- |
| 3 cups white bread flour |
| 1 cup all-purpose flour |
| 1 teaspoon salt |
| 2 tablespoons sugar |
| ½ ounce fresh yeast |
| scant 1 cup lukewarm milk |
| 1 egg, lightly beaten |
| 1 cup butter |
| FOR THE GLAZE |
| 1 egg yolk |
| 1 tablespoon milk |

Golden layers of flaky pastry, puffy, light and flavored with butter is how the best croissants should be. Serve warm on the day of baking.

**3** Punch down, re-cover and chill for 1 hour. Meanwhile, flatten the butter into a block about ¾ inch thick. Punch down the dough and turn out onto a lightly floured surface. Roll out into a rough 10-inch square, rolling the edges thinner than the center.

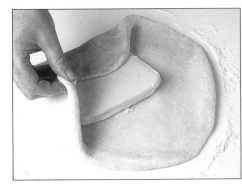

**4 ▲** Place the block of butter diagonally in the center and fold the corners of the dough over the butter like an envelope, tucking in the edges to completely enclose the butter.

~ COOK'S TIP ~

Make sure that the butter and the dough are about the same temperature when combining to ensure the best results.

**1 ▲** Sift the flours and salt together into a large bowl. Stir in the sugar. Make a well in the center. Mix the yeast with 3 tablespoons of the milk, then stir in the remainder. Add the yeast mixture to the center of the flour, then add the egg and gradually beat in the flour until it forms a dough.

**2** Turn out onto a floured surface and knead for 3–4 minutes. Place in an oiled bowl, cover with oiled plastic wrap and let rise, in a warm place, for about 45–60 minutes or until doubled in bulk.

**5 ▲** Roll the dough into a rectangle about ¾-inch thick, approximately twice as long as it is wide. Fold the bottom third up and the top third down and seal the edges with a rolling pin. Chill for 20 minutes.

**6** Repeat the rolling, folding and chilling twice more, turning the dough by 90 degrees each time. Roll out on a floured surface into a 25 × 13-inch rectangle; trim the edges to leave a 24 x 12-inch rectangle. Cut in half lengthwise. Cut crosswise into 14 equal triangles with 6-inch bases.

**7** Place the dough triangles on 2 baking sheets, cover with plastic wrap and chill for 10 minutes.

**8 ▲** To shape the croissants, place each one with the wide end at the top, hold each side and pull gently to stretch the top of the triangle a little, then roll towards the point, finishing with the pointed end tucked underneath. Curve the ends toward the pointed end to make a crescent. Place on 2 baking sheets, spaced well apart.

**9** Combine the egg yolk and milk for the glaze. Lightly brush a little glaze over the croissants, avoiding the cut edges of the dough. Cover the croissants loosely with lightly oiled plastic wrap and let rise, in a warm place, for about 30 minutes or until they are nearly doubled in size.

**10** Meanwhile, preheat the oven to 425°F. Brush the croissants with the remaining glaze and bake for 15–20 minutes, or until crisp and golden. Transfer to a wire rack to cool slightly before serving warm.

~ VARIATION ~

To make chocolate-filled croissants, place a small square of chocolate at the wide end of each triangle before rolling up as in step 8.

# French Petits Pains au Lait

**MAKES 12 ROLLS**

| |
| --- |
| 4 cups white bread flour |
| 2 teaspoons salt |
| 1 tablespoon sugar |
| ¼ cup butter, softened |
| ½ ounce fresh yeast |
| generous 1 cup lukewarm milk, plus 1 tablespoon extra milk, for glazing |

~ **VARIATION** ~

These can also be made into long rolls. To shape, flatten each ball of dough and fold in half. Roll back and forth, using your hand to form a 5-inch long roll, tapered at either end. Just before baking, slash the tops horizontally several times.

These classic French round milk rolls have a soft crust and a light, slightly sweet crumb. They won't last long!

**1** Lightly grease 2 baking sheets. Sift the flour and salt together into a large bowl. Stir in the sugar. Rub the softened butter into the flour.

**2** Mix the yeast with 4 tablespoons of the milk. Stir in the remaining milk. Pour into the flour mixture and mix to a soft dough.

**3** Turn out onto a floured surface and knead for 8–10 minutes until smooth and elastic. Place in an oiled bowl, cover with oiled plastic wrap and let rise, in a warm place, for 1 hour or until doubled in bulk.

**4** Turn out the dough onto a floured surface and gently punch down. Divide into 12, shape into balls and place on the baking sheets.

**5 ▲** Using a sharp knife, cut a cross in the top of each roll. Cover with lightly oiled plastic wrap and let rise, in a warm place, for about 20 minutes or until doubled in size.

**6** Preheat the oven to 400°F. Brush the rolls with milk and bake for 20–25 minutes or until golden. Transfer to a wire rack to cool.

# French Dimpled Rolls

**MAKES 10 ROLLS**

| |
| --- |
| 3½ cups white bread flour |
| 1½ teaspoons salt |
| 1 teaspoon sugar |
| ½ ounce fresh yeast |
| ½ cup lukewarm milk |
| ¾ cup lukewarm water |

A French and Belgian specialty, these attractive rolls are distinguished by the split down the center. They have a crusty finish while remaining soft and light inside—they taste great, too.

**1** Lightly grease 2 baking sheets. Sift the flour and salt into a large bowl. Stir in the sugar and make a well in the center.

**2** Mix the yeast with the milk until dissolved, then pour into the center of the flour mixture. Sprinkle on a little of the flour from around the edge. Let sit at room temperature for 15–20 minutes or until the mixture starts to bubble.

**3** Add the water and gradually mix in the flour to form a fairly moist, soft dough. Turn out onto a lightly floured surface and knead for 8–10 minutes until smooth and elastic. Place in a lightly oiled bowl, cover with lightly oiled plastic wrap and let rise, at room temperature, for about 1½ hours or until doubled in bulk.

**4** Turn out onto a floured surface and punch down. Re-cover and let rest for 5 minutes. Divide the dough into 10 pieces. Shape into balls by rolling under a cupped hand, then roll until oval. Lightly flour the tops. Place spaced well apart on the baking sheets, cover with lightly oiled plastic wrap and let rise, at room temperature, for about 30 minutes or until almost doubled in size.

**5 ▲** Oil the side of your hand and press the center of each roll to make a deep split. Re-cover and let rest for 15 minutes. Place a roasting pan in the bottom of the oven and preheat the oven to 450°F. Pour 1 cup water into the pan and bake the rolls on a higher shelf for 15 minutes or until golden. Transfer to a wire rack to cool.

# Swiss Braid

**MAKES 1 LOAF**

| |
|---|
| 3 cups white flour |
| 1 teaspoon salt |
| ¾ ounce fresh yeast |
| 2 tablespoons lukewarm water |
| ⅔ cup sour cream |
| 1 egg, lightly beaten |
| ¼ cup butter, softened |
| FOR THE GLAZE |
| 1 egg yolk |
| 1 tablespoon water |

This braided, attractively tapered loaf is known as *zupfe* in Switzerland. Often eaten on weekends, it has a glossy crust and a wonderfully light crumb.

**1** Lightly grease a baking sheet. Sift the flour and salt together into a bowl and make a well in the center. Mix the yeast with the water in a small bowl.

**2** ▲ Gently warm the sour cream in a small pan until it reaches 98.6°F. Add to the yeast mixture and combine.

**3** Add the yeast mixture and egg to the center of the flour and mix into a dough. Beat in the softened butter.

**4** ▲ Turn out onto a lightly floured surface and knead for 5 minutes, until smooth and elastic. Place in a lightly oiled bowl, cover with lightly oiled plastic wrap and let rise, in a warm place, for about 1½ hours or until doubled in size.

**5** Turn out onto a lightly floured surface and punch down. Cut in half and shape each piece of dough into a long rope about 14 inches in length.

**6** To make the braid, place the two pieces of dough on top of each other to form a cross. Starting with the bottom rope, fold the top end over and place between the two bottom ropes. Fold the remaining top rope over so that all four ropes are pointing downward. Starting from the left, braid the first rope over the second, and the third rope over the fourth.

**7** Continue braiding to form a tapered bread. Tuck the ends underneath and place on the baking sheet. Cover with oiled plastic wrap and let rise, in a warm place, for about 40 minutes.

**8** Meanwhile, preheat the oven to 375°F. Mix the egg yolk and water for the glaze, and brush over the loaf. Bake the bread for 30–35 minutes or until golden. Cool on a wire rack.

# German Sourdough Bread

This bread includes rye, whole-wheat and all-purpose flours for a superb depth of flavor. Serve it cut in thick slices, with creamy butter or a sharp cheese.

MAKES 1 LOAF
FOR THE SOURDOUGH STARTER
¾ cup rye flour
⅓ cup warm water
pinch caraway seeds
FOR THE DOUGH
½ ounce fresh yeast
1⅓ cups lukewarm water
2½ cups rye flour
1¼ cups whole-wheat bread flour
1¼ cups all-purpose flour
2 teaspoons salt

**1** ▲ Combine the rye flour, warm water and caraway seeds for the starter in a large bowl with your fingertips, to make a soft paste. Cover with a damp dish towel and let sit in a warm place for about 36 hours. Stir after 24 hours.

**2** Lightly grease a baking sheet. In a measuring cup, blend the yeast for the dough with the lukewarm water. Add to the starter and mix thoroughly.

**3** ▲ Mix the rye flour, whole-wheat bread flour and all-purpose flour for the dough with the salt in a large bowl; make a well in the center. Pour in the yeast liquid and gradually incorporate the surrounding flour to make a smooth dough.

**4** Turn out the dough onto a lightly floured surface and knead for 8–10 minutes until smooth and elastic. Place in a lightly oiled bowl, cover with lightly oiled plastic wrap and let rise, in a warm place, for 1½ hours, or until nearly doubled in bulk.

**5** ▲ Turn out onto a lightly floured surface, punch down and knead gently. Shape into a round and place in a floured basket, or *couronne*, with the seam up. Cover with lightly oiled plastic wrap and let rise, in a warm place, for 2–3 hours.

**6** Meanwhile, preheat the oven to 400°F. Turn out the loaf onto the prepared baking sheet and bake for 35–40 minutes. Cool on a wire rack.

~ COOK'S TIP ~

Proving the dough in a floured basket or *couronne* gives it its characteristic patterned crust, but is not essential. Make sure that you flour the basket well, otherwise the dough may stick.

# German Stollen

**MAKES 1 LOAF**

½ cup golden raisins

¼ cup currants

3 tablespoons rum

3¼ cups white flour

½ teaspoon salt

¼ cup sugar

¼ teaspoon ground cardamom

½ teaspoon ground cinnamon

1½ ounces fresh yeast

½ cup lukewarm milk

¼ cup butter, melted

1 egg, lightly beaten

⅓ cup chopped candied peel

⅓ cup blanched whole
    almonds, chopped

melted butter, for brushing

confectioners' sugar, for dusting

FOR THE ALMOND FILLING

1 cup ground almonds

¼ cup sugar

½ cup confectioners' sugar

½ teaspoon fresh lemon juice

½ egg, lightly beaten

This German specialty bread, made for the Christmas season, is rich with rum-soaked fruits and is wrapped around a moist almond filling. The folded shape of the dough over the filling represents the baby Jesus wrapped in swaddling clothes.

**3 ▲** In a small bowl, mix the yeast with the milk until creamy. Pour into the flour and mix a little of the flour from around the edge into the milk mixture to make a thick batter. Sprinkle some of the remaining flour on top, then cover with plastic wrap and leave in a warm place for 30 minutes.

**4** Add the melted butter and egg and mix into a soft dough. Turn out the dough onto a lightly floured surface and knead for 8–10 minutes, until smooth and elastic. Place in an oiled bowl, cover with lightly oiled plastic wrap and let rise, in a warm place, for 2–3 hours or until doubled in bulk.

**1 ▲** Grease a baking sheet. Preheat the oven to 350°F. Put the golden raisins and currants in a heatproof bowl and warm for 3–4 minutes. Pour in the rum and set aside.

**2** Sift the flour and salt into a large bowl. Stir in the sugar and spices.

**5 ▲** Combine the ground almonds and sugars for the filling. Add the lemon juice and enough egg to knead to a smooth paste. Shape into an 8-inch long sausage, cover and set aside.

**6** Turn out the dough onto a lightly floured surface and punch down.

**7** Pat out the dough into a rectangle about 1-inch thick and sprinkle on the golden raisins, currants, peel and almonds. Fold and knead the dough to incorporate the fruit and nuts.

**8 ▲** Roll out the dough into an oval about 12 × 9 inches. Roll the center slightly thinner than the edges. Place the almond paste filling along the center and fold over the dough to enclose it, making sure that the top of the dough doesn't completely cover the base. The top edge should be slightly in from the bottom edge. Press down to seal.

**9** Place the loaf on the prepared baking sheet, cover with lightly oiled plastic wrap and let rise, in a warm place, for 45–60 minutes or until doubled in size.

**10** Meanwhile, preheat the oven to 400°F. Bake the loaf for 30 minutes or until it sounds hollow when tapped on the bottom. Brush the top with melted butter and transfer to a wire rack to cool. Dust with confectioners' sugar just before serving.

~ COOK'S TIP ~
Dust the cooled stollen with
confectioners' sugar and
cinnamon or drizzle on glacé icing.

# German Pumpernickel

**MAKES 2 LOAVES**

4 cups rye flour

2 cups whole-wheat flour

⅔ cup bulgur wheat

2 teaspoons salt

2 tablespoons molasses

3½ cups warm water

1 tablespoon vegetable oil

---

~ COOK'S TIP ~

This bread improves if you keep it for at least 24 hours double-wrapped in plastic.

---

This famous German bread is extremely dense and dark, with an intense flavor. It is baked very slowly and is more like a steamed bread than a baked one.

**2** Mix the molasses with the warm water and add to the flours with the vegetable oil. Combine to form a dense mass.

**1** Lightly grease two 7 × 3½-inch loaf pans. Combine the rye flour, whole-wheat flour, bulgur wheat and salt in a large bowl.

**3** ▲ Place in the prepared pans, pressing well into the corners. Cover with lightly oiled plastic wrap and let sit in a warm place for 18–24 hours.

**4** Preheat the oven to 225°F. Cover the pans tightly with foil. Fill a roasting pan with boiling water and place a rack on top.

**5** Place the pans on top of the rack and transfer very carefully to the oven. Bake the loaves for 4 hours. Increase the oven temperature to 325°F. Top up the water in the roasting pan if necessary, uncover the loaves and bake for another 30–45 minutes or until the loaves feel firm and the tops are crusty.

**6** Let cool in the pans for 5 minutes, then turn out onto a wire rack to cool completely. Serve cold, very thinly sliced, with cold meats.

# Swedish Vört Limpa

This festive Swedish bread is flavored with warm spices and fresh orange. The beer and port work nicely to soften the rye taste. The added sugars also give the yeast a little extra to feed on and help aerate and lighten the bread. It is traditionally served with cheese.

**MAKES 1 LOAF**

| |
|---|
| 3 cups rye flour |
| 3 cups white flour |
| ½ teaspoon salt |
| 2 tablespoons sugar |
| 1 teaspoon grated nutmeg |
| 1 teaspoon ground cloves |
| 1 teaspoon ground ginger |
| 1½ ounces fresh yeast |
| 1¼ cups light ale |
| ½ cup port |
| 1 tablespoon molasses |
| 2 tablespoons butter, melted |
| 1 tablespoon grated orange zest |
| ½ cup raisins |
| 1 tablespoon malt extract, for glazing |

**1** Lightly grease a 12 × 4-inch loaf pan. Combine the rye and white flours, salt, sugar, nutmeg, cloves and ginger in a large bowl.

**2** In another large bowl, using a wooden spoon, blend the yeast into the ale until dissolved, then stir in the port, molasses and melted butter.

**3** Gradually add the flour mixture to the yeast liquid, beating to make a smooth batter. Continue adding the flour a little at a time and mixing until the mixture forms a soft dough.

**4 ▲** Turn out onto a lightly floured surface and knead for 8–10 minutes, until smooth and elastic. Place in an oiled bowl, cover with oiled plastic wrap and let rise, in a warm place, for 1 hour or until doubled in size.

**5** Turn out the dough onto a lightly floured surface and punch down. Gently knead in the orange zest and raisins. Roll into a 12-inch square.

**6 ▲** Fold the bottom third of the dough up and the top third down, sealing the edges. Place in the pan, cover with oiled plastic wrap and let rise, in a warm place, for 1 hour or until the dough reaches the top of the pan.

**7** Meanwhile, preheat the oven to 375°F. Bake for 35–40 minutes or until browned. Turn out onto a wire rack, brush with malt extract and let cool.

# Swedish Knackerbröd

**MAKES 8 CRISPBREADS**

| |
|---|
| 4 cups rye flour |
| 1 teaspoon salt |
| ¼ cup butter |
| ¾ ounce fresh yeast |
| generous 1 cup lukewarm water |
| 2 cups wheat bran |

A very traditional Swedish crispbread with a lovely rye flavor.

**1 ▲** Lightly grease 2 baking sheets. Preheat the oven to 450°F. Mix the rye flour and salt together in a large bowl. Rub in the butter, then make a well in the center.

**2** Mix the yeast with a little water, then stir in the remainder. Pour into the center of the flour, mix into a dough, then mix in the bran. Knead on a lightly floured surface for 5 minutes, until smooth and elastic.

**3** Divide the dough into 8 equal pieces and roll each one out on a floured surface to an 8-inch round.

**4 ▲** Place 2 rounds on the prepared baking sheets and prick all over with a fork. Cut a hole in the center of each round, using a 1½-inch cutter.

**5** Bake for 15–20 minutes or until the crispbreads are golden and crisp. Transfer to a wire rack to cool. Repeat with the remaining crispbreads.

~ COOK'S TIP ~

The hole in the center of these crispbreads is a reminder of the days when breads were strung on a pole, which was hung across the rafters to dry. Make smaller crispbreads, if desired, and tie them together with bright red ribbon for an unusual Christmas gift.

# Finnish Barley Bread

**MAKES 1 SMALL LOAF**

| |
|---|
| 2 cups barley flour |
| 1 teaspoon salt |
| 2 teaspoons baking powder |
| 2 tablespoons butter, melted |
| ½ cup light cream |
| 4 tablespoons milk |

In Northern Europe breads are often made using cereals such as barley and rye, which produce very satisfying, tasty breads. This quick-to-prepare flat bread is best served warm with butter.

**1 ▲** Grease a baking sheet. Preheat the oven to 400°F. Sift the dry ingredients into a bowl. Add the butter, cream and milk. Mix into a dough.

**2** Turn out the dough onto a lightly floured surface and shape into a flat round about ½-inch thick.

**3 ▲** Transfer to the prepared baking sheet and, using a sharp knife, lightly mark the top into 6 sections.

**4** Prick the surface of the round evenly with a fork. Bake for 15–18 minutes or until pale golden. Cut into wedges and serve warm.

~ COOK'S TIPS ~

• This flat bread tastes very good with cottage cheese, especially cottage cheese with chives.
• For a citrusy tang, add 2–3 teaspoons finely grated lemon, lime or orange zest to the flour mixture in step 1.

# Swedish Lusse Bröd

**MAKES 12 BUNS**

½ cup milk

pinch of saffron threads

3½ cups white flour

½ cup ground almonds

½ teaspoon salt

6 tablespoons sugar

1 ounce fresh yeast

½ cup lukewarm water

few drops of almond extract

¼ cup butter, softened

FOR THE GLAZE

1 egg

1 tablespoon water

~ VARIATION ~

Gently knead in 3 tablespoons currants after punching down the dough in step 4.

Saint Lucia Day, December 13th, marks the beginning of Christmas in Sweden. As part of the celebrations, girls dressed in white robes wear crowns of lighted candles and walk through the streets offering these saffron buns to the townspeople.

**1 ▲** Lightly grease 2 baking sheets. Place the milk in a small saucepan and bring to a boil. Add the saffron, remove from the heat and let infuse for about 15 minutes. Meanwhile, combine the flour, ground almonds, salt and sugar in a large bowl.

**2** In a small bowl, mix the yeast with the water. Add the saffron liquid, yeast mixture and almond extract to the flour mixture and mix into a dough. Gradually beat in the softened butter.

**3** Turn out onto a lightly floured surface and knead for 5 minutes, until smooth and elastic. Place in an oiled bowl, cover with oiled plastic wrap and let rise, in a warm place, for about 1 hour or until doubled in bulk.

**4 ▲** Turn out onto a lightly floured surface and punch down. Divide into 12 equal pieces and make into different shapes: Roll into a long rope and shape into an "S" shape; to make a star, cut a dough piece in half and roll into two ropes, cross one over the other and coil the ends; make an upturned "U" shape and coil the ends to represent curled hair; divide a dough piece in half, roll into two thin ropes and twist together.

**5** Place on the prepared baking sheets, spaced well apart, cover with lightly oiled plastic wrap and let rise, in a warm place, for about 30 minutes.

**6** Meanwhile, preheat the oven to 400°F. Brush the glaze onto the rolls. Bake for 15 minutes or until golden. Transfer to a wire rack to cool. Serve warm or cold.

# Savory Danish Crown

Filled with golden onions and cheese, this butter-rich bread ring is quite irresistible and needs no accompaniment.

**1** Lightly grease a baking sheet. Sift the flour and salt together into a large bowl. Rub in 3 tablespoons of the butter. Mix the yeast with the milk and water. Add to the flour with the egg and mix into a soft dough.

**2** Turn out onto a floured surface and knead for 10 minutes, until smooth and elastic. Place in an oiled bowl, cover with oiled plastic wrap or slide into an oiled plastic bag and let rise, in a warm place, for about 1 hour or until doubled in bulk.

**3** Punch down and turn out onto a lightly floured surface. Roll out into an oblong about ½-inch thick.

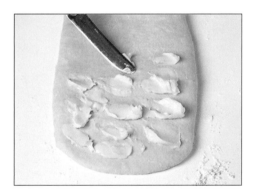

**4 ▲** Dot half the remaining butter over the top two-thirds of the dough. Fold the bottom third up and the top third down and seal the edges. Turn by 90 degrees and repeat with the remaining butter. Fold and seal as before. Cover with oiled plastic wrap and let rest for 15 minutes.

**5** Turn by another 90 degrees. Roll and fold again without any butter. Repeat once more. Wrap in lightly oiled plastic wrap and let rest in the refrigerator for 30 minutes.

**6** Meanwhile, heat the oil for the filling. Add the onions and cook for 10 minutes until golden. Remove from the heat and add the bread crumbs, almonds, Parmesan and seasoning.

**7** Mix half the beaten egg into the bread crumb mixture.

**8** Roll out the dough on a floured surface into a rectangle 22 × 9 inches. Spread with the filling to within ¾ inch of the edges, then roll up like a jelly roll from one long side. Cut in half lengthwise. Braid together with the cut sides up and shape into a ring. Place on the baking sheet, cover with oiled plastic wrap and let rise, in a warm place, for 30 minutes.

**9** Meanwhile, preheat the oven to 400°F. Brush the remaining beaten egg over the dough. Sprinkle with sesame seeds and Parmesan cheese and bake for 40–50 minutes or until golden. Transfer to a wire rack to cool. Serve warm or cool completely to serve cold. Cut into slices.

**MAKES 1 LOAF**

| |
|---|
| 3 cups white flour |
| 1 teaspoon salt |
| generous ¾ cup butter, softened |
| ¾ ounce fresh yeast |
| scant 1 cup mixed lukewarm milk and water |
| 1 egg, lightly beaten |
| FOR THE FILLING |
| 2 tablespoons sunflower oil |
| 2 onions, finely chopped |
| ¾ cup fresh bread crumbs |
| ¼ cup ground almonds |
| ½ cup freshly grated Parmesan cheese |
| 1 egg, lightly beaten |
| salt and freshly ground black pepper |
| FOR THE TOPPING |
| 1 tablespoon sesame seeds |
| 1 tablespoon freshly grated Parmesan cheese |

# Danish Julekage

**MAKES 1 LOAF**

| |
|---|
| 1 ounce fresh yeast |
| 5 tablespoons lukewarm milk |
| 4 cups white flour |
| 2 teaspoons salt |
| 6 tablespoons butter |
| 15 whole cardamom pods |
| ½ teaspoon vanilla extract |
| ⅓ cup light brown sugar |
| grated zest of ½ lemon |
| 2 eggs, lightly beaten |
| ¼ cup dried apricots, chopped |
| ¼ cup candied pineapple, chopped |
| ¼ cup red and green candied cherries, chopped |
| 3 tablespoons pitted, dried dates, chopped |
| 2 tablespoons candied ginger, chopped |
| FOR THE GLAZE |
| 1 egg white |
| 2 teaspoons water |
| FOR THE DECORATION |
| 1 tablespoon sugar |
| ½ teaspoon ground cinnamon |
| 8 pecans or whole blanched almonds |

In Scandinavia special slightly sweet holiday breads containing fragrant cardamom seeds are common. This exotic bread, enriched with butter and a selection of candied and dried fruits or "jewels", is traditionally served over the Christmas period with hot spiced punch.

**1** Lightly grease a 9 × 5-inch loaf pan. In a small bowl, mix the yeast with the milk.

**2 ▲** Sift the flour and salt together into a large bowl. Add the butter and rub in. Make a well in the center. Add the yeast mixture to the center of the flour and butter mixture and stir in enough flour to form a thick batter. Sprinkle on a little of the remaining flour and set aside in a warm place for 15 minutes.

**3** Remove the seeds from the cardamom pods. Put them in a mortar and crush with a pestle. Add the crushed seeds to the flour with the vanilla extract, sugar, lemon zest and eggs, then mix into a soft dough.

**4 ▲** Turn out onto a lightly floured surface and knead for 8–10 minutes, until smooth and elastic. Place in an oiled bowl, cover with plastic wrap and let rise, in a warm place, for 1–1½ hours or until doubled in bulk.

**5** Punch down the dough and turn it out onto a lightly floured surface. Flatten into a rectangle and sprinkle on half of the apricots, pineapple, cherries, dates and ginger. Fold the sides into the center and then fold in half to contain the fruit. Flatten into a rectangle again and sprinkle on the remaining fruit. Fold and knead gently to distribute the fruit. Cover the fruited dough with lightly oiled plastic wrap and let rest for 10 minutes.

**6** Roll the fruited dough into a rectangle 15 × 10 inches. With a short side facing you, fold the bottom third up lengthwise and the top third down, tucking in the sides, to form a 9 x 5-inch loaf. Place in the prepared pan, seam side down. Cover with lightly oiled plastic wrap and let rise, in a warm place, for 1 hour or until the dough has reached the top of the pan.

**7** Meanwhile, preheat the oven to 350°F. Using a sharp knife, slash the top of the loaf lengthwise and then make diagonal slits on either side.

**8** Combine the egg white and water for the glaze, and brush on top. Mix the sugar and cinnamon in a bowl, then sprinkle on top. Decorate with pecans or almonds. Bake for 45–50 minutes or until risen and browned. Transfer to a wire rack to cool.

~ VARIATIONS ~

• You can vary the fruits for this loaf. Try candied peaches, yellow candied cherries, golden raisins, raisins, candied angelica, dried mango or dried pears and use in place of some or all of the fruits in the recipe. Use a mixture of colors and make sure that the total weight is the same as above.
• Use walnuts instead of the pecans or almonds.

~ COOK'S TIP ~

Keep a close watch on the bread, especially during the final 15 minutes of cooking. If the top of the loaf starts to brown too quickly, cover loosely with foil.

# Scandinavian Sunshine Loaf

**MAKES 1 LOAF**

| FOR THE STARTER |
| --- |
| 4 tablespoons lukewarm milk |
| 4 tablespoons lukewarm water |
| ¼ ounce fresh yeast |
| scant 1 cup white bread flour |
| FOR THE DOUGH |
| ½ ounce fresh yeast |
| generous 2 cups lukewarm water |
| 4 cups rye flour |
| 2 cups white bread flour |
| 1 tablespoon salt |
| milk, for glazing |
| caraway seeds, for sprinkling |

~ VARIATION ~

This bread can be shaped into one large round or oval loaf, if preferred.

Scandinavia, Land of the Midnight Sun, has numerous breads based on rye. This splendid table centerpiece is made with a blend of rye and white flours, the latter helping to lighten the bread.

**1** ▲ Combine the milk and water for the starter in a bowl. Mix in the yeast until dissolved. Gradually stir in the flour with a metal spoon.

**2** Cover the bowl with plastic wrap and let the mixture sit in a warm place for 3–4 hours or until well risen, bubbly and starting to collapse.

**3** Mix the yeast for the dough with 4 tablespoons of the water until creamy, then stir in the remaining water. Gradually mix into the starter to dilute it, and then add the rye flour to form a smooth batter. Cover with lightly oiled plastic wrap and let sit in a warm place, for 3–4 hours.

**4** Stir the bread flour and salt into the batter to form a dough. Turn onto a lightly floured surface and knead for 5 minutes, until smooth and elastic. Place in a lightly oiled bowl, cover with lightly oiled plastic wrap and let rise, in a warm place, for about 1 hour or until doubled in bulk.

**5** ▲ Punch down on a floured surface. Cut the dough into 5 pieces. Roll one piece into a 20-inch "sausage" and roll up into a spiral shape.

**6** Cut the remaining pieces in half and shape each one into an 8-inch rope. Place in a circle on a baking sheet, spaced equally apart, like rays of the sun, and curl the ends around, leaving a small gap in the center. Place the spiral shape on top. Cover with oiled plastic wrap and let rise, in a warm place, for 30 minutes.

**7** Preheat the oven to 450°F. Brush the bread with milk, sprinkle with caraway seeds, and bake for 30 minutes or until lightly browned. Cool on a wire rack.

# Spanish Pan de Cebada

This Spanish country bread has a close, heavy texture and is quite satisfying. It is richly flavored, incorporating barley flour and yellow cornmeal.

MAKES 1 LOAF

FOR THE SOURDOUGH STARTER

1½ cups cornmeal

scant 2½ cups water

2 cups whole-wheat flour

¾ cup barley flour

FOR THE DOUGH

¾ ounce fresh yeast

3 tablespoons lukewarm water

2 cups whole-wheat flour

1 tablespoon salt

cornmeal, for dusting

**1 ▲** In a saucepan, mix the cornmeal for the sourdough starter with half the water, then blend in the remainder. Cook over a low heat, stirring until thickened. Transfer to a large bowl and set aside to cool.

**2** Mix in the whole-wheat flour and barley flour. Turn out onto a floured surface and knead for 5 minutes. Return to the bowl, cover with oiled plastic wrap and let the starter sit in a warm place for 36 hours.

**5 ▲** Punch down the dough and turn out onto a lightly floured surface. Shape into a plump round. Sprinkle with a little cornmeal.

**6** Place the shaped bread on the prepared baking sheet. Cover with a large upturned bowl. Let rise, in a warm place, for about 1 hour or until nearly doubled in bulk. Place an empty roasting pan in the bottom of the oven. Preheat the oven to 425°F.

**7** Pour 1¼ cups cold water into the roasting pan. Lift the bowl off the risen loaf and immediately place the baking sheet in the oven. Bake the bread for 10 minutes. Remove the pan of water, reduce the oven temperature to 375°F and bake for about 20 minutes. Cool on a wire rack.

**3 ▲** Dust a baking sheet with cornmeal. In a small bowl, mix the yeast with the water for the dough. Mix the yeast mixture into the starter with the whole-wheat flour and salt and work into a dough. Turn out onto a lightly floured surface and knead for 4–5 minutes, until smooth and elastic.

**4** Transfer the dough to a lightly oiled bowl, cover with lightly oiled plastic wrap or an oiled plastic bag and let sit, in a warm place, for 1½–2 hours or until nearly doubled in bulk.

# Spanish Twelfth Night Bread

**MAKES 1 LOAF**

| |
| --- |
| 4 cups white bread flour |
| ½ teaspoon salt |
| 1 ounce yeast |
| scant ⅔ cup mixed lukewarm milk and water |
| 6 tablespoons butter |
| 6 tablespoons sugar |
| 2 teaspoons finely grated lemon zest |
| 2 teaspoons finely grated orange zest |
| 2 eggs |
| 1 tablespoon brandy |
| 1 tablespoon orange flower water |
| silver coin or dried bean (optional) |
| 1 egg white, lightly beaten, for glazing |

FOR THE DECORATION

| |
| --- |
| a mixture of candied fruit slices |
| flaked almonds |

---

**~ COOK'S TIP ~**

If desired, this bread can be baked in a lightly greased 9½-inch ring-shaped cake pan or savarin mold. Place the dough seam side down into the pan or mold and seal the ends together.

---

**1 ▲** Lightly grease a large baking sheet. Sift the flour and salt together into a large bowl. Make a well in the center.

January 6th, Epiphany or the Day of the Three Kings, is celebrated in Spain as a time to exchange Christmas presents. Historically, this date was when the Three Wise Men arrived bearing gifts. An ornamental bread ring is specially baked for the occasion. The traditional version contains a silver coin, china figure or dried bean hidden inside—the lucky recipient is declared King of the festival!

**2** In a bowl, mix the yeast with the milk and water until the yeast has dissolved. Pour the yeast mixture into the center of the flour and stir in enough of the flour from around the sides of the bowl to make a thick batter.

**3** Sprinkle a little of the remaining flour over the top of the batter and let "sponge," in a warm place, for about 15 minutes or until frothy.

**4** Using an electric whisk or a wooden spoon, beat the butter and sugar together in a bowl until soft and creamy, then set aside.

**5** Add the citrus zest, eggs, brandy and orange flower water to the flour mixture and mix to a sticky dough.

**6 ▲** Using one hand, beat the mixture until it forms a fairly smooth dough. Gradually beat in the reserved butter mixture and beat for a few minutes, until the dough is smooth and elastic. Cover with lightly oiled plastic wrap and let rise, in a warm place, for about 1½ hours or until doubled in bulk.

**7** Punch down the dough and turn out onto a floured surface. Gently knead for 2 or 3 minutes, incorporating the lucky coin or bean, if using.

**8** Using a rolling pin, roll out the dough into a long strip measuring about 26 × 5 inches.

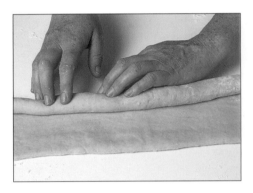

**9 ▲** Roll up the dough from one long side like a jelly roll to make a long sausage shape. Place seam side down on the prepared baking sheet and seal the ends. Cover with oiled plastic wrap and let rise, in a warm place, for 1–1½ hours or until doubled in size.

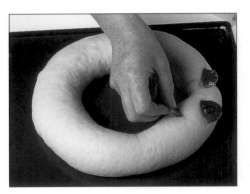

**10 ▲** Meanwhile, preheat the oven to 350°F. Brush the dough ring with lightly beaten egg white and decorate with candied fruit slices, pushing them slightly into the dough. Sprinkle with almonds and bake for 30–35 minutes or until risen and golden. Turn out onto a wire rack to cool.

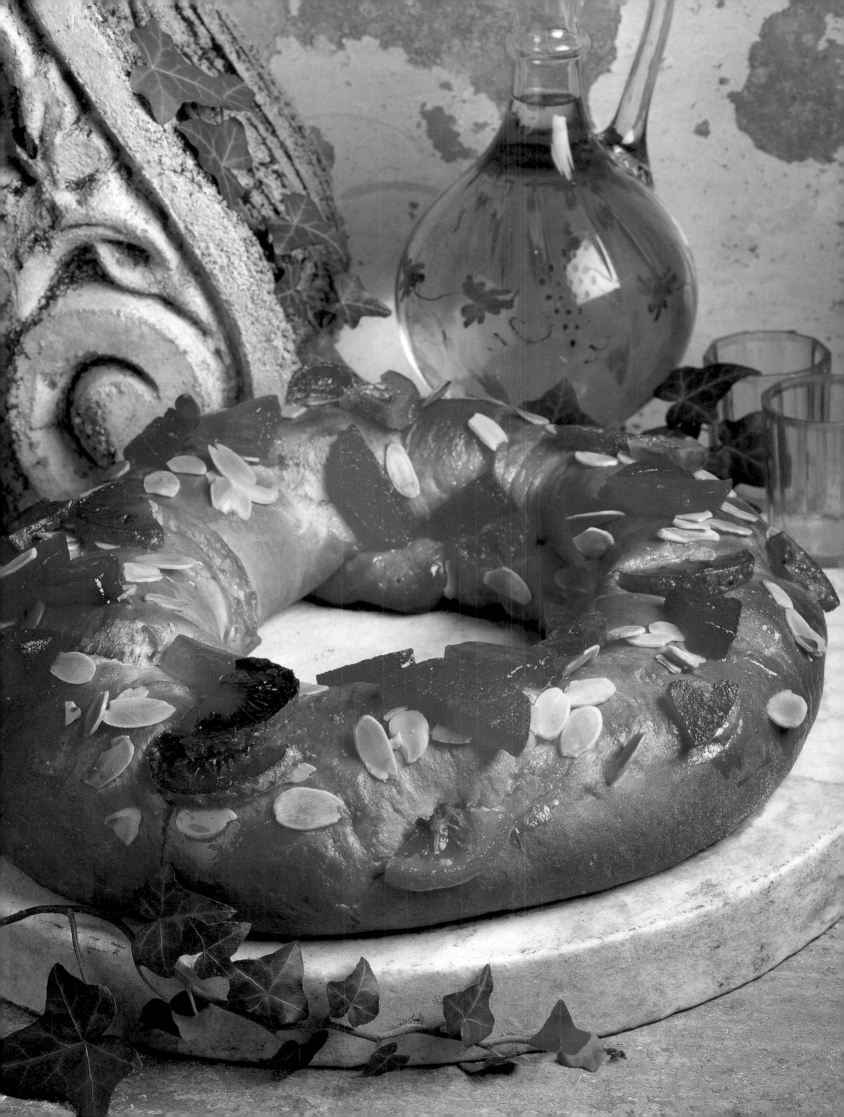

# Pan Gallego

**MAKES 1 LOAF**

3 cups white bread flour

1 cup whole-wheat bread flour

2 teaspoons salt

¾ ounce fresh yeast

generous 1 cup lukewarm water

2 tablespoons olive oil or melted shortening

2 tablespoons pumpkin seeds

2 tablespoons sunflower seeds

1 tablespoon millet

yellow cornmeal, for dusting

~ COOK'S TIP ~

You can replace the fresh yeast with ¼ ounce active dry yeast. Stir into the flours in step 1.

**1** Sprinkle a baking sheet with cornmeal. Combine the flours and salt in a large bowl.

Here, a typical round bread with a twisted top from Galicia. The olive oil gives a soft crumb, and the millet, pumpkin and sunflower seeds scattered through the loaf provide an interesting mix of textures.

**2 ▲** In a bowl, mix the yeast with the water. Add to the center of the flours with the olive oil or melted shortening and mix to a firm dough. Turn out onto a lightly floured surface and knead for about 10 minutes, until smooth and elastic. Place in an oiled bowl, cover with oiled plastic wrap and let rise, in a warm place, for 1½–2 hours or until doubled in bulk.

**3 ▲** Punch down the dough and turn out onto a lightly floured surface. Gently knead in the pumpkin seeds, sunflower seeds and millet. Re-cover and let rest for 5 minutes.

**4 ▲** Shape into a round ball; twist the center to make a cap. Transfer to the baking sheet and dust with cornmeal. Cover with an upturned bowl and let rise, in a warm place, for 45 minutes or until doubled in bulk.

**5** Meanwhile, place a roasting pan in the bottom of the oven. Preheat the oven to 425°F. Pour about 1¼ cups cold water into the roasting pan. Lift the bowl off the risen loaf and place it in the oven, above the roasting pan. Bake the bread for 10 minutes.

**6** Remove the pan of water and bake the bread for another 25–30 minutes or until well browned and hollow-sounding when tapped on the base. Transfer to a wire rack to cool.

# Portuguese Corn Bread

While the Spanish make a corn bread with barley flour, the Portuguese use white flour and cornmeal. This tempting version has a hard crust with a moist, mouthwatering crumb. It slices beautifully and tastes wonderful served simply with butter or olive oil, or with cheese.

**MAKES 1 LOAF**

| |
|---|
| ¾ ounce fresh yeast |
| 1 cup lukewarm water |
| 2 cups yellow cornmeal |
| 4 cups white bread flour |
| ⅔ cup lukewarm milk |
| 2 tablespoons olive oil |
| 1½ teaspoons salt |
| polenta, for dusting |

**1 ▲** Dust a baking sheet with a little cornmeal. Put the yeast in a bowl and gradually mix in the water until smooth. Stir in half the cornmeal and ½ cup of the flour and mix to a batter with a wooden spoon.

**2 ▲** Cover the bowl with oiled plastic wrap and let the batter sit in a warm place for about 30 minutes or until bubbles start to appear on the surface. Remove the plastic wrap.

**3** Stir the milk into the batter, then stir in the olive oil. Gradually mix in the remaining cornmeal, flour and salt to form a pliable dough.

**4** Turn out the dough onto a lightly floured surface and knead for about 10 minutes, until smooth and elastic. Place in a lightly oiled bowl, cover with lightly oiled plastic wrap and let rise for 1½–2 hours, or until doubled in bulk.

**5 ▲** Turn out the dough onto a lightly floured surface and punch down. Shape into a ball, flatten slightly and place on the prepared baking sheet. Dust with polenta, cover with a large upturned bowl and let rise, in a warm place, for 1 hour or until doubled in size. Preheat the oven to 450°F.

**6** Bake for 10 minutes, spraying the inside of the oven with water 2–3 times. Reduce the oven temperature to 375°F and bake for another 20–25 minutes or until golden and hollow-sounding when tapped on the bottom. Transfer to a wire rack to cool.

# Mallorcan Ensaimadas

**MAKES 16 ROLLS**

| |
|---|
| 2 cups white bread flour |
| ½ teaspoon salt |
| ¼ cup sugar |
| ½ ounce fresh yeast |
| 5 tablespoons lukewarm milk |
| 1 egg |
| 2 tablespoons sunflower oil |
| ¼ cup butter, melted |
| confectioners' sugar, for dusting |

These spiral or snail-shaped rolls are a popular Spanish breakfast treat. Traditionally, shortening or *saim* was used to brush over the strips of sweetened dough, but nowadays mainly butter is used to add a delicious richness.

**1** Lightly grease 2 baking sheets. Sift the flour and salt together into a large mixing bowl. Stir in the sugar and make a well in the center.

**2** In a small bowl, mix the yeast with the milk, pour into the center of the flour mixture, then sprinkle a little of the flour mixture evenly on top of the liquid. Let sit in a warm place for about 15 minutes or until frothy.

**3** In a small bowl, beat the egg and oil together. Add to the flour mixture and mix to a smooth dough.

**4** Turn out onto a lightly floured surface and knead for 8–10 minutes. until smooth and elastic. Place in an oiled bowl, cover with oiled plastic wrap and let rise for 1 hour or until doubled in bulk.

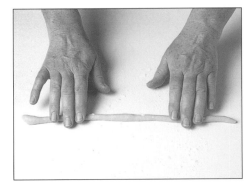

**5 ▲** Turn out the dough onto a lightly floured surface. Punch down and divide the dough into 16 equal pieces. Shape each piece into a thin rope about 15 inches long. Pour the melted butter onto a plate and dip the ropes into the butter to coat.

**6 ▲** On the baking sheets, curl each rope into a loose spiral, spacing well apart. Tuck the ends under to seal. Cover with lightly oiled plastic wrap and let rise, in a warm place, for about 45 minutes or until doubled in size.

**7** Preheat the oven to 375°F. Brush the rolls with water and dust with confectioners' sugar. Bake for 10 minutes or until light golden brown. Cool on a wire rack. Dust again with confectioners' sugar and serve warm.

# Italian Olive Bread

Black and green olives and good-quality fruity olive oil combine to make this strongly flavored and irresistible Italian bread.

**1** Lightly grease a baking sheet. Mix the flours, yeast and salt in a large bowl and make a well in the center.

**2 ▲** Add the water and oil to the center of the flour and mix to a soft dough. Knead the dough on a lightly floured surface for 8–10 minutes, until smooth and elastic. Place in a lightly oiled bowl, cover with oiled plastic wrap and let rise, in a warm place, for 1 hour or until doubled in bulk.

**3** Turn out onto a lightly floured surface and punch down. Flatten out and sprinkle on the olives. Fold up and knead to distribute the olives. Let rest for 5 minutes, then shape into an oval loaf. Place on the baking sheet.

**4 ▲** Make 6 deep cuts in the top of the loaf, and gently push the sections over. Cover with lightly oiled plastic wrap and let rise, in a warm place, for 30–45 minutes or until doubled in size.

**MAKES 1 LOAF**

| |
|---|
| 2½ cups white bread flour |
| ½ cup whole-wheat flour |
| ¼ ounce envelope active dry yeast |
| ½ teaspoon salt |
| scant 1 cup lukewarm water |
| 1 tablespoon extra-virgin olive oil, plus extra for brushing |
| 1 cup pitted black and green olives, coarsely chopped |

---

### ~ VARIATIONS ~
For a nutty flavor, add some hazelnuts or pine nuts.

---

**5** Meanwhile, preheat the oven to 400°F. Brush the bread with olive oil and bake for 35 minutes. Transfer to a wire rack to cool.

# Italian Polenta Bread

**MAKES 1 LOAF**

| |
|---|
| ½ cup polenta |
| 1¼ cups lukewarm water |
| ½ ounce fresh yeast |
| ½ teaspoon honey |
| 2 cups white bread flour |
| 2 tablespoons butter |
| 3 tablespoons pine nuts |
| 1½ teaspoons salt |
| FOR THE TOPPING |
| 1 egg yolk |
| 1 tablespoon water |
| pine nuts, for sprinkling |

Polenta is widely used in Italian cooking. Here it is combined with pine nuts to make a truly Italian bread with a fantastic flavor.

**1 ▲** Lightly grease a baking sheet. Combine the polenta and 1 cup of the water in a saucepan and slowly bring to a boil, stirring continuously with a large wooden spoon. Reduce the heat and simmer for 2–3 minutes, stirring occasionally. Set aside to cool for 10 minutes or until just warm.

**2** In a small bowl, mix the yeast with the remaining water and honey until creamy. Sift 1 cup of the flour into a large bowl. Gradually beat in the yeast mixture, then gradually stir in the polenta mixture to combine. Turn out onto a lightly floured surface and knead for 5 minutes, until smooth and elastic.

**3** Cover the bowl with lightly oiled plastic wrap or a lightly oiled plastic bag. Let the dough rise, in a warm place, for about 2 hours or until it has doubled in bulk.

**4 ▲** Meanwhile, melt the butter in a small pan, add the pine nuts and cook over a medium heat, stirring, until pale golden. Set aside to cool.

**5** Add the remaining flour and the salt to the polenta dough and mix to a soft dough. Knead in the pine nuts. Turn out onto a lightly floured surface and knead for 5 minutes, until smooth and elastic.

**6** Place in an oiled bowl, cover with lightly oiled plastic wrap and let rise for 1 hour or until doubled in bulk.

**7 ▲** Punch down the dough and turn it out onto a floured surface. Cut the dough into 2 equal pieces and roll each piece into a fat sausage about 15 inches long. Braid together and place on the baking sheet. Cover with lightly oiled plastic wrap and let rise, in a warm place, for 45 minutes. Preheat the oven to 400°F.

**8** Mix the egg yolk and water and brush over the loaf. Sprinkle with pine nuts and bake for 30 minutes or until golden and sounding hollow when tapped. Cool on a wire rack.

# Italian Prosciutto Loaf

This savory Italian bread from Parma is spiked with the local dried ham. Just a small amount fills the loaf with delicious flavor.

**1** Lightly grease a baking sheet. Sift the flour and salt together into a large bowl and make a well in the center. In a small bowl, mix the yeast with 2 tablespoons of the water, then gradually mix in the rest. Pour into the center of the flour.

**2 ▲** Gradually beat in most of the flour with a wooden spoon to make a batter. Beat gently to begin with and then more vigorously as the batter thickens. After most of the flour is incorporated, beat in the rest with your hand to form a moist dough.

**3** Turn out onto a lightly floured surface and knead for 5 minutes, until smooth and elastic. Place in a lightly oiled bowl, cover with lightly oiled plastic wrap and let rise, in a warm place, for 1½ hours or until doubled in bulk.

**4 ▲** Turn out the dough onto a floured surface, punch down and knead for 1 minute. Flatten to a round, then sprinkle with half the prosciutto and pepper. Fold in half and repeat with the remaining ham and pepper. Roll up, tucking in the sides.

### MAKES 1 LOAF

| |
|---|
| 3 cups unbleached white bread flour |
| 1½ teaspoons salt |
| ½ ounce fresh yeast |
| 1 cup lukewarm water |
| 1½ ounces prosciutto, torn into small pieces |
| 1 teaspoon freshly ground black pepper |

> **~ VARIATION ~**
>
> To make pesto bread, spread 3 tablespoons pesto over the flattened dough in step 4.

**5** Place on the baking sheet, cover with oiled plastic wrap and let rise, in a warm place, for about 30 minutes. On a floured surface, roll into an oval, fold in half and seal the edges. Flatten and fold again. Seal and fold again to make a long loaf.

**6** Roll into a stubby long loaf. Draw out the edges by rolling the dough under the palms of your hands. Place on the baking sheet, cover with oiled plastic wrap and let rise, in a warm place, for 45 minutes or until the loaf has doubled in size. Preheat the oven to 400°F.

**7 ▲** Slash the top of the loaf diagonally three or four times, using a sharp knife, and bake for 30 minutes or until golden. Cool on a wire rack.

# Italian Focaccia

**MAKES 2 LOAVES**

¾ ounce fresh yeast

1⅓–1½ cups lukewarm water

3 tablespoons extra-virgin olive oil

5 cups white bread flour

2 teaspoons salt

1 tablespoon chopped fresh sage

FOR THE TOPPING

4 tablespoons extra-virgin olive oil

4 garlic cloves, chopped

12 fresh sage leaves

~ VARIATION ~

Flavor the bread with other
fresh herbs, such as oregano,
basil or rosemary, and top with
chopped black olives.

**1 ▲** Lightly oil 2 10-inch shallow
round cake pans or pizza pans. Mix
the yeast with 4 tablespoons of the
water, then stir in the remaining
water. Stir in the oil.

**2** Sift the flour and salt together into
a large bowl and make a well in the
center. Pour the yeast mixture into
the well in the center of the flour and
mix to a soft dough.

**3** Turn out the dough onto a lightly
floured surface and knead for 8–10
minutes, until smooth and elastic.
Place in a lightly oiled bowl, cover
with lightly oiled plastic wrap or a
large, lightly oiled plastic bag, and let
rise, in a warm place, for 1–1½ hours
or until the dough has doubled in bulk.

This simple dimple-topped Italian flat
bread is punctuated with olive oil and
the aromatic flavors of sage and garlic
to produce a truly succulent loaf.

**4 ▲** Punch down the dough and turn
out onto a lightly floured surface.
Gently knead in the chopped sage.
Divide the dough into 2 equal pieces.
Shape each into a ball, roll out into
10-inch circles and place in the pans.

**5 ▲** Cover with lightly oiled plastic
wrap and let rise in a warm place for
about 30 minutes. Uncover and, using
your fingertips, poke the dough to
make deep dimples over the entire
surface. Replace the plastic wrap cover
and let rise until doubled in bulk.

**6** Meanwhile, preheat the oven to
400°F. Drizzle on the olive oil for the
topping and sprinkle each focaccia
evenly with chopped garlic. Dot the
sage leaves on the surface. Bake for
25–30 minutes or until both loaves
are golden. Immediately remove the
focaccia from the pans and transfer
them to a wire rack to cool slightly.
These loaves are best served warm.

# Italian Panini all'Olio

**MAKES 16 ROLLS**

| 4 cups white bread flour |
| 2 teaspoons salt |
| ½ ounce fresh yeast |
| 1 cup lukewarm water |
| 4 tablespoons extra-virgin olive oil, plus extra for brushing |

The Italians adore interesting and elaborately shaped rolls. This distinctively flavored bread dough, enriched with olive oil, can be used for making rolls or shaped as one large loaf.

**1** Lightly oil 3 baking sheets. Sift the flour and salt together in a large bowl and make a well in the center.

**2** In a small bowl, mix the yeast with half of the water, then stir in the remainder. Add to the center of the flour with the oil and mix to a dough.

**3** Turn the dough out onto a lightly floured surface and knead for 8–10 minutes, until smooth and elastic. Place in a lightly oiled bowl, cover with lightly oiled plastic wrap and let rise, in a warm place, for about 1 hour or until the dough has nearly doubled in bulk.

**4** Turn onto a lightly floured surface and punch down. Divide into 12 equal pieces and shape into rolls as described in steps 5, 6 and 7.

**5** ▲ For *tavalli* (twisted spiral rolls): Roll each piece of dough into a strip about 12 inches long and 1½ inches wide. Twist into a loose spiral and join the ends together to make a circle. Place on the baking sheets, spaced well apart. Brush the *tavalli* with olive oil, cover with lightly oiled plastic wrap and let rise, in a warm place, for 20–30 minutes.

**6** ▲ For *filoncini* (finger-shaped rolls): Flatten each piece of dough into an oval and roll to about 9 inches in length without changing the basic shape. Make it 2 inches wide at one end and 4 inches wide at the other. Roll up, starting from the wider end. Gently stretch the roll to 8–9 inches long. Cut in half. Place on the baking sheets, spaced well apart. Brush with olive oil, cover with oiled plastic wrap and let rise, in a warm place, for 20–30 minutes.

**7** ▲ For *carciofi* (artichoke-shaped rolls): Shape each piece of dough into a ball and space well apart on the prepared baking sheets. Brush with olive oil, cover with lightly oiled plastic wrap and let rise, in a warm place, for 20–30 minutes. Preheat the oven to 400°F. Using scissors, snip 4–5 ¼-inch deep cuts in a circle on the top of each *carciofo*, then make 5 larger horizontal cuts around the sides. Bake for 15 minutes. Transfer to a wire rack to cool.

# Italian Ciabatta

This irregular-shaped Italian bread is so called because it looks like an old shoe or slipper. It is made with a very wet dough flavored with olive oil; baking produces a bread with holes and a wonderfully chewy crust.

**1** Cream the yeast for the *biga* starter with a little of the water. Sift the flour into a large bowl. Gradually mix in the yeast mixture and enough of the remaining water to form a firm dough.

**2** Turn out the *biga* starter dough onto a lightly floured surface and knead for about 5 minutes, until smooth and elastic. Return the dough to the bowl, cover with lightly oiled plastic wrap and let sit in a warm place for 12–15 hours or until the dough has risen and is starting to collapse.

**3** Sprinkle 3 baking sheets with flour. Mix the yeast for the dough with a little of the water until creamy, then mix in the remainder. Add the yeast mixture to the *biga* and mix in.

**4** Mix in the milk, beating thoroughly with a wooden spoon. Using your hand, gradually beat in the flour, lifting the dough as you mix. Mixing the dough will take 15 minutes or more and form a very wet dough, impossible to knead on a work surface.

**5** Beat in the salt and olive oil. Cover with lightly oiled plastic wrap and let rise, in a warm place, for 1½–2 hours or until doubled in bulk.

**6** ▲ Using a spoon, carefully transfer one-third of the dough at a time to the baking sheets, trying to avoid punching down the dough in the process.

**7** ▲ Using floured hands, shape into oblong loaf shapes, about 1-inch thick. Flatten slightly. Sprinkle with flour and let rise in a warm place for 30 minutes.

**8** Meanwhile, preheat the oven to 425°F. Bake for 25–30 minutes or until golden and hollow-sounding when tapped on the bottom. Transfer to a wire rack to cool.

## MAKES 3 LOAVES

### FOR THE BIGA STARTER
¼ ounce fresh yeast

¾–scant 1 cup lukewarm water

3 cups unbleached all-purpose flour, plus extra for dusting

### FOR THE DOUGH
½ ounce fresh yeast

1⅔ cups lukewarm water

4 tablespoons lukewarm milk

5 cups unbleached white bread flour

2 teaspoons salt

3 tablespoons extra virgin olive oil

---

### ~ VARIATION ~

To make tomato-flavored ciabatta, add 1 cup oil-packed sun-dried tomatoes, drained and chopped. Add with the olive oil in step 5.

# Italian Panettone

**MAKES 1 LOAF**

3½ cups white bread flour

½ teaspoon salt

½ ounce fresh yeast

½ cup lukewarm milk

2 eggs

2 eggs yolks

6 tablespoons sugar

⅔ cup butter, softened

⅔ cup chopped candied peel

½ cup raisins

melted butter, for brushing

This classic Italian bread can be found throughout Italy around Christmas. It is a surprisingly light bread, even though it is rich with butter and dried fruit.

**2** Sift the flour and salt together into a large bowl. Make a well in the center. Mix the yeast with 4 tablespoons of the milk, then mix in the remainder.

**3 ▲** Pour the yeast mixture into the center of the flour, add the whole eggs and mix in sufficient flour to make a thick batter. Sprinkle a little flour over the top and let "sponge," in a warm place, for 30 minutes.

**1** Using a double layer of waxed paper, line and butter a 6-inch deep cake pan or soufflé dish. Leave 3 inches of paper above the top of the pan.

**4** Add the egg yolks and sugar and mix to a soft dough. Work in the softened butter, then turn out onto a lightly floured surface and knead for 5 minutes until smooth and elastic. Place in a lightly oiled bowl, cover with lightly oiled plastic wrap and let rise, in a slightly warm place, for 1½–2 hours, or until doubled in bulk.

**5 ▲** Punch down the dough and turn out onto a floured surface. Gently knead in the peel and raisins. Shape into a ball and place in the pan. Cover with oiled plastic wrap and let rise, in a slightly warm place, for about 1 hour or until doubled.

**6 ▲** Meanwhile, preheat the oven to 375°F. Brush the surface with melted butter and cut a cross in the top using a sharp knife. Bake for 20 minutes, then reduce the oven temperature to 350°F. Brush the top with butter again and bake for another 25–30 minutes or until golden. Cool in the pan for 5–10 minutes, then turn out onto a wire rack to cool.

# Italian Pane al Cioccolato

This slightly sweet chocolate bread from Italy is often served with creamy mascarpone cheese as a dessert or snack. The dark chocolate pieces add texture to this light loaf.

## MAKES 1 LOAF

| |
|---|
| 3 cups white bread flour |
| 1½ tablespoons cocoa powder |
| ½ teaspoon salt |
| 2 tablespoons sugar |
| ½ ounce fresh yeast |
| 1 cup lukewarm water |
| 2 tablespoons butter, softened |
| 3 ounces semi-sweet chocolate, coarsely chopped |
| melted butter, for brushing |

**1 ▲** Lightly grease a 6-inch round deep cake pan. Sift the flour, cocoa powder and salt together into a large bowl. Stir in the sugar. Make a well in the center.

**2** Mix the yeast with 4 tablespoons of the water, then stir in the rest. Add to the center of the flour mixture and gradually mix to a dough.

**3** Knead in the butter, then knead on a surface until smooth and elastic. Place in an oiled bowl, cover with oiled plastic wrap and let rise, in a warm place, for 1 hour or until doubled.

**4 ▲** Turn out onto a floured surface and punch down. Knead in the chocolate, then cover with oiled plastic wrap; let rest for 5 minutes.

**5** Shape the dough into a round and place in the pan. Cover with lightly oiled plastic wrap and let rise, in a warm place, for 45 minutes or until the dough is doubled.

**6 ▲** Preheat the oven to 425°F. Bake for 10 minutes, then reduce the oven temperature to 375°F and bake for another 25–30 minutes. Brush the top with melted butter and let cool on a wire rack.

> **~ VARIATION ~**
> You can also shape this bread into one large or two small rounds and bake on a lightly greased baking sheet.

# Sicilian Scroll

**MAKES 1 LOAF**

| |
|---|
| 4 cups finely ground semolina |
| 1 cup white bread flour |
| 2 teaspoons salt |
| ¾ ounce fresh yeast |
| generous 1½ cups lukewarm water |
| 2 tablespoons extra-virgin olive oil |
| sesame seeds, for sprinkling |

A wonderful pale yellow, crusty-topped loaf, enhanced with a nutty flavor from the sesame seeds. It's perfect for serving with cheese.

**4 ▲** Turn out onto a lightly floured surface and punch down. Knead, then shape into a fat roll about 20 inches long. Form into an "S" shape.

**5** Carefully transfer the dough to the prepared baking sheet, cover with lightly oiled plastic wrap and let rise, in a warm place, for 30–45 minutes or until doubled in size.

**6** Meanwhile, preheat the oven to 425°F. Brush the top of the scroll with water and sprinkle with sesame seeds. Bake for 10 minutes. Spray the inside of the oven with water twice during this time. Reduce the oven temperature to 400°F and bake for another 25–30 minutes or until golden. Transfer to a wire rack to cool.

**1 ▲** Lightly grease a baking sheet. Combine the semolina, white bread flour and salt in a large bowl and make a well in the center.

**2** In a small bowl, mix the yeast with half the water, then stir in the remainder. Add the mixture to the center of the semolina mixture with the olive oil and gradually incorporate the semolina and flour to form a firm dough.

**3** Turn out the dough onto a lightly floured surface and knead for 8–10 minutes, until smooth and elastic. Place in a lightly oiled bowl, cover with lightly oiled plastic wrap and let rise, in a warm place, for 1–1½ hours or until doubled in bulk.

## ~ VARIATION ~

Although sesame seeds are the traditional topping on this delectable Italian bread, poppy seeds, or even crystals of sea salt, could be used instead.

# Pane Toscano

This bread from Tuscany is made without salt and probably originates from the days when salt was heavily taxed. To compensate for the lack of salt, this bread is usually served with salty foods, such as anchovies and olives.

MAKES 1 LOAF

| |
|---|
| 5 cups white bread flour |
| 1½ cups boiling water |
| ½ ounce fresh yeast |
| 4 tablespoons lukewarm water |

**6 ▲** Fold the sides of the round into the center and seal. Place seam side up on the prepared baking sheet. Cover with lightly oiled plastic wrap and let rise, in a warm place, for 30–45 minutes or until doubled in size.

**7 ▲** Flatten the loaf to about half its risen height and flip over. Cover with a large upturned bowl and let rise, in a warm place, for 30 minutes.

**1 ▲** First, make the starter. Sift 1½ cups of the flour into a large bowl. Pour over the boiling water, let sit for a couple of minutes, then mix well. Cover the bowl with a damp dish towel and let sit for 10 hours.

**2** Lightly flour a baking sheet. Cream the yeast with the lukewarm water. Stir into the starter.

**3** Gradually add the remaining flour and mix to form a dough. Turn out onto a floured surface and knead for 5–8 minutes, until elastic.

**4** Place in a lightly oiled bowl, cover with lightly oiled plastic wrap and let rise, in a warm place, for 1–1½ hours or until doubled in bulk.

**5** Turn out the dough onto a lightly floured surface, punch down, and shape into a round.

**8** Meanwhile, preheat the oven to 425°F. Slash the top of the loaf, using a sharp knife, if desired. Bake for 30–35 minutes or until golden. Transfer to a wire rack to cool.

# Italian Schiacciata

**MAKES 1 LOAF**

| |
| --- |
| 3 cups white bread flour |
| ½ teaspoon salt |
| ½ ounce fresh yeast |
| scant 1 cup lukewarm water |
| 4 tablespoons extra-virgin olive oil |
| FOR THE TOPPING |
| 2 tablespoons extra-virgin olive oil, for brushing |
| 2 tablespoons fresh rosemary leaves |
| coarse sea salt, for sprinkling |

This Tuscan version of Italian pizza-style flat bread can be rolled to varying thicknesses to give either a crisp or a soft, bread-like finish.

**2** Place in a lightly oiled bowl, cover with lightly oiled plastic wrap and let rise, in a warm place, for about 1 hour or until doubled in bulk.

**1** Lightly oil a baking sheet. Sift the flour and salt into a large bowl and make a well in the center. Mix the yeast with half the water. Add to the center of the flour with the remaining water and olive oil and mix to a soft dough. Turn out the dough onto a lightly floured surface and knead for 10 minutes, until smooth and elastic.

**3 ▲** Punch down the dough, turn out onto a lightly floured surface and knead gently. Roll out to a 12 × 8-inch rectangle and place on the prepared baking sheet. Brush with some of the olive oil for the topping and cover with oiled plastic wrap.

**4 ▲** Let rise, in a warm place, for about 20 minutes, then brush with the remaining oil, prick all over with a fork and sprinkle with rosemary and sea salt. Let rise again in a warm place for 15 minutes.

**5** Meanwhile, preheat the oven to 400°F. Bake for 30 minutes or until light golden. Transfer to a wire rack to cool slightly. Serve warm.

# Moroccan Holiday Bread

The addition of cornmeal and a cornucopia of seeds gives this superb loaf an interesting flavor and texture.

**MAKES 1 LOAF**

| |
| --- |
| 2½ cups white bread flour |
| ½ cup yellow cornmeal |
| 1 teaspoon salt |
| ¾ ounce fresh yeast |
| ½ cup lukewarm water |
| ½ cup lukewarm milk |
| 1 tablespoon pumpkin seeds |
| 1 tablespoon sesame seeds |
| 2 tablespoons sunflower seeds |

**5** ▲ Turn out the dough onto a lightly floured surface and punch down. Gently knead the pumpkin and sesame seeds into the dough. Shape into a round ball and flatten slightly.

**6** Place on the baking sheet, cover with oiled plastic wrap or slide into a large, lightly oiled plastic bag and let rise, in a warm place, for 45 minutes or until doubled in bulk.

**1** Lightly grease a baking sheet. Sift the flours and salt into a large bowl.

**3** Turn out the dough onto a lightly floured surface and knead for about 5 minutes, until smooth and elastic.

**4** Place in a lightly oiled bowl, cover with lightly oiled plastic wrap and let rise, in a warm place, for about 1 hour or until doubled in bulk.

**7** ▲ Meanwhile, preheat the oven to 400°F. Brush the top of the loaf with water and sprinkle with the sunflower seeds. Bake the loaf for 30–35 minutes or until it is golden and sounds hollow when tapped on the bottom. Transfer the loaf to a wire rack to cool.

**2** ▲ Mix the yeast with a little of the water in a small bowl. Stir in the remainder of the water and the milk. Pour into the center of the flour and mix to a fairly soft dough.

> **~ VARIATION ~**
> For a plainer loaf, incorporate all the seeds in the dough in step 5 and leave the top of the loaf seedless.

# Greek Christopsomo

**MAKES 1 LOAF**

½ ounce fresh yeast

scant ⅔ cup lukewarm milk

4 cups white flour

2 eggs

6 tablespoons sugar

½ teaspoon salt

6 tablespoons butter, softened

grated zest of ½ orange

1 teaspoon ground cinnamon

¼ teaspoon ground cloves

pinch of crushed anise seed

8 walnut halves

beaten egg white, for glazing

A Byzantine cross flavored with anise seed tops this Greek Christmas bread, which is also decorated with walnuts for good fortune. The fluffy, light, butter-enriched bread contains orange zest, cinnamon and cloves—all the warm tastes associated with Christmas.

**1 ▲** Lightly grease a large baking sheet. In a large bowl, mix the yeast with the milk until the yeast is dissolved, then stir in 1 cup of the flour to make a thin batter. Cover with lightly oiled plastic wrap and let "sponge" in a warm place for 30 minutes.

**2** Beat the eggs and sugar until light and fluffy. Beat into the yeast mixture. Gradually mix in the remaining flour and salt. Beat in the butter and knead to a soft but not sticky dough. Knead on a floured surface for 8–10 minutes, until smooth and elastic. Place in an oiled bowl, cover with oiled plastic wrap and let rise, in a warm place, for 1½ hours or until doubled in bulk.

**3** Turn out onto a floured surface and gently punch down. Cut off 2 ounces of dough; cover and set aside. Gently knead the orange zest, cinnamon and cloves into the large piece of dough and shape into a round loaf. Place on the baking sheet.

**4** Knead the anise seed into the remaining dough. Cut in half and shape each piece into a 12-inch rope. Cut through each rope at either end by one-third of its length. Place the two ropes in a cross on top of the loaf, then curl each cut end into a circle, in opposite directions.

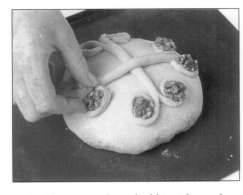

**5 ▲** Place a walnut half inside each circle. Cover the loaf with lightly oiled plastic wrap and let rise for 45 minutes or until doubled in size. Meanwhile, preheat the oven to 375°F. Brush the bread with the egg white and bake for 40–45 minutes or until golden. Cool on a wire rack.

# Greek Tsoureki

Topped with brightly colored eggs, this braided bread is an important part of the Greek Easter celebrations.

**MAKES 1 LOAF**

**FOR THE EGGS**

3 eggs

¼ teaspoon bright red food coloring

1 tablespoon white wine vinegar

1 teaspoon water

1 teaspoon olive oil

**FOR THE DOUGH**

4 cups white flour

½ teaspoon salt

1 teaspoon ground allspice

½ teaspoon ground cinnamon

½ teaspoon caraway seeds

¾ ounce fresh yeast

¾ cup lukewarm milk

¼ cup butter

3 tablespoons sugar

2 eggs

**FOR THE GLAZE**

1 egg yolk

1 teaspoon honey

1 teaspoon water

**FOR THE DECORATION**

½ cup slivered almonds

edible gold leaf, optional

**1** Lightly grease a baking sheet. Place the eggs in a pan of water and bring to a boil. Boil gently for 10 minutes. Meanwhile, combine the red food coloring, vinegar and water in a shallow bowl. Remove the eggs from the boiling water, place on a wire rack for a few seconds to dry, then roll in the coloring mixture. Return to the rack to cool and completely dry.

**2** When cold, drizzle the olive oil on absorbent paper towels, lift up each egg in turn and rub all over with the oiled paper.

**3** To make the dough, sift the flour, salt, allspice and cinnamon into a large bowl. Stir in the caraway seeds.

**4** In a bowl, mix the yeast with the milk. In another bowl, cream the butter and sugar, then beat in the eggs. Add the creamed mixture to the flour with the yeast mixture and gradually mix into a dough. Turn out the dough onto a lightly floured surface and knead until smooth and elastic.

**5** Place in a lightly oiled bowl, cover with lightly oiled plastic wrap and let rise, in a warm place, for about 2 hours or until doubled in bulk.

**6** Punch down the dough and knead for 2–3 minutes. Return to the bowl, re-cover and let rise again, in a warm place, for about 1 hour or until doubled in bulk.

**7** Punch down and turn out onto a lightly floured surface. Divide the dough into 3 equal pieces and roll each into a 15–20-inch long rope. Braid these together from the center to the ends.

**8** Place on the prepared baking sheet and push the dyed eggs into the loaf. Cover and let rise, in a warm place, for about 1 hour.

**9** Preheat the oven to 375°F. Mix the egg yolk, honey and water for the glaze, and brush over the loaf. Sprinkle with almonds and gold leaf, if using. Bake for 40–45 minutes or until golden and hollow-sounding when tapped. Cool on a wire rack.

# Greek Olive Bread

**MAKES 2 LOAVES**

6 cups white flour,
   plus extra for dusting

2 teaspoons salt

1 ounce fresh yeast

1½ cups lukewarm water

5 tablespoons olive oil

1½ cups pitted black olives,
   roughly chopped

1 red onion, finely chopped

2 tablespoons chopped fresh cilantro
   or mint

> **~ VARIATION ~**
>
> Make one large loaf and
> increase the baking time by
> about 15 minutes.

**1** Lightly grease 2 baking sheets. Sift
the flour and salt together into a large
bowl and make a well in the center.

**2 ▲** In a bowl, blend the yeast with
half of the water. Add to the center
of the flour with the remaining water
and the olive oil; mix to a soft dough.

**3** Turn out the dough onto a lightly
floured surface and knead for
8–10 minutes, until smooth. Place in
a lightly oiled bowl, cover with
lightly oiled plastic wrap and let rise,
in a warm place, for 1 hour or until
doubled in bulk.

**4** Turn out onto a lightly floured
surface and punch down. Cut off a
quarter of the dough, cover with
lightly oiled plastic wrap and set aside.

The flavors of the Mediterranean simply ooze from this decorative bread,
speckled with black olives, red onions and herbs.

**5 ▲** Roll out the large piece of dough
to a round. Sprinkle with the olives,
onion and herbs, then bring up the
sides of the circle and gently knead
together. Cut the dough in half and
shape each piece into a plump oval
loaf, about 8 inches long. Place on
the baking sheets.

**6** Divide the reserved dough into
4 equal pieces and roll each out into
a long strand 24 inches long. Twist
together and cut in half. Brush the
center of each loaf with water and
place two pieces of twisted dough on
top of each, tucking the ends
underneath the loaves.

**7** Cover with lightly oiled plastic
wrap and let rise, in a warm place, for
about 45 minutes or until the loaves
are plump and nearly doubled in size.

**8** Meanwhile, preheat the oven to
425°F. Dust the loaves lightly with
flour and bake for 35–40 minutes or
until golden and hollow-sounding
when tapped. Cool on a wire rack.

# Turkish Pita Bread

These Turkish breads are a favorite in both the eastern Mediterranean and the Middle East, and have becoome popular in England and the United States. This versatile soft, flat bread forms a pocket as it cooks, making it perfect for filling with vegetables, salads or meats.

MAKES 6 PITA BREADS

2 cups white bread flour

1 teaspoon salt

½ ounce fresh yeast

scant ⅔ cup lukewarm water

2 teaspoons extra-virgin olive oil

~ VARIATION ~
To make whole-wheat pita breads, replace half the white flour with whole-wheat flour.

**5** ▲ Roll out each ball of dough in turn to an oval about ¼-inch thick and 6 inches long. Place on a floured dish towel and cover with lightly oiled plastic wrap. Let rise at room temperature for 20–30 minutes. Meanwhile, preheat the oven to 450°F. Place 3 baking sheets in the oven to heat at the same time.

**6** Place two pita breads on each baking sheet and bake for 4–6 minutes or until puffed up; they do not need to brown. If preferred, cook the pita bread in batches. It is important that the oven has reached the recommended temperature before the pita breads are baked. This ensures that they will puff up.

**1** Sift the flour and salt together into a bowl. Mix the yeast with the water until dissolved, then stir in the olive oil and pour into a large bowl.

**2** Gradually beat the flour into the yeast mixture, then knead the mixture to make a soft dough.

**3** Turn out onto a floured surface and knead for 5 minutes until smooth and elastic. Place in a clean bowl, cover with oiled plastic wrap and let rise, in a warm place, for about 1 hour or until doubled in bulk.

**4** ▲ Punch down the dough. On a floured surface, divide it into 6 pieces and shape into balls. Cover with oiled plastic wrap; let rest for 5 minutes.

**7** Transfer the pitas to a wire rack to cool until warm, then cover with a dish towel to keep them soft.

# Polish Poppy Seed Roll

**MAKES 1 LOAF**

3 cups white flour

½ teaspoon salt

2 tablespoons sugar

¾ ounce fresh yeast

½ cup lukewarm milk

1 egg, lightly beaten

¼ cup butter, melted

1 tablespoon toasted sliced almonds

FOR THE FILLING

⅔ cup poppy seeds

¼ cup butter

6 tablespoons sugar

½ cup raisins

½ cup ground almonds

⅓ cup candied fruit, finely chopped

½ teaspoon ground cinnamon

FOR THE ICING

1 cup confectioners' sugar

1 tablespoon fresh lemon juice

2–3 teaspoons water

A favorite sweet yeast bread in both Poland and Hungary, this has an unusual filling of poppy seeds, almonds, raisins and candied fruit spiraling through the dough.

**1** Grease a baking sheet. Sift the flour and salt into a bowl. Stir in the sugar. Mix the yeast with the milk. Add to the flour with the egg and melted butter and mix to form a dough.

**2** Turn out onto a floured surface and knead for 8–10 minutes, until smooth and elastic. Place in an oiled bowl, cover with oiled plastic wrap and let rise, in a warm place, for 1–1½ hours or until doubled in size.

**3** Meanwhile, pour boiling water over the poppy seeds for the filling, then let cool. Drain thoroughly in a fine sieve. Melt the butter in a small pan, add the poppy seeds and cook, stirring, for 1–2 minutes. Remove from the heat and stir in the sugar, raisins, ground almonds, candied fruit and cinnamon. Set aside to cool.

**4** Turn the dough out onto a lightly floured surface, punch down and knead lightly. Roll out into a rectangle 14 × 10 inches. Spread the filling to within ¾ inch of the edges.

**5** ▲ Roll up the dough, starting from one long edge, like a jelly roll, tucking in the edges to seal. Place seam side down on the baking sheet. Cover with oiled plastic wrap and let rise, in a warm place, for 30 minutes or until doubled in size.

**6** Meanwhile, preheat the oven to 375°F. Bake for 30 minutes or until golden brown. Transfer to a wire rack to cool until just warm.

**7** ▲ In a small saucepan, combine the confectioners' sugar, lemon juice and enough water to make an icing stiff enough to coat the back of a spoon. Heat gently, stirring, until warm. Drizzle the icing on the loaf and sprinkle the sliced almonds over the top. Let cool completely, then serve sliced.

# Polish Rye Bread

This rye bread is made with half white flour, which gives it a lighter, more open texture than a traditional rye loaf. Served thinly sliced, it is the perfect accompaniment for cold meats and fish.

**MAKES 1 LOAF**

| |
|---|
| 2 cups rye flour |
| 2 cups white flour |
| 2 teaspoons caraway seeds |
| 2 teaspoons salt |
| ¾ ounce fresh yeast |
| scant ⅔ cup lukewarm milk |
| 1 teaspoon honey |
| scant ⅔ cup lukewarm water |
| whole-wheat flour, for dusting |

**1 ▲** Grease a baking sheet. Mix the flours, caraway seeds and salt in a bowl and make a well in the center.

**2** In a small bowl or measuring cup, mix the yeast with the milk and honey. Pour into the center of the flour, add the water and gradually incorporate the surrounding flour and caraway mixture until a dough forms.

**3** Turn out the dough onto a lightly floured surface and knead for 8–10 minutes, until smooth, elastic and firm. Place in a large, lightly oiled bowl, cover with lightly oiled plastic wrap and let rise, in a warm place, for about 3 hours or until doubled in bulk.

**4 ▲** Turn out the dough onto a lightly floured surface and punch down. Shape into an oval loaf and place on the prepared baking sheet.

**5** Dust with whole-wheat flour, cover with lightly oiled plastic wrap and let rise, in a warm place, for 1–1½ hours or until doubled in size. Meanwhile, preheat the oven to 425°F.

**6 ▲** Using a sharp knife, slash the loaf with two long cuts about 1 inch apart. Bake for 30–35 minutes or until the loaf sounds hollow when tapped on the bottom. Transfer the loaf to a wire rack and set aside to cool.

# Hungarian Split Farmhouse Loaf

**MAKES 1 LOAF**

4 cups white flour

2 teaspoons salt

½ teaspoon fennel seeds, crushed

1 tablespoon sugar

¾ ounce fresh yeast

1⅛ cups lukewarm water

2 tablespoons butter, melted

FOR THE TOPPING

1 egg white

pinch of salt

2 teaspoons fennel seeds,
    for sprinkling

A golden, fennel seed-encrusted loaf with a moist white crumb. It is equally delicious made into rolls—just reduce the baking time to 15–20 minutes.

**1** Lightly grease a baking sheet. Sift the white flour and salt together into a large bowl and stir in the crushed fennel seeds and sugar. Make a well in the center.

**2 ▲** Mix the yeast with a little water, stir in the rest, then pour into the flour. Stir in enough flour to make a runny batter. Sprinkle more of the flour on top, cover and let sit in a warm place for 30 minutes until the "sponge" starts to bubble and rise.

**3 ▲** Add the melted butter and gradually mix in with the remaining flour to form a dough. Turn out onto a lightly floured surface and knead for 8–10 minutes, until smooth and elastic. Place in a lightly oiled bowl, cover with lightly oiled plastic wrap and let rise, in a warm place, for 45–60 minutes or until doubled in bulk.

**4 ▲** Turn out onto a lightly floured surface and punch down. Shape into an oval and place on the prepared baking sheet. Cover with lightly oiled plastic wrap and let rise, in a warm place, for 30–40 minutes or until doubled in size.

**5** Meanwhile, preheat the oven to 425°F. Combine the egg white and salt and brush this glaze over the loaf. Sprinkle with fennel seeds and then, using a sharp knife, slash along its length. Bake for 20 minutes, then reduce the oven temperature to 350°F and bake for 10 more minutes or until it sounds hollow when tapped on the bottom. Transfer to a wire rack to cool.

# Russian Potato Bread

In Russia, potatoes are often used to replace some of the flour in bread recipes. They endow the bread with excellent keeping qualities.

**1 ▲** Lightly grease a baking sheet. Add the potatoes to a saucepan of boiling water and cook until tender. Drain and reserve ⅔ cup of the cooking water. Mash and sieve the potatoes and let cool.

**2** Combine the yeast, flours, caraway seeds and salt in a large bowl. Add the butter and rub in. Combine the reserved potato water and sieved potatoes. Gradually work this mixture into the flour mixture to form a soft dough.

**3** Turn out onto a floured surface and knead for 8–10 minutes until smooth and elastic. Place in an oiled bowl, cover with oiled plastic wrap and let rise, in a warm place, for 1 hour or until doubled in bulk.

**4 ▲** Turn out onto a lightly floured surface, punch down and knead gently. Shape into a plump oval loaf, about 7 inches long. Place on the prepared baking sheet and sprinkle with a little whole-wheat flour.

**5** Cover the dough with lightly oiled plastic wrap and let rise, in a warm place, for 30 minutes or until doubled in size. Meanwhile, preheat the oven to 400°F.

**6 ▲** Using a sharp knife, slash the top with 3–4 diagonal cuts to make a criss-cross effect. Bake for 30–35 minutes or until golden and sounding hollow when tapped on the bottom. Transfer to a wire rack to cool.

### MAKES 1 LOAF

| |
|---|
| 8 ounces potatoes, peeled and diced |
| ¼ ounce envelope active dry yeast |
| 3 cups white flour |
| 1 cup whole-wheat flour, plus extra for sprinkling |
| ½ teaspoon caraway seeds, crushed |
| 2 teaspoons salt |
| 2 tablespoons butter |

### ~ VARIATION ~

To make a cheese-flavored potato bread, omit the caraway seeds and knead 1 cup grated Cheddar, Red Leicester or a crumbled blue cheese, such as Stilton, into the dough before shaping.

# Jewish Challah

**MAKES 1 LOAF**

| |
|---|
| 5 cups white flour |
| 2 teaspoons salt |
| ¾ ounce fresh yeast |
| scant 1 cup lukewarm water |
| 2 tablespoons sugar |
| 2 eggs |
| 6 tablespoons butter or margarine, melted |
| FOR THE GLAZE |
| 1 egg yolk |
| 1 tablespoon water |
| 2 teaspoons poppy seeds, for sprinkling |

~ COOK'S TIP ~

If wished, divide the dough in half and make two small challahs, keeping the braids quite simple. Reduce the baking time by about 10 minutes.

Challah is an egg-rich, light-textured bread baked for the Jewish Sabbath and to celebrate religious holidays. It is usually braided with 3 or 4 strands of dough, but 8 strands or more may be used to create especially festive loaves.

**1** ▲ Lightly grease a baking sheet. Sift the flour and salt together into a large bowl and make a well in the center. Mix the yeast with the water and sugar, add to the center of the flour with the eggs and melted butter or margarine and gradually mix in the surrounding flour to form a soft dough.

**2** Turn out onto a floured surface and knead for 10 minutes, until smooth and elastic. Place in an oiled bowl, cover with oiled plastic wrap and let rise, in a warm place, for 1 hour or until doubled in bulk.

**3** Punch down, re-cover and let rise again in a warm place for about 1 hour. Punch down, turn out onto a floured surface and knead gently. Divide into quarters. Roll each piece into a rope about 18 inches long. Line up next to each other. Pinch the ends together at one end.

**4** ▲ Starting from the right, lift the first rope over the second and the third rope over the fourth. Take the fourth rope and place it between the first and second ropes. Repeat, and continue until braided.

**5** Tuck the ends under and place the loaf on the prepared baking sheet. Cover with lightly oiled plastic wrap and let rise in a warm place, for about 30–45 minutes or until doubled in size. Meanwhile, preheat the oven to 400°F. Beat the egg yolk and water for the glaze together.

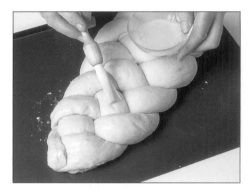

**6** ▲ Brush the egg glaze gently over the loaf. Sprinkle evenly with the poppy seeds and bake for 35–40 minutes or until the challah is a deep golden brown. Transfer to a wire rack and let cool before slicing.

# American Pumpkin and Walnut Bread

Pumpkin, nutmeg and walnuts combine to yield a moist, tangy and slightly sweet bread with an indescribably good flavor. Serve partnered with meats or cheese, or simply lightly buttered.

**MAKES 1 LOAF**

| |
|---|
| 1¼ pounds pumpkin, peeled, seeded and cut into chunks |
| 6 tablespoons sugar |
| 1 teaspoon grated nutmeg |
| ¼ cup butter, melted |
| 3 eggs, lightly beaten |
| 3 cups white flour |
| 2 teaspoons baking powder |
| ½ teaspoon salt |
| ¾ cup walnuts, chopped |

**1** Grease and neatly line a 8½ × 4½ inch loaf pan with parchment paper. Preheat the oven to 350°F.

**2** ▲ Place the pumpkin in a saucepan, add water to cover by about 2 inches, then bring to a boil. Cover, lower the heat and simmer for 20 minutes, or until the pumpkin is very tender. Drain well, then purée in a food processor or blender. Let cool.

**3** ▲ Place 1¼ cups of the purée in a large bowl. Add the sugar, nutmeg, melted butter and eggs to the purée and mix together. Sift the flour, baking powder and salt together into a large bowl and make a well in the center.

**4** Add the pumpkin mixture to the center of the flour and stir until smooth. Mix in the walnuts.

~ COOK'S TIP ~
Use any leftover pumpkin purée in soup.

**5** Transfer to the prepared pan and bake for 1 hour, or until golden and starting to shrink from the sides of the pan. Cool on a wire rack.

# San Francisco Sourdough Bread

**MAKES 2 LOAVES**

**FOR THE STARTER**

½ cup whole-wheat flour

pinch of ground cumin

1 tablespoon milk

1–2 tablespoons water

**1ST REFRESHMENT**

2 tablespoons water

1 cup whole-wheat flour

**2ND REFRESHMENT**

4 tablespoons water

1 cup white flour

**FOR THE BREAD**

**1ST REFRESHMENT**

5 tablespoons very warm water

¾ cup all-purpose flour

**2ND REFRESHMENT**

¾ cup lukewarm water

1¾–2 cups all-purpose flour

**FOR THE SOURDOUGH**

1¼ cups warm water

5 cups white flour

1 tablespoon salt

flour, for dusting

ice cubes, for baking

In San Francisco this bread is leavened using a flour and water paste, which is left to ferment with the aid of airborn yeast. The finished loaves have a moist crumb and crispy crust, and will keep for several days.

**2** Pull off the crust and discard. Remove the moist center (about the size of a hazelnut), which will be aerated and sweet smelling, and place in a clean bowl. Mix in the water for the 1st refreshment. Add the whole-wheat flour and mix into a dough.

**3** Cover with lightly oiled plastic wrap and set in a warm place for 1–2 days. Discard the crust and gradually mix in the water for the 2nd refreshment to the starter, which by now will have a slightly sharper smell. Mix in the white flour, cover and let sit in a warm place for 8–10 hours.

**4 ▲** For the bread, mix the sourdough starter with the water for the 1st refreshment. Mix in the flour to form a firm dough. Knead for 6–8 minutes, until firm. Cover with a damp towel and let sit in a warm place for 8–12 hours or until doubled in bulk.

**5** Gradually mix in the water for the 2nd refreshment, then add enough flour to form a soft, smooth elastic dough. Re-cover and let sit in a warm place for 8–12 hours. Gradually stir in the water for the sourdough, then work in the flour and salt. This will take 10–15 minutes. Turn out onto a lightly floured surface and knead until smooth and very elastic. Place in a large lightly oiled bowl, cover with lightly oiled plastic wrap and let rise, in a warm place, for 8–12 hours.

**6** Divide the dough in half and shape into 2 round loaves by folding the sides over to the center and sealing.

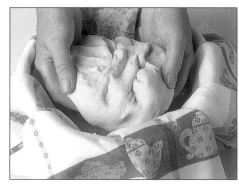

**7 ▲** Place seam side up in flour-dusted *couronnes*, bowls or baskets lined with flour-dusted dish towels. Re-cover and let rise in a warm place for 4 hours.

**8** Preheat the oven to 425°F. Place an empty roasting pan in the bottom of the oven. Dust 2 baking sheets with flour. Turn out the loaves seam side down on the prepared baking sheets. Using a sharp knife, cut a criss-cross pattern by slashing the top of the loaves 4–5 times in each direction.

**9** Place the baking sheets in the oven and immediately drop the ice cubes into the hot roasting pan to create steam. Bake the bread for 25 minutes, then reduce the oven temperature to 400°F and bake for another 15–20 minutes or until it sounds hollow when tapped on the bottom. Transfer to wire racks to cool.

**1 ▲** Sift the flour and cumin for the starter into a bowl. Add the milk and enough water to make a firm but moist dough. Knead for 6–8 minutes to form a firm dough. Return to the bowl, cover with a damp dish towel and let sit in a warm place, 75–80°F, for about 2 days. When it is ready the starter will appear moist and wrinkled and will have developed a crust.

~ COOK'S TIP ~

If you want to make sourdough bread regularly, keep a small amount of the starter covered in the refrigerator. It will keep for several days. Use the starter for the 2nd refreshment, then continue as directed.

# Boston Brown Bread

**MAKES 1 OR 2 LOAVES**

scant 1 cup yellow cornmeal

scant 1 cup white flour or
   whole-wheat flour

scant 1 cup rye flour

½ teaspoon salt

1 teaspoon baking soda

generous ½ cup raisins

½ cup milk

½ cup water

½ cup molasses

---

~ COOK'S TIP ~

If you do not have empty
coffee cans, or similar molds,
cook the bread in one or
two heatproof bowls of
equivalent capacity.

---

Rich, moist and dark, this bread is flavored with molasses and can include
raisins. In Boston it is often served with savory baked beans.

**4 ▲** Fill the container or cans with
the dough; they should be about two-
thirds full. Cover neatly with foil or
greased waxed paper and tie securely.

**5** Bring water to a depth of 2 inches
to a boil in a deep, heavy saucepan
large enough to accommodate the
container or cans. Place a trivet in
the pan, stand the container or cans
on top, cover the pan and steam
for 1½ hours, adding more boiling
water to maintain the required level
as necessary.

**6** Cool the loaves for a few minutes in
the container or cans, then turn them
on their sides and the loaves should
slip out. Serve warm, with savory
dishes or Boston baked beans.

**1** Line the base of one 5-cup
cylindrical metal or glass container,
with greased waxed paper.
Alternatively, remove the lids from
two 1-pound coffee cans, wash and
dry the cans thoroughly, then line
with greased waxed paper.

**2** Combine the cornmeal, white or
whole-wheat flour, rye flour, salt,
baking soda and raisins in a large
bowl. Warm the milk and water
in a small saucepan and stir in
the molasses.

**3 ▲** Add the molasses mixture to the
dry ingredients and combine, using a
spoon, until it just forms a moist
dough. Do not overmix.

# American Bagels

Bagels are eaten in many countries, and are very popular in the United States. They can be made from white, whole-wheat or rye flour and finished with a variety of toppings, including caraway, poppy or sesame seeds and onion.

**MAKES 10 BAGELS**

| |
|---|
| 3 cups white flour |
| 2 teaspoons salt |
| ¼ ounce envelope active dry yeast |
| 1 teaspoon malt extract |
| scant 1 cup lukewarm water |
| FOR POACHING |
| 2½ quarts water |
| 1 tablespoon malt extract |
| FOR THE TOPPING |
| 1 egg white |
| 2 teaspoons cold water |
| 2 tablespoons poppy, sesame or caraway seeds |

**5** Meanwhile, preheat the oven to 425°F. Place the water and malt extract for poaching in a large saucepan, bring to a boil, then reduce to a simmer. Place the bagels in the water 2 or 3 at a time and poach for about 1 minute. They will sink and then rise again when first added to the pan. Using a large draining spoon, turn over and cook for 30 seconds. Remove and drain on a dish towel. Repeat with the remaining bagels.

**1 ▲** Grease 2 baking sheets. Sift the flour and salt together into a large bowl. Stir in the yeast. Make a well in the center. Combine the malt extract and water, add to the center of the flour and mix into a dough. Knead on a floured surface until elastic.

**2** Place in a lightly oiled bowl, cover with lightly oiled plastic wrap and let rise, in a warm place, for about 1 hour or until doubled in bulk.

**3** Turn out onto a lightly floured surface and punch down. Knead for 1 minute, then divide into 10 equal pieces. Shape into balls, cover with plastic wrap and let rest for 5 minutes.

**4 ▲** Gently flatten each ball and make a hole through the center with your thumb. Enlarge the hole slightly by turning your thumb around. Place on a floured tray; re-cover and let sit in a warm place, for 10–20 minutes or until they begin to rise.

**6 ▲** Place five bagels on each prepared baking sheet, spacing them well apart. Beat the egg white with the water for the topping, brush the mixture on top of each bagel and sprinkle with poppy, sesame or caraway seeds. Bake for 20–25 minutes or until golden brown. Transfer to a wire rack to cool.

# American Monkey Bread

**MAKES 1 LOAF**

| |
|---|
| ¼ ounce envelope active dry yeast |
| 4 cups white flour |
| ½ teaspoon salt |
| 1 tablespoon sugar |
| ½ cup lukewarm milk |
| ½ cup lukewarm water |
| 1 egg, lightly beaten |
| FOR THE COATING |
| ½ cup golden raisins |
| 3 tablespoons rum or brandy |
| 1 cup walnuts, finely chopped |
| 2 teaspoons ground cinnamon |
| ⅔ cup light brown sugar |
| ¼ cup butter, melted |

This American favorite is also called bubble bread—because of the "bubbles" of dough. The pieces of dough are tossed in a heavenly coating of butter, nuts, cinnamon and rum-soaked fruit.

**1** Lightly grease a 9-inch springform cake pan. Combine the yeast, flour, salt and sugar in a large bowl and make a well in the center.

**2** Add the milk, water and egg to the center of the flour and combine into a soft dough. Turn out onto a lightly floured surface and knead for about 10 minutes, until smooth and elastic. Place in a lightly oiled bowl, cover with lightly oiled plastic wrap and let rise, in a warm place, for 45–60 minutes or until doubled in bulk.

**3 ▲** Place the golden raisins in a pan, pour in the rum or brandy and heat for 1–2 minutes or until warm. Do not overheat. Remove from the heat and set aside. Mix the walnuts, cinnamon and sugar in a bowl.

**4 ▲** Turn out the dough onto a lightly floured surface and knead gently. Divide into 30 equal pieces and shape into small balls. Dip the balls, one at a time, into the melted butter, then roll them in the walnut mixture. Place half in the prepared pan, spaced slightly apart. Sprinkle on all the soaked raisins.

**5 ▲** Top with the remaining dough balls, dipping and coating as before. Sprinkle on any remaining walnut mixture and melted butter. Cover with lightly oiled plastic wrap or slide the pan into a lightly oiled large plastic bag and let rise, in a warm place, for about 45 minutes or until the dough reaches the top of the pan.

**6** Meanwhile, preheat the oven to 375°F. Bake for 35–40 minutes or until well risen and golden. Turn out onto a wire rack to cool.

# New England Fantans

These fantail rolls look stylish and are so versatile that they are equally suitable for a simple snack or a gourmet dinner party!

**1** Grease 9 foil cases or a muffin sheet with 3-inch cups. Mix the yeast with the buttermilk and sugar and then let stand for 15 minutes.

**2 ▲** In a pan, heat the milk with 3 tablespoons of the butter until the butter has melted. Allow to cool.

**3** Sift the flour and salt into a bowl. Add the yeast mixture, milk mixture and egg and mix into a soft dough. Turn out onto a floured surface and knead for 5–8 minutes, until smooth and elastic. Place in an oiled bowl, cover with oiled plastic wrap and let rise, in a warm place, for about 1 hour, until doubled in size.

**4 ▲** Turn out onto a lightly floured surface, punch down and knead until smooth and elastic. Roll into an oblong measuring 18 × 12 inches and about ¼-inch thick. Melt the remaining butter, brush it over the dough and cut it lengthwise into 5 equal strips. Stack on top of each other and cut across into 9 equal 2-inch strips.

**5 ▲** Pinch one side of each layered strip together, then place pinched side down into a muffin cup or foil case. Cover with lightly oiled plastic wrap and let rise, in a warm place, for 30–40 minutes or until the fantans have almost doubled in size. Preheat the oven to 400°F. Bake for 20 minutes or until golden. Turn out onto a wire rack to cool.

## MAKES 9 ROLLS

| |
|---|
| ½ ounce fresh yeast |
| 5 tablespoons buttermilk, at room temperature |
| 2 teaspoons sugar |
| 5 tablespoons milk |
| 5 tablespoons butter |
| 3¼ cups white flour |
| 1 teaspoon salt |
| 1 egg, lightly beaten |

### ~ VARIATION ~

Add 1 teaspoon ground cinnamon to the remaining butter in step 4 before brushing over the dough strips. Sprinkle the rolls with a little confectioners' sugar as soon as they come out of the oven.

# Mexican "Bread of the Dead"

**MAKES 1 LOAF**

| |
|---|
| 3 star anise |
| 6 tablespoons cold water |
| 6 cups white flour |
| 1 teaspoon salt |
| ½ cup sugar |
| 1 ounce fresh yeast |
| ¾ cup lukewarm water |
| 3 eggs |
| 4 tablespoons orange liqueur |
| ½ cup butter, melted |
| grated zest of 1 orange |
| confectioners' sugar, for dusting |

~ VARIATION ~

Ice the bread with ½ cup confectioners' sugar and 1–2 tablespoons orange liqueur.

A celebratory loaf made for the Day of the Dead. Even though the name of this bread suggests otherwise, this holiday is actually a very happy day when Mexicans pay their respects to the souls of their dead. Traditionally, the bread is decorated with a dough skull, bones and tears.

**1 ▲** Grease a 10½-inch fluted round cake pan. Place the star anise in a small saucepan and add the cold water. Bring to a boil and boil for 3–4 minutes or until the liquid has reduced to 3 tablespoons. Discard the star anise and let the liquid cool.

**2** Sift the flour and salt together into a large bowl. Stir in the sugar and make a well in the center.

**3** In a small bowl, dissolve the yeast in the lukewarm water. Pour into the center of the flour and mix in a little flour, using your fingers, until a smooth, thick batter forms. Sprinkle on a little of the remaining flour, cover with plastic wrap and let the batter sit in a warm place for 30 minutes or until the mixture starts to bubble.

**4** Beat the eggs, the reserved liquid flavored with star anise, orange liqueur and melted butter together. Gradually incorporate into the flour mixture to form a smooth dough.

**5 ▲** Turn out the dough onto a lightly floured surface and gently knead in the orange zest. Knead for 5–6 minutes, until smooth and elastic. Shape into a 10½-inch round and place in the prepared pan. Cover with lightly oiled plastic wrap and let rise, in a warm place, for 2–3 hours or until almost at the top of the pan and doubled in bulk.

**6** Meanwhile, preheat the oven to 375°F. Bake the loaf for 45–50 minutes or until golden. Turn out onto a wire rack to cool. Dust with confectioners' sugar to serve.

# Iranian Barbari

These small Iranian flat breads can be made in a variety of sizes. For a change, make two large breads and break off pieces to scoop up dips.

MAKES 6 BARBARI

2 cups unbleached white bread flour

1 teaspoon salt

½ ounce fresh yeast

scant ⅔ cup lukewarm water

oil, for brushing

**1** Lightly dust 2 baking sheets with flour. Sift the flour and salt into a bowl and make a well in the center.

**2 ▲** Mix the yeast with the water. Pour into the center of the flour, sprinkle a little flour over and leave in a warm place for 15 minutes. Mix to a dough, then turn out onto a lightly floured surface and knead for 8–10 minutes until smooth and elastic.

**3** Place in a lightly oiled bowl, cover with oiled plastic wrap and let rise for 45–60 minutes, or until doubled.

**4 ▲** Punch down the dough and turn out onto a floured surface. Divide into 6 equal pieces and shape into rectangles. Roll each one out to about 4 × 2 inches and about ½-inch thick. Space well apart on the baking sheets, and make four slashes in the tops.

~ VARIATION ~

Sprinkle with sesame or caraway seeds before baking.

**5** Cover the breads with lightly oiled plastic wrap and let rise, in a warm place, for 20 minutes. Meanwhile, preheat the oven to 400°F. Brush the breads with oil and bake for 12–15 minutes, or until pale golden. Serve warm.

# Syrian Onion Bread

**MAKES 8 BREADS**

4 cups unbleached white bread flour

1 teaspoon salt

¾ ounce fresh yeast

scant 1¼ cups lukewarm water

FOR THE TOPPING

4 tablespoons finely chopped onion

1 teaspoon ground cumin

2 teaspoons ground coriander

2 teaspoons chopped fresh mint

2 tablespoons olive oil

The basic Arab breads of the Levant and Gulf have traditionally been made with a finely ground whole-wheat flour similar to chapati flour, but now are being made with white flour as well. This Syrian version has a tasty, aromatic topping.

~ COOK'S TIP ~

If you haven't any fresh mint to hand, then add 1 tablespoon dried mint. Use the freeze-dried variety if you can as it has much more flavor.

**1 ▲** Lightly flour 2 baking sheets. Sift the flour and salt together into a large bowl and make a well in the center. Cream the yeast with a little of the water, then mix in the remainder.

**2** Add the yeast mixture to the center of the flour and mix to a firm dough. Turn out onto a lightly floured surface and knead for 8–10 minutes until smooth and elastic.

**3** Place in a lightly oiled bowl, cover with lightly oiled plastic wrap and leave to rise, in a warm place, for about 1 hour, or until doubled in size.

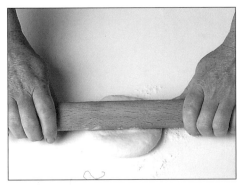

**4 ▲** Punch down the dough and turn out onto a lightly floured surface. Divide into 8 equal pieces and roll into 5–6-inch rounds. Make them slightly concave. Prick all over and space well apart on the baking sheets. Cover with lightly oiled plastic wrap and let rise for 15–20 minutes.

**5 ▲** Meanwhile, preheat the oven to 400°F. Mix the chopped onion, ground cumin, ground coriander and chopped mint in a bowl. Brush the breads with the olive oil for the topping, sprinkle them evenly with the spicy onion mixture and bake for 15–20 minutes. Serve warm.

# Indian Tandoori Rotis

There are numerous varieties of breads in India, most of them unleavened. This one, as its name suggests, would normally be baked in a tandoor—a clay oven which is heated with charcoal or wood. The oven becomes extremely hot, cooking the bread in minutes.

**MAKES 6 ROTIS**

| |
|---|
| 3 cups *atta* or fine whole-wheat flour |
| 1 teaspoon salt |
| 1 cup water |
| 2–3 tablespoons melted ghee or butter, for brushing |

~ COOK'S TIP ~
The rotis are ready when light brown bubbles appear on the surface.

**1** ▲ Sift the flour and salt into a large bowl. Add the water and mix to a soft dough. Knead on a floured surface for 3–4 minutes until smooth. Place in an oiled bowl, cover with oiled plastic wrap; let rest for 1 hour.

**2** ▲ Turn out onto a floured surface. Divide the dough into 6 pieces and shape each piece into a ball. Press out into a larger round with the palm of your hand, cover with oiled plastic wrap and let rest for 10 minutes.

**3** Preheat the oven to 450°F. Place 3 baking sheets in the oven to heat. Roll the rotis into 6-inch rounds, place on the baking sheet and bake for 8–10 minutes. Brush with ghee or butter and serve warm.

# Indian Naan

**MAKES 3 NAAN**

| |
|---|
| 2 cups unbleached white bread flour |
| ½ teaspoon salt |
| ½ ounce fresh yeast |
| 4 tablespoons lukewarm milk |
| 1 tablespoon vegetable oil |
| 2 tablespoons plain yogurt |
| 1 egg |
| 2–3 tablespoons melted ghee or butter, for brushing |

~ VARIATIONS ~

You can flavor naan in
numerous different ways:
• To make spicy naan, add
1 teaspoon each ground
coriander and ground cumin to
the flour in step 1. If you would
like the naan to be extra
fiery, add ½–1 teaspoon hot
chili powder.
• To make cardamom-flavored
naan, lightly crush the seeds
from 4–5 green cardamom
pods and add to the flour in
step 1.
• To make poppy seed naan,
brush the rolled-out naan with
a little ghee and sprinkle with
poppy seeds. Press lightly to
make sure that they stick.
• To make peppered naan,
brush the rolled-out naan with
a little ghee and dust
generously with coarsely
ground black pepper.
• To make onion-flavored
naan, add ½ cup finely chopped
or coarsely grated onion to the
dough in step 2. You may need
to reduce the amount of egg if
the onion is very moist to
prevent making the dough
too soft.
• To make whole-wheat naan,
substitute whole-wheat bread
flour for some or all of the
white flour.

From the Caucasus through the Punjab region of northwest India and beyond,
these leavened breads are served. Traditionally cooked in a very hot clay oven
known as a tandoor, naan are usually eaten with dry meat or vegetable dishes,
also cooked in a tandoor.

**1 ▲** Sift the flour and salt together
into a large bowl. In a smaller bowl,
cream the yeast with the milk. Set
aside for 15 minutes.

**2 ▲** Add the yeast mixture, oil,
yogurt and egg to the flour.

**3 ▲** Turn out the dough onto a
lightly floured surface and knead for
about 10 minutes until smooth and
elastic. Place in a lightly oiled bowl,
cover with lightly oiled plastic wrap
and let rise, in a warm place, for
45 minutes, or until doubled in bulk.

**4** Preheat the oven to its highest
setting, at least 450°F. Place 3 heavy
baking sheets in the oven to heat.

**5** Turn the dough out onto a lightly
floured surface and punch down.
Divide into 3 and shape into balls.

**6 ▲** Cover two of the balls of dough
with oiled plastic wrap and roll out
the third into a teardrop shape about
10 inches long, 5 inches wide and
with a thickness of about ¼–⅓ inch.

**7** Preheat the broiler on its highest
setting. Meanwhile, place the naan
on the hot baking sheets and bake for
3–4 minutes, or until puffed up.

**8** Remove the naan from the oven
and place under the hot broiler for a
few seconds, or until the top of the
naan browns slightly. Wrap the
cooked naan in a dish towel to keep
warm while rolling out and cooking
the remaining naan. Brush with
melted ghee or butter and serve warm.

~ COOK'S TIP ~

To help the dough to puff up and
brown, place the baking sheets
in an oven preheated to the
maximum temperature for at
least 10 minutes before baking.

# INDEX

## A

almonds:
almond bars, 93
almond cake, 255
almond syrup tart, 218
almond tiles, 66
blackberry and almond
muffins, 118
fruit and nut cake, 331
Italian almond cookies, 58
lemon almond tart, 199
nut lace cookies, 68
peach tart with almond
cream, 216
amaretti cookies: mango
and amaretti strudel, 352
amaretto liqueur: nectarine
amaretto cake, 333
anchovies:
onion and anchovy
tart, 225
onion, olive, and anchovy
pizza, 233
apples:
American-style apple
pie, 24
apple, apricot and walnut
bread, 143
apple and cherry crumble
pie, 22
apple-cranberry lattice
pie, 158
apple cranberry
muffins, 105
apple loaf, 134
apple maple
dumplings, 219
apple pie, 156
apple ring cake, 238
apple strudel, 220
applesauce bread, 413
applesauce cookies, 82
brethren's cider
pie, 176
cranberry and apple
ring, 319
open apple pie, 175
pear-apple crumb
pie, 174
pecan-apple torte, 254
spiced apple cake, 316

apricots:
apple, apricot and walnut
bread, 143
apricot bars, 92
apricot lattice pie, 25
apricot nut bread, 412
apricot and orange
roulade, 336
filo and apricot purses, 356
glazed apricot sponge, 359
pineapple and apricot
bread, 140
asparagus, corn and red bell
pepper quiche, 228

## B

bacon:
bacon and cheese
quiche, 226
bacon cornmeal
muffins, 119
spinach and bacon
bread, 394
bagels, American, 497
baguettes, French, 446
baking equipment, 12–13
baking ingredients, 10–11
baking techniques, 14–39
bananas:
banana bread, 139
banana and cardamom
bread, 414
banana cream pie, 193
banana and ginger tea
bread, 144
banana and gingerbread
slices, 334
banana lemon layer
cake, 245
banana muffins, 112
banana-oatmeal
gingerbread, 332
banana orange bread, 142
banana-pecan
muffins, 114
banana sauce, 282
chocolate banana
cake, 326
glazed banana spice
bread, 148

whole-wheat banana
nut bread, 416
bara brith, Welsh, 434
barbari, Iranian, 501
barley bread, Finnish, 458
bars:
almond bars, 93
apricot bars, 92
banana and gingerbread
slices, 334
butterscotch meringue
bars, 94
chocolate pecan
squares, 86
chocolate walnut bars, 88
fig bars, 90
five-layer bars, 72
hazelnut squares, 79
hermits, 94
lemon bars, 90
oatmeal wedges, 74
pecan bars, 89
toffee bars, 82
see also brownies
basil:
ricotta and basil tart, 224
saffron and basil
breadsticks, 408
berries:
berry shortcake, 293
lattice berry pie, 163
see also individual berries
e.g. strawberries
blackberries:
baked blackberry
cheesecake, 350
blackberry and almond
muffins, 118
blueberries:
blueberry-cinnamon
muffins, 114
blueberry-hazelnut
cheesecake, 202
blueberry muffins, 104
blueberry and orange
crêpe baskets, 354
blueberry pie, 170
blueberry streusel
bread, 147
Maryland peach and
blueberry pie, 168

bran: raisin bran
muffins, 100
brandy Alexander tart, 211
brandy snaps, 71
"bread of the dead," 500
bread-making, 36–7, 39
breads:
American monkey
bread, 498
American pumpkin and
walnut bread, 493
banana and cardamom
bread, 414
Boston brown bread, 496
braided loaf, 367
bread stick, 375
British cottage loaf, 426
British Grant loaves, 427
British harvest festival
sheaf, 430
British lardy cake, 432
British poppy-seeded
bloomer, 428
brown soda bread, 384
buttermilk Graham
bread, 374
cheese bread, 389
cheese and onion sticks, 406
corn bread, 400
Cornish saffron breads, 437
country bread, 365
Danish julekage, 462
dill bread, 388
everyday white bread, 36
Finnish barley bread, 458
flatbread with sage, 410
French baguettes, 446
French brioche, 447
French épi, 441
French fougasse, 444
French kugelhopf, 438
French pain aux noix, 445
French pain bouillie, 440
French pain de campagne
rustique, 442
French pain polka, 439
German pumpernickel, 456
German sourdough
bread, 453
German stollen, 454
granary cob, 380

Greek christopsomo, 484
Greek olive bread, 486
Greek tsoureki, 485
Hungarian split farmhouse
  loaf, 490
Indian naan, 504
Indian tandoori rotis, 503
Iranian barbari, 501
Italian ciabatta, 477
Italian focaccia, 474
Italian olive bread, 471
Italian pane al
  cioccolato, 479
Italian panettone, 478
Italian polenta bread, 472
Italian prosciutto
  loaf, 473
Italian schiacciata, 482
Jewish challah, 492
Mexican "bread of the
  dead," 500
Moroccan holiday
  bread, 483
multi-grain bread, 378
oatmeal bread, 381
onion focaccia, 402
pan gallego, 468
pane Toscano, 481
pecan rye bread, 372
Polish poppy seed
  roll, 488
Polish rye bread, 489
Portuguese corn bread, 469
prosciutto and Parmesan
  bread, 392
prune bread, 398
raisin bread, 418
rosemary bread, 386
Russian potato
  bread, 491
rye bread, 370
saffron focaccia, 404
sage soda bread, 385
San Francisco sourdough
  bread, 494
savory Danish crown, 461
Scandinavian sunshine
  loaf, 464
sesame seed bread, 379
Sicilian scroll, 480
sourdough bread, 368
sourdough rye bread, 373
Spanish pan de
  cebada, 465

Spanish Twelfth Night
  bread, 466
spinach and bacon
  bread, 394
spiral herb bread, 387
split pan, 366
sun-dried tomato
  braid, 390
Swedish knackerbröd, 458
Swedish vört limpa, 457
Swiss braid, 452
Syrian onion bread, 502
Tex-Mex corn bread, 400
three-grain bread, 376
Turkish pita bread, 487
walnut bread, 396
Welsh bara brith, 434
Welsh clay pot loaves, 435
white bread, 364
zucchini and walnut
  loaf, 397
zucchini yeast bread, 393
  see also rolls; tea breads
breadsticks, 39
  saffron and basil
    breadsticks, 408
brioche, French, 447
broccoli and goat cheese
  pizza, 234
brownies:
  chocolate chip
    brownies, 84
  marbled brownies, 85
  raisin brownies, 86
butter frosting, 30
buttermilk:
  buttermilk biscuits, 122
  buttermilk Graham
    bread, 374

C

cake pans, 14, 34–5
cake-making methods, 28–33
cakes:
  almond cake, 255
  angel food cake, 240
  apple ring cake, 238
  banana lemon layer
    cake, 245
  banana-oatmeal
    gingerbread, 332
  best-ever chocolate
    cake, 278

black walnut layer
  cake, 250
black and white pound
  cake, 241
Boston cream pie, 288
caramel layer cake, 290
carrot cake with cream
  cheese frosting, 242
carrot cake with maple
  butter frosting, 268
chiffon cake, 252
chocolate banana cake, 326
chocolate brownie cake, 285
chocolate cinnamon
  cake, 282
chocolate frosted layer
  cake, 276
chocolate-orange angel
  food cake, 328
chocolate orange sponge
  cookies, 301
coconut angel food
  cake, 258
coconut lime layer cake, 262
coffee sponge drops, 346
cranberry and apple
  ring, 319
cranberry upside-down
  cake, 264
cup cakes, 302
dark fruit cake, 247
devil's food cake, 274
devil's food cake with
  orange frosting, 277
eggless Christmas cake, 330
forgotten torte, 253
fruit cake, 31
fruit and nut cake, 331
German chocolate
  cupcakes, 300
ginger cake, 248
Greek honey and lemon
  cake, 318
heart cake, 304
huckleberry coffee cake, 281
Jack-O'-Lantern cake, 310
Lady Baltimore cake, 294
lemon chiffon cake, 320
lemon coconut layer
  cake, 260
lemon yogurt coffee
  cake, 244
light fruit cake, 246
Mississippi mud cake, 280

nectarine amaretto cake, 333
orange cake, 238
pecan-apple torte, 254
pineapple upside-down
  cake, 265
plum crumbcake, 270
pound cake, 243
raspberry-hazelnut
  meringue cake, 295
rich chocolate pecan
  cake, 284
rich, sticky
  gingerbread, 249
sachertorte, 286
snake cake, 306
sour cream streusel coffee
  cake, 267
spice cake, 266
spiced apple cake, 316
spiced date and walnut
  cake, 317
stars and stripes cake, 312
strawberry torte, 322
sun cake, 308
Tia Maria cake, 324
walnut coffee torte, 256
whiskey cake, 292
Yule log cake, 271
  see also jelly rolls;
    tea breads
caramel layer cake, 290
cardamom: banana and
  cardamom bread, 414
  cardamom and saffron tea
    loaf, 146
carrots:
  carrot cake with cream
    cheese frosting, 242
  carrot cake with maple
    butter frosting, 268
  carrot muffins, 102
challah, Jewish, 492
Cheddar cheese:
  bacon and cheese
    quiche, 226
  cheese bread, 389
  cheese and chive
    biscuits, 129
  cheese and marjoram
    biscuits, 128
  cheese muffins, 120
  cheese and onion sticks, 406
  cheese and tomato
    quiche, 230

cheese *see* individual
cheeses e.g. cream;
Parmesan
cheesecakes:
baked blackberry
cheesecake, 350
blueberry-hazelnut
cheesecake, 202
chocolate cheesecake, 296
chocolate cheesecake
pie, 204
classic cheesecake, 296
lemon mousse
cheesecake, 298
marbled cheesecake, 299
rich orange cheesecake, 201
*see also* tarts, sweet
cherries:
apple and cherry crumble
pie, 22
cherry lattice pie, 164
cherry marmalade
muffins, 117
cherry strudel, 221
dried cherry muffins, 102
rhubarb cherry pie, 159
chess pie, 186
chestnut and orange
roulade, 340
chicken-mushroom
pie, 222
chives: cheese and chive
biscuits, 129
chocolate:
best-ever chocolate
cake, 278
chewy chocolate
cookies, 48
chocolate banana
cake, 326
chocolate brownie
cake, 285
chocolate cheesecake, 296
chocolate cheesecake
pie, 204
chocolate chiffon pie, 189
chocolate chip brownies, 84
chocolate chip and
macadamia nut cookies, 63
chocolate chip muffins, 106
chocolate chip walnut
bread, 149
chocolate cinnamon
cake, 282

chocolate, date and
walnut pudding, 342
chocolate frosted layer
cake, 276
chocolate ice cream
roll, 33
chocolate lemon tart, 198
chocolate macaroons, 64
chocolate-nut refrigerator
cookies, 76
chocolate-orange angel
food cake, 328
chocolate orange sponge
cookies, 301
chocolate pear tart, 213
chocolate pecan
squares, 86
chocolate pretzels, 50
chocolate roll, 273
chocolate walnut bars, 88
chocolate walnut
muffins, 106
devil's food cake, 274
easy chocolate tart, 26
five-layer bars, 72
German chocolate
cupcakes, 300
Italian pane al
cioccolato, 479
Mississippi mud cake, 280
Mississippi mud pie, 188
mocha Victoria sponge, 28
rich chocolate pecan
cake, 284
sachertorte, 286
tollhouse cookies, 80
velvet mocha cream
pie, 212
Christmas cake, eggless, 330
Christmas cookies, 59
christopsomo, Greek, 484
ciabatta, Italian, 477
cinnamon:
blueberry-cinnamon
muffins, 114
chocolate cinnamon
cake, 282
cinnamon refrigerator
cookies, 77
snickerdoodles, 48
coconut:
coconut angel food
cake, 258
coconut cream pie, 210

coconut lime layer
cake, 262
coconut macaroons, 64
coconut oatmeal
cookies, 44
five-layer bars, 72
lemon coconut layer
cake, 260
coffee:
chiffon cake, 252
coffee ice cream
sandwiches, 78
coffee sponge drops, 346
huckleberry coffee
cake, 281
mocha Victoria sponge, 28
velvet mocha cream
pie, 212
walnut coffee torte, 256
cookies:
almond tiles, 66
applesauce cookies, 82
chewy chocolate
cookies, 48
chocolate chip and
macadamia nut cookies, 63
chocolate-nut refrigerator
cookies, 76
Christmas cookies, 59
cinnamon refrigerator
cookies, 77
coconut oatmeal
cookies, 44
coffee ice cream
sandwiches, 78
cream cheese
spirals, 51
crunchy jumbles, 44
florentines, 67
ginger cookies, 46
granola cookies, 42
lady fingers, 56
nut lace cookies, 68
oatmeal and cereal
cookies, 42
oatmeal lace
cookies, 68
old-fashioned sugar
cookies, 62
orange cookies, 47
peanut butter
cookies, 80
pecan puffs, 54
pepper-spice cookies, 72

raspberry sandwich
cookies, 70
snickerdoodles, 48
tollhouse cookies, 80
vanilla crescents, 52
walnut cookies, 56
walnut crescents, 52
*see also* bars; brownies;
macaroons
cookie cases, 26
corn:
asparagus, corn and red
bell pepper quiche, 228
corn bread,
Portuguese, 469
Tex-Mex corn
bread, 400
corn syrup:
almond syrup tart, 218
treacle tart, 209
cornmeal:
bacon cornmeal
muffins, 119
corn bread, 400
cottage loaf, British, 426
cranberries:
apple-cranberry lattice
pie, 158
apple cranberry
muffins, 105
cranberry and apple
ring, 319
cranberry orange
bread, 150
cranberry upside-down
cake, 264
cream:
sour cream streusel coffee
cake, 267
spiced whipped
cream, 248
sweetened whipped
cream, 17
cream cheese:
cream cheese
frosting, 266
cream cheese
spirals, 51
cream-puff pastry, 27
crêpe baskets, blueberry
and orange, 354
croissants, French, 448
currants: British malted
currant bread, 433

# D

dates:
  chocolate, date and
    walnut pudding, 342
  date-nut bread, 417
  date and nut malt
    bread, 141
  date oven scones, 15
  spiced date and walnut
    cake, 317
devil's food cake, 274
devil's food cake with
  orange frosting, 277
dill:
  dill bread, 388
  dill-potato cakes, 130
dried fruit *see* fruit
dumplings, apple maple, 219

# E

eggs, 35
ensaimadas, Mallorcan, 470
épi, French, 441

# F

fantans, New England, 499
feta cheese: cheese and
  chive biscuits, 129
fig bars, 90
filo pastry:
  filo and apricot purses, 356
  filo scrunchies, 357
  plum filo pockets, 358
flan, fresh strawberry, 23
flan pastry, 18, 21
florentines, 67
focaccia, 39
  Italian focaccia, 474
  onion focaccia, 402
  saffron focaccia, 404
fougasse, French, 444
frostings:
  buttercream, 30
  cream cheese frosting, 266
  orange frosting, 29, 277
  seven-minute frosting, 29
fruit:
  cranberry orange
    bread, 150
  dark fruit cake, 247
  dried fruit bread, 151
  fruit cake, 31

fruit and nut cake, 331
fruit tartlets, 196
light fruit cake, 246
nesselrode pie, 184
*see also* individual fruits
  e.g. apples; raisins

# G

ginger:
  banana and ginger tea
    bread, 144
  banana and gingerbread
    slices, 334
  banana-oatmeal
    gingerbread, 332
  ginger cake, 248
  ginger cookies, 46
  rich, sticky
    gingerbread, 249
goat cheese: broccoli and
  goat cheese pizza, 234
golden raisins:
  golden raisin bread, 420
  pear and golden raisin tea
    bread, 145
  sunflower-raisin
    biscuits, 126
granary cob, 380
Grant loaves, British, 427
Gruyère cheese: bacon and
  cheese quiche, 226

# H

harvest festival
  sheaf, British 430
hazelnuts:
  blueberry-hazelnut
    cheesecake, 202
  hazelnut squares, 79
  raspberry-hazelnut
    meringue cake, 295
  rich chocolate pecan
    cake, 284
heart cake, 304
herbs:
  herb popovers, 132
  spiral herb bread, 387
  *see also* chives; dill;
    marjoram; sage
honey:
  Greek honey and lemon
    cake, 318

orange honey bread, 134
yogurt honey muffins, 110
huckleberry coffee cake, 281

# I

ice cream:
  chocolate ice cream
    roll, 33
  coffee ice cream
    sandwiches, 78
ingredients, 10–11, 14

# J

Jack-O'-Lantern cake, 310
Jelly rolls, 33, 35
  chocolate ice cream
    roll, 33
  chocolate roll, 273
  orange walnut roll, 272
  peach jelly roll, 338
  Yule log cake, 271
  *see also* roulades
julekage, Danish, 462

# K

kiwi ricotta cheese
  tart, 206
knackerbröd, Swedish, 458
kugelhopf, French, 438

# L

Lady Baltimore cake, 294
lardy cake, British, 432
lemons:
  banana lemon layer
    cake, 245
  chocolate lemon
    tart, 198
  Greek honey and lemon
    cake, 318
  lemon almond
    tart, 199
  lemon bars, 90
  lemon chiffon cake, 320
  lemon coconut layer
    cake, 260
  lemon meringue
    pie, 180
  lemon mousse
    cheesecake, 298

lemon walnut bread, 138
lemon yogurt coffee
  cake, 244
limes:
  coconut lime layer
    cake, 262
  Key lime pie, 196
  lime meringue pie, 182
lusse bröd, Swedish, 460

# M

macaroons:
  chocolate macaroons, 64
  coconut macaroons, 64
malt breads:
  British malted currant
    bread, 433
  date and nut malt
    bread, 141
  malt bread, 136
mangoes:
  mango and amaretti
    strudel, 352
  mango bread, 152
maple syrup:
  apple maple
    dumplings, 219
  carrot cake with maple
    butter frosting, 268
  maple pecan
    muffins, 113
  maple walnut pie, 214
marjoram: cheese and
  marjoram biscuits, 128
marmalade: cherry
  marmalade muffins, 117
meringue, 17, 60
  brown sugar
    meringues, 345
  butterscotch meringue
    bars, 94
  lemon meringue pie, 180
  lime meringue pie, 182
  meringue nests, 17
  raspberry vacherin, 348
  raspberry-hazelnut
    meringue cake, 295
  snowballs, 344
  toasted oat meringues, 60
mince pies, 172
Mississippi mud cake, 280
mozzarella: tomato and
  mozzarella pizza, 38

muffins, 16
  apple cranberry
    muffins, 105
  bacon cornmeal
    muffins, 119
  banana muffins, 112
  banana-pecan
    muffins, 114
  blackberry and almond
    muffins, 118
  blueberry-cinnamon
    muffins, 114
  blueberry muffins, 104
  carrot muffins, 102
  cheese muffins, 120
  cherry marmalade
    muffins, 117
  chocolate chip
    muffins, 106
  chocolate walnut
    muffins, 106
  crunchy muesli
    muffins, 16
  dried cherry muffins, 102
  maple pecan
    muffins, 113
  oatmeal buttermilk
    muffins, 108
  prune and candied peel
    cookies, 126
  prune muffins, 110
  pumpkin muffins, 108
  raisin bran muffins, 100
  raspberry crumble
    muffins, 101
  raspberry muffins, 116
  yogurt honey
    muffins, 110
mushrooms:
  chicken-mushroom
    pie, 222
  mushroom quiche, 226

### N

naan, Indian, 504
nectarine amaretto
  cake, 333
nuts:
  date and nut malt
    bread, 141
  *see also* almonds;
    hazelnuts; pecans;
    walnuts

### O

oats:
  coconut oatmeal
    cookies, 44
  oatmeal bread, 381
  oatmeal buttermilk
    muffins, 108
  oatmeal and cereal
    cookies, 42
  oatmeal lace cookies, 68
  oatmeal wedges, 74
  toasted oat meringues, 60
olive oil: Italian panini
  all'olio, 476
olives:
  Greek olive bread, 486
  Italian olive bread, 471
  onion, olive, and anchovy
    pizza, 233
onions:
  cheese and onion
    sticks, 406
  onion and anchovy
    tart, 225
  onion focaccia, 402
  onion, olive, and anchovy
    pizza, 233
  Syrian onion
    bread, 502
oranges:
  apricot and orange
    roulade, 336
  banana orange bread, 142
  blueberry and orange
    crêpe baskets, 354
  chestnut and orange
    roulade, 340
  chocolate-orange angel
    food cake, 328
  chocolate orange sponge
    cookies, 301
  orange cake, 238
  orange cookies, 47
  orange frosting, 29,
    277
  orange honey bread, 134
  orange raisin scones, 124
  orange tart, 200
  orange walnut
    roll, 272
  orange wheat
    bread, 399
  rich orange
    cheesecake, 201

### P

panettone, Italian, 478
Parmesan cheese:
  cheese popovers, 132
  Parmesan popovers, 131
  prosciutto and Parmesan
    bread, 392
pastry:
  basic pie pastry, 18
  cream-puff pastry, 27
  tart pastry, 19
  techniques, 20–5, 171
  *see also* filo pastry; pies;
    tarts
peaches:
  featherlight peach
    pudding, 343
  latticed peaches, 360
  Maryland peach and
    blueberry pie, 168
  peach jelly roll, 338
  peach leaf pie, 166
  peach tart with almond
    cream, 216
  peach torte, 269
peanut butter:
  peanut butter cookies, 80
  peanut butter pie, 194
pears:
  caramelized upside-down
    pear pie, 178
  chocolate pear tart, 213
  pear-apple crumb pie, 174
  pear and golden raisin tea
    bread, 145
  walnut and pear lattice
    pie, 171
pecans:
  banana-pecan
    muffins, 114
  chocolate pecan
    squares, 86
  date-nut bread, 417
  maple pecan muffins, 113
  pecan-apple torte, 254
  pecan bars, 89
  pecan nut tartlets, 21
  pecan puffs, 54
  pecan rye bread, 372
  pecan spice muffins, 113
  pecan tart, 215
  pecan tassies, 55
pepper: pepper-spice
  cookies, 72

peppers: asparagus,
  corn and red bell
  pepper quiche, 228
*see also* strudels
pies:
  American-style apple pie, 24
  apple and cherry crumble
    pie, 22
  apple-cranberry lattice
    pie, 158
  apple pie, 156
  apricot lattice pie, 25
  banana cream pie, 193
  black bottom pie, 190
  blueberry pie, 170
  brethren's cider pie, 176
  brown sugar pie, 192
  caramelized upside-down
    pear pie, 178
  cherry lattice pie, 164
  chess pie, 186
  chicken-mushroom
    pie, 222
  chocolate chiffon pie, 189
  lattice berry pie, 163
  lemon meringue pie, 180
  lime meringue pie, 182
  Maryland peach and
    blueberry pie, 168
  mince pies, 172
  Mississippi mud pie, 188
  nesselrode pie, 184
  open apple pie, 175
  peach leaf pie, 166
  peanut butter pie, 194
  pear-apple crumb
    pie, 174
  plum pie, 162
  pumpkin pie, 185
  rhubarb cherry pie, 159
  rhubarb pie, 160
  shoofly pie, 187
  walnut and pear lattice
    pie, 171
  *see also* pastry; tarts
pineapple:
  pineapple and apricot
    bread, 140
  pineapple upside-down
    cake, 265
pita bread, Turkish, 487
pizzas, 38, 232
  broccoli and goat cheese
    pizza, 234

onion, olive, and anchovy
pizza, 233
tomato and mozzarella
pizza, 38
plums:
plum crumbcake, 270
plum filo pockets, 358
plum pie, 162
polenta:
corn bread, 400
Italian polenta bread, 472
popovers:
cheese popovers, 132
herb popovers, 132
Parmesan popovers, 131
poppy seeds:
British poppy-seeded
bloomer, 428
Polish poppy seed roll, 488
potatoes:
dill-potato cakes, 130
Russian potato bread, 491
pound cake, 243
pretzels, chocolate, 50
prosciutto loaf,
Italian, 473
prosciutto and Parmesan
bread, 392
prunes:
prune bread, 398
prune and candied peel
cookies, 126
prune-filled coffee cake, 422
prune muffins, 110
puddings:
chocolate, date and
walnut pudding, 342
featherlight peach
pudding, 343
glazed apricot sponge, 359
pumpernickel, German, 456
pumpkin:
American pumpkin and
walnut bread, 493
pumpkin muffins, 108
pumpkin pie, 185

Q
quiches:
asparagus, corn and red
bell pepper quiche, 228
bacon and cheese
quiche, 226
cheese and tomato
quiche, 230
mushroom quiche, 226
quiche Lorraine, 231
see also tarts, savory

R
raisins:
hermits, 94
oatmeal buttermilk
muffins, 108
orange raisin scones, 124
raisin bran muffins, 100
raisin bread, 418
raisin brownies, 86
sweet potato and raisin
bread, 419
raspberries:
raspberry crumble
muffins, 101
raspberry-hazelnut
meringue cake, 295
raspberry muffins, 116
raspberry sandwich
cookies, 70
raspberry tart, 208
raspberry vacherin, 348
rhubarb:
rhubarb cherry pie, 159
rhubarb pie, 160
ricotta cheese:
kiwi ricotta cheese
tart, 206
ricotta and basil
tart, 224
rolls, 37
American bagels, 497
French croissants, 448
French dimpled rolls, 450
French petits pains au
lait, 450
granary rolls, 382
Italian panini
all'olio, 476
Mallorcan
ensaimadas, 470
New England
fantans, 499
Scottish morning
rolls, 436
Swedish lusse bröd, 460
rosemary bread, 386
rotis, Indian tandoori, 503

roulades:
apricot and orange
roulade, 336
chestnut and orange
roulade, 340
strawberry roulade, 337
see also jelly rolls
rye breads:
French pain bouillie, 440
German pumpernickel, 456
pecan rye bread, 372
Polish rye bread, 489
rye bread, 370
Scandinavian sunshine
loaf, 464
sourdough rye bread, 373
Swedish knackerbröd, 458
Swedish vört limpa, 457

S
sachertorte, 286
saffron:
cardamom and saffron
tea loaf, 146
Cornish saffron breads, 437
saffron and basil
breadsticks, 408
saffron focaccia, 404
sage:
flatbread with sage, 410
sage soda bread, 385
schiacciata, Italian, 482
scones, 15
baking powder
biscuits, 122
buttermilk biscuits, 122
cheese and chive
biscuits, 129
cheese and marjoram
biscuits, 128
date oven scones, 15
orange raisin scones, 124
sunflower-raisin
biscuits, 126
sweet potato biscuits, 121
whole-wheat scones, 124
sesame seeds:
sesame seed bread, 379
sweet sesame bread, 411
shoofly pie, 187
shortbread, 74
berry shortcake, 293
strawberry shortcake, 96

snake cake, 306
snowballs, 344
soda breads:
brown soda bread, 384
sage soda bread, 385
sourdough, 368
German sourdough
bread, 453
San Francisco sourdough
bread, 494
sourdough bread, 368
sourdough rye bread, 373
spinach and bacon
bread, 394
spongecakes, 32, 35
see also cakes; jelly rolls
stars and stripes cake, 312
stollen, German, 454
strawberries:
fresh strawberry flan, 23
frozen strawberry
pie, 204
strawberry roulade, 337
strawberry shortcake, 96
strawberry torte, 322
strudels:
apple strudel, 220
cherry strudel, 221
mango and amaretti
strudel, 352
sugar:
brown sugar
meringues, 345
brown sugar pie, 192
old-fashioned sugar
cookies, 62
sun cake, 308
sunflower-raisin
biscuits, 126
sweet potatoes:
sweet potato biscuits, 121
sweet potato and raisin
bread, 419

T
tartlets:
fruit tartlets, 196
latticed peaches, 360
pecan tartlets, 21
pecan tassies, 55
tarts, savory:
onion and anchovy
tart, 225

ricotta and basil tart, 224
*see also* quiches
tarts, sweet:
  almond syrup tart, 218
  brandy Alexander tart, 211
  chocolate lemon tart, 198
  chocolate pear tart, 213
  coconut cream pie, 210
  easy chocolate tart, 26
  frozen strawberry
    pie, 204
  Key lime pie, 196
  kiwi ricotta cheese
    tart, 206
  lemon almond tart, 199
  maple walnut pie, 214
  orange tart, 200
  peach tart with almond
    cream, 216
  pecan tart, 215
  raspberry tart, 208
  treacle tart, 209
  velvet mocha cream
    pie, 212
  *see also* cheesecakes; pies
tea breads, 16
  apple, apricot and walnut
    bread, 143
  apple loaf, 134
  applesauce bread, 413
  apricot nut bread, 412
  banana bread, 139
  banana and ginger tea
    bread, 144
  banana orange bread, 142

blueberry streusel
  bread, 147
chocolate chip walnut
  bread, 149
cranberry orange
  bread, 150
date-nut bread, 417
dried fruit bread, 151
glazed banana spice
  bread, 148
golden raisin bread, 420
lemon walnut bread, 138
mango bread, 152
orange honey bread, 134
orange wheat bread, 399
pear and golden raisin tea
  bread, 145
pineapple and apricot
  bread, 140
sweet potato and raisin
  bread, 419
sweet sesame bread, 411
whole-wheat banana nut
  bread, 416
zucchini bread, 152
*see also* breads; cakes;
  malt breads
Tia Maria cake, 324
toffee:
  butterscotch meringue
    bars, 94
  toffee bars, 82
tomatoes:
  cheese and tomato
    quiche, 230

sun-dried tomato
  braid, 390
tomato and mozzarella
  pizza, 38
torte, peach, 269
treacle tart, 209
tsoureki, Greek, 485

## V

vacherin, raspberry, 348
vanilla crescents, 52
Victoria sponges, 28–9
vört limpa, Swedish, 457

## W

walnuts:
  American pumpkin and
    walnut bread, 493
  apple, apricot and walnut
    bread, 143
  apricot nut bread, 412
  black walnut layer
    cake, 250
  chocolate chip walnut
    bread, 149
  chocolate, date and
    walnut pudding, 342
  chocolate walnut bars, 88
  chocolate walnut
    muffins, 106
  French pain aux
    noix, 445
  lemon walnut bread, 138

maple walnut pie, 214
orange walnut roll, 272
pecan-apple torte, 254
spiced date and walnut
  cake, 317
walnut bread, 396
walnut coffee torte, 256
walnut cookies, 56
walnut crescents, 52
walnut and pear lattice
  pie, 171
whole-wheat banana
  nut bread, 416
zucchini and walnut
  loaf, 397
whiskey cake, 292

## Y

yeast, 36–7
*see also* breads
yogurt:
  lemon yogurt coffee
    cake, 244
  yogurt honey
    muffins, 110
Yule log cake, 271

## Z

zucchini:
  zucchini bread, 152
  zucchini and walnut
    loaf, 397
  zucchini yeast bread, 393